Introducing
MORAL
THEOLOGY

Introducing
MORAL
THEOLOGY

True Happiness *and the* Virtues

William C. Mattison III

BrazosPress
a division of Baker Publishing Group
Grand Rapids, Michigan

Published by Brazos Press
a division of Baker Publishing Group
P.O. Box 6287, Grand Rapids, MI 49516-6287
www.brazospress.com

Printed in the United States of America

Library of Congress Cataloging-in-Publication Data
Mattison, William C., 1971–
   Introducing moral theology : true happiness and the virtues / William C. Mattison III.
     p. cm.
   Includes bibliographical references (p.   ) and index.
   ISBN 978-1-58743-223-1 (pbk.)
   1. Christian ethics—Catholic authors. I. Title.
BJ1249.M195 2008
241′.042—dc22
                   2008025502

14 15   8 7

To my parents,
Joan and Bill Mattison,
with immense gratitude for their love and support.
These, my first teachers of a morality of happiness,
demonstrate what lives of faith, hope, and
love marked by joy look like

CONTENTS

ACKNOWLEDGMENTS

Gratitude is a true privilege. We often speak of a "debt of gratitude," and the debt of gratitude I owe for this work is enormous and widespread. But one of the points of this book is that living virtuously is life-giving for all involved. I can only hope that the following people have found the interactions which constitute their contribution to this book even a fraction as life-giving as they have been for me. It is a privilege to acknowledge my indebtedness in gratitude to the following.

I would first like to thank the students from my classes for whom this book was written, and who have shaped its entire content with their questions, contributions, and wonderful conversations. The book is truly the percolation of these classes and so would not be possible without the students. Many students were particularly generous in giving me explicit and written feedback on earlier versions of the text. With apologies to any I may have missed, special thanks to Alex Bautz, Liz Casey, Marian Cassilly, Mary Cohill, Mel Corley, Laura Davidson, Wil Donahue, Emily Dufficy, Rachel Dunphy, Mark Fellin, Ryan Frederickson, Philip Ilg, Rachel Jacobs, LeighAnne Kauffman, Peter Mercatanti, Kaylie Metz, Caitlin McKeon, Ellen Rawson, Dimitrie Samata, Emilee Senkevitch, J. Silverman, Lynne Simmons, and Kirsten Toth. Teaching assistants Matt Haven and Donna Moga also provided valuable feedback.

Many colleagues in the field of moral theology were generous in helping to shape the course out of which this book grows, and/or commenting on earlier versions of this text. Special thanks to David Cloutier, Tom Leininger, David McCarthy, John Grabowski, Bill Barbieri, and Jim Halstead. Friends at New Wine, New Wineskins, the annual symposium at Notre Dame for pretenure Catholic moral theologians, have also made important contributions in more ways than one. I cannot fail to mention the three mentors who have been so generous with me throughout my own formation in moral theology, and without whom I would never have been able to take on this project: Jean Porter, Servais Pinckaers, OP, and James F. Keenan, SJ. In terms of publishing and editing this book, Jeremy Langford and Rodney Clapp have been indispensable. I am grateful for their diligent work and especially for their friendship. Chris Blake and Mount St. Mary's University generously provided grant money, in addition to a wonderfully hospitable intellectual environment, for the development of this book. Friends at Georgetown University's Office of Campus Ministry also provided a home in Healy Hall for the writing of this book. Finally on the professional side, it seems fitting to thank those whose work has been so formative on my teaching this course and thus writing this book. It is ludicrous to thank such cornerstones of the tradition as Augustine and Aquinas, and even those more recent intellectual giants such as Josef Pieper and C. S. Lewis who have gone before us. But it does seem appropriate to acknowledge contemporaries such as Robert Barron and Paul Wadell, whose works have been models of how to teach the riches of the Christian tradition to undergraduates in an accessible and attractive manner.

Lastly I would like to express my gratitude to those people who, while all intellectuals in the best sense of the word, have influenced me and therefore this work not primarily through their intellectual activity *per se*, but through the witness of their lives. My own vocation to study and teach moral theology has been born from the faith and love of these people who taught me through their examples how a life of virtue in Christ is indeed a truly fulfilling life. First mention must go to my wife Courtney who constantly teaches me about the virtuous life, in ways she does not describe with theological terminology but nonetheless speaks more vividly in her actions. Teachers and friends Stephen Balletta, SM, Otto Hentz, SJ, Timothy Scully, CSC, Sean McGraw, CSC, Lou Delfra, CSC, Brian Daley, SJ, and Cathy Kaveny have all helped teach me the content of this book with their lives and friendships, and for each of them I am eternally grateful.

Perhaps the best example from my own experience of people teaching with their lives has been that of my parents, Joan and Bill Mattison. With no theological training whatsoever, they are nonetheless the people in my life whose faith and love are so constitutive of who they are that they taught me more than anyone what it means to live a life of Christian virtue. In more ways that I can mention here or even perhaps recount, I owe the good things of my life to them. And thus it is to them that this book, a small token the life they have borne in me, is dedicated.

INTRODUCTION

I wrote this book as an exercise in hospitality. With it I invite readers into a conversation on the basic human question, what is a good life? The book strives for an intentionally welcoming tone in two ways. First of all, a good host listens to his or her guests and appreciates wherever they are in their lives. This book grew out of just such listening to over five hundred students in twenty course sections over six years at four American universities (University of Notre Dame, Mount St. Mary's University, Catholic University, and Georgetown University). It has grown and developed dramatically such that the present book, which follows this course's most recent version, is radically different from its first presentation to the students who took it and helped shape it. Its overall structure, the layout of individual chapters, and certain distinct points echo specific contributions of particular students over these past few years. It is born out of a conversation, and so its tone is one of walking with, rather than preaching at.

Second, a welcoming host does not simply listen, but also offers and contributes. By arranging space and furniture in a certain way, offering food and drink, and joining in conversation, a good host nourishes whatever venture he or she shares with the guests, be it the enjoyment of friendship, a better understanding of themselves and the world, support in times of trial, a common cause to make changes in the world, or all of these together. In this book I attempt to make a contribution to that ultimate adventure shared by readers and myself, that of understanding and living a good life. I offer my own experience (as a teacher), but more importantly share—in an accessible and relevant way— the wisdom of smart and holy people who have gone before us on this common quest. The manner this is done in is not a simple presentation of information. It is rather adding voices to our conversation, a conversation that includes renowned thinkers, but as importantly the voices of us today who

11

enjoy reflecting on and struggling with the question, what is a good life? I hope readers will join with me and past students in building a habit of reflection on this question as one component of the answer to that question.

Speaking of answers, this book is not a manual offering technical procedures and solutions to how to live a good life. This is largely due to that fact that this ultimate question defies technical solutions. It should not be placed in the how-to section of a bookstore next to books on home repair or writing a good resume. That is not to say there are no answers, or that this book makes no contribution to such answers. Given the nature and complexity of the question, no short synopsis is offered here by way of conclusion. Yet before proceeding to describe more specifically the goals and format of this book, allow me to note two foundational ideas of the book's response to this question.

First, simply put, the answer to the question of what constitutes a good life is happiness. A good life is a fulfilling, satisfying, rewarding, flourishing—in short, a happy—life. This may seem so obvious as to be no answer at all. But recall this is a book on moral theology. The word "moral" has not yet appeared in this introduction. Some people may connect morality with living a good life. But morality as being happy? That is exactly the contention of this book. It is by no means an innovative contribution of this particular book. Great thinkers throughout history—Christian and non-Christian alike—have understood the moral life to be one and the same as the happy life, even if this claim does not initially resonate with what many of us today think of when we say morality. We see already the benefit of inviting those historic voices into our conversation. A main claim of this book is that it makes no sense to say, "this will make you truly happy, but the morally right thing to do is something else." There are plenty of obstacles to happiness in this life, but morality rightly understood is not one of them. This point is not uncontested. As seen in chapter 1, some people today and throughout history have not understood morality as constitutive of living happy lives. Nonetheless, one central idea of this book is that determining how to live morally is a matter of determining how to be genuinely happy.

The second foundational idea of this book is that living happily depends upon a truthful understanding of ourselves, the world around us, and anything beyond this world we live in. This is not to say that people with more schooling or higher SAT scores are therefore happier. Nor is it to say that happiness cannot be experienced in this life until we know everything. It is to say that determining how to live morally, and thus what constitutes genuine happiness, entails determinations of whether or not how we live our lives reflects accurately who we are, what the world around us is like, and what is true beyond the world around us. This claim permeates the entire book, but is addressed most directly in chapters 1, 5, 10, and 11. Having presented two cornerstone ideas of this book, and already begun to mention specific chapters, we turn now to the main goals of the book and its organization into different chapters.

The Goals and Format of the Book

There are five large goals driving the tone and structure of this book's exploration of the central question, what is a good life? The first echoes what was said above: to present the riches of the Western (particularly Christian) traditions of moral thought in an accessible and hospitable manner. Our answers to everyday contemporary questions about how to live our lives can be nourished by seeking the guidance of the smart and holy people who have gone before us. Thus the starting point for this book is not an assumed knowledge of or even interest in traditional sources such as Plato, Aristotle, St. Augustine, or St. Thomas Aquinas. The starting point here is own our lives and the questions that inevitably arise as we live our lives. Hence, examples are generally taken from everyday experiences. The thought and terminology of those who have gone before us is then only employed to the extent that it helps us better understand and answer the questions we face. As noted above, it is assumed here that everyone—however articulately or even consciously –is seeking how to live a happy, fulfilling life. This provides a common starting point for our reflection and a reason to appeal to classical sources in the tradition in a manner that applies to our experiences. When moral theology is understood in this way it is not only accessible but hospitable.

Second, this book presents moral theology as informing the common everyday questions of our lives primarily through the concept of virtue. The notion of virtue is explained more fully in chapter 3. Virtues (such as the seven that help structure this book: faith, hope, love, prudence, justice, fortitude, and temperance) are stable qualities a person has that enable him or her to live a good life. One benefit of approaching moral theology through the virtues is that living virtuously (which is the same as living morally) accounts for the importance of rules without reducing the entire moral life to rules. Furthermore, focusing on virtue enables us to attend to the sorts of persons we become, and not simply the sorts of acts we perform. Finally, describing the good life through the virtues provides both a way to describe the commonalities between people of varying or no religious tradition, and a way to delineate the distinctiveness of the virtuous Christian life. As seen below, the very twofold structure of the book reflects this latter concern.

The third goal for this text is to present a comprehensive account of moral theology. Despite its reliance on a virtue perspective of morality, this text boldly seeks to present all important topics in the field of moral theology. Reminiscent of the first goal, the purpose of this text is not to present an academic field of inquiry called moral theology. Its starting point is the set of questions that our lives pose to us. But that starting point provides the context for exploring all of the main concepts of which any student of the discipline moral theology should grasp.

Fourth, a foundational claim of this book is that living a good life requires a truthful grasp of the way things are in reality. This claim is true not only with regard to the necessity of having an accurate grasp of ourselves and the world around us, but also with regard to the moral importance of our answers to what are called here "big-picture" questions: is there a God and if so what is God like? What is the meaning of human life? What happens after death? Our answers to these ultimate questions have enormous impact on what we think constitutes living a good life. While the first half of the book demonstrates how our understanding of "the way thing are" concerning worldly matters is morally important, the second half explains how critical for our lives are our big-picture beliefs about the way things are. Given this claim, a basic account of the Christian story of the way things are is offered here, along with more extensive treatments of key features of the Christian vision of the way things are.

The fifth goal of this book is to examine several particular moral issues. Many texts on moral theology (or Christian ethics) begin with, and perhaps rest exclusively with, particular contested moral issues. This is understandable, since any fruitful discussion of moral theology must eventually engage concrete issues. However, particular cases are purposely not the starting point of this book. They are treated only after extensive discussion of the virtues. The purpose of the four "test case" chapters in this book is not to offer an exhaustive treatment of each of those four issues (drinking alcohol, the use of the atomic bomb in 1945, when to have sex, and euthanasia). The purpose is twofold. First, each test case does indeed aim to offer practical guidance as to each of these actions or decisions. But second, this is done in a manner that attempts to illustrate the important difference it makes to attend to virtue in moral theology. It is hoped the discussion of cases in this book accomplishes that, in addition to (in fact, as a means of) offering persuasive positions on each of the issues.

The structure of the book flows directly from these goals. The book is divided into two halves based upon two types of virtue: cardinal virtues and theological virtues. The first half focuses on cardinal virtues, which are qualities that enable persons to do well those worldly activities that are part of any human life in any time or culture, including eating, drinking, sex, making decisions, relating with others, and facing difficulties. This half of the book describes simply how human persons function regarding such activities, and what qualities enable us to function well. The first three chapters address how human persons think and act in practical matters by addressing the topics: "why be moral?" (chapter 1), intentionality and freedom (chapter 2), and the nature and types of virtue (chapter 3). There is also a chapter on each of the four cardinal virtues: temperance (chapter 4), prudence (chapter 5), justice (chapter 7) and fortitude (chapter 9). Finally, both in order to demonstrate how the claims of these chapters play out and to offer practical guidance on particular issues, there are chapters on drinking alcohol (chapter 6) and the dropping of the atomic bomb in World War II (chapter 8).

The second half of this book begins with an explanation of how big picture beliefs are important for shaping practical reasoning in worldly matters, and how the Christian story in particular shapes the life of virtue (chapter 10). It then proceeds with chapters on each of the three theological virtues of the Christian life: faith (chapter 11), hope (chapter 13), and love (chapter 15). These are interspersed with chapters on key themes in the Christian story which, if a central claim of this book is true, are enormously important for living a life of Christian virtue: sin (chapter 12), Jesus Christ (chapter 14), and grace (chapter 16). Finally, there are two chapters on specific moral issues, again, both to offer practical guidance and to demonstrate how the claims of the chapters in this part of the book impact the questions of when to have sex (chapter 17) and how to best make end of life decisions, particularly concerning euthanasia (chapter 18).

As should be clear, the second half of the book is far more distinctively Christian than the first half. But for reasons mentioned in the following section and explained more fully in chapter 16, this should by no means be taken to imply that how we live out the cardinal virtues has nothing to do with Christianity and the theological virtues. The twofold division of this book does indeed signify an importance difference between the cardinal and theological virtues. But that difference should not lead one to conclude that the material of the second half has no bearing on the first half of the book. To the contrary, Christianity and the theological virtues transform and perfect how we live the cardinal virtues.

Finally, the epilogue addresses an otherwise neglected topic in this book: the importance of prayer, liturgy, and the sacraments for living the virtuous Christian life. Since this topic is way beyond the scope of a single chapter, the epilogue simply provides an example of the seamless integration of prayer and the virtuous Christian life by demonstrating how words of the Lord's Prayer, or the Our Father, both exemplify and further illuminate the seven virtues that help structure this book.

Caveats and Suggestions for Using the Book

(Especially for Moral Theologians)

The primary audience for this book is people who are not trained in the academic discipline of moral theology. Though the fruits of that discipline make up the content of the book, every attempt is made to start not from the methods and debates of the academic discipline, but rather from the more common everyday questions and experience that engender those academic debates. In sum, though this is a book of moral theology, its primary goal is not to help train people in the discipline of moral theology, but rather to enable people to understand and utilize their practical reasoning better so as to live more virtuous lives. That said, this present section is the only one in the entire book addressed primarily to teachers and practitioners of the field of moral theology. Its goal is to explain why the book has been written as it has, to enable this particular audience to better understand why (and possibly to critique so as to improve how) it appears in the form it does. Though all are of course welcome to read on within this section, be aware that the tone and content of the remainder of this introduction is not replicated in this book. The disparate topics addressed warrant a list.

1. As mentioned above, the book proceeds in two parts. What this distinction reflects is the relationship between nature and grace. This topic is treated directly in this book, but climactically in chapter 16. This could leave the reader to think for fifteen chapters that the importance of the topic is unrecognized or, even worse, that grace floats above, without transforming and perfecting nature. This would be a mistaken impression. In fact, each chapter on a theological virtue attempts to show how the natural capacities and longings of human persons are fulfilled and even elevated by grace. Furthermore, chapter 16 explains in detail how grace transforms human nature and the worldly activities of the cardinal virtues. The structure of this book as a whole actually makes an argument on how this question can be fruitfully addressed with the target audience of this book. In a manner reflective of chapter 11's read of John Paul II's *Fides et Ratio*, it starts from common human experiences to show how grace perfects nature. Another approach would be to start with the theological virtues and grace. The reasons for the approach adopted here are primarily strategic, given the target audience of the book. For a large majority of American university students today the claims of Christianity are at least somewhat alien. Christianity is thus most intelligible and compelling when presented as the completion and perfection of common human experiences, even though the person of Christian faith affirms that human nature originates in, and is only fully understood in the context of, grace.

2. Those familiar with traditional thought on virtues, and especially that of St. Thomas Aquinas, know that there is a particular order of the virtues. That order is respected in the second half of the book on theological virtue: faith, then hope, then love. It is not respected concerning the cardinal virtues, which in the Thomistic tradition are ordered: prudence, justice, fortitude, then temperance. Temperance is treated first among cardinal virtues for two reasons. First, its object of sensual pleasure is a particularly accessible one for contemporary readers and so it is a helpful way to start analysis of particular virtues. Second, temperance provides a perfect occasion to examine the moral importance of emotions, which continues the theme of the previous two chapters on the importance of interiority for the moral life. This chapter on temperance thus serves as the perfect transition from action theory to particular virtues.

3. Speaking of action theory, the primary task of this book is not to inaugurate its readers into technical debates among practitioners of the discipline of moral theology. Thus there is no adjudication of important debates between virtue ethicists and either consequentialists or deontologists, or on the existence of intrinsic evils, or on the distinctiveness of Christian ethics. One's positions on these debates obviously shape how one presents an accessible vision of moral theology. In fact, though the guiding task of this text is not to address these more technical debates, the vision presented in this book clearly takes positions on each of these, and other, debates. In other words, there is indeed an underlying argument in this book concerning the distinctiveness of Christian ethics, the existence of intrinsic evils, and other such questions. Nonetheless, the task of this book is not to explain the different sides of those debates or substantiate this book's stance on them.

4. Related to these debates, trained moral theologians will immediately note that three of the four test case chapters (8, 17, and 18) address absolute norms on different issues. People who deny the existence of absolute norms could reject this approach out of hand, or more subtly argue that the approach presented here is not truly a virtue ethic, but an old-fashioned (perhaps natural law) approach to moral theology that is simply dressed up with chapters on different virtues while actually being driven by the norms themselves. This particular criticism reflects a poor understanding of virtue ethics as unable to account for absolute norms. Each of these three chapters attempts to demonstrate that an absolute norm (such as no intentional killing of the innocent) is justified by the incompatibility of the action prohibited with the good goals of the activity at hand, be it waging war, having sex, or caring for the dying. Obviously these are hard cases (and chosen for that reason), so many will disagree with the conclusions drawn, and perhaps the approach employed here. But it is not an accurate critique to claim the positions herein are only extrinsically relayed to the methodology espoused in other chapters.

5. As for the test case chapters, the order they appear in the book basically reflects the order they are taught in the class. It would be ideal to have all the material in the other chapters assimilated before treating any one case, but this seems to lose students and readers, so the test cases are interspersed throughout the book. The chapter on drinking alcohol has limited treatment of justice and fortitude since it precedes chapters on those two virtues for precisely this reason. But students and readers benefit from examining an issue earlier on in the class. The chapter on the atomic bomb fits logically after that on justice, and thus precedes the discussion of fortitude in the following chapter. The two test case chapters in the second half of the book are placed after chapter 16 so readers can benefit from that chapter's material on grace and infused cardinal virtues while engaging questions of sex and end-of-life decision-making. In sum, while the order or presentation of the non-test case

chapters is part of the underlying argument of this book, the order of the test cases is intentional but not part of that underlying argument.

6. Finally, the tone of this book is purposely casual to make it accessible and inviting. This is a danger with regard to the precision of terminology. Some crucial terms in this book have common usages that are close in meaning to, but not exactly the same as, their meaning in this book. Examples include morality, intention, habit, passion, prudence, temperance, and so on. The confusion which may result from this reveals why some academics are drawn to devising technical terms which purposely do not relate to common usage. For both readability and methodological reasons, that step is not taken here and commonly used terms are employed technically, with every attempt made to be precise about their meaning in this context, often with attention to how that is similar to, yet different from, the meanings of more common usage.

Furthermore, sometimes in this book more casual terms are used as technical terms. The best examples are "big picture beliefs" and "innerworldly" activities. The former term refers to beliefs concerning what *Fides et Ratio* has called "ultimate" (or "big picture") questions. The latter term comes from *Veritatis splendor* and designates activities that people of any time and culture engage in since they are accessible to unaided human reason. This topic is taken up in chapter 3.

1

MORALITY, HAPPINESS, AND THE "GOOD LIFE"

*How Do I Live My Life,
and Why Do I Live That Way?*

In the opening lines of his autobiographical book *Confessions*, African bishop and theologian St. Augustine of Hippo describes the human heart as restless. We are restless, longing to be satisfied, to have our desires fulfilled and to be content in perfect happiness.[1] Italian friar and theologian St. Thomas Aquinas similarly begins his examination of morality with the observation that people long to be happy.[2] Contemporary priest and spiritual writer Ronald Rolheiser picks up this consistent theme and describes the longing that all people have. He claims that spirituality, far from some esoteric interest for New Age folks who burn incense in their rooms, is simply how we live out that restlessness, or longing, in our actions. It is what we do with our desires. Put

1. Augustine, *Confessions,* trans. Maria Boulding, OSB (New York: Random House, 1997), I.1.
2. Thomas Aquinas, *Summa Theologiae*, English Dominican trans. (New York: Benziger, 1948), I–II 1.

19

in this way, Rolheiser makes it clear that everyone has a spirituality. Everyone has some set of desires and some way of living out those desires.[3]

In one sense of the term, morality is simply spirituality, the having and living out of desires in life. In this general (descriptive) sense of the term, everyone has some sort of morality. Rolheiser makes this point by looking at the lives of Mother Theresa, Princess Diana, and 1970s rock 'n roll rebel Janis Joplin. He shows how each of these women had identifiable sets of desires in life, and distinct ways of living out those desires. Thus they each had a distinct spirituality, or what is called here morality.

Of course, this use of the term "morality" is more descriptive than normative. In other words, saying that all people have some identifiable ways of living their lives (the descriptive sense) is not the same as saying all people live the way they should live their lives (the normative sense). Consider any organized crime movie or television program (*The Godfather*, *The Sopranos*, or *Goodfellas*). There are usually very clear and defined ways to live, or rules, that dictate what one who lives the life of organized crime should and should not do. One of the oddly appealing things about such stories is the way the individuals' lives are so thoroughly integrated or ordered by their involvement in the mob. There is a clear mob morality, or set of rules, that dictates what should and should not be done, and it completely governs the lives of those involved. But with a moment's reflection we see how warped these lives are. The goals they are oriented toward include violence, exploitation, theft, and corruption. Though there is a clear morality here in the descriptive sense of the term, normatively speaking we may say things like, "These people have no morals!"

The fact that everyone has some morality, in the descriptive sense of the term, is an important point that will be revisited again later in this chapter. It also leads us immediately to ask normative questions: which ways of living are better than others? Are there some ways of living that should always be avoided? Awareness that there are different moralities in the descriptive sense invites analysis as to how to adjudicate them, to figure out which ones (surely there are many) are good ways to live, and which are not. This is what we normally think of when we think of morality—determining which ways to live are good. This book obviously engages in such analysis. But in order to be able to do so, some reflection is first necessary on a more basic question: why be moral? in the normative sense of the term. Why be morally good? We all know certain basic rules in life that we should follow: do not kill, do not betray your friends, do not lie, do not use others for your own purposes, and so on. Where does the "should" come from? Many of these are codified into civil law, and the reasons for obeying such rules may seem more obvious. But even beyond civil statutes, what is the origin or source of the moral rules, or

3. Ronald Rolheiser, *The Holy Longing: The Search for a Christian Spirituality* (New York: Doubleday, 1999), 3–19.

norms, to which we so frequently conform our lives? Identifying where these rules come from will help us to realize why we do (or do not) follow them, and help us to better adjudicate which ones are best to follow.

Much of moral theology is concerned with specifying exactly what the rules are. Is drinking alcohol OK, and if so under what conditions? Is killing by the state ever justified, as in warfare? When should one become sexually active with another person? Is it ever OK to purposely end a dying person's life at their request to put them out of tremendous suffering? The rules concerning these specific questions will all be discussed later in this book. But in this first chapter it behooves us to explore why we have any such rules at all. Why "should" we do anything? Where do these rules come from, and why follow them?

The first part of this chapter considers two answers to the question, why be morally good? and the resulting two approaches to morality. It begins with a famous text from Plato as an entry point to this question. The second section of this chapter relies on the lessons from the first half and attempts to more precisely define terms such as "morality" and "rules" in order to prepare the reader for how these topics are approached in the rest of this book.

Why Be Morally Good?

This may be one of those questions that is so basic you have never thought about it. "Why be morally good? Because that's what you do! Because you have to!" OK, but *why*? In the Western tradition of moral philosophy and theology there are two basic answers to the question of why be moral. Though there are important differences among the thinkers who represent each of the two answers, all representatives of each answer agree in their basic approach to this question. The two basic answers to this question then engender two basic approaches to morality. The famous *Ring of Gyges* story discussed below helpfully exemplifies these two basic approaches. After examining this story (which it would be helpful to read on your own), this section goes on to delineate what are called here a "morality of obligation" vs. a "morality of happiness." It then briefly explores the relationship of each to religion before asking you to reflect on which approach you espouse in your own life.

Glaucon vs. Socrates and the Ring of Gyges Story

Though a wide variety of answers to this question have been offered throughout history, Greek philosopher Plato's classic dialogue *Republic* features a debate between the characters Socrates and Glaucon that helpfully illustrates two basic answers to the question of why be morally good.[4] These two answers are still evident in how we think of morality today. In articulating his position, Glaucon first argues why he thinks people are morally good, or just (as in justice), and then tells the famous *Ring of Gyges* story to support his claim.

Glaucon claims that an ideally good life is getting whatever you want. Someone who had the power to get whatever he or she wanted would not worry about what is just, or what one should do. Why, then, do people worry about being moral, in the normative sense of the term (i.e., morally good)? Glaucon claims that though the best thing in life would be to do and get whatever you want even at the expense of others, the worst thing would be to have others who are stronger than you do and get whatever they want at your expense. He claims that the suffering involved in the latter far exceeds the good gained by the former. Therefore, people enter into agreements to neither do nor suffer injustice. These rules are enforced not only by laws but also by societal expectations and pressures, upbringing, and the like. This is the origin of laws and moral norms, and the reason why people generally obey them.

Therefore, being morally good is not what everyone wants, according to Glaucon. Morality is a second-best compromise. It is a sort of compromise between the best and worst extremes; it does protect us from suffering injustice at the hands of others (which would be the worst), but the cost is sacrificing the fully good life that we all *really* desire (which would be the best). As evidence of this claim, Glaucon cites the legendary *Ring of Gyges* story. The story serves as a sort of thought exercise to prove his point. In this tale, a shepherd finds a magical ring that gives him the power to become invisible. He can therefore do whatever he wants without suffering the consequences. Sure enough, Glaucon claims, the shepherd kills the king, seduces the queen, and takes over the kingdom. In short, he does whatever he wants because now he can.

Glaucon argues that if there were two such rings, one found by a just person and another by an unjust person, the two people would not act any differently once they had the ring. No one, he claims, is so incorruptible that she would continue to live in a morally good manner when she could take whatever she wanted, have sex with whomever she wished, harm whomever she wished, or "do all the other things that would make her like a god among humans."[5] Indeed, if a person with such power did not exercise it to her benefit, Glaucon claims, people would secretly think her stupid, even though they would publicly praise her in order to maintain the facade of their belief in morality to hopefully avoid suffering future injustices.

---

4. Plato, *The Republic* II.359–60, in *Great Dialogues of Plato*. ed. Eric Warmington and Philip Rouse (New York: Signet, 1984). Note that the book is by Plato, but it is the protagonist Socrates whose view is presented as opposed to Glaucon (though scholars claim Plato would agree with Socrates here).

5. Plato, *The Republic* II.359–60. The gender of the pronouns in this passage has been changed to fit with the rest of the paragraph.

This may seem shocking to us. We may say to ourselves, "I would never kill, rape, and steal even if I could do so without suffering consequences." Perhaps, but maybe this is because the very societal conditioning of which Glaucon speaks works so well. It does seem that at times we knowingly break the rules if we know we can get away with it. This may happen on small everyday matters, or on an even larger scale with drastic consequences. If you have ever asked a friend, "If you knew no one could find out and you could get away with it, would you . . ." then you have basically asked them whether or not they would behave as Glaucon suggests people would. Could it be that Glaucon is right, that we all really desire a good life constituted by getting whatever we want, and acting morally good is something we all do simply as a compromise, or because we fear suffering the legal or societal consequences of acting immorally?

In response to Glaucon, the character Socrates offers another view on the question, why be morally good? Socrates argues that the just, or moral life, *is* the good life. The most fulfilling and happy life is the virtuous life. In fact, our word "virtue" comes from the Latin (and ultimately Greek) word for excellence. As Socrates famously says in the *Crito*, the most important question is not simply how to live, but how to live well.[6] How can we have excellent, happy lives? For Plato, his student Aristotle, and later, Christian thinkers such as Augustine and Aquinas, the answer to this question is by living virtuously, or in a morally good manner. From this perspective, contrary to Glaucon, it simply makes no sense to speak of the good life as impeded by or distinct from the morally good life. The two are one and the same.

How would Socrates respond to Glaucon's *Ring of Gyges* story? We can imagine that he would say one of two things. First of all, if a just person did indeed turn to injustice once there was no threat of suffering consequences for such injustice, then he was not truly just in the first place. He was simply performing just acts so as not to get caught doing otherwise. Second, a truly just person would continue to act justly, even with the newfound power. A good example of this would be the movie *Superman 2*. Superman has powers akin to the ring bearer in that he can do practically whatever he wants and suffer no consequence for it. And yet he still protects justice. The three other people who arrive from Krypton dressed in black, however, would be more akin to Glaucon's ring bearer. Once they realize their powers on earth, they set out doing whatever they want. Socrates would not deny this possibility, of course, but would say both that these three characters were not just and that therefore they were not actually living fulfilling, satisfying lives.

6. Plato, *Crito* 48–49.

Two Different Visions of Morality

Socrates and Glaucon offer two strikingly different responses to the question, why be morally good? They offer radically different visions of the origin and purpose, if you will, of morality (in the normative sense) and moral rules. According to Glaucon, morality is a set of externally imposed obligations that we may agree to, but ultimately is not what we truly want. According to Socrates, living a moral life is actually what we all want (or should want), since it is the way to live the most satisfying, fulfilling, good life.

The approach to morality envisaged by Glaucon is called by one contemporary thinker a *morality of obligation*.[7] This is not simply a claim that being morally good at times feels like a burden, or an obligation. No one would contest that. Rather, the claim is that following moral rules is experienced as an obligation because following the rules is not what we really want to do since it is not the path to true happiness. We may obey willingly, to get a future reward or avoid punishment. But even in these cases it is not living morally that we want, but what living morally gets us, which is good enough to prompt us to endure following the rules in the meantime.

Socrates' view of morality is called here a *morality-of-happiness* approach. The main claim here is not necessarily that we feel happy whenever we act morally. Rather, the claim is that following genuine moral rules is what we all truly want since it itself constitutes living a good, truly satisfying life. From this perspective, it would make no sense to say, "Yes, that will make you happy, but you are not allowed to do that." The rules given by God—and by just governments, families, institutions, and the like—are themselves guides to living a good and happy life.

Consider an example to see how these two different visions play out in real life. Any college student knows that you should not cheat on your boyfriend or girlfriend if you are in a committed relationship. But why not? According to Glaucon, you may very well want to cheat on him or her, and there is nothing inherently "wrong" with that. The problem is, you may also be the one who gets cheated on. And you really do not want that. In order to protect ourselves from such suffering, there are societal expectations about being a faithful boyfriend or girlfriend. You can defy them, but you will suffer consequences. In this case, perhaps people will look down on you. Or it may be tough to get a future date. Of course, if you are sure you can get away with it, with no one finding out, all those reasons to restrain yourself disappear. You would be like the wearer of the invisible ring in Glaucon's *Ring of Gyges* story. In that case, you would be foolish not to do whatever you want, though publicly we would all praise you for doing the moral thing.

7. Servias Pinckaers, OP, *Sources of Christian Ethics* (Washington, DC: Catholic University of America Press, 1995), 14–22.

Socrates would approach this quite differently. He would say that there is a better reason for the rule not to cheat on your boyfriend or girlfriend. Living in right relationship with others is not some externally imposed obligation that impedes the good life. It *is* the good life. Being unfaithful may be alluring at times, but it is not the way to live a satisfying good life. It is not what you really want, because it is ultimately not the path to a good life. Of course, there are times when what we do want is not ultimately most fulfilling for us, like when we are tempted to cheat in a relationship. That is why good moral rules are there, to guide us when our own desires would lead us astray. Such rules are not impediments to, but aids toward, the happy life.

Religion and the Two Approaches to Morality

It may be tempting to think that one of these two perspectives is religious and one is not. But that is not true. For instance, the debate outlined above happens within pagan Greek culture. On which side does Christian morality fall concerning this question? Historically, and even today, Christians can be found on both sides of the question, why be morally good? For instance, believers who think that they should follow moral rules solely because God tells them to do so are reminiscent of Glaucon. In their case, the rules come from God and not simply from people's attempts to protect themselves from others. This is an important difference from Glaucon. But the similarity is that moral rules are externally imposed obligations that exist in tension with our wills, which are actually fulfilled when doing whatever we want. Perhaps there is some reward for following the rules, like going to heaven. But this reward is not intrinsically related to following the rules. Following the rules is not the good life. At best it is something we do to get rewarded. Whether it is held by religious or non-religious people, this approach to morality is rightly labeled a morality of obligation.

Similarly, both pagan and Christian thinkers alike have—and do—adopt a morality-of-happiness approach. It is Socrates' view of morality. Aristotle began his most famous book on ethics with a reflection on happiness.[8] It is also how most Christian thinkers through history have understood the Christian moral life. St. Augustine assumes in his main discussions of morality that the starting point for such reflection is how to live a happy life, and explains why the love of God and neighbor that Christ commands in all four gospels is the true path to happiness.[9] St. Thomas Aquinas follows Aristotle in be-

8. Aristotle, *Nicomachean Ethics,* in *The Basic Works of Aristotle. ed.* Richard McKeon, 935–1112 (New York: Random House, 1941), I.

9. Augustine's *On the Way of Life of the Catholic Church* (Washington, DC: Catholic University of America Press, 1966). There Augustine arrives at the great commandment to love God and neighbor as the summation of the happy life. Recall Augustine's opening lines of the *Confessions,* that our hearts are restless until they rest in God. Finally, for a more complicated

ginning his most famous discussion of morality with a treatise on happiness, and concludes with Augustine that God alone can fulfill the restlessness and longing that marks all human persons.[10]

What unites these thinkers who hold a morality-of-happiness approach is the assumption that reflection on human happiness leads naturally to morality and ethics as a path to that good life, rather than some impediment to it. Living morally (in the normative sense) is not an instrumental path to something else. Living morally is itself a response to the natural human longing for happiness and fulfillment. Of course, there is great diversity among these and other morality-of-happiness thinkers as to what exactly constitutes living a good life, and therefore what moral rules serve as the path to that happiness. Those differences are not dismissed here. Indeed they will be a major focus of the second half of this book.

But the twofold division between morality of happiness and morality of obligation is emphasized at the start of this book because people are sometimes surprised to hear that the dominant strain of the Christian moral tradition essentially addresses the question, how can we be happy? Or, as phrased in the Christian scriptures, how can we "live abundantly" (John 10:10) or gain "eternal life" (Mark 10:17; Matt. 19:16; Luke 18:18)?[11] To many people discussions of morality, and especially religious discussions of morality, tend to sound onerous and focus on obligation rather than happiness. We often simply assume that acting in a morally good manner is not what we really want to do! There are historical and theological reasons for the rise of a morality of obligation approach, reasons which we need not engage here. Much recent scholarship on both non-Christian and Christian morality laments this turn and suggests that a morality of happiness approach is more fruitful.[12] The main point here is that although discussions of morality can indeed take on a tenor of obligation, they need not.

Some people also wonder if and where the Bible speaks of living a happy life. Passages are actually not difficult to find, as indicated by the scriptural references in the last paragraph. Consider first the New Testament. In the Gospel according to John, Jesus tells his disciples he has come "that they might have life, and have it more abundantly" (John 10:10). Any rules Jesus offers are given so that people may live more fully. In fact, he enjoins his disciples the

---

examination of how different schools of thought seek happiness, see *The City of God* (New York: Penguin Books, 1984), xix.

10. Aquinas, *Summa Theologiae* I–II 1–5.

11. The latter quotation comes from the story of the rich young man in the synoptic Gospels. Pope John Paul II began the major moral theology encyclical of his pontificate, *Veritatis Splendor* (Encyclical Letter, 1993. Available online at www.vatican.va), with a reflection on this very passage.

12. From a Christian perspective see Pinckaers, *Sources of Christian Ethics*. For related themes concerning Greek ethics, see Julia Annas's *The Morality of Happiness* (New York: Oxford University Press, 1993).

night before his death to follow his commandments "so that my joy might be in you and your joy might be complete" (John 15:11, cf. 1 John 1:4). In Matthew, Jesus begins the famous Sermon on the Mount with the Beatitudes, each of which begins, "happy are those who . . ." (Matt. 5:3–10; cf. Luke 6:20–22). In Mark, Jesus responds to the rich young man's question about how to live a good life by offering him the commandments (Mark 10:17–19). In sum, the life of discipleship to which Jesus invites his followers in the gospels entails rules and commandments, but all in the service of living more abundantly, more joyfully.

As for the Old Testament, it is the book of Deuteronomy where God's commandments are most extensively presented. There we find several reasons why the Lord has given the Israelites the law, and why the Israelites should follow it (see Deut. 5–6). We do find injunctions to avoid the wrath of God (5:9; 6:2; 6:15) and obtain his mercy (5:10; 6:3). The Lord also contextualizes the commandments there as part of an ongoing relationship between the Israelites and their God who took them out of slavery (5:6; 5:15; 6:21–23). But the most common reason given here for why the Israelites should obey the commandments is to live a long life and prosper (5:16; 5:29; 5:33; 6:3; 6:18), and even to have a happy life (6:24).

Why Am I Morally Good?

Before proceeding in this book, it would be helpful to pause here and reflect on whether you hold a morality of obligation or morality of happiness perspective. Recall that those who take a morality of happiness perspective follow the rules they do because they think that doing so will lead to a most fulfilling, satisfying life. They know, of course, that living morally may often be experienced as an obligation: they may not feel like working out at times, or visiting a sick family member, or doing some service work, or holding their tongues while in an argument. But they know that they follow these rules, which can at times feel obligatory, ultimately because living according to such rules is the most fulfilling, happy life. In my own life, I know at times I do not feel like praying, but am always more fulfilled when I do. I know at times I do not feel like patiently listening when my wife is distressed, but know that when I do our relationship, and therefore my own life, is more genuinely happy.

Those who live out a morality of obligation are also trying to a live a good life that is most satisfying and fulfilling. They, too, are willing at times to follow rules that they do not feel like following. So they do not cheat on exams (even though it would be nice to get better grades) because they might get caught or, worse yet, because if everyone could cheat maybe they'd be even lower on the curve! They follow laws not because living justly is actually good for them, but because as part of society they will play by the rules everyone does so as not to be punished, or so as not to suffer injustice at the hands of others. They listen to parents or respected people in life not because it is a better way to live, but for some other purpose (free college tuition? to look like a good son or daughter? simply because it is the right thing to do?). They go to church not because nourishing one's relationship with God within a community is inherently part of a fulfilling life, but rather because it is respectable, or what their parents or grandparents would want. Note that in all of these cases one may follow the rules willingly. But doing so is still living a morality of obligation (rather than a morality of happiness) because there is no inherent connection between the rules and the happiness one seeks. Rather, one follows rules because it is what one ought to do, or because it will get one something that one really seeks, reasons unrelated to living according to the rules themselves.

Why Everyone Lives Some Sort of Morality, and Why That Matters

This reflection from Plato's *Republic* on "why be moral?" perfectly sets the stage for the way morality is approached in this book. The *Ring of Gyges* story makes it clear that everyone—even the shepherd with the power of the ring—has some vision of what it means to live a good life that results in some way of living to best achieve that good life. The diversity of visions of the good life leads to basically two types of reasons why people are moral. The story prompts us to reflect on where we have derived the moralities we live by and, relatedly, why we follow the rules we do. In particular, it prompts us to reflect on whether we live by a morality of happiness or a morality of obligation. The second half of this chapter frames these questions a bit more precisely in preparation for the rest of the book's discussion of morality and theology.

Everybody Has a Morality—Yes, Even That Guy

Why bother asking the basic questions "what is morality?" and "why be morally good?" to start this book? One of the main goals of this chapter is to expand the sense of terms such as "morality" and "rules" beyond the narrower, and in many ways limited, ways we may now understand them. By doing so, it becomes clear that everyone has a stake in discussing morality, whether they know it—or like it—or not. In the broad descriptive sense of the term, *morality* just means some identifiable way to live one's life, evident through the myriad of choices one makes. We decide to act or not to act. We decide when and how to act. We have to decide how to treat our friends or parents, whether or not to be loyal to a significant other, if and how to use alcohol, and if and how to become sexually active. Since everybody in life makes such decisions in one way or another, everyone has some morality in this descriptive sense of the term. Note this is as true of the shepherd in Glaucon's story as it is the people who obey the rules out of fear of the consequences of breaking them. Though only the latter are moral in the normative sense of the term we are accustomed to (i.e., morally good), all in the story have some sort of morality in the descriptive sense (and some form of morality of obligation at that!).

If we take a moment to examine the way we normally do things in different areas of our lives, we will be able to identify basic rules or guidelines we follow, even if these rules are not explicitly articulated, and/or we generally follow them unconsciously. Whatever guides our decision-making in those moments are the rules we live by. Much as we often think of morality in the too narrow sense of a set of obligations that limits us from doing what we really want (i.e., Glaucon's view), we too often understand rules simply as constraints that cramp our style and limit our fun. Though this can be the case, it is not necessarily so. When you want to be healthy, and thus decide to work out a few times a week, you are following a rule: work out in order to be healthy. If you want to be a loyal friend, you decide not to talk behind a friend's back. You are following a rule here. A *rule* is simply some sort of principle that guides our action. Note that in this broader (descriptive) sense, rules can be (normatively) good or bad. Even people whose rules we may disdain as deplorable nonetheless follow them. Hitler guided an entire society according to rules we now see as wretchedly wicked. On a less drastic and more everyday level, if you want to be healthy but also do not want to work out when you do not feel like it, your rule is do what you feel like doing at the moment. It may be a bad rule, but it is a rule. You may be willing to take something that is not yours if you really want it and deem it would not be missed by its owner. You are following a rule here: take what I want. Of course, people may look down on you, and depending on the situation you may be prosecuted for breaking the law. But in any case you are following some sort of rule; it simply may be a bad rule.

In these senses of the terms "morality" and "rules," everyone lives by rules and everyone has some sort of morality that describes their set of rules. Some claim that they would prefer to opt out of the whole morality conversation altogether. "Why can't we just eat, drink, and be merry?! What if I do not want to live by any rules? *Carpe diem*—seize the day! Live and let live! Of course you can approach life in this way. Many people do. But do not delude yourself that you are not living by rules. They are just different rules. For instance, the carefree perspective just described means that you should do what you feel like doing at any moment. (That's a rule.) It means you should not subject other people's acts and decisions to scrutiny. (That's a rule too.) It probably means you should not listen to any authority (parents, school administrators, law enforcement officers, church officials, etc.) that you do not want to heed (another rule). The point here is, there is simply no opting out of morality and rules in life, in the descriptive senses of those terms. There is plenty of variation as to what type of moralities we espouse, and what rules we follow.

But that's simply a different way of living out a morality, and not an opting out of morality.

Understanding morality and rules in these broader senses has the effect of getting everyone into the conversation about morality. This is an essential point for this book. For instance, when we debate the use of military force in a later chapter, we will see that the debate is not between people who attend to morality in warfare, and those who do not. The debate is between rival sets of rules, or moralities, in warfare. Some may say, "do not intentionally kill innocent people." Others may say, "win at all costs." But in the descriptive senses of the terms, both these sides have rules and moralities. Debate between them is not whether there should be morality in warfare or not; it is between what morality a person or society follows. The same could be said of those who support euthanasia (note it is always under very specific conditions, or rules) vs. those who do not, or those who think sexual activity belongs solely in marriage vs. those who think it can be done well outside marriage (but only under such conditions as consent, some sort of commitment or exclusivity—more rules!). For reasons discussed in the next chapter on intentionality and freedom, human persons are the sorts of creatures who operate according to rules of one sort or another.

Another effect of such a broad understanding of morality and rules is that it expands the conversation to include not only those who may be decried as immoral or amoral (in the normative sense), but also those activities in our lives that many do not see as in the realm of morality. One of the most important teachers in my life, Fr. James Keenan, SJ, taught me that morality is not simply about when you have sex, if you do drugs, whether you'd have or support an abortion, or whether or not you support the death penalty. These typical moral issues are indeed important, and are helpful to examine, as this book will, because as debated issues they illuminate the important points of difference between people whose rules differ from one another.

But if this is what morality were all about, over 90 percent of our lives would be morally irrelevant! What about the ways we treat our immediate friends and families? What about the ways we use and pursue financial resources? What about the host of daily practices and habits that we engage in? It is the claim of this book that these are morally important. Notice some of the examples above regarding the broader sense of morality and rules: how we pursue our health, how we talk to others about our friends, and how we use alcohol. These are very ordinary, everyday activities. But for reasons and in ways described more extensively in the following two chapters, how we conduct ourselves in these matters—in other words, the rules we live by in such matters—is crucial to shaping the types of persons we become and the types of moralities we live by. So this section concludes by noting not only that everyone has some sort of morality and rules they live by, but also that the scope of actions considered moral is far more broad than many of us imagine.

Who's Your Daddy? Or Where Does Your Morality Come from?

Having established that everyone has a morality, or ways of living out their lives that entail rules to guide their behavior, it is worth pausing a moment to ask where we get our moralities. Again, this will ultimately facilitate the task of adjudicating which moralities and rules are best. The rules we live by may be provided by parents, a religious community, a nation, a peer group, and/or other significant influences in our lives. College students are generally very attentive to the fact that the way they live their lives is greatly influenced by particular, contingent influences such as the parents they have, the religion they were brought up in, and the broader American culture in which they have been raised. (Interestingly, they are often all too oblivious of the at least as strict ways that their peers' expectations structure their lives!) All of these influences may be called *authorities* in that they shape how we live our lives, either formally or informally. Especially when we are growing into adulthood, but really at any point in our lives, we simply do not have all the answers we seek as to how to best live our lives. Thus we consciously or unconsciously (usually the latter) invest certain persons and institutions in our lives with authority, allowing them to shape how we live our lives under the assumption, even trust, that they present good ways to live.

Of course, we know that oftentimes authoritative influences like those mentioned above shape us in ways that are not good. They can corrupt us with their influence. Parents can be abusive rather than nurturing. Religious communities can foster bias or arrogance rather than virtue. Nations can lead their citizens to atrocities and injustice rather than justice. Historical and contemporary examples of all of these are easy to find. In reaction against both the at times corruptive nature of authorities, and even the fact that our lives are so powerfully influenced by such historically contingent forces as being born to particular parents with a particular religious tradition in a particular nation, young adults commonly respond in better or worse ways.

What sort of reaction is described here as "worse?" Sometimes people resist the very fact *that* their lives are so powerfully shaped by authoritative influences. Such people point to the very existence of authority itself as evidence that anyone who is so influenced is brainwashed, or simply conforming to societal (or religious, or family) expectations. There is at least an implicit suggestion here that if you do not strike out on your own and do things the way you want to, without the guidance of any authorities, you are not truly free. In fact, it almost seems that unless you end up opposed to influences commonly regarded as authoritative, you are simply a conformist.

But this is wrong on a couple of different counts. First, it seems to assume the problem is not how one is influenced by an authority, but that one is so influenced. There is, ironically, a very particular vision of morality latent here. It assumes that people are all first and foremost individuals who autonomously generate their rules, and only then possibly share their lives with others who have similar rules. But this is not right. People who hold such a view only do so because they themselves were influenced by different authorities who led them to see the attractiveness of this view, be it a particular set of parents, college professor, and/or peer group that revels in being countercultural. Note that the point here is not proving that these people are wrong in how they live. It merely demonstrates that what they should be reacting against are the specific rules and moralities their former authorities presented them with, rather than the fact that as social creatures we derive and sustain our moralities from some sort of social framework.

Second, this approach fails to consider that what an authority presents as a good way to live may actually be a good way to live! It may not be of course, but it also may be. Therefore, the better response to the fact that we are powerfully influenced by authorities is not to reject their influence completely, but rather to scrutinize the ways they influence us to ensure to the best we can that they are indeed offering good ways to live rather than destructive ones. This is a difficult task precisely because we are so influenced by our particular communities. But for that reason it is all the more important we do so. This leads us to the next claim about the purpose of this book on morality.

Why Bother with All This Reflection?

Perhaps by now your head is spinning and you are wondering, "why bother with all this?" Don't most people in our time and in past ages simply go through life without worrying about moral theology and all this reflection on morality and rules? Enough!

It is certainly the case that many do go through life unreflectively. It is even true that granting some very fortunate influences in your life, this may work out OK and lead you to a good life. But it is more likely that Socrates was right in his famous dictum that the "unexamined life is a life not worth living."[13] It may be a bit drastic to say that such a life is not worth living. But the basic claim that it is better to live a reflective life—that it is better to think about the ways we act and why we act that way—is wholeheartedly affirmed here. Why?

First of all, sometimes we have indeed been formed in corrupt ways, and without being challenged to reflect on our lives we will remain in the dark. Education serves this function superbly, illuminating unquestioned assumptions we hold as members of particular families, communities, and nations that may indeed need to be questioned because they are actually distorted ways of seeing things, resulting in distorted ways of acting. The growing realization over the past few decades of the ways racial biases distort our thinking and behavior is a perfect example of this.

13. Plato, *Apology*, 38a.

Second, there are many moments in one's life where big decisions have to be made that have everything to do with the sorts of moralities we espouse, the rules we want to follow, and the sorts of persons we want to be. What sort of career should I pursue, or is it time to switch to another? Do I want to be married, and if so is this the right person? What are my religious and spiritual convictions, and how is it best for me to live them out? These are important questions in our lives that are tough to answer. One of the reasons for that difficulty is that our answers to these questions will engender or reaffirm all sorts of specific rules about how we live our lives. Often the best data for discerning the answers to these questions is reflecting on ways we are already living, and asking which option to a question at hand enables us to continue those ways of living that we find life-giving, or truly happy, and to embark on new ones that we are attracted to as life-giving. But you have to have some sense of why you do what you do in order to make decisions well.

In fact, these comments on making important decisions accurately describe the methodology, or approach, of this entire book on morality. The basic goal of this book is to equip you to better understand the ways you act (your rules) and why you act that way, whether it be in everyday matters or in more drastic or dramatic situations. This will enable you to decide whether that is the way you *want* to live your life or not. God willing, in many areas of your life you will find your reflection consoling, affirming that you have indeed been living the way you would hope. In others arenas, you will likely become aware of ways you are unable to live up to the good rules you hold yourself to, and ways that the rules you have been living by are not most life-giving.

How the Rules We Live by Reflect How We "See" Things

As may already be clear from Glaucon's *Ring of Gyges* story, determining the best rules for living our lives is usually not simply a choice among options with no basis for choosing. The rules we live by generally point to certain things we think are true about the world we live in. This is why thinkers from the Greeks through Aquinas and beyond have consistently claimed that the good life is a life lived in accordance with reason. With the possible exception of Stoic and Kantian morality, this is not an injunction to live rationalistic lives devoid of passion and imagination. It is rather a plea to live in a manner that reflects an accurate grasp of the "way things are" around us, which our capacity to reason helps us to grasp. It is seen in Christ's injunction to "know the truth and the truth will set you free" (John 8:32).

As an example of living in accordance with the truth, or reason, consider the racism example mentioned above. If people of different races really are unequal and differ in dignity, then what we call "racism" is an appropriate rule to live by. Of course, thankfully, we have increasingly come to realize this is *not* the case. Racial differences, while culturally important for how we live our lives, do not differentiate levels of human dignity. There is equality among different races. So if I were to reflect on how I live and realize that I do judge people unequally based upon race, deciding whether to commit myself to live by a different rule or not is actually a judgment—explicit or implicit—that I think people of different races are equal or not. In this case, as with so many of the rules we live by, the best rule reflects the most truthful judgment about the "way things are" in the world around us.

This is certainly true of Glaucon in the story above. Recall that Glaucon thinks morality, or justice, consists of that set of rules we live by not because we think it the path to a good life, but rather because it is the best we can hope for given the sorts of persons we are and the sort of society we live in. After all, we all really desire to get whatever we want. And since that is true of everyone else, then the best we can hope for is a society where people live by rules that protect us from being victims of others' desires, even if that means we can never fully achieve our own. Note the assumptions here. People are most fulfilled in satisfying their every desire, whatever that may be (which in his story consists of murder, seduction, and theft). Society is a fragile balance of self-indulgent egos living in the uneasy tension of restrained rivalry. And, of course, there is no God offering any guidance or final judgment that might impact why and how people do what they do.

This is clearly not a Christian vision of reality. It is not even the view of non-Christians such as Plato and Aristotle. It rests on certain assumptions about the "way things are" concerning ourselves, society, and God. If Glaucon is right that this is how things are, the vision of morality he presents makes perfect sense. If people really are most fulfilled doing whatever they want, and society really is a balance of competing interests, and if there is no God to consider in these questions, then Glaucon is right as to where moral rules come from and why we follow them. If you or I found a ring of Gyges, we would indeed be fools not to act as the shepherd did! But of course, if Glaucon is wrong in his vision of the way things are, this way of life is not only sadly unfulfilling, but actually false.

Christians, as well as non-Christian opponents like Socrates, must take seriously the fact that Glaucon could be right. If he is, the way of life he espouses follows naturally. Of course, on this question Christians (with Socrates) argue Glaucon is wrong. Here is a great example of how our moralities are shaped not only by how well we see visible things around us (like race), but also how we understand the answers to big-picture questions about the nature of the person, society, God, the afterlife, and so on. Demonstrating the connection between morality and those big-picture questions is the main task for the second half of this book, and thus we leave it aside for the moment. For now we can simply take away the point that determining the best rules to live by in matters such as race relations, drinking alcohol, having sex, going to war, and the like, entails making judgments concerning what is true about the world around us.

Adjudicating Different Moralities and Different Rules

This chapter began with the claim that everyone has some sort of morality and rules to guide them in living that morality. That observation led to an obvious question: how do we evaluate and adjudicate between different moralities? If a simple answer to the basic question, how should I live? could be offered at this point, there would be no reason to read any further. Only through more detailed examination of different virtues and particular issues can we answer that question with any specificity. Nonetheless, some basic insights on adjudicating different moralities can be offered from this chapter's analysis.

Determining the best way to live depends a great deal on why you think you should be moral in the first place. If you hold a morality-of-obligation perspective, then determining which rules should be followed is a matter of determining who or what the proper authority is in some situation, and what that authority says to do. It may be God, the church, one's family, the nation's laws, or (for someone like Kant) one's pure practical reason. Whatever their source, the rules are imposed on us as obligations according to this perspective because they are not inherently connected to the further goal of human happiness and flourishing. Therefore, determining which rules are best is less a matter of demonstrating their connection to human flourishing than it is an issue of who or what has proper jurisdiction in the area under consideration, and what does that authority dictate.

Yet from a morality-of-happiness perspective, living morally is simply living a most fulfilling, happy life. Rules that we follow not only point us toward that further goal, but are a very participation in that goal, rather than simply a means to some extrinsically related end. So different moralities and rules are adjudicated by determining which one, or ones, best lead to true human happiness or flourishing. In this approach, authorities are indeed important. We heed them because we do not know fully by ourselves the best way to live. But authorities are heeded not simply due to their status (as my God, my church, my family, or my nation), but as conduits to a better life. And they are able to lead us in such a way to the extent that they represent a truthful grasp of the way things are in the world, and thus what constitutes true human happiness.

Of the two paths described here, the one endorsed in this book is clearly the morality of happiness. For reasons explained more fully in the following chapter, this approach seems to best explain why people do the things they do, even when they seek happiness poorly. Nonetheless, it should be recognized at the outset that this is not to say there is no room in a morality-of-happiness perspective for rules that are experienced as obligations. Particularly with children, and even for us adults who are less mature in certain areas of our lives, sometimes we follow the rules at moments when their connection to happiness is not at all clear. Yet even when this occurs, from a morality-of-happiness perspective the hope is that our following the rules (likely in deference to some trusted authority) will lead us to eventually see and experience how doing so is indeed constitutive of true happiness.

Concluding Thoughts

We now end where we started, with the two different approaches to morality suggested by the *Ring of Gyges* story. Given that all have some sort of morality, why are we moral in the particular way we are? The second half of this chapter has gotten us to the point where we may fruitfully apply the lessons of Plato's story to our own lives. We now see that everyone has a morality, some set of rules that they live by. We are more attuned to how different communities and persons influence us in obtaining and sustaining these rules. We hopefully see the value in reflecting on the way we live our lives so as to realize how we live, how we learned to live that way, and whether or not we want to keep living that way in the future. How we determine the way we want to live will be in large part shaped by what we think is true about the world around us.

Study Questions

1. Does everyone have a "morality?" Use the terms "descriptive" and "normative" to explain your answer.
2. According to Glaucon, what does the "good life" that all people really want look like? Is it the same or different than the "moral" (or "just") life? How does he use the *Ring of Gyges* story to make his point?
3. According to Glaucon, why are there laws and moral norms? Why does he call justice a "mean between two extremes"?
4. Why does Socrates think people are moral? How does he understand the relationship between morality and the good life? Imagine how he would tell the *Ring of Gyges* story to make his point.
5. Describe the similarities and differences between a person who lives a "morality of obligation" and one who lives a "morality of happiness."
6. Which of these two approaches do religious people hold? Explain.
7. Why is it the case that everyone lives according to certain rules? Use the terms "normative" and "descriptive" to explain.
8. Where do people learn their moralities (in the descriptive sense)? What problems does this pose, and what is the best way to address such problems?
9. What do most classical thinkers mean when they say it is best to live "in accordance with reason"? Give an example to explain it.

Terms to Know

Glaucon, *Ring of Gyges* story, morality of happiness, morality of obligation, morality (descriptive vs. normative sense), moral rules (descriptive vs. normative sense), authority

Questions for Further Reflection

1. Early in the chapter it is claimed that the recognition that there are many moralities, in the descriptive sense, invites normative analysis of which moralities are better or worse. How would you respond to someone who said they did not want to judge which ones are better or worse? What drives this impulse in people? What dangers are there in failing to identify certain moralities that are worse?
2. If everyone has some sort of morality, in the descriptive sense of the term, does that mean there is no way to adjudicate which moralities are better or worse (in the normative sense of the term)? If it can be done, how so?
3. What are some concrete examples of how authorities in our lives can be questioned in a manner that is not simply dismissive?
4. What would you say to someone who says that everyone really follows a morality of happiness approach, since they follow the rules they do ultimately to pursue their own happiness?

Further Reading

It would certainly help to read the brief *Ring of Gyges* story from Plato's *Republic* in conjunction with this chapter. (I have used the excerpt of it from the Guignon text cited below.) More broadly, the work of Fr. Servais Pinckaers, OP, is the driving force behind the chapter. Of course, his claim is that the morality of happiness approach is actually most true to great Christian and non-Christian thinkers such as Plato, Aristotle, St. Augustine, and St. Thomas Aquinas, and thus he is simply helping us read these authors the way they intended to be read. For a significantly shorter version of the extensive argument he presents in *Sources of Christian Ethics*, see his brief *Morality: A Catholic View*. Any of the classic texts cited in this chapter can then be read with Pinckaers' argument in mind. A fine collection of relevant texts from throughout the Western tradition and beyond can be found in Editor Charles Guignon's *The Good Life*.

2

INTENTIONS, GOOD ACTS, AND HUMAN FREEDOM

In the last chapter we claimed that everyone has some sort of morality, or set of rules, to live by. We then looked at why people follow the sets of rules they do, and found an important difference between a morality of obligation and a morality of happiness. But though we spent some time reflecting on why people are moral in general, we spent no time figuring out how to determine the different particular ways people do what they do. How do we specify the types of people that we and other people are? How can we ascertain what our different actions mean in order to try to evaluate those actions as good or bad?

This chapter continues our preparation for more specific evaluation of particular virtues and moral issues. The purpose of this chapter is not to claim that all people have desires that they live out in certain ways (the point of last chapter) but rather to describe how we can identify the different desires people have in life, how they give meaning to our actions, and how they give each of us a certain character. This is necessary in order to be able to evaluate different moralities and different actions. To that end we explore two crucial concepts in moral theology here: intention and freedom. The first half of this chapter explains what an intention is, and how intentions render our actions both intelligible (i.e., understandable or meaningful) and open to moral evaluation. In fact, through examining intentions in our lives, we can arrive at a stable vision of our characters, or "what we are all about." The second half of this chapter examines the notion of freedom. After defining freedom and offering three classic terms to help describe free actions, the chapter concludes with a challenging discussion of two different types of freedom.

Intentionality: People as Purposeful Creatures

Consider an everyday occurrence you might witness in a hallway before class. A young lady is walking along when she suddenly drops her books and they scatter across the hallway. A young man witnesses the situation, stops, and bends down to help the young woman pick up her books. This is a seemingly straightforward event. But what exactly happened here? Does this situation have any moral relevance, beyond simply serving as some random act of kindness? The last chapter implied that morality is at least as much about everyday occurrences as it is about intensely contested ethical issues; is that true in this case? The first part of this chapter will help us better understand this event, our own actions, and even how all our actions fit together to make up our character. It will do so by exploring a crucial concept in moral theology: intention.

What is an Intention?

An *intention* is a goal or purpose toward which we direct ourselves. It is the specification of our desire. It answers the question, "what do you want?" or in Jesus's own very first words in the Gospel according to John, "What are you looking for?" (John 1:38). You want to become a teacher, to do service work, to be a good friend, to go and work out at the gym, and so on. Notice that you do not simply want, or desire in general. You desire something. And what you want is grasped, or understood, as something more or less specific. That is why we say that acting intentionally not only involves pursuing, or fleeing, something, but also a grasp of what it is we pursue or flee. For human persons, this means that acting intentionally is a function of our wills whereby we move toward, or away from, something, and our intellect or reason whereby we grasp or comprehend what we are pursuing or avoiding. For example, I want to be a good friend to someone. And I understand that being a good friend means helping my friend move into a new house, sharing my hopes and fears, and listening when he or she is in need. Therefore I pursue or seek (with my will) those things I grasp (with my intellect) as making me a good friend.

Notice also that intentions exist at a variety of levels. You can intend (or in Jesus's words, "look for") something very limited and immediate (say, to go work out), or something far longer term and more important (say, to be a teacher). Furthermore, some of our more immediate intentions are for the sake of longer term intentions. So you may come to class regularly because your further goal is to succeed in the class and get a good grade. You intend to succeed in class and get a good grade because you desire the even further goal of becoming an educated person and graduating with a degree.

To explicitly connect this analysis to the previous chapter, we intentionally seek goals because we seek our own happiness. Whatever we intentionally do we do because we think it leads to our happiness, either directly or as a means to that happiness. Note that this does not contradict the preceding chapter's distinction between a morality of happiness and a morality of obligation. People who live a morality of obligation still do things intentionally, and do them ultimately to be happy, whether they recognize that is what they are doing or not. We say they espouse a morality of obligation rather than happiness not because they do not seek happiness; after all, even Glaucon wanted to be happy and live a good life! Rather, their morality is one of obligation because the moral rules they obey—the things they do to be morally good—are seen at best as things to be grudgingly endured on the path to happiness, or at worst as impediments to or (as in the case of German philosopher Immanuel Kant) a separate realm from that happiness.[1] The point is, to recall opening words of this book, people are restless, longing to be happy and have their desires fulfilled. The intentions we have in life reveal what we think will make us happy and how we pursue that happiness in our actions.

That is why—though as noted above intentions exist on a variety of different levels—what they all have in common is their power to guide actions. You only have an intention in the proper sense of the word when it drives an action, or purposeful inaction. This is one way in which the use of the term "intention" in moral theology differs from common usage. Sometimes we speak of "good intentions," as when we hear "the path to Hell is paved with good intentions." This phrase implies that you have some intentions that never translate into action. That is not an intention in the technical sense of the term. An intention is a purpose or goal you have that drives some sort of action. You hope or wish for things all the time that you never pursue. Properly speaking, you only have an intention if it guides your action or purposeful inaction.

Intentions Make Our Actions Meaningful

The intricate connection between intention and action leads to a further point about intention. Not only do intentions prompt actions, but they also make those actions intelligible, or meaningful. Human persons are the sorts of creatures that act for purposes, and you cannot fully understand their actions without some sense of their purposes. Therefore, intentions are what make our actions intelligible (literally, "understand-able"), or meaningful.

---

1. The Stoic school of philosophy is an interesting challenge to this dichotomy since they claim that acting virtuously *is* happiness (and so seem to espouse a morality of happiness), and yet hold such an idiosyncratic view of what constitutes happiness that they seem disconsonant with other adherents of that approach.

Recall the above example of the young man helping someone pick up her books. What is happening here? We can easily describe what the young man did here: help someone pick up her books. But we really do not have a sense of what this act means without looking at his intentions. Why did he help her pick up her books? Is he simply a considerate person who saw someone in need, and responded with what help he had to offer? Was he trying to impress the young woman to get a date, or impress someone who was watching close by? Was he concerned that someone watching might know that he is active in church and campus ministry activities, and think him a hypocrite if he did not stop to help? All of these are different intentions that might have prompted the same act of helping the young woman pick up her books. Needless to say, that same act could have very different meanings based upon the intention at hand. It could be an act of generosity, or a clever move to get a date, or a façade before others to evade charges of hypocrisy. That is why we have to attend to people's intentions to truly understand what their actions mean.

Consider another example. Every term I teach in college, I find the students generally quite motivated to succeed in the course. Yet there are many different reasons that could be driving them to do their reading, study for tests, write good papers, and the like. Some students rely heavily on their parents' affirmation, and good grades gain that affirmation. Other students want to get good grades to get into the best law school possible, in order to eventually make the most money possible. Some students study to maintain athletic eligibility, which is what they really desire above and beyond their education. Other students want to learn the material in the class to have a better understanding of themselves and the world. We can therefore only really understand the meaning of these different students' actions (in this case, studying for class) by attending to their larger goals for those actions.

Because intentions are so crucial in giving human actions their meaning, they also help us evaluate actions as good or bad. For instance, we can judge if the purpose driving the act is praiseworthy or blameworthy. If I do all sorts of nice things because I want people to think I am generous, we will likely think less of those acts, and me as a person, than if I did the same thing in order to help someone in need. Realizing people's intentions can also help us determine if the actions they perform are effective ways of achieving that purpose or goal. When we eventually adjudicate between different moralities and rules, a key part of that task will be determining which goals are good or bad, and more or less important. From a morality of happiness approach, what this means is determining which goals contribute to or detract from, and are more or less constitutive of, human happiness and flourishing. Knowledge of intentions not only enables us to evaluate the goodness and relative importance of those intentions, but also how effectively or ineffectively our chosen courses of action lead to those goals.

At this point students commonly wonder about mixed intentions. What if I was trying to help the person in need, but also did it to feel good about myself, and so that others would think me compassionate, and perhaps even to get a date out of it! It is surely the case that we commonly have many reasons to do a certain act. But remember that intentions are properly understood to be action-guiding. So though we may have various hopes or wishes that accompany an act, what intentions are actually driving you to do the act? Would you do it if no one else were around? If so, that wish to appear compassionate before others may be present, but it is not the intention driving the act.[2] You would have done it otherwise. Would you have done it had you not been attracted to the person you were helping? If so, the hope for a date may have been there, but it was not driving the act. Of course, sometimes different circumstances may reveal that we would not have done the act, and that does indeed reveal something about our true intentions.

Another way our intentions give our actions meaning is by shaping how they are done. For instance, if a student's goal in class is to achieve good grades for the sake of admission to a prestigious graduate school, then truly learning the material, rather than simply preparing to put right answers on the test, would be less important. One might even be willing to cheat to secure those grades. Doing either of these would of course be nonsensical if one's true intention were to learn more about one's self and the world through understanding the course material. We could also imagine two seniors who already have jobs approaching their studies at the end of the spring term quite differently based upon their intentions for college study. All of these reflections reveal why it is that intentions make our actions intelligible, or give them their meaning.

Intentions Shape Who We Are

When we think of human actions, we most likely think of what effect or change people's actions make in the world around them. What do people's actions accomplish? What good or harm do they do? These are of course crucial questions since it does indeed matter how our actions effect change in the world around us. Recall the example above. When the young man helps the young woman with her books, one effect of this action is that the books get picked up. It would certainly be a very different situation if he kicked her books down the hall and jeered at her! Thus our actions have what is called a *transitive* effect; by our actions we make changes in the world around us.[3]

2. This is why the word "wish" is used here rather than intention, an important distinction for later discussion of euthanasia.

3. The "transitive/intransitive" distinction used here was found in Paul Wadell's book *The Primacy of Love* (New York: Paulist, 1992). He cites its origin as John Finnis's *Fundamentals of Ethics* (Washington, DC: Georgetown University Press, 1983).

But our actions do not only impact the world around us; they also impact our very selves. Our actions shape who we are.[4] By performing certain acts, we shape the sorts of persons we are, for good or bad. In the above example of picking up books, if the young man acts for the purpose of being generous, it helps to make him a more generous person. He is a different person than he was before the act, since now he is more considerate. If he had helped the young woman simply to look compassionate in the eyes of others, he would also shape his very self, though in a different way. Such an act would make him more of the sort of person who does good things to impress others. The impact that our actions have on ourselves is called an *intransitive* effect.

It is not simply the type of action performed that shapes our very selves. This should be clear by the fact that the same external act can shape us in varying ways. Rather, it is the intentionality of the act that both gives it meaning and determines what sort of way it will shape who we are. What we do is guided by intentions that reveal what we hold to be important. Acting on those intentions not only reveals what we think is important, but also further ingrains that purpose or goal in our lives. The next chapter will explore the dynamics of how exactly this happens by examining habits, virtues, and vices. For now it suffices to note that due to intentionality, our actions not only impact the world around us (the transitive effect) but also shape our very selves (the intransitive effect).

Intentions and Our Character

In the myriad of activities we perform through a day, year or life, we see reflected a multitude of different goals or purposes that drive us to action. By examining the different purposes in our lives we can discover who we are by what is important to us, by what drives our actions. Attending to intention gives us a very realistic account of who we are. Since intentions are action-guiding, discerning who we are by the multitude of goals and purposes in our lives means that who we are is not some idealized or abstract account, but rather is determined by what we do and why we do it. This is why we become what we do.

If our lives are made up of a multitude of goals and purposes, how can we give any consistent sense of who we are? Doesn't this imply that our identity is constituted simply by what we are doing at the moment? Though our goals exist on a variety of levels and change over time, there is a consistency to our character since some goals are more important than others and some persist over time. To get a sense of what purposes in life are more important to you, consider what you prioritize when a conflict arises and you have to choose one. For instance, faith, family, work, friendships, home, leisure, exercise,

4. For a beautiful discussion of this point, see Paul Wadell, *The Primacy of Love*, 29–36.

and service work may be purposes that are all important to you, and which guide actions in your life. Will your studies come first or your leisure time with friends? When time with family and your work conflict, which generally wins out? Making, say, family most important in your life certainly does not mean you are not devoted to work, your friends, etc. But it does mean when conflicts arise that family generally wins out.

By reflecting on what the goals are in our lives that drive our actions, and what relative importance we attach to each of these purposes, we obtain a sense of our character. Each of us is a constellation of intentions lived out in varying ways and with varying priorities. We might imagine them pictured as a triangle, with our less important (but still action-guiding) intentions at the bottom (taking care of my car, keeping up with a favorite team, occasional tennis with a friend, etc.), more important ones toward the middle (spending time with friends, exercising, etc.), and the most important ones at the top (family, faith). Goals toward the top of the triangle are our higher priorities that win out when conflicting with other goals. As noted above in the case of college students who study to learn versus those who study to eventually get a high-paying job, higher priorities not only win out over lower ones, but also shape how those lower ones are done. How we live out our set of priorities reveals our character.[5]

Though thinkers have debated this question for millennia, a broad stream of the Western tradition has maintained that each of us has one ultimate goal or purpose in life.[6] We might describe this as "what we're all about." What do you believe is your greatest good, or purpose, to which you are most consistently turned because you believe it best for you? For some it may be their faith. In fact, the Judeo-Christian tradition interprets the great command to love God with all your heart, your mind, and your soul as indicative of the believer's highest goal in life: God. For some, it may be one's family. We hear some people say, "there is nothing I would not do for my family." For others it may be money, or power, or status, or pleasure. All of these are common answers people live out to the question, what are you all about?

Why insist that each of us has one ultimate goal in life? Isn't it clear from what was said above that we have a multitude of intentions governing our lives? Claiming that we are each ultimately "all about" one ultimate purpose does not mean such a person has only one intention in life. It simply means it

5. Many thinkers are attracted to the terms "story" and "narrative" to describe both how particular actions fit into our overall lives, and how our lives of a multitude of goals and desires can still be coherent. For a helpful introduction to "narrative theology," see Stanley Hauerwas and Gregory Jones, eds., *Why Narrative? Readings in Narrative Theology* (Grand Rapids: Eerdmans, 1989).

6. For examples of this claim, see Aristotle's *Nicomachean Ethics*, in *The Basic Works of Aristotle*, ed. Richard McKeon (New York: Random House, 1941), I. and Thomas Aquinas, *Summa Theologiae*. English Dominican trans. (New York: Benziger, 1948) I–II 1.

is the overarching goal that shapes all others. It wins out when other priorities conflict with it. Furthermore, it even shapes how we do other things. The person of faith, for instance, can be a devoted family member, employee, reliable bowling partner, and so on. But all those lower goals of varying levels stand in relation to her ultimate goal, and are related to—or at least do not interfere with—that ultimate goal. A fine example of this is the troubling story of Jesus seemingly denouncing his mother and brothers, and saying that you cannot follow him without "hating" your family (Luke 14:26). A categorical rejection of family simply does not make sense given Jesus's life (see John 19:26–27). But what makes perfect sense of this troubling claim is Jesus's consistent refusal to put anything—even his family—before his mission to spread the kingdom. When a conflict between family and mission arose, there was no doubt which would win out for him.

Conversely, a conniving status seeker can at times care for his family, exercise, go to church, and so on. But when push comes to shove, any of these varying lower priorities will yield to an opportunity to gain status. In fact, how each of those lower goals is lived will be shaped by the ultimate goal of seeking status, such that church may be also an opportunity to look wholesome, and exercise may be a way to become more attractive and charming. One's ultimate goal in life does not simply win out when intentions conflict. It also shapes, or governs, how the goals that are below it are lived out and pursued.

This is precisely why the Sermon on the Mount's words on putting God above all else are so important. Christ exhorts his followers to put the kingdom of God first, and not let anxieties over mundane or even other important matters interfere with discipleship: "seek first the kingdom of God and His righteousness, and all these [other] things will be given you besides" (Matt. 6:33). He implores his followers to store up heavenly, rather than worldly, treasure, since "where your treasure is, there also will your heart be" (Matt. 6:21). Finally, the governing importance of one's highest goal in life is nowhere more obvious than in Christ's famous claim that "no one can serve two masters. He will either hate the one and love the other, or be devoted to one and despise the other. You cannot serve God and mammon [money]" (Matt. 6:24).

By attending to what intentions guide our actions in life, how they are lived out particularly in relation to each other, and what constitutes our ultimate goal in life, we obtain a sense of our character. What we hold important and why we do what we do is revealed to us. In short, it reveals what we think true happiness consists in and how we pursue it. This is the essential starting point for any moral self-reflection. Who are we, what do we do, and why? By attending to these questions and their honest answers, we can begin to determine the ways that we are proud of our characters and hope to further ingrain them, and the ways we realize the need to change to live better lives.

Some Qualifiers on this Vision of Intention

This vision of intention, and how our goals are prioritized to reveal our characters, may seem rather static and deductive, as if we go through life in a staid manner, mechanistically acting out more important goals over lesser ones. This is not the case. The claim here is that people act for purposes. These intentions are specific, which enables us to morally evaluate them. They not only guide our actions but shape our very selves, making us certain sorts of people. Furthermore, our goals may be prioritized hierarchically to reflect what intentions are more or less important to us. Finally, we all have some highest good, ultimate aim, or overall plan in life that governs all other intentions.

Nonetheless, though the above claims are all indeed affirmed here, the following qualifications, or caveats, must be kept in mind. First, we generally do not self-consciously understand all our actions as hierarchically ordered, and then make choices with some vision of this triangle in mind. If we pause to reflect on what we do, and what takes precedence in our lives, we will indeed discern some sort of prioritization in our lives revealed by our actions. Nonetheless, this is lived out dynamically and often without thinking, rather than self-consciously and deductively.

Second, our actions do not reflect the whole of our hierarchy or goals, in proper proportion, at each moment or day or week. Exercise may be an important, but not really important, goal in your life. But when you are working out, you are likely focused on it alone. During exam week, studies may consume our lives in vastly disproportionate ways given the impending exams. But this is not an indication of their consistent relative importance in our lives. In other words, at certain times lower or middle goals may assume seemingly disproportionate importance. This may well be a function of time frame, and not an indication of their relative importance in our lives. Part of the virtuous life is having the practical wisdom to determine what those times are, a topic discussed in a later chapter.

That said, even while focused disproportionately on certain goals at certain times, one should not act in ways that positively defy and deny higher purposes in one's life. It is one thing to see less of my friends or spouse during a stressful time in the term. It is another to steal those same friends' notes due to my more immediate goal of passing finals, or to let the stress of added work make me cruel or short-tempered with my spouse. These ways of pursuing the immediate goal at hand would positively defy the higher goals, rather than be insistences where they are temporarily on hold.

Third, it is not the case that we always act in a manner that is perfectly consistent in reflecting our higher and lower intentions. Even the most reliable among us deviate from our integrity and act against goals that we hold as important to us. Sometimes we get caught up in a moment and lose our sense of priorities by focusing on lower goods over ones we know to be more important. The reasons why this happens are examined in a later chapter. Though ignorance and immaturity are common causes, the Christian tradition affirms that the most common cause is human sin. Of course, if acting against goals we hold highly important happens consistently enough, it is no longer accurate to say that the goal is truly more important to us. But apart from that, sometimes we are simply inconsistent in how we pursue the most important goals in our lives.

Fourth, this chapter's claims about possessing a consistent character, or triangle of purposes in our lives, should not be taken to deny that people change over time. Sometimes this happens developmentally, or through stages in life. To use an obvious example, married parents have priorities in life (spouse, child) that simply did not exist before they had those people in their lives. Sometimes these changes are equally obvious but not simply developmental, as when someone suddenly gains or loses faith. Someone could develop an addiction, as to alcohol, or cease such an addiction. These sorts of changes impact one's entire triangle not only by introducing or eliminating a higher level goal, but also in the resulting impact of that change on the other goals in one's life. That said, though people certainly change over the course of their lives, the attention to character examined here is not so fluid as to be something that changes daily.

Fifth, notice that there has been no discussion here of whether one's higher goals in life are actually good or not. More obvious examples are given here, such as the development or curing of an addiction, or performing good acts for recognition or out of genuine generosity. But the detailed task of evaluating one's particular life goals and their relative importance is not the task of this chapter. Later chapters will examine what constitute good and bad intentions and actions concerning issues such as drinking alcohol, waging war, having sex, and making end-of-life decisions. The goal of this chapter is to illuminate the dynamic of how people's intentions shape their lives, so that you can become aware of what to look for in assessing your own life, and then do so in the company of family, friends, mentors, and the like.

Freedom and Human Action

What does this chapter's discussion of intentionality have to do with human freedom? Since most of the above discussion of intention is equally a discussion of freedom, it would help to pause and define freedom, especially in relation to intentionality. As noted above, an intention is most properly a goal directing an action and making that action meaningful. Something is grasped and pursued, or fled. In this broader sense, animals can be said to act intentionally. Beavers build dams; birds seek food for their young; sheep run from wolves; salmon swim upstream to spawn, and so on. These animals all have some grasp of something, and then seek or avoid it. All of these actions are goal directed, and their proper meaning is grasped only by understanding that goal.[7]

But of course we would not describe the beaver, bird, sheep, or salmon as "free" in these instances. Free action is goal-directed activity, but not simply that. It is the activity of a person who understands the goal of an activity and therefore does, or does not, do it with a certain understanding of that goal in mind. Animals have some grasp of the goal they pursue, but it is supplied by their instinct, or at times by training from humans. They do not properly understand what they are pursuing as one option among many, so as to be able to choose otherwise. We might picture two circles, one larger, with the smaller one inside the larger. The larger circle would represent intentional action, while the smaller subset would represent free action. All free action is intentional, but not all intentional action is free.

The discussion of intentionality in the entire first section of this chapter, since it focuses on human intentionality where the goals are understood and embraced by the one acting, is actually a discussion of free intentional action. Though we often speak of free will, our wills are free due to the power of reason, by which we understand the goals we embrace. In fact, it is precisely the human power of reason that distinguishes us from animals and makes us truly free. It is our reason that gives us free choice, since it enables us to understand different goals, and pursue one or the other—or none at all. This is why the *Catechism of the Catholic Church* defines freedom as "the power, rooted in reason and will, to act or not act, to do this or that, and so to perform deliberate actions on one's own responsibility. By free will one shapes one's life."[8]

Helpful Terms in Evaluating Free Action

Moral theology is all about understanding and evaluating free actions, the things we do intentionally in our quest for happiness in life. With the above discussion of intentionality and a precise definition of freedom in mind, you are now ready for several terms that will help you morally evaluate different actions and situations. These terms will be invaluable in later chapters' discussions of issues such as drinking alcohol, having sex, making end-of-life decisions, and waging war justly. In discussions of moral theology, for an act to be "good," it must be good in *object*, *intention*, and *circumstances*. Though these terms may sound foreign, you actually use these ideas all the time. To understand

7. For a fascinating discussion of intentional action in dolphins, and an exploration of the pre-rational roots of practical reasoning, see Alasdair MacIntyre, *Dependent Rational Animals* (Chicago: Open Court, 1999).

8. *Catechism of the Catholic Church*. 2nd ed. (Vatican City: Libreria Editrice Vaticana, 1997), 1731.

what each of these means, consider a classic example used by both Aristotle and St. Thomas Aquinas.[9]

A ship captain is out at sea. A terrible storm arises, such that the lives of his crew as well as the safety of the cargo are dangerously threatened. When it seems the ship may indeed sink, the captain orders the crew to throw all the cargo overboard to lighten the ship and keep it afloat. Though Aristotle and Aquinas use this case to make a slightly different point, it perfectly illustrates our three terms.

The *object* of an act is what is actually done. Identifying the object can be a tricky matter. The trick is to name the action in the most specific way possible, without reference to longer-term goals. Yet the act must still be described in a rich enough matter that it has meaning. For instance, if asked upon return to port what he had the crew do, it would be a poor description of object for the captain to say, "I had them save the ship." While true, this is not specific enough to name the particular act that was done. It is a longer- term goal. On the other end of the spectrum, it would also be accurate but unhelpful for the captain to say, "I had the crew lift up and drop boxes of cargo." While true, this does not describe the crew's actions in a meaningful way. The object here is throwing cargo overboard. This names the specific action that is done in a meaningful way.

What is the intention? The *intention* is the goal or purpose we have in mind for doing an action. Often we use phrases such as "in order to" or "to" or "so that" when we reveal our intentions. In the above scenario, the cargo was thrown overboard to lighten the ship and keep it afloat. Thus the intention here is to save the ship and its crew by lightening the ship.

Finally, what are the circumstances of an action? *Circumstances* are features of the situation which, although secondary, help determine the morality of an act. This case, like all cases, is full of them. How bad was the storm? How heavy was the cargo? Would sending crew on deck put them in more danger? As indicated by these questions, the circumstances are crucial in determining whether the object of a particular action is a wise way to achieve even a good intention. As should be clear after explaining these terms, one must consider all three features of moral action. For an action to be labeled good it must be good and fitting in object, intention, and circumstances.

Though these terms are technical, they help us sort through the moral evaluation of activities with greater ease. You actually do this all the time, even if you are just now learning the names of these three terms. Recall the case of the young man helping to pick up books. When we say it is important to know whether he kicked the books further or helped pick them up, we are asking what the object of the action was. What did he do? When we give various reasons

---

9. This example can be found in Aristotle's *Nicomachean Ethics* III.1 1110a, and Thomas Aquinas's *Summa Theologiae* I–II 6,6.

for why he might have done that act, we are inquiring as to his intention. If you have ever said something like, "She was really trying to . . . ," what you were saying is that the intention was not as it seemed. Finally, circumstances are also important. Even if the young man did this act with a good intention, if it was done while he was delivering insulin to someone in diabetic shock, we will probably protest that given the circumstances, he could have let the young woman pick up her own books!

Therefore, when people act freely, they knowingly engage in a certain activity (object), for a purpose (intention), with a good grasp of the situation (circumstances). When this occurs, we say they are responsible for their actions, and we may praise or blame them depending on the sorts of actions they perform or the purposes they hold. When we are responsible for our actions, they do not just happen to us but are done by us and thus shape who we are (as mentioned above and described in detail next chapter). When we act freely we ourselves are the source of an action. Therefore free actions reflect and further ingrain who we are.

Becoming Free: Two Types of Freedom

Talk of "becoming free" may seem odd to certain people. Many think that freedom is like a light switch. It is on or off. You are free or not. You are free when you act without any external influences such that your action is just from you. You are not free when you are forced by some influence or state of affairs to do something that you yourself would not want to do. There are clearly some cases where you act intentionally but are not free. For example, if you are passing by a bank one morning and some bank robbers grab you at gun point and force you to drive their getaway car, are you free? You understand the goal of getting the robbers safely away from the scene of the crime, and you act toward that goal by driving them. Therefore, this is an intentional action. In fact, you presumably could have acted otherwise, refusing to participate, even at the possible cost of your life. But if you were to participate, it would not accurately be labeled a free action because it happened *to you*, rather than arising *from you*. It was forced upon you rather than chosen. The technical term for some external force or pressure that leads you to do something in a manner that lessens, or even removes, your responsibility for an act (praise if it is good, blame if it is bad) is *duress*. In the case of your coerced participation in the bank robbery, we would say you acted under duress and thus are not responsible for (in this case blameworthy for) the act. Even though you did it, it was not your act.

It is easy to see in this case how you are not responsible for your act, and therefore not free. But other instances from our lives reveal that the variety of influences in our lives are far more subtle, and so it is not accurate to group all our actions into two black-and-white categories—free or not free—depending on whether or not we were coerced by external pressure. For instance, what of other pressures like peer pressure, or that exercised by a boyfriend or girl-friend? What of the pressure to be financially secure, or receive our parents' approval? These external influences certainly impact how we act. Do they make us less free, and therefore less responsible for our actions? What of a series of bad influences in one's life back through childhood (absent parents, abusive siblings, manipulative teachers.)? For that matter, what of good influences such as loving parents, good teachers, financial security, and others? Do these bad or good influences make us less free for our actions since they are shaped by external influences? At what point do those influences become duress and lessen our responsibility for our actions?

The point here is not to claim that since we are all subject to external influences we can never hold people responsible for their actions. The point is that freedom is best understood not as a binary capacity that is either on or off, but rather as a capacity we have by which we understand and internalize as our own the actions we do. Even when we are the recipients of bad or good influences, to the extent that we are mentally capable of understanding our actions and that we take on, or internalize, the goals and meanings of those actions as our own, then we are responsible for our actions, and we act freely. It is true that this process of internalization is a continuum rather than an on/off switch. It is also true that at some point on that continuum people are determined to have taken on their actions adequately enough as their own that they are responsible, even despite the presence of significant external influences. If this were not the case, we could not, for instance, have courts and jails. But nonetheless, people can become more free to the extent that their actions are understood and undertaken as their own.

There are other reasons why people can be more or less free in the sense of having our actions be our own. Chapter 5 will examine different forms of ignorance, and explain to what extent we are, or are not, blameworthy for ignorance that impedes our ability to live well. That chapter will also briefly explore the influence of unjust social structures on how we live. Nevertheless, the presence of any external influence whatsoever does not "turn off" our freedom; our actions are generally shaped by external influences rather than simply originating from us alone. The point here is that human persons are free because we have the capacity to understand and undertake our actions as our own, and we are more or less free in particular situations to the extent that our actions are indeed our own.

According to one perspective on the meaning of human freedom, as long as your actions are truly taken on as your own, then you are fully free. In this view, it does not matter what you choose to do; as long as the action is truly your own, you are free. This perspective is called *freedom of indifference*, because you are free no matter what you choose (hence "indifference"), as long as it is your choice.[10] However, according to a second perspective on freedom, being truly free depends not only on whether the action is your own, although that is certainly necessary too. It also depends on what you choose. This perspective is called *freedom for excellence*. The assumption here is that freedom is a human capacity with a purpose: the happiness and flourishing of the human person. So it is fully exercised not only when actions are taken on as our own, but when those actions contribute to our happiness and flourishing (hence "excellence"). On this view, the person who chooses what is true and good is actually more free.

To illustrate the two different approaches to freedom, consider the story of the rich young man in the Gospel according to Mark (Mark 10:17–22; cf. Matt. 19:18–22 and Luke 18:18–23). A young man approaches Jesus and asks how to inherit eternal life. Christ exhorts him to follow the commandments. When the man says he has done so since his youth, Jesus "looked at him, loved him, and said to him, 'You are lacking in one thing. Go, sell what you have, give it to the poor and you will have treasure in heaven; then come, follow me.'" We read that the rich young man's face fell and he walked away sad, "for he had many possessions."

This extraordinary passage could be pondered for countless insights about the moral life. But for our purposes in this chapter, the key question is, "Was the rich young man free when he walked away?" We assume he never came back, though we cannot know for sure. We do know he went away sad, and we have no evidence that he was dragged away against his own will. In other words, he clearly chose to walk away. The question is, when he made that choice, was he fully free?

It depends on which perspective on freedom you hold. From a freedom of indifference view, the rich young man is clearly free. He chooses to walk away; no one drags him. You may reply that he seems torn or conflicted by that decision since we read he walked away sad. Maybe so, but that inner conflict is his own rather than imposed on him. The story clearly implies he can choose to follow Jesus, but does not. According to a freedom of indifference perspective, the rich young man is indeed free, since the choice to walk away is his own.

However, according to the freedom for excellence perspective, it is not enough for an action to be one's own in order for a person to be fully free. That is certainly necessary, and if an action is not truly one's own, then the person is not fully free (or even free at all). But in addition to this condition, to be fully free a person must not only choose, but also choose what is good. Thus from this perspective, assuming Christ's invitation was

---

10. For extensive work on the two different types of freedom discussed here, see Servais Pinckaers, OP, *The Sources of Christian Ethics* (Washington, DC: Catholic University of America Press, 1995), 327–378.

indeed the path to eternal life, the rich young man actually acted against his own freedom.

This very way of speaking sounds oxymoronic to some. How can a person act against his own freedom, if the act is chosen by him? True, if freedom is just the ability to do whatever you want, you cannot act against your own freedom. But if freedom is the ability to choose to act well in pursuit of truth and true happiness, then not only can you choose to defy your freedom, but positively you can continually grow in his freedom through good choices.

The question here is what is the purpose, or point, of human freedom. If human freedom is simply a capacity to choose, then one is free no matter what one chooses. This is what the freedom-of-indifference perspective claims. Note that these people do not say that any exercise of freedom is equally good. They also hope people use their freedom for good choices. But even when they do not, they are still fully free since they have used their freedom to exercise a choice.

The freedom-for-excellence perspective holds that the point of human freedom is not simply its exercise, but its use for the flourishing and happiness of the human person. They of course recognize that people can choose badly. And they even admit that when people choose poorly they may well be free in the more limited sense of making the choice themselves. (Otherwise they could not blame people for choosing wrongly.) But they also claim that since the point of freedom is to contribute to the happiness of the person rather than simply to be used in no matter what way, then people are more free to the extent that they choose what is true and good and thus leads to happiness. From this perspective freedom is more like a skill to be developed than a binary capacity that is either on or off like a light switch. This perspective is seen perfectly in the *Catechism* when it says:

> Human freedom is a force for growth and maturity in truth and goodness; it attains its perfection when directed toward God, our beatitude [happiness]. (1731)

> The more one does what is good, the freer one becomes. There is no true freedom except in the service of what is true and just. The choice to disobey and do evil is an abuse of freedom and leads to the "slavery of sin" (cf. Rom. 6:17). (1733)

> By deviating from the moral law man violates his own freedom. (1740)

Appealing to some common experiences may help make this claim more understandable. Surely all of us have experienced failing to refrain from acting on a bad habit that we knew we possessed and were trying to change. Some examples are trying to quit smoking, or stopping a habit of procrastination, or trying to avoid losing your temper. When you fail to avoid these things, you are not only acting badly, but actually defying your own freedom by doing so, even if it is you yourself who is making the choice. Of course, some might reply that this is only because we possess some sort of desire to not act in that manner. But according to the freedom-for-excellence perspective, it is also true that we can defy our freedom even when we act willingly and without hesitation or remorse. Perhaps you have had the experience of seeing a friend engage in behavior you know to be wrong. Though she may not see it and thus acts willingly, from your perspective you can see how the behavior, though freely chosen, is not in her true best interest. Thus she is acting in a manner that is keeping her from living as rewarding and satisfying a life as possible. And so she is defying her own freedom. An extreme case would be watching someone willingly develop a drug habit. You might wonder how she could limit herself like that, how she could do that to herself. If you have ever had a response like this, toward your own actions or toward those around you, your response reveals your awareness that true freedom is not only doing what one wants, but wanting what is genuinely best. That is freedom for excellence.

One more case will help illuminate the difference between freedom for excellence and freedom of indifference, and also prepare us for the following chapter on virtue. Consider two spouses. The husband struggles to be faithful to his wife. He is constantly tempted to cheat on her. But he never acts on his temptations. His wife, on the other hand, experiences no such temptations. She knows she wants to be with her husband, and after years of marriage has become so accustomed to their life together that she does not even imagine, let alone experience a temptation to, being in a sexual relationship with some one else. The question is, who is more free?

From a freedom-of-indifference perspective, you could say both are equally free. Both make their choices and do what they want. Perhaps the husband is even a bit more free. Choosing to sleep with someone else is a live option for him and so he has more choices, whereas in the sense of entertaining various options the wife seems to have fewer choices and thus less freedom. Yet from a freedom-for-excellence perspective, it is abundantly clear that the wife is more free. She easily chooses what is good for her. She may seem to have fewer choices, since she never considers being with someone other than her husband. But since this fidelity is both chosen by her, and what is truly good for her (assuming that is the case), she is actually more fully free than her husband. The following chapter on virtue will continue this line of thought by explaining how it is that people can reach the point where doing good becomes ingrained in them, as it is in this case with the wife.

This treatment of the two perspectives on human freedom is very challenging to people. Some insist it is not right to insert into our understanding of freedom notions of goodness or badness, such that acting poorly is a failure to be fully free. Such freedom-of-indifference proponents may indeed agree that it is best to use freedom for the good, but also think that you are fully free even if you choose poorly, as long as it is your choice. Yet proponents of the freedom-for-excellence perspective insist that the human capacity for freedom is integrated with, rather than apart from, the sets of goals that lead a person to happiness. Either way, since both sides agree it is best to exercise one's capacity for freedom by choosing what is good, it is not necessary to decisively settle this difference here before proceeding with the rest of the book, and in particular the next chapter on how to become the sorts of persons for whom choosing well is easier and more consistent.

Concluding Thoughts

We have now come full circle back to the topic that began chapter 1 of this book. Is morality the path to happiness? Or is morality a matter of obligations that limit our happiness? The former perspective is that of Socrates and leads to a morality of happiness. The latter is that of Glaucon and leads to a morality of obligation. Each of the two types of freedom seems more at home in one of these perspectives on morality than the other. The morality of obligation perspective reflects the freedom-of-indifference view, since the exercise (or not) of one's freedom has no connection to one's happiness. Yet the person who holds a morality of happiness would surely say that only choosing to live the moral life, which is the truly happy life, makes one fully free. While the immoral person may be called free in some sense because he is responsible for his actions, he is not fully free since freedom is a human capacity that is meant to be exercised in a manner that leads to our fulfillment. The exercise of choice alone is not the point of this capacity. It is to choose well. The following chapter explains how choosing well shapes us into certain sorts of people by developing habits in us called virtues.

Study Questions

1. Define intention. How do intentions render our acts meaningful?
2. Describe how our various goals in life are related to each other such that we can get some coherent sense of a person's character.
3. Define freedom. Why is it important that freedom is an act of will and reason?
4. Define object, intention, and circumstances, and use an example to illustrate each.
5. What is the difference between freedom of indifference and freedom for excellence? Be able to use the story from Mark 10:17–31 to explain each one.

Terms to Know

transitive and intransitive features of human action, intention, free will, freedom of indifference, freedom for excellence, object, circumstances, duress

Questions for Further Reflection

1. Do any human actions have no intention? Do any significant human actions have no intention? If not, why not? If so, what do they look like?
2. Need it be the case that each person has one ultimate goal in life? Is it possible to have a set of balanced priorities without naming something as overarching? Explain.
3. Freedom is described here as a human (rather than animalistic) sort of acting intentionally. What ramifications of this analysis are there for better understanding child development and parenting?
4. Which perspective—freedom for excellence or freedom of indifference—do you espouse and why?

Further Reading

For a helpful and accessible survey of the morality of human acts and human freedom, see the *Catechism of the Catholic Church* 1730–1761. Thomas Aquinas's *Summa Theologiae* is the classic source for the action theory described here, but the text is very difficult. Daniel Westberg's *Right Practical Reason* and Charles Pinches' *Theology and Action* are helpful, though also challenging, expositions of Aquinas's thought. An accessible explanation of intentionality is found in Paul Waddell's *Primacy of Love*. Servais Pinckaers, OP, explains the different notions of freedom in his *Sources of Christian Ethics*. Finally, Pope John Paul II's encyclical *Veritatis Splendor* is an important exploration of Catholic moral theology, the entire first section of which is a detailed analysis of the rich young man story from Mark.

3

WHY VIRTUE?

The Moral Life as More Than Actions

In the previous chapter we examined the intentionality of human action. There we claimed that intentional action is intransitive as well as transitive, in that our behavior not only impacts the world around us, but shapes our very selves. In that chapter's treatment of freedom, we saw the *Catechism* claim that "by free will one shape's one's own life." As of yet there has been no discussion of exactly how this works. Why is it that our intentional actions shape our very selves? What does this matter for moral theology?

This chapter explores these questions through an examination of virtue. As noted in the introduction, the topic of virtue, through the seven main virtues of the Christian tradition, structures this entire book on moral theology. So this chapter is foundational for the rest of the book. It also provides a lens through which to examine the moral life in a richer way than approaches that concentrate solely on actions, rules, and contentious cases (abortion, death penalty, etc.). To explain why this is the case, the first section examines the relationship between persons and their acts by defining the tricky term "habit." The second section briefly defines virtue and then answers the "why bother?" question by explaining why attending to virtue—rather than simply good acts—is an important task for moral theology. The third section distinguishes between two categories of virtue: cardinal (these four virtues structure the first half of the book) and theological (these three virtues structure the second half of the book). The fourth section gives basic definitions for each of the cardinal virtues. The fifth and final section examines why the four cardinal virtues have been such a consistent way to characterize the good life in the Western tradition, and yet why there are important differences in naming the specific acts of those virtues.

Acts, Persons, and Habits

In the words of one contemporary moral theologian, we human creatures are "underdetermined."[1] We have many capacities: to eat, make decisions, allot goods, have sex, and so on. How well or how poorly (and in what particular ways) we develop these capacities depends on how our freedom is exercised—or, in the terms of chapter 1, what morality we have and what rules we live by. We have capacity for greatness, and also great destructiveness, to both ourselves and others. Particularly in the formative college years, but even throughout our lives, our lives are unfinished, and each of us can become the sort of person who is pleased with, or who regrets, who he or she is.

This is really a lofty way of saying we are free. But we are free not only in what actions we perform, but also in the very selves that we sculpt. As the *Catechism* claims, by our freedom we shape not only what we do, but who we become. How does this happen? Obviously our actions are crucial to who we are. As the gospel says, a tree is known by its fruits (see Matt. 7:17–18 and 12:33; Luke 6:43–44). No discussion of who a person is can neglect what she does. It would be ludicrous to label someone cruel who always genuinely acts generously to others. That said, we commonly speak as if someone should not be equated with her acts. We know that a cruel person can perform a considerate act, and a just person can break the law. We even say things like, "she's not like that!" when we observe a discrepancy between a person's act and who she is. But how do we ascertain who she is, and how does she get that way?

Western thinkers from Greeks such as Aristotle, through medievals such as Aquinas, and up until today have used the term "habit" to describe an abiding quality a person has that characterizes who he is.[2] We often refer to mindless activities like biting your nails, or vices like smoking as habits. But the term has a broader, richer meaning in moral theology. "Disposition" and "inclination" are also terms that capture the meaning of the technical term "habit," though the latter is used here since it the most common translation of the original

---

1. See Paul Wadell, *The Primacy of Love* (New York: Paulist, 1992), 106–24.
2. The classic text in Aristotle where he explains the moral importance of habit is books II and III of the *Nicomachean Ethics* in *The Basic Works of Aristotle*, ed. Richard McKeon (New York: Random House, 1941), 927–1112. See also Aristotle's *Categories*, especially chapter 8, 1–137 of the same volume. For Aquinas's most systematic thought on habits, see his *Summa Theologiae* (New York: Benziger Bros., 1948), I–II 49–54.

Latin term *habitus*. Habits are a sort of middle ground between a person and the person's acts. They are more stable qualities of the person than particular actions. So when our friend arrives late and we say, "that's not like him," we are saying that he was late in this particular action, but he is not the sort of person who is late. Habits are the more enduring qualities that make you a certain sort of person. Yet they are still changeable. One can be a stingy person, and later in life become quite generous. Hence habits are more indicative of who we are now than individual actions, and still may be changed over time.

How do we obtain habits? A very common way of obtaining a habit is through repeated actions. Consider the example of developing the habit of exercise in order to be healthy. Initially this may involve the first step of over-coming a contrary habit, such as your inclination to sit on the couch, watch TV, and not worry about exercise. You resist this and go to the gym instead because you know you want to be healthy. The second step would be repeat-ing this act over and over to ingrain it, so it becomes more natural to you. You may eventually arrive at the third and final stage in the development of a habit, when the habit becomes such a part of who you are that you exercise effortlessly—with pleasure and promptness—such that you even feel "off" if you stop exercising regularly. Good habits make us the types of persons who do good things readily.

Consider another example. Your friend Joe continually has the capacity and opportunity to donate money to those less fortunate, and yet consistently refuses to do so. Joe develops the habit not of generosity but of stinginess. We would call Joe cheap, and though he might perform an occasional act of generosity, such as picking up a tab for his friends at a restaurant, we would be surprised if he did so and say, "that's not like Joe!" Of course, if Joe began to perform generous acts repeatedly, eventually we would stop saying it was out of character and call Joe generous. But that would entail first overcoming his habit of stinginess, then repeating generous actions to ingrain the new habit, and eventually—and ideally—doing generous acts with pleasure and promptness.

As noted above, sometimes when we hear the English word "habit" we can think of simple, mechanistic repeated actions. I might say I have a habit of tapping my pen on the desk when I read. But the term habit, as it is used in moral theology to apply to persons with reason and will, has a richer sense that includes not only consistent external actions but also their corresponding intentionality. For instance, consider two other people besides your friend Joe who is cheap. Mary is generous, and does as much as she can to help those in need. While Joe is, unfortunately, still cheap, Mary is generous.

A third person, Lucy, is also accustomed to donating money to charitable causes. Yet in Lucy's case, she only does this in public settings, as when the collection goes around in church, or when a club is raising money in her dorm. She is doing it in order to look generous in front of others. In fact, if she had an opportunity to be generous with no one watching, there is little chance she would donate the money. She does not have the same habit as stingy Joe, because she does indeed donate money at times. But neither does she develop the same habit as generous Mary, even though both consistently perform similar acts of donating money to those in need. The difference between these latter two is their intentionality. As a stable quality of a person, a habit consists not only of what exterior acts one does, but also of the intentionality of the act (its "intransitive" feature). Lucy consistently donates money to the poor, but since she does it to look good in front of others, she does not develop the habit of generosity. Of course, it is better for Lucy to occasionally donate money to those in need (even if it is done to look good in front of others) than, say, steal from those in need. But she is not rightly called a "generous" person because though the object of her action (giving money) may help others, the goal (intention) of her action is not for the good of those in need. That fact will impact how and when she gives money to those in need. Note that Lucy does indeed develop a habit—but it is the habit of doing good acts to be seen by others. We might use the terms two-faced, hypocritical, or self-promoting to name the habit Lucy develops with regard to helping those in need.

Therefore a habit should not be thought of as a mechanistic rut where meaningless actions are performed repeatedly. The reason habits develop has everything to do with intentionality. In the above example, Joe, Mary, and Lucy all have different intentions. Recall an intention is an act of will and reason since something is pursued or avoided (will) as it is understood to be (reason). How people consistently act reflects and further ingrains the way they see situations. The stingy person (Joe) sees his resources as solely for his own use, and he acts accordingly. The generous person (Mary) sees her resources as there to serve her own needs but also those of others, and she acts accordingly. The person who gives only to appear generous (like Lucy) sees her resources as aimed at the further goal (intention) of aiding her reputation, and acts accordingly. By repeatedly acting on these intentions, they ingrain in themselves a way of seeing things, and thus a settled way of acting in similar situations.

Thus habits are related to, but not equated with, performing certain types of actions. This relationship is cyclical. It is often through repetition of intentional actions of a certain type that habits develop in the first place. Then, once one possesses a certain type of habit, one is inclined to do more such actions in the future. Again, habits of character do not operate deterministically. In other words, though they incline one to more such actions in the future, one can act out of character. Nonetheless, the influence of our habits is such that Aristotle famously called habits "second nature."

It is this point that makes attention to habits in moral theology so important. Recall from the last chapter that each of us is a constellation or triangle of different goals or priorities that stand in different degrees of relative importance. Pursued intentionally, these attachments or priorities shape who we are.

Taken as a whole, these stable characteristics or habits represent a person's moral character since they reflect (and when acted upon further ingrain) not only what the person does but also who the person is. The various habits a person possesses are the way to ascertain the person's character, what he or she is all about.

Focusing on Virtue: Why Bother?

Having come to an understanding of habit, we are ready to understand what a virtue is. Simply put, a virtue is a good habit. Since a habit is an abiding quality in a person that inclines one to act in a certain way, a virtue is a habit that inclines one to act in a good manner (both externally and intentionally). Conversely, a vice is a bad habit. It was noted above that we humans have a multitude of capacities (eating, making decisions, allotting goods, having sex, etc.). What acts we perform from a certain capacity, and how we understand those acts, defines the habit we have regarding that capacity. A good habit is a *virtue*, and a bad one a *vice*. These virtues and vices often have common names. Generosity is using one's resources well with genuine concern to help others. Stinginess is using one's resources poorly by refusing to help others when one can. Determining exactly what acts characterize a virtue versus a vice is a task for discussions of specific issues. For example, chapter 6 will explore what virtuous drinking of alcohol looks like versus vicious, or vice-like, drinking. The task here is to explain exactly what a virtue is, and argue what difference it makes to attend to virtue in moral theology.

What difference does it make to think about morality from the perspective of virtue? Chapter 2 provided us the resources to evaluate particular actions as good or bad—object, intention, and circumstances. If morality is about how to live, why bother attending to what virtues (or vices, for that matter) people have? Isn't this just another way of saying that someone performs a certain good (or bad) action frequently?

The resources for answering this question have already been mentioned in the previous section on habit. A habit is not simply a way of calculating how frequently a person performs a certain type of activity in a certain way. A habit is an abiding disposition that changes who a person is. It resides in a person like a second nature, according to Aristotle. Therefore, the virtuous person is not simply someone who consistently performs good actions, although that is certainly the case. Having a virtue also changes who one is. Understanding this is crucial not only for evaluating specific cases, but also for helping ourselves become virtuous people. Therefore, some word on the difference between being a virtuous person, and simply performing good actions, is necessary here.

C. S. Lewis uses the example of playing tennis to differentiate someone who has a virtue from someone who simply performs good actions.[3] Imagine two people playing tennis. One is an accomplished player, and the other unskilled. Surely the good player may miss a shot. And the poor player may occasionally hit a good shot. But it is the good player who will reliably hit good shots, and the poor player who will not. This is a perfect example of how the sort of habits one has—in other words, the sort of person one is—may not be accurately represented in a particular action. The virtuous person is obviously akin to the good player.

Why is being a good player in life more important than simply doing good things? The first reason Lewis mentions is reliability. The person with a virtue, like the good tennis player, does good actions more frequently and consistently. This is surely important. But it is actually a consequence of having one sort of habit over another. The virtuous person's goodness abides in the self in the form of a habit, rather than simply in the acts. There is something different about who the person is. Aristotle says that the person with a virtue has that quality even when it is not being exercised. So a mathematician is a mathematician even in her sleep. On Lewis's example, the good tennis player is such even while he is not playing tennis. He is in shape, has certain muscle memory, a well-trained eye, a sense of tennis strategy, and so on. Having a virtue—or a vice, for that matter—changes who you are, and it is that change that leads to a greater frequency of good acts.

There are further consequences of the fact that having a virtue changes who one is. Having a virtue is not simply an indicator of past action, but more importantly a dynamic disposition to act well in the future. The virtuous person, due to who she is, enters a new situation already inclined to respond virtuously. On Lewis's example, the abiding qualities in the trained tennis player lead him to see situations on the court in such a way that enables him to play well. He does not come at the game from scratch, but rather already inclined to serve well, volley well, and the like. The same is true of the virtuous person. Every new opportunity for moral action is not begun from scratch, but rather with an inclination to act well. Her virtue provides this inclination.

In fact, having a virtue usually enables one to do good acts spontaneously and automatically. A good tennis player seems to hit effortlessly and reacts automatically. But effortlessness and spontaneity are results of training. The same is true of the virtuous person, who seems to do good things easily and without thinking.

Furthermore, the virtuous person's inclination to act well is easily "spreadable" to related areas in life. We can easily imagine an excellent tennis player using his athletic skills to excel in other sports. In fact, in university intramural

---

3. See Lewis's *Mere Christianity* (San Francisco: HarperSanFrancisco, 2001), 79–80. The same could of course be said concerning having a vice versus performing bad actions.

programs, varsity athletes in other sports are often the most proficient in the different intramural sport at hand. Their skills transfer, if you will, to help them in new sports. The same is true of the virtuous person. Even with no prior experience in the exact activity at hand, the virtuous person's habit of acting well in similar situations will tends to spread into the new area so that she acts well. This is why prospective employers, for instance, seek recommendation letters from those who know an applicant. The recommender cannot know how the applicant will do in the exact job being applied for, since the applicant has never done it. But an employer trusts that the habits the applicant demonstrates in former positions will spread to their work in the new job. And so they seek recommendations to know if an applicant is lazy or diligent, punctual or constantly late.

An ordinary example will help illuminate these differences. As mentioned below and discussed extensively in a later chapter, chastity is the virtue for using one's sexuality well. The lustful person uses his sexuality poorly. Determining what exactly constitutes chaste vs. lustful behavior is a task for later in the book, but an obvious example will help us here. Consider two men. Matt is chaste and thus accustomed to treating women with dignity. He is not prudish, but neither does he see women as objects for his sexual enjoyment. He has gained this habit through repeated past actions. Jim, on the other hand, is lustful. He is able to act in a friendly manner toward women, but through repeated past actions he tends to see, and thus treat, women primarily as potential sexual partners for his own enjoyment. These two men are marked by their respective habits (one a virtue, the other a vice), even as they sit together in a room talking.

Suddenly they look up at the door and see a very attractive woman enter the room. Jim immediately sees this woman as someone who can satisfy him sexually. He does so automatically, without thinking. In fact, he has never even seen this woman before, but his vice of lust inclines him to approach such situations in this manner. Matt, on the other hand, immediately sees this woman certainly as attractive, also as a person with dignity who is not simply there for his own sexual satisfaction. He does not have to think about this; it is just how he spontaneously responds. His abiding habit of chastity inclines him to act in this new situation in the way he generally has in the past, and he treats the woman accordingly.

This simple example shows exactly why it is important to attend to virtue and vice in moral theology. People do not enter situations from scratch, but rather already inclined to act well or poorly.[4] By examining particular actions alone, this broader scope is neglected. Indeed, both Jim and Matt might politely greet the woman when she enters the room. They may both

---

4. Another interesting fact not explored further here is that other people often easily pick up on how we react—chastely or lustfully, generously or with stinginess, and so on.

chat casually with her when she sits down. But those similar external acts may have different meanings given the different habits underlying them. Matt is genuinely interested in the woman for far more than her sexuality. Jim's vice, however, shapes how he engages the woman in conversation. Even if he does not eventually "hook up" with the woman, that further goal still shapes his interactions with her. Therefore, attending to external actions is indeed crucial for moral theology. But the habits that abide in us are what incline us to act in one way or the other, and the intentionality that they hold gives meaning to how those external acts are done. Ironically, we do not even understand particular acts well without attending to habits, whether virtues or vices, and the intentionality they hold.

All of these reasons reveal why it is important in moral theology to focus on developing virtues rather than simply performing good acts. What must not be forgotten is that one's habits reveal not only what acts one frequently performs, but how one sees things and why one does those acts. The virtuous person not only does the right thing, but does so for the right reasons, willingly, with the right attitude.

In sum, attending to virtue means attending to who a person is, inside as well as out, in a manner that counting good actions alone cannot do. The importance of such interiority is particularly evident in Christ's Sermon on the Mount in Matthew. Many are shocked when they hear Christ criticize people who pray, fast, and give money to the poor.[5] That is exactly what Christ does. But his dismissals in all three cases are of those who do these good acts "so that others may see them" (see Matt. 6:2; 6:5; 6:16). Like Lucy in the example above, the hypocrites decried in Matthew 6 do good acts but for the wrong reasons. Christ says "they have received their reward" because they are indeed seen by those in front of whom they pray, fast, and give alms. That was why they acted (their intention), and that purpose is achieved.

Christ instead praises those who do good things in secret, telling them they will be rewarded by their heavenly Father who "sees in secret." Is Christ telling us here that all public good works are morally bankrupt? No. The examples from the gospels where Christ praises public acts are too numerous to allow us to draw this conclusion. After all, Christ sees—and praises—the poor woman in the temple when she donates two small coins (see Luke 21:1–3). But Christ is indeed saying that if our good acts are done to be seen, such that they would not be done in secret, then they are not emblematic of the persons Christ calls His followers to be.

5. These three activities, discussed in Matt. 6, are central to the Christian life, but especially important for Catholics in the observation of Lent. Aquinas thought these acts, done in the proper manner, in some way govern the whole Christian life. Prayer indicates right relationship with God. Giving alms indicates right relationship with others, especially the poor. And fasting indicates a proper ordering of self-regulating desires.

This emphasis on persons rather than acts alone is also quite evident in the Beatitudes, which are the opening lines of the Sermon on the Mount in Matthew. The Beatitudes are those famous verses where we read, "happy are those who . . ." The fact that it is happiness to which Christ calls his listeners here is extraordinary, and reminds us of the claim, in chapter 1, that the moral life is one of true happiness. But these verses are quite relevant for this chapter as well. For Christ clearly praises people, and not simply acts, in these lines. He does not say happy are those who act peacefully or mercifully. He says "happy are the peacemakers" and "happy are the merciful."[6] These people will, of course, perform such types of acts. Yet they are not merely performing external acts. They are marked by the interior transformation, the habits (in this case virtues), that are so important to fully understanding the moral life.

Different Types of Virtue

Having come to an understanding of virtue, and why it is so important for moral theology, the next task is to name, define, and categorize different particular virtues. Recall that this chapter began with the claim that we have capacities for all different sorts of activities, and that these capacities can be developed for good or ill. The former are virtues, the latter vices. A virtue or vice is said to govern, or direct, a particular human capacity for certain types of action. There are many ways to group virtues and vices into categories. One of the most important is by the type of activity that is being done well (or poorly, in the case of a vice). There is a virtue for using one's sexuality well ("chastity— which does not mean simply, "don't do it"), for enduring suffering well (patience), for believing true things about God and God's relationship to humanity (faith), for seeking pleasures well (temperance), for seeking union with God in this life, and fully in the next (hope), for distributing goods well among others (justice), and so on. In each of these cases, the virtue is named for the sort of activity that is being done well. A technical name for the sort of activity is the "object." You recall this term from the previous chapter.

The numerous virtues can all be placed into two broad groups based on whether their type of activity, or object, falls into one category or the other. The first category is called *theological virtue*, and includes the virtues faith, hope, and love.[7] What distinguishes these virtues is that their activities, or

6. The *Catholic Study Bible* edition, which is the New American translation, uses the term "blessed are those...." The Greek term *makarios* means "happy" or "blessed." Properly understood, the two are actually synonymous. But "blessed" is often chosen since it connotes a more exalted happiness that is not simple revelry in base pleasures. It connotes *"truly* happy are those who. . . ." For more on the continuity between simply earthly pleasure and full happiness promised by Christ, see Josef Piper's *Happiness and Contemplation* (South Bend, IN: St. Augustine's Press, 1998), esp. 13–19.

7. The classic place these are found in scripture is 1 Cor. 13:13. But see also 1 Thess. 1:3.

objects, all concern God directly.[8] These virtues are examined more carefully in the second part of this book.

The second category of virtue consists not of virtues that concern God directly, but those that concern innerworldly activities. Such activities include eating, drinking, engaging in sexual relations, distributing goods, making practical decisions, and facing difficulties. Anyone who lives in our world engages in these activities.[9] Hence the objects of these virtues are called "innerworldly."[10] The group of virtues concerning such activities has often been labeled moral virtue. Given that the term moral is used so frequently and broadly, moral virtues will be called *cardinal virtues* here.

The number of moral virtues is rather numerous, since there are so many innerworldly activities. The cardinal virtues are four particular moral virtues (prudence, justice, fortitude, and temperance) that have long been posited in the Western tradition as encapsulating the virtuous life in this world.[11] Aquinas claimed that all other virtues concerning innerworldly activities could be grouped under one of these four virtues.[12] So generosity is a sub-virtue of justice; chastity a sub-virtue of temperance; patience a sub-virtue of fortitude; and, foresight is a sub-virtue of prudence. Therefore, what distinguishes cardinal virtues from theological virtues is that the objects of cardinal virtues are innerworldly activities. The next section defines the four cardinal virtues in more depth, since those four cardinal virtues are used to structure the remaining chapters in the first half of this book.

The Four Cardinal Virtues

The four cardinal virtues are justice, prudence, temperance, and fortitude. Each of these is easily misunderstood, so it is worth pausing to state exactly what type of innerworldly activity is done well by the person with each of these virtues.[13] First, consider *justice*. Aristotle famously claimed that we humans are social animals. Our lives are interdependent, such that living

---

8. See Aquinas's *Summa Theologiae*, I–II 62 for a detailed discussion of the theological virtues.

9. This would be true even of those who apparently renounce certain activities, such as the celibate person or the pacifist.

10. The term "innerworldly" is taken from John Paul II *Veritatis Splendor* (Encyclical Letter, 1993), 65.

11. This is seen in the work of Aquinas, who actually uses the term "moral virtue" to refer to virtues concerning innerworldy activities, but on certain occasion employs "cardinal virtue" to avoid confusion. See *Summa Theologiae* I–II 61. Thomas examines all moral virtues under the auspices of one of the four cardinal virtues. See his *Summa Theologiae*, II–II 47–170.

12. Again here he is following the likes of Gregory the Great and Cicero, both of whom he cites at *Summa Theologiae* I–II 61,2 and 61,3 respectively.

13. C. S. Lewis's brief chapter on the cardinal virtues in *Mere Christianity* (76–81) was formative for this section.

a good life must entail good relationships with other people. Justice is the virtue that inclines us to good interactions and relationships with others. We may immediately think of the courts and the law when we hear "justice," and such matters do indeed fall under justice. But any activity where we give another his or her due is a matter of justice. Honesty, generosity, keeping promises, being a loyal friend, and respect between parents and children are all matters of justice.

Another central component of human life in this world is bodily desire. We desire and act to obtain things that are pleasant to touch, taste, or experience. Such objects of our desire include food, drink, sex, and recreation. Any good life in this world will be marked by such desires, but these desires must also be well-ordered. *Temperance* is the virtue of well-ordered desires for pleasures. When we hear the word "temperance," we may think solely of alcohol, or even more specifically of the temperance movement in the early part of the twentieth century in the United States. A moderate desire for alcohol is indeed important for temperance, but temperance also includes desires for food, sex, and recreation. The person who drinks too much is acting intemperately. But so too is the person who is obsessed with video games, or who neglects important duties to spend leisure time with friends.[14]

Life in this world entails facing difficulties. *Fortitude* is the cardinal virtue that enables us to face difficulty well. "Courage" and "bravery" are synonyms of fortitude. When we think of bravery we may immediately think of a soldier on the battlefield risking her life for her friends and nation. This is indeed an example of bravery. In fact, since the greatest danger we can face in this life is our own death, a willingness to literally lay down one's life has always been seen as the paradigmatic act of fortitude. Yet this virtue may also be demonstrated in any difficulty in life, such as a sick person facing his sickness well, a student stepping up during stressful exam periods to perform well, or a person enduring pain after a hard breakup. These are all examples of fortitude.

The final cardinal virtue is perhaps the most difficult to understand. In all areas of life, we have to make practical decisions that guide our actions. Even if we mean well and have good desires, we must choose well in order to effectuate those good desires. *Prudence* is the virtue of choosing well, or doing practical decision-making well. When we hear the word "prudence," we commonly think of being cautious and wary. At times the virtue prudence may indeed call for cautious hesitation. But it may also call for decisive action. In all cases, we act prudently when we accurately size up the situation at hand and make good practical decisions. This virtue is particularly important because

---

14. We commonly assume that vices are always examples of excess—in the case of temperance, excessive desire for pleasure. This is understandable since this problem is by far the most common. But Aristotle and Aquinas are clear that one can be "intemperate" by having *too little* desire for, and initiative seeking, pleasure. This is clearly the case with eating, but can even be true of people who prudishly condemn anything pleasurable as sinful.

it is required for the exercise of the other cardinal virtues.[15] One may desire to drink moderately, but without an accurate grasp of what constitutes moderate drinking, one cannot effectuate that desire. One may desire to help those in need by giving money to a charity. But if one contributes to a fraudulent charity, then the poor are never served. Surely we can make poor decisions out of unavoidable ignorance.[16] But the prudent person uses the good sense she is capable of in order to choose well concerning all activities in this world.

Cardinal Virtues as the Path to the Good Life in This World

The cardinal virtues may rightly be called the path to the good life, or happiness, in this world. These four virtues, and all of the sub-virtues under each of the four, cover all aspects of a good life as it concerns activities in this world (innerworldy activities). In fact, the very term "cardinal" comes from the Latin "hinge" since a good life is said to hinge upon these virtues. There is actual remarkable consistency throughout the Western tradition in affirming the centrality of these virtues for the good life.[17] They may be found in scripture, where the book of Wisdom, describing God's spirit of wisdom, claims "she teaches moderation and prudence, justice and fortitude, and nothing in life is more useful for men than these" (Ws 8:7). Plato uses these four virtues to describe both the well-ordered society and the well- ordered individual.[18] Roman philosopher Cicero also reduces all virtues to these four.[19] Saints Augustine, Gregory the Great, and Thomas Aquinas are just a few Christian thinkers who appeal to the four cardinal virtues when describing the moral life.[20] Thus there is a remarkably consistent emphasis in the Western tradition, Christian and non-Christian alike, on the crucial importance of the cardinal virtues in the moral life.

15. For this reason prudence has traditionally, in both Christian and non-Christian sources, been called the "charioteer of the virtues." See, for instance, the *Catechism of the Catholic Church*, 2nd ed. (Vatican City: Libreria Editrice Vaticana, 1997), 1806.

16. We see here the close relationship between prudence and conscience. These topics will be treated together in chapter 5 on prudence.

17. There are even important commonalities between Western thought on the cardinal virtues and non-Western thought. See, for example, Lee H. Yearley's *Mencius and Aquinas: Theories of Virtue and Conceptions of Courage* (Albany, NY: State University of New York Press, 1990).

18. See book iv of Plato's *Republic*, trans. G. M. A. Grube (Indianapolis: Hackett Publishing, 1974), 85–109. This is one of the reasons why early Christians such as Justin Martyr thought Plato was exposed to the Old Testament (which is not true!).

19. Aquinas makes this claim at *Summa Theologiae* I–II 61,3, where he cites Cicero's *De inventione rhetorica* ii.

20. See Augustine's *On the Way of Life of the Catholic Church* (Washington, DC: Catholic University of America Press, 1966), i.15, 19–28. See Gregory the Great's *Morals on the Book of Job*, ii, is cited at Aquinas *Summa Theologiae* I–II 61,2. Aquinas's own treatment of the cardinal virtues is cited above.

What can account for this consistency? Since the cardinal virtues concern innerworldly activities, any person or society, regardless of varying beliefs or religious commitments, must have some vision (explicitly stated, or just implicit in how people act) of how to engage in these activities well. All persons everywhere face difficulties, desire sensual goods, relate to others, and make practical decisions. Living in this world necessarily entails these activities. For this reason, doing such things has traditionally been called "natural" for human beings. The norms or guidelines that dictate how to do them well have been called the "*natural law*." Of course, just because an activity is natural does not necessarily mean that every person does it well, or even knows exactly how to do it well. Yet since all rational persons engage in these activities and can at least in principle discern how to do them well, the cardinal virtues are said to be accessible to reason.

Nevertheless, it would not be accurate to say that therefore all these voices in the Western tradition share a solitary vision of what is morally right and wrong. This points us to another observation about the cardinal virtues—and indeed the natural law. The cardinal virtues incline their holder to act well in different areas of life: making practical decisions, desiring pleasures, relating to other, and facing difficulties. Yet specifying good action in particular cases is not necessarily and immediately evident to all people. What exactly constitutes acting well concretely in each of these areas? The traditional answer to this question has been that virtue resides in the mean, or middle, course between excess on one side and excess on the other. In other words, the brave person (the one with fortitude) is neither too cowardly nor too foolhardy. The chaste person is neither too promiscuous nor too prudish. Virtue lies in the mean between two extremes.

Perhaps we can all agree on this claim that virtue lies in the mean. But this really just pushes back one further step the problem of naming specific acts as good or bad. What constitutes promiscuity, or being too prudish? A virtue approach to morality has the advantage of being supple. It can accommodate individual, as well as cultural, differences as to what constitutes, say, temperance concerning alcohol. But some have criticized the virtue approach to moral theology for not offering specific enough rules to guide our lives in practical situations. Is this criticism accurate? Yes and no.

First, consider why this criticism is not accurate. Though supple, a virtue approach is not so abstract or formal as to render anything potentially virtuous. Two things guard against such a "content-less" morality. The first is the reliance of the virtue approach on exemplary, or paradigmatic, actions to exemplify each virtue.[21] For instance, fortitude is the virtue of facing difficulty well, but its exemplary, or paradigmatic, act is the willingness to lay down one's life for

---

21. For more on this point, see Jean Porter's *Nature as Reason: A Thomistic Theory of the Natural Law* (Grand Rapids: Eerdmans, 2005), 190–203.

an important cause. We can certainly debate which of our country's wars are just and thus warrant laying down one's life, or whether the circumstances in a particular battle justify a retreat. But bravery will always be a willingness to lay down one's life for a truly important cause. On no one's terms is it brave to abandon one's country mates in the heat of battle in an important fight. That is cowardice.

The second and related guard against a virtue approach being completely abstract, and content free, is the naming of certain actions that are necessarily incompatible with, and thus opposed to, virtuous activity. A classic example here is the intentional killing of innocent persons. This is always unjust.[22] As noted in a later chapter on justice and fighting war justly, there are great debates on whether and when it is ever virtuous to kill in the name of justice. Some think pacifism alone is fully virtuous. Others think waging war, even with its necessarily killing, can be fully virtuous, but even these people grant that the virtue of justice shapes and indeed limits how war may be waged. Surely in the Christian tradition and arguably beyond, it is never just to intentionally kill innocent people in the name of justice.[23] This is called an *absolute norm* (a norm is a rule), since it can never be violated by the virtuous person. Even phrasing it in this way reveals why. Justice guards the value of human life in society by inclining people to right relations with others. Intentional killing of the innocent is necessarily opposed to that protection, to such right relation. This is why St. Paul famously warns that one must not—because it makes no sense—"do evil that good come of it" (Rom. 3:8). Therefore, due to its reliance on paradigmatic acts, and its recognition of certain absolute norms, a virtue approach to morality is not completely content free.

In another sense, however, the criticism that a virtue approach lacks specificity is accurate. But the problem, if it can be called that, is not one with virtue but rather with real life. Aquinas famously argued that in concrete individual cases, there is so much contingency and detail that general rules are liable to fail.[24] In other words, saying "be temperate in your use of alcohol" is a good start, but more is needed. Identifying the relevant virtue, and any relevant absolute norms, is only the start of the process of discerning how to act well in a particular situation. A norm particular to the exact situation must be formulated in order to act well.

22. See Pope John Paul II's encyclical *Evangelium Vitae* (Encyclical Letter, 1995) on this topic. Aquinas names this act as always immoral in his *Summa Theologiae* II–II 64,6. There has been a contentious debate in Catholic moral theology over the past few decades on the existence of, and process of naming, intrinsically evil acts.

23. This claim will be explored in great detail in chapter 8 on the bombing at Hiroshima.

24. See *Summa Theologiae*, I–II 94,4. For more on this difficult topic of the relationship between law and prudence, see Thomas Hibb's *Virtue's Splendor: Wisdom, Prudence and the Human Good* (New York: Fordham University Press, 2001), 88–108.

For instance, virtue discussions of alcohol use assume there is a mean of temperance, and ways to deviate in excess or defect. But where to draw the lines is something that needs to be specified through further examination of the particular activity at hand. For what purposes is alcohol being used? How does alcohol impact the body? What social forces are at work inclining one toward or preventing one from alcohol use? What influence does an individual's history or physique have on the decision to use alcohol? Further reflection, at both the individual and communal level, serves to clarify the mean of, in this case, temperate alcohol use, and establish specific norms for the situation at hand.[25] The ability to formulate particular rules concerning activities accessible to reason, and the very rules themselves, is what is meant by *natural law*. It is the possession of the cardinal virtues that enables one to identify and observe it.

Therefore, it is indeed accurate that a broad discussion of virtue, such as found in this chapter, cannot provide specific rules to dictate how to act well in any situation. Life is varied and rich enough that, though means can be stated and absolute norms heeded, the virtue of prudence is needed to specify virtuous action in particular situations. This is one important and unavoidable reason why moral theology relies on virtuous people (authorities, to recall chapter 1) for specific norms. It is also a reason why, even in matters of natural law, there will be better and worse ways people live out their lives.

Not all differences in how people live out the cardinal virtues can be accounted for by the varying contingencies of particular cases. Why is that so? If the cardinal virtues concern innerworldly activities that are in principle accessible to reason, why are there so many different understandings of what constitutes a just, or brave, or prudent, or temperate act? How can some societies regard hari-kari as honorable, and others condemn suicide as wrong? How can certain societies differ so radically on their views of gender or race relations, or of what constitutes virtuous sexuality or alcohol use? Some individual and communal differences as to what constitutes virtuous action reflect the simple truism that the good life has many expressions. But other differences seem incompatible with each other, and not so easily explained.

Even though an activity is innerworldly and in principle accessible to unaided human reason, the way things really are concerning that activity may be contested. For instance, what is the true purpose of sexuality? Different people may disagree on this, or even that there is a real purpose of sex. Are men and women truly equal, and if so how should that equality be instituted in a society? Clearly people continue to disagree on this. This does not necessarily mean there is no such thing as temperance or justice. It simply means

25. For the importance of the community in such reflection, see Pamela Hall's *Narrative and Natural Law: an Interpretation of Thomistic Ethics* (Notre Dame, IN: University of Notre Dame Press, 1994).

that people disagree on the meanings of innerworldly activities. There are many possible explanations for these differences, such as malice, ignorance, evil social structures, and the like. As examined in a later chapter, the Christian tradition holds that human sin is one major cause of these differences.

Another important cause is that one's understanding of the way things really are concerning innerworldly activities is importantly shaped by one's beliefs about the way really things are concerning God and God's relationship to humanity. In other words, what one believes about God shapes how one regards innerworldly activities, and how one judges whether or not they are being done well. Of course, all differences about cardinal virtues such as temperance and justice do not boil down to differences of faith. However, to neglect the impact of faith on how one lives in this world leads to an impoverished view of the cardinal virtues. In the second section of this book we will attend more explicitly to exactly how different faith commitments and the possession of the theological virtues shape how one practices the cardinal virtues.

Concluding Thoughts

We have come a long way since the beginning of this chapter. Recall the opening question for this chapter: why is it that by exercising our freedom we shape not only how we act, but our very selves? By understanding the concept of habit, and how habits connect persons and their particular actions, this question has been answered. We were also able to describe why it is important to attend to habits—be they virtues or vices—in moral theology, rather than simply examining particular actions.

Defining virtue as a good habit also led us to two categories of virtue: theological and cardinal. Theological virtue is a subject for the second half of this book. The four cardinal virtues, however, were briefly defined in preparation for the rest of the first half of the book. These virtues are literal mainstays in the Western tradition, and describe the path to the good life in this world. We now turn to the first of these cardinal virtues, temperance, which will be especially useful in a later discussion of drinking alcohol.

Study Questions

1. What is a habit? Describe how a habit is related to a person's particular actions.
2. What steps are given in this chapter to describe the development of a virtue? Give an example.
3. Give at least three reasons why it is important to focus not just on particular actions, but on virtues, in doing moral theology. Use an example

to show how having a virtue is not the same as simply performing good actions.

4. What is the difference between theological and cardinal virtue?
5. List and define each of the four cardinal virtues. For each, tell how some people commonly misunderstand it, and why it actually means more than that.
6. Why are people of any time or place said to have some vision of the cardinal virtues?
7. Define natural law. How is it related to the cardinal virtues?
8. Why do different people define the acts of the cardinal virtues differently at times? Give three reasons.

Terms to Know

habit, virtue, vice, theological virtue, cardinal virtue, justice, temperance, fortitude, prudence, natural law, absolute norm

Questions for Further Reflection

1. One potential problem with virtue approaches to morality is circularity: you can only perform good acts with pleasure and promptness if you already have a virtue, but obtaining a virtue generally occurs by performing good actions! Is this a fatal problem for virtue ethics? What contribution might rules and authorities make toward a solution to this dilemma?
2. Some people criticize virtue approaches to morality by saying they cannot account for occasions when we act for reasons that are not clear to ourselves, or from unconscious motives. Can a virtue approach explain these situations?
3. With the section "Focusing on Virtue: Why Bother?" in mind, explain what difference—if any—attending to virtue makes in discussing a particular moral issue like drinking alcohol or deciding when to have sex or whether euthanasia should be legal.
4. How helpful are the cardinal virtues as starting points for cross-cultural or interreligious dialogue over ethical issues? What is attractive about this approach, and what limitations are there?

Further Reading

The driving influence behind this chapter is again the *Summa Theologiae* of Thomas Aquinas. See his discussion of habits and virtues at I–II 49–70. The entire *Secunda Secundae* is structured according to the theological and cardinal virtues. For detailed work on the cardinal virtues, see II–II 47–170. See also Aquinas's treatises *On the Virtues in General* and *On the Cardinal Virtues*. For a helpful introduction to the moral importance of virtue, see Paul Wadell's *Primacy of Love*, esp. 106–124. The *Catechism* has a brief sketch of virtue and the types of virtue at 1803–1845. For extended treatments of each virtue, see Josef Pieper's *Faith, Hope and Love*, and his *Four Cardinal Virtues*. For more on the complicated issues surrounding the specificity of virtue ethics, the need for prudence in norm specification, and the relationship between virtue and natural law, see both Thomas Hibbs' *Virtue's Splendor* and Jean Porter's *Nature as Reason*.

4

The Virtue of Temperance

Living a Passionate Moral Life

One of the main organizing concepts of this book is virtue. The four cardinal virtues are treated in the first half of the book and the three theological virtues in the second half. This chapter is the first one based on one of the virtues. Temperance is examined before the other three cardinal virtues for two reasons. First, as the virtue that helps us desire and enjoy pleasures well, it is relatively straightforward. Examples of it—and of its opposing vice, intemperance—are easy to find from our experience. Second, since temperance most properly concerns sensual pleasures, it affords us an opportunity to examine how all our desires are relevant for moral theology. In the broad sense of the term, desire refers simply to something we want. It could be far off and lofty (to serve humanity), less far off and more practical (to go shopping and get some new shoes) or very immediate and carnal (to eat this food). When chapter 2 explored how our characters are ascertained through the different desires we have, and the different priorities we give them, it was referring to desire in this broad sense. But desire can also refer more specifically to those bodily longings or aversions we have that we often call feelings or emotions. This chapter not only examines the virtue of temperance, but also uses that occasion to explore whether and how our desires (in this more immediate sense meaning emotions or feelings or passions) are important for morality.

The first section of this chapter defines and explains the virtue temperance. The virtue temperance concerns not only external acts and intentions (recall chapters 2 and 3) but also our desires, our emotions. That recognition prompts the second section, which explains what exactly our emotions are and whether or not it makes sense to label them moral. In other words, does it make any sense to praise or blame someone for how they feel? Perhaps surprisingly to you, the answer offered here is yes. That leads us to the third section on how we can direct or shape our emotions so that they are more virtuous. The fourth section will answer the question, why bother? If we have already established in this book that morality is not only about exterior actions but also our intentions driving those actions, why do we need to examine another facet of how we act by looking at desires or emotions? We will actually find that the answer to this question has everything to do with a morality of happiness. For thinkers like Aristotle and Aquinas, a fully virtuous life means not only doing the right thing for the right reasons, but also doing it with "pleasure and promptness," which comes from having well-ordered passions and desires.

The Virtue of Temperance: Acts, Intentions, and Desires

Temperance is a virtue, which we know from earlier chapters is a stable tendency, or habit, to do a certain type of activity well, with good intentions. Temperance, in particular, is the virtue that inclines us to desire and enjoy pleasures well. It enables us to regulate our actions, and even our desires, concerning pleasurable activities so that they are reasonable, or in accord with the way things really are. Four key questions and points arise from this definition of temperance.

First, what are such pleasurable activities? Aquinas, following Aristotle, claimed that temperance is most properly about how we seek and enjoy the sensible pleasures of food, drink, and sex. These are the most obvious examples in our lives where our desires are not cold and detached, but entail immediate, bodily longings. With such activities our mouths water, our hearts race, our stomachs churn, or our skin flushes. We might think of other pleasures in our lives besides food, drink, and sex that arouse in us such bodily longings, such as other recreational activities. Aquinas also recognized that we have passionate longings for other things in life that engage us in such an immediate, bodily way. So he was willing to speak of being virtuously passionate for justice; that is, being neither too angrily vengeful nor too flaccidly unresponsive. Therefore, temperance most properly concerns immediate sensual pleasures such as food, drink, and sex, but in a broader sense concerns other desires we have in our lives that entail immediate, bodily longing. Temperance is the virtue of desiring these things in a reasonable or moderate manner.

This raises the second question, namely, what constitutes a reasonable, or moderate, desire? In the above definition, temperance is said to dispose us to enjoy and desire pleasures reasonably, or in accordance with the way things are. What exactly is that? In the last chapter's examination of virtue in general, we saw that virtue lies in the mean. So the temperate person desires and enjoys pleasures not too much and not too little. While this is interesting, it does not help us specify exactly what constitutes too much or too little food, or sex, or alcohol, or some other pleasurable activity. As noted in that chapter, such exact specification is impossible without a more detailed inquiry into the particular activity under consideration. We will do this with alcohol in chapter 6.

But perhaps we can say a bit more about how to think about what is unreasonable or immoderate by looking back further to chapters 1 and 2. There we claimed that people have all sorts of different purposes or desires in life. What they are, and how they are ordered, or prioritized, in relation to each other forms our character. Recall the triangle image from chapter 2. Hopefully, the purposes we seek are ordered so as to guide us to a genuinely happy life. Pleasurable activities surely fit into this constellation. Our desires for pleasurable activities can be called immoderate or unreasonable either when they displace goals or purposes we claim to hold more important, or when they displace goals or purposes we should hold more important. To use an obvious example, if someone is playing ten hours of computer games per day, he is clearly allowing that pleasure to displace other purposes in life—there are only so many hours in a day! Perhaps studying falls by the wayside, or leisurely time with friends, or exercise, or healthy eating. Whichever the case may be, this is unreasonable, since the person chooses to elevate something fun but ultimately not that important above other more worthy goals in life. We say this desire is not in accord with the way things really are, under the assumption that those other goals really are more important than playing video games, even though one's desires fail to reflect that truthful evaluation of things.

The same may be said when excessive, or minimal, eating impedes one's health, or when sexual activity impedes healthy relationships with others, or when drinking alcohol impedes friendships or family commitments. These pleasures become unreasonable, or not in accord with the way things are, not because they are a no-no, and earn us someone's disapproval. Rather, they elevate what is less important to one's happiness and living a good life above what is truly important. Obvious examples of intemperance are given here to make the point. Determining the exact line where one crosses into intemperance is more difficult, requiring the more detailed examination of a particular activity mentioned above. For now it suffices to note that temperance disposes us to enjoy and desire pleasures reasonably, or in accordance with how things really are.

Third, despite our proclivity toward excessive desire of, and engaging in, pleasurable activities, temperance is not simply about prohibiting such desire and enjoyment, nor all about limiting it. The vice of intemperance is most often a matter of excessive desire for and enjoyment of pleasures, but it can also be a matter of too little desire and enjoyment of pleasures. This is a perfect example of the last chapter's claim that virtue lies in the mean, or middle. This may seem odd. What if I do not like to play computer games? What if I do not choose to drink alcohol? What if I choose a celibate life as a priest or nun, and therefore give up sexual activity? None of these need be examples of intemperance. But pleasures can be renounced in an intemperate way as, for instance, if one thinks all sexual activity is dirty and sinful. One might fail to appreciate any positive role for sexuality in one's marriage. Sadly, it is all too common that people can be intemperate in their lack of eating. As said above, examination of the particular activity at hand would be necessary to give more details, but the point here is that intemperance can be a matter of too little desire for and engaging in pleasurable activities.

Fourth and last, this treatment of temperance repeatedly refers to desire for and engaging in pleasurable activities. The term "engaging" is used here to refer to the actual partaking in the pleasure, as opposed to the mere desire for the pleasure. Yet though these two are distinct, temperance concerns both a moderate partaking in pleasures, and a moderate desire for such pleasures. In other words, the temperate person not only acts well concerning pleasurable activities, but even desires them appropriately—not too much, not too little, and in the right situations.

This observation on enjoying vs. desiring prompts us to the rest of this chapter's exploration of whether and how we can order, or influence, the desires we have. In chapters 2 and 3 we saw how the moral life is not simply a matter of performing good actions, but also doing those acts for the right reasons and developing habits to do so consistently. In this chapter we examine not intentionality but a different sort of interiority: our desires, or feelings. To understand the difference between these two different interior facets of human action—intention and desire—consider this example. Lauren performs good acts by going to the gym regularly. She even does so for the right intentions; for example, to stay healthy. Yet she hates doing so. It is struggle each time she goes. She does the right thing, for the right reasons, but without accompanying desires. Her friend Kathy, however, not only does good acts (goes to the gym) for good reasons (to be healthy), but she also enjoys it. She has good desires because she feels like going each day, and is even disappointed if she cannot for some reason. In this case, both women act well and have good intentions. Surely that is what is most important. But only Kathy has good desires, or feelings. How can we account for this difference, and is it at all important?

The virtue temperance is about not only doing pleasurable activities for the good reasons, but also having the desires to act well, and not having desires to act poorly. So this chapter affords us the perfect opportunity to explore the related but distinct question of the role of our desires, or feelings, in the moral life. What are our passions or desires, and can we ever label them morally good or bad? Is it possible to shape our desires so that we not only do good things for good reasons, but even have good desires; and if so, how? And why does it matter? These are the three questions that the following three sections address.

Feelings as Moral Phenomena—Isn't That "Just How I Feel"?

What are our emotions, or desires, and what sense does it make to call them "moral"? In other words, can people really be praised or blamed for their emotional responses in different situations? After all, we constantly hear people retort, "but that's just how I feel," as if to say that we cannot hold it against them. This section explains what is meant here by feelings, and argues that we may indeed be responsible for how we feel. True, our control over our emotional responses is not as great as, say, our deliberate decisions. Nonetheless, if we attend carefully to the nature of our emotions, it will be clear in what ways it does indeed make sense to praise or blame people for how they feel.

Preliminary Point One: Distinguishing Emotions and Ensuing Actions

Before tackling the nuanced question of whether or not our emotional responses are moral in the sense of being praiseworthy or blameworthy, two preliminary points must be made. First, what we are examining here is the morality of an emotional response itself, and not any subsequent action we may take that is prompted by the emotion. This is seen quite clearly in Christ's words on anger in the Sermon on the Mount, where he says:

> You have heard that it was said to your ancestors, "You shall not kill; and who-ever kills will be liable to judgment." But I say to you, whoever is angry with his brother will be liable to judgment, and whoever says to his brother, "Raqa," will be answerable to the Sanhedrin, and whoever says, "You fool," will be liable to fiery Gehenna. (Matt. 5:21–22)

Christ clearly condemns actions taken by people who are unjustly angry.[1] In this case, he mentions those who lash out verbally in anger. But note that his

---

1. The reader may wonder why the term "unjustly" is used here when that does not ap-pear in the biblical text. With few exceptions, thinkers throughout the Christian tradition have interpreted this passage not as a condemnation of all anger but only of vicious anger, the sort that leads to murder, as mentioned in this passage. The broad question of whether anger is compatible with the Christian life is beyond the scope of this chapter. For more on this topic, see William C. Mattison III, *Christian Anger? A Contemporary Account of Virtuous Anger in the Thomistic Tradition* (PhD diss., University of Notre Dame, 2003). See also William C.

first targets are those who are simply unjustly angry, even if they do not act on this anger.

This is an important point, since students who are asked whether or not their emotions may be praiseworthy or blameworthy almost universally respond by referring to actions done in their emotional state. They will say things like, "It is wrong to feel that way if you act on it." Or, "it is OK to feel that way as long as you do not act on it." This reflects an important insight. To anticipate the final section of this chapter, our actions are indeed closely related to our feelings. People commonly act based upon how they feel. Hence in his commentary on this passage in Matthew, Aquinas claims that Christ, like a good physician, seeks to alleviate not only the symptom of murder but also the underlying cause of murder, which may be unjust anger. It is natural and good that we so intimately connect internal feelings and external actions.

Nonetheless, they can and should be distinguished. One can be enraged and act on it by doing physical violence, or by verbally lashing out. Or one can restrain one's self so as not to act on the anger. In the latter case, the unjust anger still exists. The crucial point is, it is this emotional response, regardless of any subsequent action, that can also be morally good or bad, as Christ clearly indicates in Matt. 5:22 and as this chapter further explains.

Preliminary Point Two: What Exactly Are Emotions?

The next preliminary point of this section addresses the question, what exactly are emotions? For the purposes of this chapter, the terms "passion," "emotion," "feeling," and "desire" are used interchangeably. This topic is being addressed in a chapter on temperance because the virtue temperance concerns activities toward which we experience very immediate, bodily longings or aversions (food, drink, and sex). Our emotions (or feelings, desires, passions) are also generally manifest in immediate, bodily changes. When we are overjoyed our hearts leap. When we are angry our blood boils. When we are afraid, our hearts race and our senses become acute. Like our desires for sex, food, and drink, our emotions are bodily longings or aversions to things we encounter.

Note that though all these desires do indeed entail bodily, including hormonal, changes, they are not mere rushes of adrenalin, or blind surges. They are consistently identifiable responses to certain types of stimuli (persons, events, memories, etc.), prompting us toward certain types of actions. In other words, you get angry (or scared, or overjoyed, or sad) at certain types of events, and such events prompt you toward certain types of action (to rectify the injustice, flee the threat, rest in a good thing, or shun what causes sorrow) This is the very reason why we can even consistently label different emotional responses

---

Mattison III, "Christian Anger? Beyond Questions of Vengeance," *Journal for the Society of Christian Ethics* 24, no. 1 (Spring, 2004): 159–79.

in the first place. It would be nonsensical if you told a friend you were sad and she said, "how wonderful!" Similarly, if you told her you were overjoyed you would not expect her to reply, "Quick! Get away!" The reason you can count on your friend knowing what you are experiencing is that each emotion is understood by us as a response to a certain sort of stimulus.

Though we are not accustomed to thinking of them in this way, our desires or emotions are forms of judgment. They make a claim, if you will, about the thing they respond to. Consider fear. This is a bodily response to a perceived source of danger, which includes an inclination to flee. Our hearts beat faster, our palms become sweaty, and our senses become acute in response to the perceived threat. Thus, the presence of fear in us is a sort of judgment—granted, a judgment automatic and often nonconscious—that whatever arouses our fear threatens us, so we need to flee. Of course, there may or may not actually be a threat. And we may or may not act on the emotion. Nonetheless, though an emotional response is a passive reaction in response to a situation, it is still an identifiable, or intelligible response. It is a sort of claim, or bodily judgment,[2] that the perceived event or entity really is a certain sort of thing.

The moment we recognize that our emotional responses are bodily judgments of the situation at hand, we can then say that these judgments are more or less accurate. Consider a person sitting next to you on a plane who is afraid of flying. You and he are in the exact same situation. You perceive no danger, yet he is terrified. Which is an accurate perception of the situation? Should you be more scared? Should he calm down a bit? Obviously, people's varied histories shape their perceptions of their situations. Perhaps your plane mate was involved in a near miss on a previous flight. Nonetheless, you are both in the presence of the same event—in this case, an impending flight—at the same time. Who perceives the situation more accurately?

To conclude this second preliminary point, since emotions are not blind surges of affect but intelligible responses to particular types of situations, we can indeed label particular occasions of emotion as more or less accurate responses to the situation at hand. In extreme cases of fear we may label someone phobic, meaning the person has irrational fears that do not reflect how things really are. In more ordinary examples we may simply counsel someone not to be so afraid of their first day on the job, or of what will happen if they dare to ask someone on a date. We are implicitly saying that the threat perceived by the scared person is either nonexistent or at least not as threatening as the person's fear suggests.

---

2. Every judgment is embodied in some sense, since we persons are embodied. But feelings are more obviously embodied, since they are partially constituted by the bodily changes we associate with different emotions. This explains the slew of psychological studies where subjects report feeling angry when certain brain and bodily changes are induced by an experimenter, even without a genuine cause of anger being present.

Few of us would consider a fear of flying, or of asking someone out, an important moral question. But consider another case that will shift our attention from the nature of emotions to their moral significance. You and a friend meet someone who makes a racial slur. Though the comment did not please you, it did not upset you either. But your friend becomes rather angry. Whose response is more accurate? The emotion of anger is an embodied response to a perceived injustice that inclines us to rectify the injustice. Is your friend's anger appropriate for this situation or not? Is it an accurate judgment about the comment that was made?

Can Our Emotional Responses Really Be Morally Good or Bad?

We are now ready to explain the central claim for this section, and indeed this chapter. Granting that emotional responses are identifiable bodily reactions constituting an appraisal of one's situation, and that they may be examined regardless of whether or not they lead to external actions on the part of the one experiencing the emotion, does it make sense to praise or blame someone for their emotional responses? After all, as the very name "passion" indicates, it would seem that we are passive in our emotional responses, simply responding to the stimuli, or situations, in which we find ourselves.

This is usually the point where people protest that only actions ensuing from emotional responses are morally praiseworthy or blameworthy. This reaction is understandable for two reasons. First, people often assume that many of our emotional responses are not morally important. You may fear spiders and I do not. You may like vanilla and I chocolate. Unless your fear of spiders leads you to do something harmful, or your love of vanilla lead you to steal ice cream, who cares? It is granted here that many of our emotions and desires are not morally important. Second, many people assume that we are only praiseworthy or blameworthy for our actions since we can control them, whereas emotions and desires just seem to arise in us. Though it is granted here that some of our emotions and desires are wholly beyond our control, it is also argued here that most are not wholly beyond our control.

Consider again the example at the end of the previous part, where you and a friend heard someone make a racial slur. This example usually leads people to think twice. They may try to reason that certainly what is most important is that either friend, whether they are angry or not, confront the racist on her comment—granted. But should we praise the one friend for feeling angry at the comment? Or consider the racist herself. Even if she did not make the racial slur, what if she simply felt hatred toward members of a certain racial group? Can we blame her for simply feeling that way, even if she never acts on it? This is the central question of this section.

To answer it, we must identify what sorts of human activities are praiseworthy or blameworthy, or, in other words, moral. We label those activities moral that we are responsible for, because they are in some way reflective of our freedom. They are in some sense our own, rather than simply happening to us. Many people use the term "control" in this discussion (see two paragraphs above) and say we are praised or blamed for only those actions we can control. Yet that term is generally avoided here, because even deliberate decisions are rarely fully under our control. We are limited by our capacities, our knowledge of the situation, the options available to us, and so on. As described in the discussion on freedom in chapter 2, responsibility for our acts is more like a continuum. At one end are the deliberate decisions for which we are clearly responsible (even if all facets of the situation are not under our control). At the other end are activities like reflexes. Someone may have better or worse reflexes, but it would be nonsensical to praise or blame someone for their reflexes! We are not responsible for them.

The classic way of describing the difference between moral and non-moral human activities is to say only those activities that involve our reason and will (the capacities that engender our freedom) are properly called moral, and thus praised or blamed. By reflectively understanding the world around us (with our reason) and making choices based upon that understanding (with our will), we exercise our freedom and are responsible for our activities. Deliberate decisions are clearly expressions of our free will, whereas reflexes just as clearly are not.

Where do emotional responses fit on this continuum? They are certainly not deliberate decisions. You cannot tell yourself at this moment, "get angry at this," or, "desire that" and expect it to happen. Emotions are responses to stimuli perceived as, say, arousing anger or desire. And so they depend on the presence of such a stimulus, even if it is simply our memory or imagination of such a stimulus.

Yet neither are they completely passive responses which, like reflexes, cannot at all be shaped by our reason and will. Though they arise in response to our perception of some stimulus, we can indeed through our reason and will influence if and how we perceive the people, events, and stimuli that arouse our emotions. When our emotional responses are shaped by our higher powers of reason and will, then they are rightly called moral phenomena, and appropriately praised or blamed.

This shaping of our emotions can happen in several ways. First, some desires and emotions arise spontaneously, without any engagement of our reason and will, but then are sustained and encouraged by us. Perhaps we feel a rush of sexual desire for someone in an inappropriate situation. To the extent that we dwell upon and cultivate that initial feeling, we may be called responsible for the ongoing desire, even if we never act upon it. We would be lustful, even if we never committed any sexual act. (In fact, Christ explicitly warns us about just such desire that doesn't lead to action when he says, "everyone who looks at a woman with lust for her has already committed adultery with her in his heart," Matt. 5:28.) This also commonly happens with anger. We may feel an initial surge of anger at someone, but then feed it by brooding over it, and ruminating over all the other things that person has done to offend us in the past. To the extent that we willfully sustain and arouse an emotional response, we are praiseworthy for it if it is good, or blameworthy for it if it is bad.

Another way that our emotions are shaped by our reason and will is when we intentionally put ourselves in situations where predictable desires will be aroused. In the previous example, a desire or emotion already arose and our responsibility was for nurturing it further. Here we are responsible for the initial desires that arise, since they are aroused due to a situation we intentionally place ourselves in. If I read racially supremacist literature and choose friends who are racist, then when I feel hatred toward another race that emotional response is not purely passive, but is rather a reflection of past willful decisions. The next time I see a member of a different race and I experience feelings of hatred, this response, while not deliberately chosen at the moment, is shaped by prior deliberate acts and is therefore rendered morally blameworthy.

Finally, in some cases even when we do not intentionally place ourselves in situations where predictable emotions will be aroused, we may still be rightly called responsible for our spontaneous emotional responses. While emotions are responses to perceived events, how we perceive things is not simply a matter of the senses. Our perception of events through the senses is shaped by our beliefs. An obvious example is the passenger afraid of flying. If both his and your senses are working properly, why does he perceive a threat and you do not? His perception of the situation reflects certain implicit beliefs he must have about the safety of airplanes, beliefs which you do not share. Thus, the final way our spontaneous emotional responses are governed by reason and will is when those responses reflect beliefs we have that give ruse to the emotional reactions, beliefs which could (and perhaps should) be revised.

Again, we would not label the belief of the frightened passenger blameworthy. But what about the racist mentioned above? A feeling of hatred or fear when seeing a person of another race reflects her belief that the person seen is inferior, or threatening. Thus, when she sees such a person, she responds with hatred or fear. If the belief is accurate, this is actually an appropriate emotional response. But in this case, the racist's belief is not only inaccurate, but morally blameworthy. Assuming the racist is not a very young child who could not have known better, she should know that not all persons of one particular race are threats, or inferior. Therefore, to the extent that an emotional response arises due to her clinging to her beliefs, the response itself may be praised or blamed depending on the moral quality of the belief that engenders the emotional response.

How to Develop Virtuous Emotions

The previous section explained what exactly is meant by an emotion (or passion, desire, feeling), and why people can indeed be praised or blamed for their emotional responses. This is the case because our emotions often reflect decisions or beliefs about morally important matters for which we are clearly responsible. Granting that our desires are truly moral facets of human living, how can we shape or change our emotional responses to different situations? After all, it would be cruel to claim that we can be blamed for our desires, and yet fail to offer some guidance as to how we can shape those desires to be more virtuous. How can we develop a virtue to experience, say, sexual desire at the right time, at the right place, for the right reasons, at the right persons, to the right degree, and so on? The short answer is, of course, to have our desires increasingly shaped by our reason and will, such that they are accurate responses to the world around us. While the previous section argued that this is possible, this section explores in more detail how it is possible.

At the beginning of this chapter we observed that emotional responses, and the actions toward which they prompt us, are intricately related and yet distinguishable. This point is crucial for developing good habits for our desires, or "habituating" our emotional responses to become virtuous. People are clearly more free to determine their actions than their emotional responses. Yet it turns out that our actions then have an impact on those very emotional responses. This section offers four sequential stages in which people's actions and emotions are increasingly virtuous.

Four Stages in the Development of Virtuous Desire

We begin at a stage furthest from full virtue: *intemperance*. Any person or act that is not moderate with regard to pleasurable activities can be called intemperate. But in the fullest sense of the term, intemperance is a vice, a stable habit leading one to perform such immoderate acts. Not only does the intemperate person perform bad acts, but he also intends and desires to perform such acts. Consider the example of anger. You may have a habit of becoming enraged at a sibling, and spew venomous words toward him. You are always convinced you are being offended, and so you consistently feel disordered anger and act on it without hesitation. Note that your anger is disordered in this case because in reality there was no offense. But you are so convinced you are right that you fail to see it that way, and experience anger, lashing out anyway. This is a clear example of intemperance: you have bad desires, and bad actions arising from those desires.

The next stage toward the development of virtuous passion appears similar to intemperance, for it too is constituted by bad desires and bad actions ensuing from those desires. Yet in the case of *incontinence*, which is the second stage, though you experience disordered emotions and act on them, you are aware that your desires and actions are wrong. In fact, you often pledge not to be that way again, and regret it when you nonetheless succumb, and act out your vicious anger. In the case of your anger with your sibling, you may know you are prone to rage and vow not to get angry and act on it again. But alas, an occasion arises where you do just that, and regret it afterwards. What distinguishes this second stage of incontinence from the first stage of intemperance is knowing that your acts and desires are wrong, and having some desire to change them. You have not been able to change them as of yet, but this step is a crucial step toward doing so, since you cannot advance toward full virtue without both realizing your acts and desires are wrong, and wanting to change them.

The third stage, *continence*, is equally crucial for moral development. The continent person still has disordered desires, but manages to contain (hence continence) the disordered desires so as not to act on them. The continent person performs good acts (with good intentions), even though bad desires are present. In the anger example, perhaps the next time you feel yourself becoming flush with rage, you somehow manage to restrain yourself and avoid lashing out. This stage most clearly demonstrates the distinction between emotional responses and actions, since the continent person has disordered desires even while restraining them so as to act well.

Some people would say that reaching stage three constitutes moral completion, since a person is indeed acting well, even if there are still disordered desires. Yet Aquinas, following Aristotle, sees an even higher stage of virtue, which he calls temperance. Aquinas certainly praises continence. Since all people will at times experience anger, hatred, sexual desire, or desire for food and drink that is disordered, or immoderate, the ability to contain such desires and act well is crucial in order to live virtuously. But Aquinas claims that continence is not full virtue, since not all of one's capacities are in accordance with virtue, as evidenced by the disordered desires. He argues it would be better to not only do the right thing for the right reason, but also to feel desire to do the right thing, with no conflicting disordered desires impeding one's good actions.

This describes the fourth and final stage of *temperance*. We can refer to any person or act that is moderate with regard to pleasurable activities as temperate. But in the fullest sense of the term, temperance refers to the virtue, or good habit, where a person not only performs good actions for the right reasons, but also has virtuous desires to perform those actions. There are no conflicting desires as found in the continent person. To continue with the angry sibling example, if you were fully temperate, not only would you not lash out at your brother in anger, but you would never actually experience the arousal of unjust anger in the first place. Since we are assuming in this case there is no true occasion for anger (hence our calling it unjust), if you were temperate you would not ever experience a desire to right a perceived injustice. Your emotions would arise in accordance with the way things really are, and not in a warped manner perceived by you for the seeming benefit of yourself.

Though it has been mentioned above, it bears repeating here that temperance is not simply the absence of disordered desires, but also the presence of well-ordered desires and emotions. The person who experiences real sexual passion for their spouse whom they love dearly is temperate. The person who desires and enjoys a nice meal is temperate. The person whose ire is raised at injustice is temperate, as is the person who fears things that ought to be feared. Temperance is not an absence of passion or emotion, but rather well-ordered desire. So progress in the habituation of emotion can be seen both as ridding one's self of disordered desires, and the development of virtuous desires.

How to Move from One Stage to the Next

Given this four-stage vision, how can we progress from one stage to the next? The jump from intemperance to incontinence is subtle, but crucial. We have to realize that our desires and actions are disordered, and feel some desire to be relieved of them. Even though the incontinent person still desires and acts badly, the realization that this is so is what makes any further change even possible. This is why the crucial first step in the famous Alcoholics Anonymous Twelve Step Program is admitting that there is a problem. Without such recognition, change is not possible. How does it happen? It may come from a friend, parent, or mentor who points out our behavior to us. We may see the problems in some behavior exhibited in others, and realize we too are guilty of such acts and desires. The negative consequences of our own acts may finally catch up to us, so that we realize the error of our ways. We may hear a powerful sermon, read a probing book, or come to a realization in times of prayer. Whatever the source, the key features in moving from intemperance to incontinence are our realizing that our acts and desires are indeed disordered and then wanting to change.

Yet this realization is not enough, as evidenced by the incontinent person who knows her acts and desires are wrong but persists nonetheless. The movement from incontinence to continence seems simple. Just stop performing the bad action. Yet anyone who has struggled with a vice—be it greed, envy, lust, rage, or some addiction—knows that this can be most difficult. The key step in stopping the habit of smoking is simply not having another cigarette. Or for the enraged it may mean holding one's tongue. Or for the envious it may mean resisting the urge to gossip. Whenever you resist the bad urge and thus contain your disordered desire, you have entered into the state of continence. Sometimes you can do this with raw willpower. Sometimes the support of others helps, perhaps even of those who share the bad habit. Occasionally even chemicals can help, as when drug addicts use replacement substances, or smokers try nicotine patches or pills to limit cravings. But however you do so, you become continent when you stop acting on a bad desire. Note that you do not yet have virtuous desires. But by ceasing to act on the disordered desires, you stop further ingraining those desires and make it possible to alter the desires themselves.

At the stage of continence, a person is acting well despite disordered desires. The last stage in the advance to full virtue is temperance. According to Aquinas, the temperate person not only does the right thing for the right reasons, but also desires to do it from one's heart.[3] The term "heart" is a reference to one's emotions. Yet though we can control our actions so as to do the right thing despite bad desires, it seems impossible to control one's desires. The very name for emotions in Latin, *passiones*, indicates that our emotions are passive responses, and thus seemingly beyond our control.

But as the previous section on the morality of the emotions made clear, this is not the case. Though our emotional desires are not under our control in the same way that deliberate decisions are, they may nonetheless be shaped or governed by our higher powers of reason and will. How can we shape our desires so that they arise in accord with what is best for us? As noted above, a crucial weapon in eliminating disordered desires is refusing to put one's self in those situations where they tend to arise. This is the most obvious way to prevent bad desires from arising in the first place.

Though it is more difficult and takes more time, we can even exercise some responsibility over how our emotions arise spontaneously in unexpected situations. Recall that we do not respond emotionally to stimuli directly in a strict stimulus-response mechanical manner. Rather, we respond emotionally to persons, events, situations, by how we cognitively perceive those objects. The point of contrast would be the reflex. If you hit someone's knee in the proper place, it will reflexively jerk upward. One has no control of this response without coercively holding the knee down. It does not matter how one perceives the strike of the hammer—it will achieve its desired effect.

But this is not the case with our emotions. It is quite common that two persons can be in the exact same situation and respond with different emotions. Recall the airplane example. Being on an airplane may be terrifying for one person, and yet pose no threat to another. Despite the fact that both are in the exact same situation, one responds with fear, and the other does not. This is because both perceive the situation differently, likely due to their different histories. This indicates that we can change our emotional responses to a situation if we can change how the situation is perceived. In fact, this is exactly what you do when the person in the seat next to you is afraid to fly. You tell him it is safer than any other form of transportation. You assure him of the airline's safety record. What you are doing here is trying to change

3. See Thomas Aquinas, *Summa Theologiae*, English Dominican trans. (New York: Benziger, 1948), I–II 24,3.

how he imagines the situation, namely, as less of a threat. If it works, he will experience no more, or at least less, fear.

This process of reimagining a situation which results in changes in one's very emotional response is called by psychologists *cognitive manipulation*.[4] A person is reimagining, or manipulating, how one cognitively grasps a situation. Since the event, person, or situation is perceived differently, one's emotional response also changes. Therefore, cognitive manipulation is the key to how we can habituate our emotional responses to better conform to the way things really are.

As an example of moving through all four stages, recall the example about your anger at a sibling. When your brother offers a simple instruction or observation, you too often lose your temper and lash out. Let's say your friend sees you do this, and assures you that you are becoming angry for no good reason. You realize your friend is right, and you try to avoid lashing out in the future. For a time you are regrettably unable to control your lashing out. This is incontinence. But soon you are able to control yourself, and refrain from lashing out, even though you are still flush with anger at the most minute comment from your brother. This is continence. How can you get to the point where your vicious anger does not even arise in the first place?

What happens when unjust anger arises is that you perceive what is in reality a harmless comment to be a slight or insult. Anger is a desire for justice in response to a perceived offense or slight. In this case, the perceived insult is not truly an offense. You misperceive it. When you calm down, you realize that and regret getting angry, even as you are grateful you refrained from lashing out. You can then begin to reimagine the situation. You recall what your brother said, and realize it was not done maliciously. Perhaps you reflect on what about yourself makes you prone to hear such comments as offenses. You reflect on how your brother loves you, and how he was not trying to attack you in that case. All of this is cognitive manipulation.

Of course, all this is happening after the unjust anger has already arisen. What is done is done. But through cognitive manipulation, you can shape how you will perceive the next such comment you hear, either as an offense or a harmless comment. If you successfully reimagine the situation to get a better grasp of what really happened, the next time your unjust anger will not flare up or, more likely, it will flare up less strongly. Eventually it will not be aroused at all. And thus over time you will have habituated your anger so that eventually it is virtuous, and arises only at the proper time, in the proper place, at the right person, and in the right degree.

Through cognitive manipulation, or reimagining the different situations that arouse your emotions, you can indeed shape not only your actions but your desires themselves. This ability to shape your emotions is not direct control.

---

4. Some psychologists call this "cognitive behavior therapy."

You cannot command your emotional responses, such that they will obey you immediately, as for instance your arm will obey your command when you want to raise it up. Indeed, due to the responsive nature of our emotions, they will never be fully under your complete control. But that is far from saying they are wholly beyond your control. Through such means as cognitive manipulation emotional responses can be well habituated so as to support your quest for the good life.

Why Bother Talking about the Emotions in Moral Theology?

This last section briefly explores the question, why bother? Previous chapters in this book have already expanded the scope of the moral life so as to include not only what actions we perform, but also what we intend by those actions. The moral life has already been shown to be a matter of interiority as well as external action. With this attention to interiority in place, why bother attending to another sort of interiority, that of our desires? What is gained by such attention? Or, better, what is missing if we do not understand, and in our lives attend to, the sorts of desires we have? In order to answer this question, a brief survey is offered here of three prevalent visions of the role emotions play in the moral life, held by various thinkers throughout the Western tradition. This book argues for the third approach described below.

First, recognizing that emotional attachments are responsive and therefore never fully under our control, some thinkers (such as Stoic philosophers) hold the view whereby the emotions are always seen as inordinate attachments that should be eradicated to the greatest extent possible. Emotions, simply put, only get in the way. We hear echoes of this view when people tell us, "Stop being so emotional! Think rationally!" Surely at times our emotional distress can hinder our ability to think straight. But this advice can also indicate that emotions only get in the way of our thinking straight, and thus we need to extinguish them as fully as possible. Of course, people who espouse this Stoic view know that eradicating emotions altogether is never fully possible. But the more we can be apathetic, the better. Emotions only get in the way.

A second vision of the role of the emotions in the moral life was held by Immanuel Kant, and arguably Plato. According to this view, emotions are not necessarily obstacles to virtuous living. They may be, but they might even help one act virtuously at times. However, since they are unreliable they should be reined in by one's reason. Most important for this approach to the emotions, when they are absent from virtuous action there is nothing missing without them.

Aristotle and Aquinas represent a third vision of the role of the emotions in the moral life. They would agree that emotions can at times mislead us. They would also agree that the most important thing for virtuous living is good action and intention, even if unaccompanied by well-ordered desires. But they differ from the previous school of thought in two ways. First, they claim that our desires and emotions can indeed be transformed by our higher powers so as to participate in one's higher powers, rather than merely being reined in by those powers. They recognize that when we have unruly desires, reining in may be the best we can do. That is why continence is virtuous, even if not fully virtuous. But they claim that having desires that are shaped by reason is even better. Why? This leads us to their second difference from the previous school of thought. Both Aristotle and Aquinas claimed that without virtuous emotions and desires something important is missing.

To understand what they say is missing, consider an example used both by Aquinas and Kant. When giving alms to the poor, is it best to feel sympathy for those in need? Kant recognizes that we are often sympathetic, but worries that if our emotions are the main drive behind our good acts, we might not do our duty and give to those in need at times when we do not feel like it. So he actually claims that since it is best to do good out of duty and not simply because of one's feelings, the person who gives to the poor purely out of duty and without any sympathy is more praiseworthy. Aquinas, of course, agrees that it is most important to do the good act, even if one does not feel like it. But he argues that the fully virtuous person not only does the right thing for the right reasons, but also with the right emotions. In other words, almsgiving without sympathy, while still praiseworthy, is not as fully virtuous as doing so with the corresponding well-ordered emotions. Something would be missing without them.

This naturally raises the question, what would be missing? If in both cases good acts are being done for good motives, what is missing in the person without the corresponding emotions? Aquinas is never clear enough in explaining this, except to say that since we were created as embodied persons, it is more fitting that we should do good not only with our wills but also with our hearts, by which he meant our emotions. But we can speculate on a further answer that would be in accord with Aquinas's (and Aristotle's) thought.

Both Aquinas and Aristotle thought that the fully virtuous person acts well with "pleasure and promptness." For them, the moral life need not be, indeed should not be, burdensome. Well-ordered emotions grant to the virtuous person a *facility*, an ease of action, not present in the person who acts on rational deliberation alone. The person with virtuous emotions responds nimbly to her environment such that doing good acts is not only done consistently and for the right reasons, but is also done easily, promptly, and with pleasure. The emotions serve just such a purpose for the human person. True, poorly habituated desires can do just the opposite, leading one facilely to activities that hinder the good life. But this is actually all the more reason to attend to how our desires are habituated, lest they encumber us in our desire to live most fully.

Much is at stake in attending to, or failing to attend to, our emotions. It is true that the continent person is evidence enough that one can indeed restrain one's desires so as to act well in spite of those desires. But not only is such a life burdensome, it will likely not last. Eventually we will be worn down and succumb to those desires. Or, if we consistently resist those desires, the disordered desires themselves will likely diminish, and that should be enough reason to attend to important role our emotions play in the virtuous life.

Concluding Thoughts

This chapter is the first one devoted to a specific cardinal virtue: temperance. The first section offers a largely straightforward discussion of temperance, noting that temperance is not only about right actions and intentions, but also about right desires. The rest of this chapter springboarded off this fact to: (a) define emotions or desires and explore whether and why we are praise-worthy or blameworthy for those we have; (b) explore how we can develop good habits in our desires and emotions; and, (c) what difference it makes for the moral life if we do so.

After the preceding analysis, one obvious question remains. It concerns the possibility of self-deception and delusion while engaging in cognitive manipulation. A scene from the movie *A Beautiful Mind* illustrates this pos-sibility well. It is the story of mathematical genius and Nobel Prize winner John Nash, who also suffers from severe psychiatric problems. In this scene, Nash's wife is asked by a friend how she is doing throughout John's bouts of schizophrenia and periods of institutionalization. She admits to feelings of obligation, guilt for wanting to leave him, and anger at him and God for his condition. Of course, she has not left John, and so this is a perfect example of continence. She is containing these desires and staying with her husband. She then provides a perfect example of cognitive manipulation. After admit-ting her feelings, she says:

> I think often what I feel is obligation. Or guilt over wanting to leave. Rage, against John, against God. But then I look at him and I *force myself to see* the man that I married. And he becomes that man. He's transformed into some-one I love. And I'm transformed into someone who loves him. It's not all the time—but it's enough.[5]

Here is a classic example of how someone reimagines a situation, such that her emotions themselves are transformed. Yet students who have seen this clip, perhaps prompted by the occasion of a woman convincing herself to stay with her husband, have asked an excellent question. What if cognitive

---

5. *Beautiful Mind*, scene 15 (1:21:00 into film) (emphasis added).

manipulation is used to deceive or delude one's self? For instance, what if we hear these words from a victim of abuse convincing herself to stay with her violent spouse?

This question reveals that cognitive manipulation can indeed be used poorly, to delude one's self and possibly even harm one's self or others. Does this mean one should avoid any such reimagining? No, since it is the same sort of cognitive manipulation (in reverse) that can enables an abused spouse to overcome her emotion of fear to get help. There is a guard against such harmful cognitive manipulation. It is to ensure that one is reimagining the situation more, and not less, truthfully. How to know when that is the case? This is exactly the point of the following chapter, on the virtue of prudence.

Study Questions

1. Define temperance. What sorts of acts does it cover? In what different ways can one fail to be fully temperate?
2. Does temperance concern only external acts? Explain. What two types of interiority are distinguished in this chapter?
3. What are passions, or emotions? Give some examples. How are they related to external actions?
4. Can one ever be responsible for an emotional response? Explain. Give an example.
5. Explain how virtuous emotions can be developed, and be sure to use the following terms: intemperance, incontinence, continence, temperance.
6. What is essential for advancing from each step to the next in the development of virtue? Give one example for each step of advancement.
7. Give three different models for the role of the emotions in the moral life. State who holds each one, and explain what distinguishes each view.

Terms to Know

temperance, passion, incontinence, continence, intemperance, cognitive manipulation, facility

Questions for Further Reflection

1. Think of some occasions in your life when you possessed a disordered desire, even if you did not act on it. What did it prompt you to do? Why didn't you do that? Could you have avoided the desire in the first place?

2. Think of some occasion in your life when you progressed through the different stages of developing virtuous emotions. Explain what helped you move from step to step.
3. Can the steps outlined here be used to develop increasing disordered passions? Try to think of an individual or communal example of such a case.
4. Can one intermittently go forward and backward with regard to the virtuousness of one's desires?
5. Are there some areas in people's lives where continence may be the highest possible state to achieve?
6. What ramifications on parenting are there for this chapter's work on developing the emotion? In other words, try and answer the "why bother" question of the last section with regard to child development.

Further Reading

Thomas Aquinas is again the driving force behind this chapter. See in particular his "Treatise on the Passions," I–II 22–48 in his *Summa Theologiae*. The *Catechism of the Catholic Church* has a helpful and concise section on the passions, sections 1762–1775. For helpful contemporary moral theologians on the emotions, see Diana Fritz Cates' *Choosing to Feel* as well as her article "Temperance" in Stephen J. Pope's (ed.) *The Ethics of Aquinas*. See also G. Simon Harak's *Virtuous Passions*.

5

THE VIRTUE OF PRUDENCE

Knowing the Truth and Living It

In her brief article entitled "The Lady in the Mirror," Lorraine Murray offers a powerful account of how, like so many women in our society, she has struggled much of her life with being acutely conscious of her weight. Though she never claims she had a clinical eating disorder, she poignantly describes the trials of her journey from an overweight childhood to a normal- sized adulthood where she still continues to obsess over what she should, and should not, be eating.[1] At one point she reveals how exactly this fixation continues to play out in her adult life. "Although I was delighted to wear smaller sized dresses and jeans, when I looked in the mirror I didn't see the new me. Instead, I saw a fat lady staring back."

There are numerous facets of her story that invite analysis: social pressure on women to have a certain body type, whether one should obsess over eating even if one is overweight, and the like. But the part of this story that nicely introduces this chapter concerns how Murray saw herself—"the trouble is that when I gaze into the mirror, a fat lady stares back." Murray's obsessions about her diet and body are the result of how she sees herself. Even though she knows she is not overweight, since it is she who reports her adult dress sizes, she also admits that she still sees herself in another fashion. It is the latter

---

1. Lorraine Murray. "Loving the Lady in the Mirror," *America,* Feb. 17, 2003, 14–16.

way of seeing, or grasp of how things are, that drives her actions. Thus it is sadly no surprise that she continues to obsess over her eating, even when the tags on her dresses have smaller numbers. The relevant lesson for this chapter is that how we see the way things are, whether our vision is accurate or not, drives how we act.

Given how Murray says she sees herself, it is less surprising that she agonizes over her weight. One contemporary moral theologian describes the moral importance of how we see things and claims it is crucial that we have "truthful vision."[2] Put simply, we cannot act rightly if we do not see rightly. If we do not have an accurate grasp of the way things are, it is impossible to act virtuously. So the question for Murray is, why does she see things in the way she does? Why doesn't she just open her eyes and see things rightly? Then she would not obsess so about her eating!

Using a story of a woman who struggles with her weight and diet to introduce the meaning of a virtue may seem offensive. Is Murray sinful because she saw herself as fat? This is a legitimate question, and the issue of what someone like Murray is responsible for in how she sees things will be addressed below in a discussion of conscience. However, this question may also reveal a morality-of-obligation perspective, focused primarily on following rules and assigning blame. Though these are important, moral theology is presented here first and foremost from a morality-of-happiness perspective as a way to live a good life. It is a life that is most in accord with the truth, or the way things are. Blameworthy or not, Murray is not living in accordance with the truth. She is not seeing herself rightly, and it is impeding her ability to live a good life.

Consider another example of the moral importance of seeing things rightly. In the last chapter's discussion of habituating virtuous passions, cognitive manipulation was suggested as a way to shape your emotions by reimagining how you see a situation. We even saw an example from the movie *A Beautiful Mind*, where a wife employed this technique to change how she saw, and thus felt about, her husband struggling with schizophrenia. But this also raised a disturbing possibility. Can't someone reimagine a situation in a manner that is not virtuous, but self-destructive? Indeed, this happens with many victims of spousal abuse, who convince themselves that "he doesn't really mean it" or "this isn't who he is; he is just under stress." Does the possibility of such self-delusion mean that one should not ever re-imagine situations?

The guard against self-deception and delusion is not, of course, refusing to see things differently. That may at times be needed to get one out of self-deception. The key is to reimagine things accurately, so that our grasp of situations is more, not less, in accordance with the truth of how things

2. Paul Wadell, *Becoming Friends: Worship, Justice, and the Practice of Christian Friendship* (Grand Rapids: Brazos, 2002), 121–30.

are. So if we were friends with the wife in *A Beautiful Mind*, we would try to help her ensure that she understood her relationship with her husband more, not less, accurately. If we were friends with Lorraine Murray, we would help her see herself more truthfully, as a woman who need not obsess over her eating. In both cases, we would be helping people see things more truthfully, more accurately, so that they could then act well. The key insight for this chapter is a simple phrase used by one twentieth-century thinker who wrote extensively on virtue: "the true precedes the good."[3] Doing good actions requires a truthful grasp of the way things are around us. As Murray's story sadly illustrates, and the wife's cognitive manipulation in *A Beautiful Mind* suggests, a failure to see things rightly is a great impediment to the good life.

This chapter explores two crucial topics in moral theology that both pertain to seeing things rightly. The first is the virtue prudence, which enables us to both see things rightly concerning practical matters, and to translate that truthful grasp of things into action. It is so important to the virtuous life that it has consistently been seen in the Western tradition as pre-eminent among the cardinal virtues. The first half of this chapter defines prudence, explains its importance, and provides some examples of ways to be prudent or imprudent.

The second half of this chapter examines the meaning of a related term: conscience. This section will explain the meaning of the term and explain why the Christian tradition makes the radical claim that one must always follow one's conscience. Nonetheless, that tradition has also maintained that one's conscience can be in error, setting up the disturbing possibility that one may follow one's conscience, and in doing so may actually be acting wrongly. Explaining how and why this is so, and how we can determine blame in such situations, is the last task for the second section of this chapter.

Prudence: Seeing and Acting Truthfully

The purpose of this first section is to explain the meaning of the cardinal virtue, prudence. Being a prudent person is what enables one to see rightly and translate that truthful vision into action. After defining this crucial virtue, the section goes on to explain the different ways prudence operates, why it is preeminent among the cardinal virtues, and how the right seeing of prudence is related to being smart. It concludes with examples of skills needed to be prudent and ways of being imprudent to help fill out your understanding of the virtue prudence.

3. Josef Pieper, *The Four Cardinal Virtues* (Notre Dame, IN: University of Notre Dame Press, 1966), 2. Later, Pieper (23) offers a different formulation of this same claim based upon a quote from Thomas Aquinas: "the good presupposes the true."

Defining Prudence

Even more so than temperance, prudence is a virtue that is easily misunderstood, given the English translation of the term. The Latin term *prudentia* does not simply mean, as the English term "prudence" often does, being cautious or wary. *Prudentia* is better translated "practical wisdom," or as one recent moral theologian prefers, "good sense."[4] Nonetheless, the translation "prudence" is still used here, given its prevalence as the English term for this virtue.

What is prudence? Prudence is the virtue that disposes us to see rightly, the way things are in the world around us, and to employ that truthful vision to act rightly. It enables us to size up a situation accurately, to determine the best course of action, and to embark upon it.[5] It is practical wisdom because it is not simply an aloof knowledge about how things are. It is what the *Catechism* (citing Aquinas) calls "right reason in action."[6] This is an absolutely crucial point in understanding prudence. If prudence were simply right knowledge about what to do, it would be possible to have this virtue and never put the knowledge to use by acting rightly. We see the importance of this point in Murray's depiction of her struggle with her weight. If asked, she knows the truth about her weight and how she should thus act. But that is not what she puts into action. Prudence is not simply knowing better, in the sense that Murray knows better that she is not overweight. Sadly, Murray is not prudent. Prudence is not only good deliberation about a situation and settling on the best course of action; it is also acting well based on that deliberation.

Why do we need to see rightly, or have a truthful grasp of things, in order to act well? Shouldn't we just do what is good? And can't we just follow the rules to be sure to do what is good? It is certainly true that the prudent person knows what the rules are. And at times it is abundantly clear how to follow the rules. Yet prudence is not simply the deductive, mechanistic application of general rules to particular situations. Prudence is the ability to see and act out what is good in specific situations. For instance, a consistent theme in this book thus far has been that virtue resides in the mean. Virtue is having well-ordered, or reasonable desires, for things such as eating or drinking. But of course that simply raises the question, what constitutes a proper or well-ordered desire? For instance, what constitutes moderate drinking of alcohol? Or in the case of Lorraine Murray described above, what is the true way things are concerning her body size, and how does that determine what she should eat? The prudent person sees the mean in particular situations and puts it into action.

4. Herbert McCabe, OP, *God Still Matters* (London, Contimuum, 2003), 152–65.

5. For three stages of prudence, see Thomas Aquinas *Summa Theologiae* (New York: Benziger Bros., 1948) II–II 47,8. For an outstanding (and difficult) contemporary discussion of prudence, see Daniel Westberg's *Right Practical Reason: Aristotle, Action, and Prudence in Aquinas* (Oxford: Clarendon Press, 1994).

6. *Catechism of the Catholic Church*, 2nd ed. (Vatican City: Libreria Editrice Vaticana, 1997), 1806.

Prudence is therefore a more elusive virtue to understand than, say, temperance. It is easier to call to mind ways our sensual desires have, and have not, been virtuous. Occasions of moderate or immoderate eating, drinking or sexual desire are immediately obvious to us. Actually, occasions of prudence or imprudence are just as prevalent, but they may be less obvious due to the type of activity governed by this habit. Prudence is the virtue that disposes us to do practical decision-making well. Practical decision-making, or practical reasoning, is our capacity to effectuate our desires, or put them into action effectively. It concerns not what we desire, but how to achieve it.

Consider the example of a mother with two teenage daughters. She loves her children dearly. Her family knows this. But it is also clear to her family that despite how much she loves her children and wishes them well, she continually makes poor decisions to live out that love effectively. At times she is very lax in setting rules such as curfews, not out of indifference but because she wants her children to enjoy themselves and not be burdened by too many rules. At other times she worries she is being too lax and thus sets overly strict rules for her girls out of a genuine concern for their own good.

The problem is that, though intended for their own good, these practical decisions on how to raise teenagers actually harm these girls. The lack of consistency of the rules makes the girls distrust their mother and wonder if she really wants what is best for them. Furthermore, the lack of coherence in the rules prevents the girls from understanding and adopting for themselves the purpose and meaning of those rules. Sadly, the mother fails to see the inconsistency of her rules, and how it actually hurts her daughters. Though the mother has good desires, and truly does love her daughters, those good wishes are not enough to effectuate her desires. Despite what the Beatles' sang, it is not true that "all you need is love." The mother needs prudence to be able to make good decisions that will put her love of her girls into action effectively. If the mother did her practical decision-making well, we would call her prudent. But in this case she is imprudent.

The Preeminence of Prudence

As is clear in this example, prudence is needed to effectively exercise any virtuous action. Raising kids (a matter of justice), pursuing pleasures moderately (temperance), and facing difficulties well (fortitude) all require a truthful grasp of the way things are in order to put virtuous inclinations into action effectively. For precisely this reason, prudence has consistently been called preeminent among the other cardinal virtues. It has been labeled the "charioteer of the virtues."[7] In other words, it is needed to steer, or guide, the other virtues into action. Without it, they flounder and remain ineffective.

---

7. *Catechism of the Catholic Church*, 1806. See also Aquinas, *Summa Theologiae* II–II 47. The image of charioteer is likely taken from Plato's *Republic*. Though Western thinkers have

How exactly does prudence help effectuate virtuous action? One contemporary moralist claims it is not enough to understand prudence simply as setting the path for our virtuous desires. That is one role, but she suggests three in all. [8] The first is indeed setting a specific means or path to putting a virtuous desire into action. Imagine you wish to give money to help victims of a recent natural disaster. This is a generous intention. But of course, you have not yet effectuated that virtuous goal. If you give the money to an unknown person with no credentials who claims to be raising money for those victims, it may never find its way there and thus you never serve those you intended to help. So a potentially generous act is done imprudently, and thus not done well. But if you give the money to Catholic Charities or the Red Cross in one of their drives to aid victims of that disaster, you can be reasonably sure, given the history and reputation of these organizations, that the money will find its intended target. Here a virtuous inclination is effectuated with good practical decisions, so that a virtuous act actually happens with the guidance of prudence. This example reveals one of the tasks of prudence: how to carry out a virtuous intention.

In this first role for prudence, it is clear how to act generously, and what needs to be seen rightly is simply how to carry out that action. A second example reveals that sometimes prudence helps us determine what a virtuous act is in the first place. Consider the example of a father who wants both to provide for his son financially, and also to teach the son an appreciation for the value of money. Should the father provide the son's college spending money, if possible? Would that be generous? Or should he require the son to work, so as not to spoil him? Like the first example, prudence is needed in this case for a well-meaning person to know what decisions to make. But in this second role for prudence, the issue is not simply setting the path for an obviously good action, but rather determining what counts as a virtuous action given the particular situation at hand. This is a second way that prudence functions to enable us to make good decisions.

Consider a third way that prudence is needed for good practical reasoning. In real life, our reflection about how to make practical decisions does not always concern executing an obviously good act (giving money to charity) or figuring out what actions are virtuous given the particularities of one relationship (the father and son). Prudence is often a matter of properly balancing many diverse commitments and projects in one's life. For example, toward the end of an academic term I commonly have a student tell me he wants to come to my office to explain why he has completely fallen behind in my class. Quite

consistently understood prudence as preeminent, they do so in different ways, a point not necessary for our analysis (though hinted at in the final section of last chapter on the difference between Plato/Kant and Aristotle/Aquinas).

8. See Jean Porter, *Nature as Reason* (Grand Rapids: Eerdmans, 2004). The following examples also come from Porter, 313–16.

often this is neither a health or family emergency, nor a case of negligence or indifference. Frequently students simply get overwhelmed by their commitment to various good projects, and find themselves unable to balance them all. As a result, they neglect an important task (like a course), or manage to do all of their projects but none of them well. This is a perfect example of the third role for prudence. The prudent person sees rightly what the truly most important projects are in one's life, and knows how to prioritize them accordingly. That may indeed mean not being able to participate in something worthy. It may entail saying no. But the prudent person neither neglects important commitments nor gets overextended. This necessitates seeing things rightly and deciding accordingly.

Are Only Smart People Holy?

These examples hopefully illuminate why the prudent person's seeing rightly is not simply a matter of opening her eyes. Prudence is not a matter of eyesight, but rather of good sense. It means having an accurate grasp of the way things work in the world. Some immediately wonder if this means that one has to be smart to be holy. If seeing things truthfully is so important for living virtuously, are intelligent people at an advantage? Two twentieth-century Christian authors (Herbert McCabe, OP, and C. S. Lewis) address this question beautifully. It is obviously not the case that people who score higher on their SAT's are necessarily more holy. So if by smart is meant book smarts, smarter people are not necessarily more virtuous. As McCabe says, "what is in question is not theoretical thinking and the handling of concepts and words, but practical shrewdness and common sense in matters of human behavior."[9] Lewis says bluntly that "God will not love you any less, or have less use for you, if you happen to have been born with a very second-rate brain."[10]

Nonetheless, Lewis goes on to say, "He has room for people with very little sense, but He wants every one to use what sense they have." McCabe is even more direct, when he claims "no stupid person can be good." McCabe indicates that the issue is not only using what sense you have, but also the type of sense or smartness truly necessary to be virtuous, when he goes on to say, "Unreasonableness, pig-headedness, bigotry, and self-deception are all in themselves blameworthy, and are constitutive of the kind of stupidity that is a vice."[11] The reason these latter are types of stupidity is that they are inaccurate grasps of the way things are. You are not always right (pig-headedness). People of different races are not unequal (bigotry). And refusing to see that you might be wrong leaves you ignorant as well as blameworthy (self-deception).

9. McCabe, *God Still Matters*, 155–56.
10. C. S. Lewis, *Mere Christianity* (San Francisco: HarperSanFrancisco, 2001), 77.
11. McCabe, *God Still Matters*, 155.

As McCabe notes, "there is a sense of 'education' (rather different from the one in common use) in which the educated person does indeed have a moral advantage over the uneducated; if this were not so, education would not be a serious human endeavor."[12] This sheds some light on why Aristotle famously claimed that the young could never be fully wise.[13] It takes life experience to understand how people behave, to be able to foresee consequences of one's acts, and to learn what is truly important. And these skills, among others, all enable us to see things rightly and act accordingly. They are parts of prudence, and thus needed in order to be virtuous, since prudence is the charioteer of the virtues.

Before elaborating on some of the specific skills prudence entails, two observations are warranted. First, it should be noted that practical decision-making is as much a communal activity as it is an individual one. Therefore, prudence is thoroughly social. In one sense this is obvious. We often consult others for guidance that shapes the decisions we make. But in an even deeper sense, how we see the way things are and thus act is deeply shaped by our formative communities. We learn how to raise children by how we ourselves were raised, and how we see others do it. We may even learn to view members of one race a certain way by growing up in a certain society at a particular time period. All of this is simply to say that how we see things and act accordingly is very much shaped by the communities in which we live, for better or for worse.

As for the second observation, it is appropriate to end this section with some words on the moral importance of education. As McCabe notes, the common use of the term education—meaning the formal sense of going to a school and taking classes—has little to do with virtue. But in the broader, informal sense he prefers, education is crucial for becoming virtuous. It is through education in this broader sense that we learn about how our family, churches, and society all see things and live out that vision. The way certain activities such as sexual activity, alcohol use, and eating food are all modeled, shapes how we see what those activities mean and what their place is in a good life. How we see the poor, children, spouses, and those of other races treated by those around us shapes how we see and relate to others, and thus our capacity for justice. In all of these senses, formal education, like informal education, can be a powerful tool for passing on truthful or deceived ways to see things. Both can also equip one with the vision to see falsity in prevailing practices. In this larger sense, there is no more morally important endeavor than education.

Parts of Prudence and Types of Imprudence

Before moving on to conscience, it is worth pausing to give examples of some parts, or sub-virtues, of prudence. Recall that Aquinas claims each cardinal

12. Ibid., 156.
13. Aristotle, *Nicomachean Ethics*, in *The Basic Works of Aristotle*, ed. Richard McKeon (New York: Random House, 1941), 1142a.

virtue covers a host of related virtues. Any habit of doing practical reasoning well is rightly called a part, or sub-virtue, of prudence.[14] We will consider three such sub-virtues of prudence here, and note the Latin equivalents of these terms to be precise as to what each one does and does not mean. The three are memory (*memoria*), docility (*docilitas*), and nimble decisiveness (*solertia*).[15] A quick look at these sub-virtues will further illuminate exactly how prudence enables, and imprudence impedes, truthful action.

It may sound odd to call *memory* a virtue. Isn't memory simply a container where things are stored and later accessed? Where is there room for praise or blame with such a capacity? This sense of memory may be the case with basic pieces of information, like phone numbers. Though one could forget a number, or remember it wrongly, it seems odd to blame someone for that. But truthful memory is also crucial for being able to make good decisions, and at times this may indeed be a matter of praise or blame. Ask two friends who are in a fight what happened to get them there. Chances are you will receive two stories that are similar but importantly different. People tend to remember what happened in ways that benefit themselves. They tend to make themselves look better by neglecting things they might have done wrongly and accentuating what they have suffered unjustly at the hands of others.

This happens not only on the individual, but also on the communal, level. Look at a pre-1950s American textbook on slavery to see how we remembered what happened in the slave era. Look at even more recent Japanese textbooks for what happened in China before World War II, and you will fail to find mention of Japanese atrocities committed there. In these cases you will read communal memories where truth is skewed. Failing to remember history accurately inhibits one's ability to make good practical decisions. Thus the virtue of truthful memory is needed to exercise prudence, at both the individual and communal levels.

A second sub-virtue of prudence is *docility*. This word commonly connotes slavish following of others. That is not the sense of the term here. Docility as understood here is an open-minded willingness to accept guidance from others. If having a true sense of how thing are is needed to act rightly, and if we grant that we do not know it all, it follows that we should be willing to enlist the help and guidance of others in order to see things more truthfully and thus act more rightly. This is what chapter 1 described in its discussion of authority. Of course, this entails an act of trust, and one can be deceived. Indeed, having the sub-virtue of docility includes a sense of whom to trust

14. The classic treatment of this topic in Aquinas is found in his *Summa Theologiae* II–II 48–9. Thomas uses the term "part" in a technical sense that is not necessary to explain for our purposes.

15. See Pieper, *The Four Cardinal Virtues*, 14–18. Though this chapter follows Pieper in selecting which three parts from Aquinas to explain more fully, the explanation here extends beyond what Pieper does in his own text.

for guidance and when to seek it. For failing to hear others out of fear of deception leaves one close-minded and half blind. We consult friends, mentors, and teachers regularly in coming to a better sense of how things are. Docility is simply the skill of seeking and accepting guidance well.

Finally, the term *solertia* has no obvious English cognate. It seems best translated as "nimble decisiveness."[16] *Solertia* is the ability to quickly size up an unexpected situation and act well to achieve one's good goals. Consider a mundane example of this. You and your seven friends are meeting in a campus parking lot to drive into town together for dinner. One person unexpectedly cannot come, and she, with you, was one of the drivers. What to do? The person with *solertia* is the one who steps up to evaluate the situation and make happen what you all had planned, given the new circumstances. They can quickly assess possible actions. Is there someone else with a car? Can someone use their roommate's car? Do you go somewhere closer and walk? Though such a case is morally insignificant, this sub-virtue is needed in cases where the good of all involved is morally significant. One could easily imagine a boss having to address the sudden boorish behavior of a worker to her peers, or a parent of four having to react quickly and decisively to tend to an injured child while not neglecting the other three. The prudent person who displays *solertia* makes good practical decisions in such unexpected situations.

Of course, one can also be imprudent, which is simply the name for the vice of not doing practical decision making well. There are also several types of imprudence, but two nicely encapsulate the essential features of prudence as both seeing things rightly and allowing that practical knowledge to drive good action. The person with the vice of *thoughtlessness*, on the one hand, acts quickly but without adequately attending to the situation, and thus often fails to attain a truthful grasp of the situation to guide his action. On the other hand, the person with the vice of *irresoluteness* deliberates endlessly over what to do, but never lets such deliberation translate into action. Thus even if there is seeing rightly it is not in action. Both of these habits, in this case vices, are examples of different types of imprudence.

Conscience: Knowing the True to Do the Good

"Conscience" is a commonly used but often misunderstood term. We hear people speak of guilty consciences, and wonder in exasperation if others around them doing wrong action have any conscience. There are better and worse ways to understand conscience, so this second section of the chapter takes on the important task of explaining this term. It is relevant here because, like prudence, conscience is crucial for seeing rightly so that we may

---

16. This is in line with Pieper's thought, though his term is "nimbleness" (ibid., 17).

act rightly. For this reason, conscience has always been a foundational term in moral theology.[17]

Defining Conscience

In a helpful introductory article on conscience, one contemporary moral theologian asks what constitutes the main challenge to living the virtuous life.[18] Many assume that it is resisting temptation. The familiar image of deciding what to do with an angel on one shoulder and a devil on the other comes to mind here. In this model, we know the right thing to do—the angel tells us. Yet we are also tempted to do what we want to do; that is what the devil encourages. The similarity to Glaucon's vision of morality and the good life should be clear. In this model, what we really want to do is in tension with what we should do. The little angel telling us what we should do in this model is our conscience.

We have all surely been in exactly such a situation where we felt tempted to do what we knew we should not do. Resisting temptation is indeed an important part of living virtuously. Of course, reminiscent of chapter 1, the claim of this book is that the little devil is not encouraging us to do what is truly best for us. It may seem to be what we want for the time being, but what we really want (reminiscent of Socrates) is to be virtuous, not only because it is the morally good thing to do, but because living virtuously is what leads to genuine happiness.

But note that in this first model of the main challenge to living virtuously, the right thing to do is already clear to us. It may be experienced as a burden or obligation (even though it is truly not), but there is no doubt as to what living virtuously entails. Yet often the main obstacle to living virtuously is not knowing what the right thing to do is in the first place. For instance, perhaps a college student is considering becoming more sexually involved with her boyfriend. (A later chapter examines sex in more detail, so this case will be purposely vague as to what exactly is being considered.) She has well-intentioned reasons to become more sexually involved. She cares for him deeply and wants to physically express her love for him. She also has well-intentioned hesitations about doing so. She knows it will have a huge impact on their relationship and is not sure how exactly their relationship will handle it, or indeed what their long-term plans together are. Again, this is not simply a case of knowing the right thing to do and convincing one's self to do otherwise, as we all have

17. The basis of the term conscience in the Christian tradition is a scripture passage where St. Paul affirms that those who do not have the law of God still have the moral law "written on their hearts" (Rom. 2:14–16), to which their consciences bear witness. Conscience also plays an important role in 1 Cor. 10.

18. Darlene Fozard Weaver, "Conscience: Rightly Formed and Otherwise" *Commonweal*, September 23, 2005, 10–13.

done when we fail to resist temptation. This is a matter of being able to truly determine what exactly constitutes the virtuous thing to do.

This second scenario reveals another important obstacle to living virtuously, not knowing what exactly is the good thing to do. Unlike the first model, here the person does not have the right answer already, so to speak. The virtuous life is a matter both of resisting temptation to do what we know is wrong, and knowing what is right in the first place. Knowing what is right is the domain of conscience. Simply put, "conscience is a judgment of reason whereby the human person recognizes the moral quality of a concrete act that he is going to perform, is in the process of performing, or has already completed."[19] It is what we honestly and sincerely think to be right, despite any temptations, peer pressures, or other challenges. It is what we think in our gut, in our heart of hearts, is the right thing to do. Sometimes the challenge to living virtuously is following what one's conscience says is the right thing to do, since we want to do otherwise. Yet sometimes the challenge is developing, or forming, one's conscience so we know what is right to do in the first place.

It is easy to see why conscience and prudence are being treated together in the same chapter. Both prudence and conscience entail seeing things rightly concerning practical matters for the sake of good action. But there are also important differences. Conscience is your ability to make judgments about whether a particular act is right or wrong, and the particular judgment you make in a certain circumstance. You can have a conscience that makes accurate judgments about what constitutes a good act, and still decide not to follow it and act well. In other words, you can do what you know in your heart of hearts is not the right thing to do. But the same is not true of prudence. Prudence is not simply deliberating and deciding well, but also putting right reasoning into action. Prudence requires a well-formed conscience, but more—if you do not act well, you are not prudent. The main point of this second half of the chapter is describing and evaluating how consciences are formed well or poorly, and explaining whether you are blameworthy or not if your conscience is poorly formed.

Does Everyone Have a Conscience?

The need for formation of conscience, discussed explicitly in the *Catechism*, surprises many people who assume that one's conscience is simply a given.[20] Don't we all simply know what is right and wrong? And if people differ on what they think is right and wrong, doesn't that simply mean that on some questions (like perhaps our college student considering her sexual relationship with her boyfriend) different answers can both be right? In other words,

19. *Catechism of the Catholic Church*, 1778.
20. *Catechism of the Catholic Church*, 1783–85, 1798. The formation of conscience is called a lifelong task (1784).

the underlying question is, can a person think they are right in what they are doing and actually be wrong?

One way to approach this issue is by asking if everyone has a conscience that tells them what is truly right. The answer is yes and no. Everyone has the general capacity to judge right and wrong, and does so in particular situations. The general capacity has traditionally been called *synderesis*. All have this awareness of the general principles of right and wrong, and the ability to make judgments based on that knowledge in particular cases. However, at the level of particular cases, people may indeed come to different judgments as to the rightness or wrongness of an act. Again, we are not speaking here of the obvious fact that people do wrong actions as well as right ones. We are making the stronger claim that some people sincerely judge, in their heart of hearts, that some particular act is good while other people sincerely judge the same act wrong.

Of course, there are many occasions where such diversity is legitimate, even beautiful. You may know in your conscience that it is right for you to enter religious life, while I know in mine that I am called to get married. You may judge it is best not to drink alcohol at all, while I judge it right for me to drink moderately. In these cases, personal differences, such as one's vocation, or the nature of a particular activity, such as drinking alcohol, may allow or even call for different actions on the part of different people.

But are there occasions when presumably well-intentioned people differ on the judgment of some particular act, so one must be right and the other one wrong? This is indeed the case. In fact, it can happen not only in individual cases, but even wholesale at the societal level. The case that best illustrates this point is slavery. Consider a slaveholder in 1700 America who genuinely believes in his heart of hearts that owning his slaves is a virtuous act. He treats them fairly and humanely. Today we would clearly say that this person was performing bad actions (buying and selling human beings, controlling their freedom, etc.), even though he really did not think he was wrong. In other words, he acted wrongly even though his conscience told him he was acting rightly. Whether or not we should blame this person for being wrong is a further question which will be addressed below. For now, note the simple claim that one can really judge with one's conscience that one is acting rightly, even though one is actually not.

The slavery case makes a crucial point. There may indeed be a right thing to do, even if we are not aware of it. The view that there are objectively right and wrong things to do, regardless of whether or not people realize it, is called *moral realism*. There really is a morally right thing to do, even if one does not see it at times. Unless you wish to argue that systems like slavery, or societal policies like the Holocaust, are morally right as long as people engaged in them genuinely believe them right, then you are a moral realist. Thankfully, I find few, perhaps no, students who are not moral realists. Of course, moral realists may disagree on the questions for which there is only one right way, and which way that is. But as long as you are willing to say there are at least some things that are really wrong, even if the person committing them thinks them right, you are a moral realist. The basic insight here, which is crucial to the Christian tradition, and indeed most of the Western moral tradition, is that one's judgment about what is right and wrong does not make it so.[21] The judgment of one's conscience is an alarm about what is the case, and it may be accurate or inaccurate. This point must be kept in mind in the following discussion of following one's conscience, and the possibility of erroneous conscience.

Follow Your Conscience—Always!

The recognition that one can err in a judgment of conscience would seem to indicate that one should not always follow one's conscience, but only when it is accurate. But this position actually makes no sense. One's conscience is one's most sincere judgment, in one's heart of hearts, of what the right thing to do is. There is no getting underneath one's conscience. Telling someone not to follow his conscience would, in effect, be telling someone to not do what he sincerely thinks is right. And this would make no sense. Hence, Christians have famously affirmed that one should always obey the certain judgment of one's conscience.[22]

Of course, the injunction to always follow one's conscience, coupled with the realization that one's conscience can be in error, sets up a disturbing possibility. One can follow one's conscience, and in doing so honestly think in one's heart of hearts one is acting well, and yet be acting wrongly. The reason the Christian tradition has maintained that people should always follow their consciences is largely due to a trust that they generally do indeed know what is right and wrong, even if they do not always act on it. But nonetheless, one can have, and act on, what has traditionally been called an *erroneous conscience*. In this situation one acts wrongly but "doesn't know better." One honestly thinks that one is acting rightly. The case of the slaveholder above is an example of an erroneous conscience—assuming he really thought that his actions were virtuous. This raises a further question: Is a person blameworthy for following an erroneous conscience?

The short answer to this is, it depends on why one's conscience is erroneous. If one should have known better, then one is blameworthy for following an erroneous conscience, even though the person really did not know better. This ignorance is called *vincible ignorance*, since it is conquerable if someone is duly attentive and conscientious. Yet if one could not have known better, the ignorance is called *invincible ignorance* (unable to be conquered), and one is not blameworthy. An example may help make this distinction.

21. See John Paul II, *Veritatis Splendor* (Encyclical Letter, 1993), 60, on this point.
22. For a recent example of this claim, see *Catechism of the Catholic Church*, 1790.

Say you are driving down a road and are pulled over by the police. The officer says you were speeding, doing 45 in a 30 mph zone. You could respond that you did not know the speed limit, so you should not get a ticket. But, of course, you are going to get a ticket. As a driver, it is your responsibility to know the speed limit, to keep an eye out for signs and drive accordingly. Note that the assumption here is that you truly are ignorant, and not lying to the officer. You really thought, in your heart of hearts, that the limit was 45 mph, and acted accordingly. Here is a simple example of following your conscience when it is an erroneous conscience. The ignorance is vincible, and you are morally responsible for not knowing better.

But perhaps you were paying attention, and the last sign you saw did indeed read 45 mph. Since the road did not significantly change, you assumed that was still the limit. It turns out, there was a sign marking the change to 30 mph, but when you drive back out of frustration to see if you were truly inattentive, you find the sign was knocked over in an accident. Indignant, you take pictures of the spot, go to court on your hearing date, and explain the situation to the judge. Now note, you were still speeding and violating the law. The question is not whether you violated the law—you did. The question is whether you are accountable, or blameworthy, for that violation. In this case, you truly had no way of knowing the law. You acted sincerely out of an erroneous conscience. You acted wrongly, but are not blameworthy since the ignorance was invincible.

What this language of vincible and invincible ignorance provides is a way of evaluating situations where people are acting in good faith but doing morally wrong things. A perfect example would be the slavery example. Surely slavery was wrong then, as it is now. Let's also assume that there were some people back then who honestly thought that owning slaves could be a morally good thing to do. They were wrong. It remains to be determined, of course, whether their ignorance is vincible or invincible. Should the slaveholder of the 1700s have known that slavery is wrong and not participated in the system willingly? If so, it would be vincible ignorance, and the person is blameworthy.[23] If such a stance were not possible given societal conditions, upbringing, and so on, the person would be invincibly ignorant and thus not blameworthy. As the slavery case makes clear, a lack of moral responsibility certainly does not mean one is acting rightly.

This discussion of slavery and the question of vincible/invincible ignorance prompts two observations before closing this section. First, the fact that slave owners several centuries ago seem to have genuinely thought they were acting rightly raises some humbling questions about our own contemporary societal

---

23. Even if someone is blameworthy in a case of vincible ignorance, societal forces can impact someone's freedom to lessen—though not remove—morally blameworthiness. For there to be no blame, the ignorance must be invincible.

practices. What are the things we do today that instrumentalize and victimize people—ourselves included—even though we do not see it? And should we see it? Do our national or international economic policies cause real harm to people in ways we do not see? Is the current U.S. penal system something people will look back on centuries later with horror? What about the place of alcohol in our society, particularly among college students? Is it dehumanizing people in ways we do not see clearly? What about common sexual practices, such as premarital sex? Again, the question here is not whether people are doing things they know are wrong. People are doing, have always done, and always will do things they know in their heart of hearts (in their consciences) to be wrong. The question is whether we are doing things we sincerely think are good, but which actually corrupt us, others, and society as a whole.

Another point revealed by the slavery example is that the point of moral theology is not determining whether we can praise or blame someone. This is important, for sure. But it is possible to act wrongly, even if one is not blameworthy. If acting wrongly simply meant being blameworthy, this would make no sense. But as we know from chapter 1, acting wrongly means acting in a manner where the genuine happiness of ourselves and others is impeded. This is certainly true in the slavery example. Even if slaveowners in the year 1700 were not blameworthy, they would still be inflicting enormous harm on other people (the slaves), themselves (by being deprived of seeing, serving, and enjoying the dignity of these people right before their eyes), and society. Or consider the Lorraine Murray example at the beginning of this chapter. Let's assume that her struggle with eating is the result of biological and familial influences for which she is not to blame. Nonetheless, even if not blameworthy, she is certainly acting in a manner that is harmful to herself. Saying she is not blameworthy does not mean she is acting rightly. Therefore, though determining blame is an important exercise for us who have freedom and are responsible for our actions, it is not the primary point of moral theology. The main goal is, as Socrates said, to live well.

Concluding Thoughts

The basic insight of this chapter is that an accurate, or truthful, grasp of the way things are is necessary in order to act well. The true precedes the good. We cannot act rightly if we do not see rightly. Your conscience is both the general capacity to know whether acts are good or bad, and the concrete determinations on various occasions of whether specific actions are good or bad. You should always follow your conscience, because your conscience tells you what you truly and honestly think is the right thing to do. However, since your conscience recognizes, rather than determines, what is the right thing to do, it is possible that in following your conscience you are doing what is wrong. This is called an erroneous conscience, and you are blameworthy for it if you should have known better (vincible ignorance) but not blameworthy for it if you could not have known better (invincible ignorance). This is why a good formation of conscience is so important, so that we can make accurate judgments about what is right and wrong, and live accordingly.

Of course, one can have a well-formed conscience and thus know what is truly right and wrong, and yet still not act on that knowledge. Prudence is the virtue that enables us not only to see rightly what is right and wrong, but also to act rightly based on that knowledge. If you have a well-formed conscience, it is possible to not be prudent. But it is impossible to be prudent without having a well-formed conscience. Though prudence is just one of the cardinal virtues, one that enables us to do practical decision-making well, it is actually preeminent among the cardinal virtues, because without it we cannot effectively live out temperance, justice, or fortitude. The virtuous person must be prudent in order to be able to see rightly and act accordingly.

Although it is prudence that sets the course of action for one who lives out good desires, this chapter on prudence has still been rather general in explaining how that happens. The examples used here are all rather obvious; no one claims that slavery is actually a good thing! It may be frustrating to the reader that even with a chapter on the virtue that sets the specific course for virtuous actions, we have still not gone into detail on any issue and said exactly what is right or wrong. These first five chapters were required in order to even start to do that. Later chapters will be necessary to do it even better. But at this point we are adequately equipped to begin that task, and the next chapter does so by looking at the place of alcohol in the virtuous life.

Study Questions

1. Why is seeing rightly essential for acting virtuously?
2. Define the virtue prudence. What human capacity does it govern?
3. Why is prudence called preeminent among, or charioteer of, the virtues? Give three ways that prudence helps effectuate virtuous action.
4. Are smart people more holy? Explain.
5. Why is prudence a communal activity?
6. Name and describe three sub-virtues of prudence, and two types of imprudence.
7. Define conscience. Why does a conscience need to be formed? Does everyone have a conscience? Explain.
8. Should one always follow one's conscience? Why or why not?
9. Is one blameworthy for following an erroneous conscience? Explain.

Terms to Know

prudence, charioteer of the virtues, docility, *solertia*, memory, irresoluteness, thoughtlessness, conscience, *synderesis*, moral realism, erroneous conscience, invincible vs. vincible ignorance

Questions for Further Reflection

1. If prudence is so central to living virtuously, is it the only virtue you need? Put another way, are there examples of failing to live virtuously that are not simply examples of poor practical decision-making?
2. To what extent can prudence be taught? Can you think of examples of where you were helped to live more prudently?
3. Give some examples of when people seem to know what is best to do, but then not act on that knowledge? When is this a failure to be prudent?
4. Reminiscent of the example given of *solertia*, where you are trying to go out with friends and face an unexpected situation, what are some skills you may develop in life that do not at first seem to be about morality, but which are related to important moral skills?
5. Some people deny the possibility of an erroneous conscience by claiming that on any significant moral issue, it is clear to all thinking persons how to act rightly, and if they do not do so they are choosing wrongly and always blameworthy. How would you respond to such a person?
6. How can this chapter's discussion of erroneous conscience help explain seemingly intractable debates over hotly contested ethical issues (like abortion)?
7. Can you think of some common contemporary activity (that is not a hot-button ethical issue) where people are acting wrongly even though they may be invincibly ignorant? If you recognize this activity is wrong, can some people doing it be vincibly ignorant? What would render other people invincibly ignorant?

Further Reading

The main contours of this treatment of prudence and conscience are again from Aquinas's *Summa Theologiae*. The *Catechism* contains concise introductory material on these topics (1776–1802; 1806). The most formative twentieth-century texts on this chapter have been Josef Pieper's *The Four Cardinal Virtues*, Daniel Westburg's *Right Practical Reason*, and Herbert McCabe's *God Still Matters*.

6

ALCOHOL AND AMERICAN COLLEGE LIFE

Test Case One

This first chapter that addresses a concrete issue is a perfect place to offer a disclaimer. All of the issues examined in this book are far too broad to be fully understood and sorted out in one chapter. Furthermore, if a main claim of this book is true, namely, that the way things are as ascertained by prudence is essential to acting virtuously, then good moral theology requires a thorough understanding of the particular issue at hand, using the fruits of different disciplines (history, sociology, biology, etc.). Each test-case chapter in this book cannot hope to provide all the information needed to accurately examine the issue at hand. So the necessarily brief virtue analyses offered in these chapters should be supplemented with outside reading.

Each test-case chapter, including this one on drinking alcohol, has two goals. First, each attempts to offer concrete guidance on the issue at hand, with a goal of living a better life. Second, each chapter tries to exemplify the virtue-centered morality-of-happiness approach of this book to the concrete issue at hand. Again, the goal is not—indeed could not be—a complete treatment of each issue. But each such chapter will model how to examine a particular contested issue in a manner that is attentive to rules, but always in the broader context of intentionality, virtue, and what rule-directed ways of living lead to genuine happiness.

Speaking of rules, this chapter on drinking alcohol is distinct from the other three test-case chapters in an important way. The analysis in each of the other three chapters focuses on whether a particular absolute norm is defensible from within a virtue perspective or not. For example, can the innocent ever be targeted in a just war? Can it ever be virtuous to intentionally end a dying patient's life to ease his suffering? Is sex outside of marriage ever virtuous? One question to ask concerning an absolute norm with regard to drinking would be: is there ever a virtuous use of alcohol? The position held in this chapter is that there can indeed be virtuous drinking. Thus the argument here is less one of articulating and defending an absolute norm than it is seeking to better understand drinking practices, why we do what we do, and what sorts of persons we become in doing so. This is not at all to say that every way of drinking is virtuous. Indeed, the point of this chapter is to pose questions to readers to help them determine whether or not the way they drink alcohol, or refrain from it, is fully virtuous. Though the remaining three test-case chapters do focus on whether or not an absolute norm exists, each of those issues could and should also be engaged with an analysis akin to this chapter's, where we probe our practices concerning the issue at hand (waging war, having sex, and caring for the dying) to determine how to live most virtuously regarding that activity.

To do this with drinking alcohol, the chapter unfolds in four sections that correspond roughly to the preceding chapters in this book. The first section explores what rules we follow in our drinking, where we got them from, and why we follow them. The second section explores why we drink, and thus examines intentionality and freedom. The third section looks more at the intransitive effects of drinking and employs the language of habit and virtue to determine what sorts of persons we become through our drinking practices. Finally, the fourth section explores the relevance of each of the four cardinal virtues for drinking alcohol. Before proceeding in this manner, it should be reiterated that this chapter grows out of experience teaching undergraduates in American universities, and thus it is shaped by this audience. Given common drinking practices in this audience, this is a particular, and often extreme, drinking environment. However, the benefit of the origin of this chapter is not only that it grows out of the real experience of a set of people, but also that its focus on that often more extreme drinking environment helps illuminate dynamics that are also prevalent but less obvious in other environments.

Why Do I Follow the Rules That I Do?

Perhaps the best way to illustrate that Glaucon's *Ring of Gyges* story accurately describes why some people are moral is to look at the drinking habits of many freshmen in college. As you recall from chapter 1, Glaucon said that people who are just (or moral, or who do the right thing) do so not because it is what they truly want to do. It is not what they think constitutes happiness, or a good life. Rather, they do so because they fear the consequences of acting immorally. Society places certain rules in place to keep people in line, and enforces those rules in varying ways (laws, school rules, parents, etc.). To avoid the negative consequences of breaking those rules, people stay in line, but would surely do whatever they wanted the moment they could be sure they would not face negative consequences.

For college freshman that moment has come. Outside the watchful eye of parents, and usually residing on insulated college campuses technically ruled by state laws on drinking age that realistically offer little enforcement of those laws, college freshmen have, in effect, found their Ring of Gyges. What happens? They too often mimic the shepherd from Glaucon's story and do whatever they want. The central problem is not that they begin using alcohol while legally underage. The problem is how they use it. Freed from all the influences that had previously limited their use of alcohol (parental consternation, the need to drive home from high-school parties, greater enforcement of underage drinking, the need to get up early the next morning, etc.), there are no resources left to govern, or rather limit, their drinking except bodily limits—and even those are fully stretched and sometimes crossed at students' peril. Freshmen drink the way they do because they can, and it is only through learning new reasons to limit their drinking that they will eventually, one hopes, do so.

Of course, not all freshmen experience and live out the sort of freedom from these obligatory rules. Some have managed to learn how to drink more moderately before college. Others (actually, a greater percentage of college students than often assumed,[1] though still a minority) decide for one reason or another not to drink alcohol at all. But the dynamic described here is common enough to need no further justification to those familiar with college students. What does it say about why we drink?

Recall that the key distinguishing feature of a morality-of-obligation perspective is that moral rules may be followed voluntarily, but even when they are it is not with the understanding that following such rules is constitutive of living a happy life, or what one really wants. At best, following the rules is endured in order to receive rewards (heaven, parental approval, a clean record, etc.) that are not inherently connected to following the rule. The behavior of too many college freshmen reveals that their limitations on alcohol use before

1. See studies generated by Harvard University's college alcohol study for exact numbers of college students who drink. There is a significant minority who do not. And over two thirds of all alcohol consumption is done by a mere 20 percent of college students. See especially H. Wechsler et al. "College Alcohol Use: A Full or Empty Glass?" *Journal of American College Health* 47, no. 6 (1999): 247–52, and M. Kuo et al.'s "More Canadian Students Drink but American Students Drink More: Comparing College Alcohol Use in Two Countries" *Addiction* 97, no. 12 (2002): 1583–92.

college were rules understood from a morality-of-obligation perspective. Note that generally rules do remain governing their alcohol use. Perhaps they are limited by what money they have to spend. They are certainly concerned with how their peers view them (though ironically this peer pressure may lead to increased, not decreased, alcohol use). Hopefully they observe the thankfully widely accepted norm among college students that you do not drive under the influence. Maybe they occasionally refrain from drinking due to an upcoming big paper or difficult exam. But so often in each of these cases, the dynamic in play is refraining from what they really want to do (drink and party) for a reason experienced as an obligation rather than a way to live a fulfilling life.

Before we take too much pride in having a laugh at college freshmen, it should also be noted that upperclassmen and adults are far from immune to this dynamic. The reasons for limiting drinking may become more sophisticated. We become aware of our limits. We take on responsibilities (job, children, etc.) that limit our use of alcohol. But the similarity in the dynamic is that these limitations are experienced as just that—limitations from what we really would like to do. In fact, during the socially acceptable occasions to let go of such externally imposed limitations ("thank God it's Friday!," senior week activities, work happy hours, weddings, weekend getaways, etc.), we do just that. What this reveals is that on occasions where we observe rules for limiting our drinking, these rules are not seen as guiding us toward what is a genuinely fulfilling way to live (i.e., moderate drinking), but rather externally imposed obligations that we would, and do, quickly dispense with on occasions where that is possible.

This is not to say that virtuous drinking is incompatible with drinking more or less on different occasions. It is through prudence that we determine if and how alcohol fits into our living out a good life, and that determination does indeed take into account circumstances such as a job, family, and occasions for celebration such as reunions and weddings. But see how differently this is worded from the above depictions of freshmen or adults living out of a morality-of-obligation perspective. From this latter perspective, what we really want to do (drink a lot) is impeded by obligatory concerns, and when those concerns are not present we can (finally!) let loose. From a morality-of-happiness perspective, the fact that we limit our use of alcohol due to factors such as our jobs, families, being concerned with how we act in front of peers, and so on, is a matter of prudently living out a genuinely fulfilling life. On occasions where drinking would indeed impede these other commitments, there is not even a draw or desire to drink alcohol (if our desires and actions are temperate). If drinking alcohol were instead seen as something we hold more important than things such as our jobs, families, and friendships, then we must address how inflated a place drinking alcohol has assumed in our lives, a task for the next section. If we know what is truly important but have inordinate desires nonetheless, and therefore experience limitations on alcohol use as obligatory, then the task is to set about habituating our desires more virtuously, a topic addressed in a later section. And as for exactly how much to drink and on what occasion, yet another section below on prudence will address these questions.

The purpose of this first section is to ascertain how we drink the way we do, and in particular why we observe whatever rules we do concerning drinking alcohol. What are the rules we observe concerning our use of alcohol? When do we drink, and what determines when we drink, how much we drink, and what else we do when we drink? Why do we limit our use of alcohol? Drinking alcohol is an activity where it is particularly helpful to note the influence of authorities in our lives. As explained in chapter 1, an authority is any influence on us about how we live our lives. The connotation of the word "authority" is onerous and heavy-handed; as it concerns drinking you may immediately think of authorities such as law enforcement, university staff, and parental expectations, appropriate influences that do shape if and how we drink.

But despite the connotation of the word, authorities are not simply re-strictive. Other influences shape how we drink as well, often in ways that are encouraging rather than restrictive. For instance, what models of the role of alcohol in life were provided to you by your parents growing up? Your family lived by some set of rules concerning alcohol, and given the importance of our families in our lives, their influence can be quite powerful, whether we take on their ways of drinking or react against them. Another powerful influence is our peers. As social animals it is completely appropriate to take cues on how to act from those close to us—but of course this can be for better or worse. Our peers can be a positive influence on us ("you drove while you were drunk? How could you!"), or a negative influence. Though we all like to think we are not subject to peer pressure in the crude sense of adolescents telling their friends they are not cool unless they follow along with everyone else, it would be foolish to ignore how formative on our lives our peers are. Where, when, and how often we drink alcohol, and what types of activities go along with it, are all deeply shaped by our peer groups. Since, as in the case of our parents, this can be a good or bad influence, we should be aware of it so we can reflect on that influence to either mitigate it or be thankful for and foster it.

Other authorities could be named as well. For instance, what cultural stories and images about drinking are prevalent in our minds? These are often obtained from songs, television, and movies (consider the movies *Old School* and *Animal House*). What ways does advertising shape our understanding of what role alcohol plays in having a good time? Indeed what are the goals of advertisements for alcoholic beverages? As we look at our own lives to deter-mine what rules we follow in our drinking, being aware of the influence of authorities in our lives is helpful in gaining some perspective on those rules.

Once aware of the particular rules we live by (whatever they may be—lax, moderate, or strict abstinence), and where we obtain them, chapter 1 presses us to ask: why do we live by them? Do we live out of a morality of obligation or a morality-of-happiness perspective? This book argues that living according to a morality-of-happiness perspective is not only a path to a more fulfilling life, but also gives the rules we follow intelligibility. In other words, from this perspective virtuous people do not simply obey the rules as obligations. They not only follow them willingly, but also see how the rules they live by are part of living out, rather than obstacles to, a genuinely fulfilling life. They follow rules they assimilate as their own, and do not simply act the way they do to impress others, please their parents, avoid problems with the law, or not offend religious sensibilities. Observing the way you do or do not use alcohol, why have you adopted the path you have? Is it to obey some externally-imposed obligation, or to live out a genuinely fulfilling life? If the latter, is the path you have chosen truly leading you in that direction or not? If you approach the issue of drinking alcohol this way, then you have adopted the virtue-centered morality-of-happiness approach at the heart of this book.

Why Do I Drink?

A foundational claim of this book, in line with great thinkers such as Aristotle and Aquinas, is that human persons are purposeful creatures. We do things for reasons, and those reasons, or intentions, render our actions meaningful. So the first task in examining any particular moral question is to ask why. What goals are we pursuing here? That way we can examine whether it is a worthy goal (intention) and if it is being pursued well (a task for prudence). So when it comes to drinking alcohol, why do we drink, or choose not to drink? Are these good reasons, and if they are, are our actions in line with those goals? These are such basic questions that some people never stop to ask them. Drinking alcohol is so common in our society that most of us are simply brought up to understand that drinking alcohol has some place in life. But it is incumbent upon us to reflectively examine what we do and why we do it. The previous section examined why in general we follow the rules we do concerning drinking. This section explores more specifically the reasons why we use alcohol.

First, we should acknowledge and dismiss some reasons occasionally offered for why people drink. Though these reasons may in fact hold true for a miniscule portion of the drinking population, they are clearly not the driving force behind the drinking patterns of most people. Some claim it is for the taste. Surely some people develop sophisticated tastes for wine, beer, or scotch. But this is not the same as saying it is the driving force behind why they drink. For instance, we might ask if the same quality drinks were available in non-alcoholic form, would people still drink them? Even if some few would, it seems that most would not. Some people also cite health reasons for drinking alcohol. It is commonly claimed that a glass of wine per day, for instance, is actually good for one's health. My own great-grandmother had a glass of port wine each night before bed; she lived to ninety! Perhaps a few do indeed drink alcohol for this reason. But the practice of drinking alcohol that is examined here is the broadly prevalent drinking that goes on at social events, in homes, at restaurants, and elsewhere. For the vast majority of those who drink alcohol, taste and health are not the reasons driving their actions.

Why do people generally drink? The biblical psalmist speaks of wine as a gift to "gladden the heart" (Ps. 104:15). Alcohol changes the way people feel, and that is why people generally consume it. No hard evidence of this claim is offered here; it simply seems evident that if the alcoholic drinks we consumed were not alcoholic, they would be consumed far less frequently. Many reasons for drinking alcohol rely on this effect. People drink at social occasions to celebrate and to foster cheer. We drink alcohol as something to do together, to lubricate, if you will, our social interactions. We drink to enjoy others' company and share stories. We drink to relax and unwind. All of these reasons ring true. Yet they all revolve around alcohol's effects on how we feel. Presumably alcohol would not be such a staple in social situations if it did not have these effects.

If the crux of alcohol use comes down to its effects on our state of mind, one question to ask is whether or not intentionally altering our state of mind is inherently bad. In other words, is consuming alcohol always contradictory to the very purposes for which we use alcohol, such as better conversations, enjoyable time with friends, relaxation, and so on? If so, we would have an absolute norm: do not drink alcohol. The term absolute norm was introduced in chapter 3, but its meaning is tied deeply to intentionality. Some things are always wrong, not because they are taboo because of some whimsical, externally imposed obligations. Rather, they are always wrong because they are inherently contrary to the good purposes we claim to be pursuing in doing that action. The remaining three test cases in this book all deal with absolute norms. Although some faith traditions prohibit the use of alcohol absolutely, the position held in this chapter is that drinking alcohol is not inherently wrong. In other words, it is possible to drink alcohol, and in doing so alter our mental state, in a manner that does indeed facilitate relations with others, foster conversation, and relax us. That does not, of course, mean that alcohol is never used in a manner that is harmful to our good purposes. It just means it is not inherently harmful and can be done well.

The main guideline offered here to examine whether or not our use of alcohol is virtuous or not entails, first, answering the simple question, why do I drink? Second, it involves examining if the way I drink leads to those goals, or actually impedes them. What this is doing is simply looking at the intention and object of our drinking. First, what goals do we pursue in drinking? It is assumed here that there are virtuous goals for drinking alcohol, such as those mentioned above. However, surely there are also vicious goals. These might include: drinking to escape reality by no longer being coherent enough to think about our situation; drinking to impress, keep up with, fit in with, or look better than others; drinking to lose our inhibitions so as to be able to do things that we would not normally do (esp. true with regard to sexual intimacy).

Of course, on closer examination these bad intentions are all awfully close to the reasons people drink that are affirmed here as good. What is the line between feeling relaxed and escaping reality? What is the line between drinking to further enjoy the company of others, and drinking to impress or keep up? And in some sense don't all of us who drink do so in order to be able to do things we would not normally do, even if it is simply be more talkative? If not, why bother drinking at all? It is granted here that it is a fine line between virtuous and vicious drinking. That is why we are not dealing with an absolute norm. That said, when the line is crossed (the determination of which requires prudence, as seen in a later section) we are indeed engaging in behavior that is harmful to our ability to live well, namely, pursue and enjoy good and worthy things in our lives.

So the first thing we should look at in our drinking in order to assess whether or not it is virtuous is why we drink (intention). The next thing to examine is what exactly we do when we drink (object). Examining how we drink reveals whether or not our actions are really serving the goals we say we are seeking. For instance, if we say we are drinking to enjoy the company of friends, but inevitably our drinking leads to arguments or states of mind where we can no longer relate to, or remember relating to, our friends, can we still truly be said to be drinking to enjoy them? If we say we drink alcohol to relax and unwind after a long week, but the way we drink leads us to feel exhausted and sick the next day, are we really drinking to relax? In both of these cases, the way we drink (object) is actually counterproductive for the goal we say we are pursuing (intention). This means one of two things: we are either being imprudent in how we drink, or we really have other goals for our drinking and are deceiving ourselves by offering acceptable goals to explain why we drink. Either way, a simple look at object and intention helps illuminate the morality of our actions.

How do I determine, you may ask, whether either my goals for drinking or the ways I drink are impeding my happiness and therefore are not virtuous? It may help here to recall the triangle of goals in our lives from chapter 2. What are the things in my life that are more or less important? When people are asked where alcohol fits into their triangle, they generally say it is rather low. Even if they drink regularly, they commonly claim their use of alcohol is there merely to facilitate other more important goals in their lives, such as friendship, leisure, and the like. If alcohol really is used simply as a service to these more important goals, and does not impede them or take over for them, than alcohol is indeed playing a helpful role in a virtuous life. However, also as noted in chapter 2, our triangle is best represented not simply by what we say it is, but by how we actually live our lives, which may or may not correlate with what we say we are all about. If drinking is simply a fun activity for me in the context of friends, how willing am I to do things with friends that do not involve drinking? If drinking is the common variable at all my social activities, is it possible that enjoying alcohol together is becoming the point of why my friends and I get together, rather than simply a non-essential support of our interaction? Is alcohol needed to have that good time, and not simply an aid to enjoying time with friends? If so, then drinking has crept up higher on our triangles than we might care to admit. And if we still insist we do not need alcohol for leisure time with friends, even if it is always present on such occasions, we must ask ourselves why it is always present.

This may indeed be the best concrete guideline this chapter can offer on drinking alcohol. If alcohol is needed in order to relax or have fun, then it has assumed too high an importance in our lives. Furthermore, if drinking is really an enjoyable activity that is truly at the service of larger goals like family, friendship, and leisure, then those larger goals will dictate that our drinking does not disrupt them. It is when drinking becomes an end in itself (perhaps as an escape, or as the central activity among friends), that the way it is used becomes destructive to those goals that in our better moments we would put first in our lives. We see how importantly linked object and intention are in the moral life. This connection is seen in the advice of the scripture author on good and bad uses of alcohol:

> Wine is very life to man if taken in moderation. Does he really live who lacks the wine which was created for his joy? Joy of heart, good cheer and merriment are wine drunk freely at the proper time. Headache, bitterness and disgrace is wine drunk amid anger and strife. More and more wine is a snare for the fool; it lessens his strength and multiplies his wounds. (Sir 31:27–30)

When drinking becomes the point, our very freedom is endangered. This is not just true of those people who develop addictions, where freedom is drastically threatened.[2] Recall the discussion of types of freedom in chapter 2. Freedom can be inhibited in different ways. Sometimes our free choices impede our ability to have different choices in the future. This is an obvious way that people who develop drinking addictions can find their freedom impeded.[3]

2. The most obvious example of this is the alcoholic. Obviously, much of this chapter has direct bearing on alcoholism. However, the primary purpose here is not to examine alcoholism (or its causes, treatment, etc.), but rather to critically examine more widespread drinking practices that may or may not be problematic, but do not rise to the level of alcoholism.
3. There is extensive discussion today of the degree to which alcoholism is a disease, and indeed few people today doubt it is. That is not contested here. The observation is simply made that developing this disease does involve free choices, choices that can lead to later impediments to one's freedom. No discussion of culpability—a separate task—is engaged in here.

People with addictions are obviously less free (in the freedom-of-indifference sense) in having fewer choices. But recall that from a freedom-for-excellence perspective, freedom can also be inhibited by our failure to choose what is true and good for us. In this sense, even people without addictions can be less free due to their drinking, by making choices regarding the use of alcohol that eclipse other worthy and important—and indeed more fulfilling and genuine satisfying—goals in their lives. In other words, they are still acting in a manner that is truly their own, yet their specific choices are impeding their fulfillment.

It is therefore true, from a freedom-for-excellence perspective, that people who may not be addicted but whose drinking impedes them from pursuing the goals they hold most dear, are less free in the sense of impeding themselves from attaining the point of their freedom; that is, living a truly happy life. This constitutes being too attached to drinking. But need this be the case? Perhaps, you may say, your occasionally heavy drinking does not displace those higher goals, and that you just like to get really drunk once in a while because it is fun. Surely it is true that people can drink excessively on occasion and not displace more important goals in life. But given the lessons of chapter 3 on the formation of habits (virtue or vices), such occasional action can be isolated, but given human actions are intentional, it also easily builds into a habit. These observations lead us to the next section on the formation of habits.

Drinking and the Formation of Habits and Desires

One common assumption that people make when examining drinking alcohol as a moral issue is that drinking itself is not morally right or wrong. Rather, it is simply what happens when people drink (especially when they drink too much) that makes alcohol a moral issue. No one can contest that drinking alcohol causes great harm to individual persons, and to society as a whole. According to the World Health Organization, each year almost two million people die as a result of alcohol-related incidents.[4] Alcohol is especially dangerous in its effects on driving. But it is also a factor in a large number of incidents of sexual and domestic violence. Alcohol causes health problems, is a major factor in students dropping out of college, and has other consequences. These claims refer to hard facts, and difficult to deny. Hence they are often the basis of education programs that target excessive drinking, especially among young people.

However, an unintended consequence of statistical arguments against alcohol is that many people assume that if you can remove these negative consequences from alcohol use, then you have eliminated anything problematic

---

4. For these and other statistics on alcohol-related problems, see Christopher Cook's *Alcohol, Addiction, and Christian Ethics* (Cambridge: Cambridge University Press, 2006), esp. 7, 9–35.

about drinking. A great example of this is the decrease in recent history of the number of alcohol-related traffic fatalities. Organizations such as MADD and SADD have done a marvelous job raising awareness of the problem of drunk driving, and even stigmatizing it. I find students today, more so than when I was in college, refusing to consider or even condone drunk driving. Obviously that is not to say it never happens anymore. But young people are generally aware of the danger of drunk driving, and demonstrate their commitment against it through naming designated drivers and being willing to take a friend's car keys. This is surely a rule we can all applaud. Another example of preventing alcohol consumption from leading to big problems is the common practice I hear among students of being sure they are with a close friend if they are drinking heavily. This helps them ensure they get home OK, and (especially for women) ensure they are not victims of sexual assault by someone taking advantage of their condition.

All of these practices are good. Who could be against such ways to protect ourselves and others? Note that they all presume that drinking alcohol, to use the terminology from chapter 2, has transitive effects. Drinking alcohol can lead to dangerous driving, sexual assault, vandalism, and so on. These are the effects of our drinking on the world around us, and practices such as those mentioned above aim to limit or remove the bad consequences of our drinking. One interesting observation about these strategies is that they assume some intimate connection between drinking alcohol and these destructive effects. Yet the strategies all seek to limit the bad effects while enabling people to keep drinking in a manner that leads to those effects. In our society we do dangerous things all the time and hope to limit bad effects. We drive cars, fly airplanes, but generally it is done with some important goal in mind that makes us willing to risk the bad effects (such as car accidents and plane crashes). It is worth considering what important goals are at stake in drinking alcohol that prompt us to develop strategies to keep drinking and mitigate the bad effects.

The focus of this section is on the intransitive effects of our drinking. One question is, why is drinking alcohol worth it despite the negative effects of its use, and how we can minimize those effects? Another question, addressed in this section, is what sort of persons do we become given the ways we use alcohol? The best way to understand the relationship between the actions we do and the persons we become is through the notion of habit (be it a virtue or a vice), a topic explored in chapter 3. Habits are stable qualities that mark who we are. They are generally developed through repeated intentional action. Our intentional acts reflect our goals, our priorities. Our consistent actions not only reflect those priorities, but also further ingrain them so that we develop habits to act that way again in the future. Habits do not mechanistically force us to act a certain way. Rather, they incline us to act a certain way in the future; because the habits that mark who we are reflect how we see things and therefore how we act. This dynamic development of habits happens with countless activities in our lives, including our use, or purposeful nonuse, of alcohol.

The point is, that even if you could eliminate all the negative transitive effects of drinking alcohol—by drinking in a safe environment, avoiding driving, somehow avoiding the arguments or overly emotional scenes that so often accompany excessive drinking, and so on—the way we drink still shapes the type of persons we are. It reflects and further ingrains the role we see for alcohol in our lives, its place on the triangle of our priorities. The habits we develop while drinking become second nature to us, so that acting that way in the future is what feels natural to us. This of course can be good, if our drinking habits are virtuous and reflect a proper role for alcohol in our lives. But to the extent that our actions reflect too great an importance of alcohol (even if we say otherwise), then this way of acting becomes natural to us.

The habits we develop with regard to drinking also affect other activities to the extent that they are associated with drinking. For instance, our friendships can be deeply intertwined with our drinking habits. The friends we make depends in part on the sorts of things we enjoy doing with other people. This is all well and good if our drinking habits are virtuous. But if we place too much importance on drinking and it is the main form of leisure for us, then our friends will likely share that perspective and act accordingly. It is easy to see how alcohol becomes further embedded in our lives by shaping the friends we make and the things we commonly do with them.

Another example of the impact of drinking on our other activities is our sexual practices. For many people alcohol is an indispensable part of relating to people with whom they are or may become sexually involved. Alcohol can become so enmeshed with our romantic attachments that it can be difficult or awkward to relate to people intimately on any level (sexually, emotionally, etc.) without the presence of alcohol. Even if a couple can avoid the sexual violence or even lapses of judgment that so often accompany the mixing of alcohol and sexual activity, what sort of relationship will develop when drinking is so intertwined with how the couple relates?

The argument of this section is more subtle than the standard listing of the bad effects of alcohol use. The goal here is to explore how the drinking habits we develop reflect and ingrain the role alcohol plays in our lives, and impact other activities that are important to us. This is a particularly important task for college students, who so often see that period of their lives as separate from "real life." Not only do they live in a somewhat idyllic setting surrounded by friends and with plenty of leisure time; they also assume that this situation affords them the opportunity to live in a manner they will not be able to in the "real world." College life is seen as in some ways a bubble, to be enjoyed fully before it is left behind after graduation. The problem with this view is that it fails to attend to the ways that we develop habits and shape our characters, even while in the bubble.

And though the structure of students' lives may change after graduation, the persons they have become is something that lasts. The drinking habits they develop in college are still there after graduation, and so too is the impact of those habits on other important things in life, like friendships and romantic relationships.

Why become one sort of person now, and another later? If living a life with alcohol high on our triangles is something we strongly favor, why not try and continue that way of living later in life rather than simply going through the motions of the so-called right thing to do by getting a job, having a family, engaging in non-alcohol focused communal activities, being fiscally responsible, and so on, out of some morality of obligation? If alcohol is truly that important, more people should have the courage not to sell out and live respectably! But, of course, if other things in life are actually more important than drinking alcohol (jobs, family, friendships, faith, intellectual life, etc.), then why not engage in activities in college where we can begin to participate in those activities, and at least shape ourselves into persons who are prepared to more fully participate in those activities in the future (through study, genuine friendship, and enriching leisurely activities)? Alcohol may well be involved here, of course, as it is later in life. But in these latter situations it would be decorative garnish to the feast of life, rather than a, or the, central component of the meal. If the genuinely happy life is focused on partying with alcohol, it seems we should be up front about this and arrange both our college and post-college lives accordingly. But if it is not, why live as if it is during the college years?

Whatever triangle of priorities we live out during college, it will shape the sorts of persons we become, and this inclines us to see things and act in certain ways beyond college. This is true even if the responsibilities taken on after college keep someone from acting in all the ways they did during college. For instance, perhaps having to get up early for work means fewer nights to go out. But in this case the desires are still there since, as noted in chapter 4, habits concern not only our actions and intentions but also the desires we have. Even if we are continent regarding the drinking habits developed in college, we are not yet fullly virtuous One can develop continence into temperance as noted in that chapter. But often enough the limitations on what we really want to do (in this case, drink alcohol more often) are experienced not as guides to living more virtuously but rather as obligations. It is easy to see here how a morality-of-obligation perspective develops when people limit what they want to do for the sake of their responsibilities, but actually think their full happiness would entail being able to act on their desires (go out whenever one wants) without suffering the consequences (like poor job performance or even being fired). This language reminds us directly of Glaucon, so it is clear how far we have strayed from the morality-of-happiness perspective promoted in this book.

The point here is that the habits we develop arise from and further ingrain the way we see and act in situations that pertain to drinking alcohol. Though attending to the transitive effects of alcohol use is very important—particularly since these effects can be so destructive—an adequate discussion of the morality of drinking alcohol must also attend to the fact that how we use alcohol shapes who we are and how we will act in the future by the development of habits. It may be tempting to think that how we act only a couple nights a week, or for a few years while in college, is simply a passing matter. But this neglects the formative influence of our intentional actions on our characters.

Drinking and the Cardinal Virtues

Drinking alcohol is an innerworldly activity in that human persons of any time and culture are exposed to it and must determine whether or not to engage in it; and if so, how. Societies and individuals develop practices, or ways of going about (or purposely not going about) drinking alcohol that reflect an explicit or, more commonly, an implicit understanding of where alcohol fits into a good life. Thus, drinking alcohol is a matter of natural law. It is done well by possessing the cardinal virtues. This is not to say that one's religious convictions are irrelevant to what one understands to be virtuous alcohol use. For instance, most Christians use wine in celebrations of the Eucharist, while Muslims endorse the prohibition of alcohol at all times. How religious belief shapes the practice of the cardinal virtues is examined in far greater detail in the second half of this book. Since drinking alcohol is an innerworldly activity, it can be discussed intelligently without necessarily referring to theological commitments.

The first virtue that comes to mind when discussing alcohol is temperance. Temperance is the virtue that enables us to desire, intend, and partake in sensual pleasures well, and alcohol as mind-altering strong drink falls under sensual pleasures. What does it mean to desire and use alcohol well? We have actually been discussing temperance in the last two sections on intentionality and habit. We have good desires and actions regarding our alcohol use when our goals for its use are good, and when our actions effectively pursue those goals. We will turn to how to pursue those goals in the next few paragraphs on prudence. In terms of goals, as noted above, there are good and bad reasons to use alcohol. Furthermore, it can occupy an appropriate or disproportionate place on our triangle of priorities. The way to ascertain this is to see whether our alcohol use is appropriately governed by more important goals (family, friendships, school work, health, and job) or whether it gets in the way of these more important goals. Once we have these goals regarding alcohol use, we develop habits (virtues or vice) that both shape how we see situations involving possible alcohol use, and that incline us to consistently desire and act in some particular way with regard to alcohol. These habits can be changed, but doing so means overcoming the former habit. As should be clear, how we see alcohol and its place in our lives is crucial for the virtues or vices we develop concerning alcohol use. This is the domain of prudence, the charioteer of the virtues, to which we now turn.

Prudence is seeing an activity (such as drinking alcohol) rightly so as to be able to act rightly. How we see an activity plays out on a variety of levels, as you recall from chapter 5. One important task for our practical decision-making, which is the capacity that prudence enables us to exercise well, is to set a path for how to act out our desires and intentions. For instance, if we seek to enjoy alcohol during conversation with friends at a dinner party, then we must understand things about the potency of alcohol and its effects on us in order to use it well in that context. If we think that consuming several bottles of wine is the best path for us in this context, then we will have imprudently acted in a manner that made us dangerously drunk and created an obstacle to our good intentions of enjoying alcohol over conversation with friends. In one sense, prudence sets the path to acting well concerning alcohol. A perfect example of learning prudence in this sense is alcohol education that explains things like blood-alcohol content, the amount of alcohol present in different quantities and types of liquor, and the notion of tolerance.

This is a relatively simple function for prudence. But it helps illuminate a couple of important dynamics present in more complex functions of prudence. We see here what things about alcohol must be known in order to act well. We also see the importance of experience and education for becoming prudent. Finally, we see the formative (i.e., authoritative) role of our communities (families, peers, university, American society, and church) in our becoming prudent or imprudent. Another way that we can be prudent or imprudent concerns how accurately we see and live out particular ways of using alcohol that fit in with other life goals. For instance, if I grow up in a family where wine is enjoyed on occasions of celebration and conversation, and consumed in amounts that lighten people's hearts and facilitate conversation without getting in the way of either those goals or others, then I have learned through this experience how to prudently drink wine for the sake of these goals. However, if I grow up in a family where celebratory drinking means consuming alcohol to the point where people have shady memories, become overly emotional, tend to get into disagreements, and find themselves regularly having to undo (or at least forget and move past) what happened while under the influence, then I have learned ways to engage in celebratory drinking that are actually imprudent.

A family example was used here, but certainly examples could be drawn from our peer circles as well. How do we learn to use alcohol with our friends? How are the drinking practices, or ways of using alcohol in my broader social scene and among my immediate friends shaping me? The ways we socialize are generally entered into rather than concocted by us beforehand. How are these common practices leading us to see and use alcohol? These questions have everything to do with the formation of conscience discussed in chapter 5.

Our conscience is our ability to judge particular acts right or wrong, regardless of whether or not we then follow the judgment of our conscience. It is clearly the case that, concerning alcohol, people can do things they know they should not do. But more interesting and disturbing is the fact that many of us likely engage in certain ways of drinking that we do not judge are wrong, but are in fact detrimental to the good and worthy goals that we ourselves want to pursue in our lives. In other words, many of us likely have erroneous consciences related to drinking alcohol. Given the powerfully formative influence of authorities like our parents, peer groups, and even broader societal images of, for instance, what college is supposed to be like, many of us surely think that certain ways of drinking alcohol are normal and good when in fact they are not. Again, recall that the perspective of this book is a morality of happiness. Thus saying many of us likely engage in vicious (opposite of virtuous) drinking practices is not simply saying that there are rules out there we are unaware we are breaking. The claim is that even if we sincerely do not see it, we are engaging in patterns of behavior (in this case with alcohol) that are impeding our ability to live as happy and satisfying lives as we can. The primary point of this comment is not to assign blame. That would require us to determine if our erroneous conscience was a result of vincible or invincible ignorance. The point is for us to scrutinize the way we do things, and to look at other ways of using alcohol, to try and determine if our practices are helping or impeding us in our efforts to live fulfilling lives.

One common way to scrutinize our practices is to try and identify absolute norms in order to see if we are observing them or not. The position of this chapter is that there is no absolute norm that says, "do not drink alcohol." But there may be others. For instance, "avoid drunkenness." Given that the mean of alcohol use depends on so many factors (body size, tolerance level, etc.), it is impossible to name exactly how many drinks constitute drunkenness. Perhaps we can say that when we are unable to relate well to others, or cannot remember things, or harm our health, then surely our use of alcohol has eclipsed any good reasons there might be for drinking. Surely we could name acts associated with drinking alcohol as absolute norms: do not drive under the influence; do not become physically, emotionally, or sexually violent; do not destroy property. These things are far less likely to happen if we avoid drunkenness, but it may help to name these absolute norms as well.

But concerning drinking, it is less interesting to focus solely on absolute norms than it is to examine our practices to see what trajectories our drinking impels us toward. If we drink to fit in, how will we stop ourselves from participating if others are drinking in a destructive manner? If we drink to lose our inhibitions, perhaps to free us to interact more easily with potential romantic partners, how will we be able to continue to observe lines we know ought not to be crossed, such as casually hooking up or even becoming coercive with another? If we drink to escape, what will stop us from drinking until we cannot remember, or until we pass out? Hopefully, the virtue perspective offered here is seen as more fruitful than simply offering a bunch of rules (do not pass out, do not hit people, etc.) There is still certainly a place for rules in a virtue approach. But those rules are better understood not as ends in themselves, but as constitutive of living of living in pursuit of the good goals and priorities which the rules serve and guard.

Having spoken extensively, though not at all exhaustively, of the importance of prudence for virtuous drinking, we turn now more briefly to the two remaining cardinal virtues. Justice is the virtue that disposes us to right relationships with others. The relevance of justice has been referenced several times already. The basic question here is, in what ways does alcohol impact our relationships with others? People may immediately think of more legal and drastic aspects of this question. Does one's drinking lead to driving drunk, or vandalism, or physical altercations? These are all ways of being unjust in one's alcohol use. But justice extends far more broadly than these questions. For instance, how are the drinking practices of some group of mine helping or hindering the good relations among the members? How does my own drinking impact how I relate to others, both while drinking, and even as I plan how and with whom I will spend my free time? How do my drinking practices impact my family commitments (especially if there are children), or my friends who may struggle with alcohol? To what extent am I willing to change my drinking practices if they pose an impediment to someone close to me, such as someone with a drinking problem who is trying to avoid alcohol? All of these are questions of justice. To the extent that alcohol influences our relations with others, we can say that we are just or unjust in our drinking based upon the nature of that influence.

Fortitude is the virtue than enables us to face difficulties well. It may be more difficult to imagine how fortitude is relevant for the issue of drinking alcohol, when our common models of fortitude (or courage) are soldiers or firefighters. But as explained in chapter 9, fortitude enables us to face any difficulty well, even if it is not life-threatening. What are some difficulties posed by alcohol? It may take tremendous courage to tell a friend that her drinking practices are harming others, or to speak out against a social scene that is corroding a community. Simply not participating in an environment where alcohol is used destructively is an act of courage, as it is hard to be left out and seen as an outsider. Finally, it can take great courage to live out virtuous drinking in one's own life. This is certainly true of people who have to overcome destructive drinking habits. But on a more mundane level, it is true when we are willing to suppress a desire to have a drink, or another drink, for some good reason. Though the difficulty faced here may seem miniscule, it is through facing such small difficulties well that one becomes habituated to face larger ones well.

In sum, all four cardinal virtues are quite important for drinking alcohol virtuously, even though drinking is an innerworldly activity that fits most properly under temperance. This reflects a thesis explained at the end of chapter 9: the unity of the virtues. Though each different activity falls primarily under one cardinal virtue or another, all cardinal virtues are needed to practice any particular activity in a fully virtuous manner. This is largely due to the inter-relatedness of the different facets of our lives. Our desires impact our decision making and vice versa. Our relations with others shape and are shaped by how well we face difficulties and pursue sensual pleasures, and so on. As the good life is an integrated whole, doing any particular activity—such as drinking alcohol—in a fully virtuous manner means integrating it appropriately with the set of goals and purposes that make up our lives. Therefore, to do a particular activity well, all four cardinal virtues are essential.

Concluding Thoughts

Needless to say, there are many topics concerning drinking alcohol that have not been addressed here. As noted in the introductory comments to this chapter, the main goals here have been to offer some concrete advice on how to determine whether or not we drink virtuously, and to demonstrate what difference it makes to examine this question from a morality-of-happiness and virtue-centered perspective. You may have expected this chapter to focus on sorting through the scattered biblical verses on alcohol to arrive at some rules. Or you may have expected extensive references to sociological data on drinking in our society to determine some rules to avoid the problems drinking causes. These tasks are indeed important, should be done, and are not opposed to the approach of this chapter. But the approach of this chapter is too often neglected when people seek to articulate and justify particular norms from authorities—be they religious or scientific—without attending to happiness, intentionality, and the formation of habits. As the readers' thoughts and conversations on this topic continue, it is hoped the approach of this chapter will inform that conversation and ultimately help people live happier lives.

Study Questions

1. What are some reasons that people follow the rules they do concerning drinking alcohol? What do you find to be better or worse reasons for people to follow the rules they do? Given examples of rules that exemplify both a morality of obligation and a morality-of-happiness approach.

2. Give examples of ways that authorities (in this book's general sense of that term) shape our drinking practices.

3. What occasions (everyday or out of the ordinary) are compatible with virtuous drinking? What do these occasions tell us about the virtuous reasons people drink alcohol? What are some reasons to drink alcohol that are not virtuous?

4. Evaluate a common practice concerning alcohol in your experience. Name intention and object and evaluate it accordingly.

5. Are there ways of drinking alcohol that inhibit our freedom? Explain.

6. What are some transitive effects of drinking alcohol? How can negative ones be mitigated?

7. Explain how our intentional use of alcohol (intransitively) shapes who we are.

8. For each of the cardinal virtues, give an example of some drinking-related act or goal that illustrates or defies that virtue.

Terms to Know

There are no new terms to know in this chapter. But it may be helpful to review previous chapters' terms with the specific case of drinking alcohol in mind. For instance, explain how each of the following is now better understood with specific regard to alcohol: morality of happiness, morality of obligation, authority, absolute norm, intention, object, freedom of indifference, freedom for excellence, transitive and intransitive facets of human action, temperance, continence, incontinence, intemperance, conscience, erroneous conscience, vincible vs. invincible ignorance.

Questions for Further Reflection

1. Is it ever virtuous to intentionally alter one's mental state with alcohol? Why or why not? If it can be, what, if any, limits should there be in doing so?

2. Name two prevalent authorities in your life that have shaped how you use, or do not use, alcohol. Explain how and why they have shaped you so.

3. Granting all the negative consequences that flow from drinking alcohol for many people, is it worth it? Why not? Or if it is, what goods are achieved by our drinking alcohol that make it worth it?

4. Put another way from the previous question, can one live just as virtuous and happy a life without ever drinking alcohol? If not, why not? If so, why do those of us who drink alcohol bother drinking?

5. Give an example of where our stated goals for alcohol use are actually subverted by the ways we drink. Try to explain why this happens.
6. Reexamine which view of freedom you hold (indifference or excellence) with examples of drinking alcohol in mind.
7. How would you respond to a close friend or sibling who was consistently engaging in drinking behaviors he or she understood to be extreme, and yet claimed it was just being a college student?
8. Though we have not yet examined the thesis, unity of the virtues, mentioned at the end of this chapter, you already have some sense of its meaning. Why would it be difficult for someone to be fully virtuous with regard to drinking alcohol if they seriously lacked any one of the four cardinal virtues?
9. What difference does a virtue approach make in examining the morality-of-alcohol use?
10. This chapter purports to offer concrete guidance on how to live a good life as it concerns drinking alcohol. Yet the practical claims are spread throughout the chapter. Consider the follow non-comprehensive list of some of the practical injunctions throughout the chapter. Which do you agree or disagree with? Which other ones would you add?
    • Drink alcohol the way you want to because you believe in your conscience that your use, or purposeful nonuse, of alcohol helps you live a more fulfilling, happy life.
    • Do not gripe about the influence of authorities when you can avoid being shaped by them. If you are twenty-one and can drink legally, stop griping about how the law fosters underage drinking by making it alluring, and use, or don't use, alcohol for reasons that you want to. If you think parents or college administrators treat you without respect for your maturity and adulthood, shirk it off and drink in a manner that reflects that maturity.
    • Do not let your use of alcohol displace or impede things in your life that you would recognize as more important than drinking: family, friendships, studies, health, and the like.
    • Related to the prior rule, examine how your drinking shapes (even if not displaces or impedes) other important things in your life. Do not let alcohol be a driving factor in how you are a friend, which friends you have, how you pursue romantic relationships, and so on.
    • Be honest (remember truthful memory as a sub-virtue of prudence?) in examining your practices concerning alcohol so you can evaluate them accurately. Employ the help of others (remember docility?) to help ensure you are seeing things accurately as it concerns your drinking.
    • Do not think that you can repeatedly act in a manner without impacting your character and your habits. Even if you think, "this is

college" or "I'm just blowing off steam," know well how your actions intransitively shape who you are.

- Be generous and understanding rather than judgmental in evaluating the influences around you—parents, peers, or wider society. Nonetheless, do judge which ones you wish to emulate and which you want to resist.
- Have friends who not only share a basic similar approach to drinking with you, but also with whom you can discuss this topic.
- Be aware of and live up to occasions for fortitude concerning my use of alcohol.

Further Reading

There are far too few texts available that examine the use of alcohol from a moral theological (and especially virtue) perspective. One excellent text is Christopher Cool's *Alcohol, Addiction, and Christian Ethics*. It contains some quality data on alcohol use (in a British context), as well as moral analysis. There are some helpful official Roman Catholic Church statements available. Most recently, the Irish bishops released the 2007 document "Alcohol: the Challenge of Moderation." The diocese of Green Bay and the bishops of New Zealand are other sources of Episcopal statements on alcohol. There are some powerful narratives of the impact of alcohol on certain persons lives, which are often the best way to examine alcohol in the virtue context suggested in this chapter. See, for instance, Caroline Knapp's powerful 1997 autobiographical account, *Drinking: A Love Story*. Finally, there is an enormous amount of social scientific data on alcohol use and abuse. See for instance Harvard University's School of Public Health's ongoing College Alcohol Study for data focused on alcohol use in higher education environments.

7

THE VIRTUE OF JUSTICE
AND JUSTICE IN WAGING WAR

In an apt metaphor, C. S. Lewis begins his discussion of morality with the image of a fleet of ships to explain what he calls the different parts of morality. He claims that several things need to happen in order for the fleet to function effectively.

> The voyage will be a success only, in the first place, if the ships do not collide and get in each other's way; and, secondly, if each ship is seaworthy and has its engines in good order. As a matter of fact, you cannot have either of these two things without the other. If the ships keep on having collisions they will not remain seaworthy very long. On the other hand, if their steering gears are out of order they will not be able to avoid collisions.[1]

Lewis goes on to describe a third part of morality. To continue the fleet analogy, we must know where the fleet is trying to go and be sure it is getting there. "However well the fleet sailed, its voyage would be a failure if it were meant to reach New York and actually arrived at Calcutta."[2]

Lewis is trying to make the point that morality is not, contrary to what many people think, simply about relationships between people. Relationships

1. C. S. Lewis, *Mere Christianity* (San Francisco: HarperSanFrancisco, 2001), 71.
2. Ibid.

134

between people are indeed crucial to morality, and are represented, in his analogy, by the fact that the ships do not collide. But it is also important that the ships reach the proper destination. What the human destination, or destiny, is will be primarily addressed in the second half of this book, though we have already seen the topic arise in chapter 1 with rival visions of what people and society are all about. It is also important that individual ships are in good working order. The point for morality is that it is important not just how well you relate to others, but that your own ship is in order. In fact, as Lewis notes, it is difficult or even impossible to have one without the other. This is why we examined the virtue of temperance in chapter 4, since that virtue concerns not only how one's pursuit of sensible pleasures impacts others, but also how well one's own desires and emotions are ordered. We will examine the virtue of fortitude in chapter 9, which is also concerned with keeping one's own ship in good working order.

Justice is the virtue that inclines us to good relationships with others that, in other words, "avoid collisions." It is such a fundamentally important virtue that for many thinkers, the term justice is simply equated with morality in general. Recall from the Glaucon/Socrates exchange in chapter 1 that the main question under examination was, why be just? rather than why be moral? This makes sense if we keep in mind Lewis's claim that our relationships with others are deeply intertwined with our overall destiny in life, and with how well our own ships are in good working order. But we must be careful to avoid a common modern assumption that morality is simply about our relations with others. You may hear people say, "I wasn't hurting anyone!" Or, "what right do others have to tell me what to do when it doesn't concern anyone else!" These comments reflect an assumption that there is only one part of morality—relations with others. Yet this neglects two other essential parts of morality described by Lewis. It neglects how our overall direction in life shapes our interactions with others. It also neglects how one's habits and character, even in seemingly private matters, shape one's interactions with others and thus do indeed have societal impact. When Aquinas refers to justice, he is aware of and affirms that it can in a sense be equated with all morality. But his main use of the term corresponds to Lewis's first of three parts of morality. Justice in its most exact sense is one of the four cardinal virtues, namely, the one that inclines us to good relations with others.[3]

The purpose of this chapter is to examine the cardinal virtue justice. The chapter is divided into two main sections. The first explains in greater detail the nature of the virtue justice. As with temperance, we will find that a general treatment of justice does little by way of providing specific norms for difficult

---

3. For a helpful discussion of the understanding in Aquinas of justice, in both the general and particular senses described here, see Jean Porter, "The Virtue of Justice," in *The Ethics of Aquinas,* ed. Stephen J. Pope (Washington, DC: Georgetown University Press, 2002), 272–86.

situations where one struggles to determine what is just. Thus, the second half of the chapter examines the issue of warfare in the context of justice, and explains different positions on the issue of whether or not there is such a thing as a "just war," and, if so, what characterizes it. Though the second section will not tackle any particular historical case, it will leave us prepared to do exactly that in chapter 8.

The Virtue Justice

This opening section proceeds in three parts. The first offers a careful definition of justice. The second part revisits the Glaucon/Socrates debate from chapter 1, and explores where our sense of justice comes from by explaining the ancient question of what it means to say that justice is "natural" to us. Finally, the third part points out the varying ways justice is lived out in different social contexts and according to different rules. Though we may think of civil law when we hear the term "justice," the virtue concerns far more than that. Nonetheless, this part explains how careful thinking about what constitutes good civil law can help further illuminate justice in the broader sense.

Defining Justice

Aquinas adopts a classic Latin phrase to describe justice: "*suum cuique*," which means "to each his due." Any act of justice gives another what they deserve. As a virtue, *justice* is a steady disposition (a habit) in someone to give other people their due. There is an obvious problem with this definition, however. If justice concerns giving others their due, what exactly is due to other people? The traditional answer to this question is that the goal of justice, or what the just person seeks in her acts, is "*ius*." *Ius* is the Latin term that is the origin of English words like justice and justify. It is commonly translated "right," as in the just person seeks what is right in her relationships with others. This is somewhat misleading, both since we use the term "right" in so many ways today, and because the Latin term *ius* is a noun rather than an adjective. *Ius* refers to the "proper order of things," or "the way things were meant to be." It is a state of affairs marked by peace, or harmony, since there exist genuine right relations with others. The just person seeks such a state in all her acts.

Of course, saying that what is due to another person is *ius* does not really answer our question. It just pushes it back one step further. If the just person acts toward establishing *ius*, or rightly ordered relationships, what constitute rightly ordered relationships? There are several general rules that help us answer this question. Most famous is perhaps the Golden Rule: "Do unto others as you would have done unto you" (Matt. 7:12). There is also the part of the greatest commandment relating to love of neighbor, where Jesus says, "love your neighbor as yourself" (Matt. 22:39; Mark 12:31; Luke 10:27). Immanuel Kant articulated a famous philosophical maxim called the categorical imperative to guide people's actions: "act only according to that maxim whereby you can at the same time will that it should become a universal law."[4] All of these general principles are very useful in helping people to act justly since so often our actions, upon a moment's reflection, would be seen to be violating these relatively straightforward principles.

But though these succinct guides are helpful in identifying more obvious cases where we are acting unjustly, they are far less helpful in tough cases where it is not so clear what we would want to make a universal law, or how we would want others to treat us. Or, to put this in the language of chapter 5, these rules may help us when we know what the just thing to do is, but are less helpful when we are trying to figure out what exactly is the just thing to do. Is the death penalty just or unjust? What economic policies are just to all involved? Is it ever permissible to go to war and intentionally kill people? If so, are there any methods or occasions of killing that are unjust? It seems that offering a basic definition of justice, and even some tried-and-true general guidelines for living justly, does not get us as far as we often need to go in determining how to live virtuously. This is not the first time we have run into this problem in this book. We spoke extensively about temperance, but it took another whole chapter on drinking alcohol to find more specific guidance on how to drink virtuously. A prudent examination of the specific activity under consideration is required for specific norms that go beyond general guidelines. The same is true of the treatment of justice. We will indeed delve more deeply into one such activity, waging war, later in this chapter. And chapter 8 will explore a very specific case in the waging of war. But before turning to these more detailed examinations, some further words are needed on the virtue of justice in general.

Doing Justice, "Naturally": Justice as Constitutive of Living a Good Life

Though it may be challenging to define exactly what constitutes what is due another in a particular case, the basic notion of deserving something is very accessible to us, for it is deeply ingrained in us. To get a sense of how readily we evaluate actions in terms of giving others their due, think of how commonly you hear people frame situations in terms of what they deserve. Even children on the playground will yell things like, "he deserved it!" meaning that whatever was done was due the other child. We may hear the familiar exchange among children: "Mine!" "No, mine!" Here we have competing claims

---

4. Immanuel Kant, *Grounding for the Metaphysics of Morals*, pp. 1–62 in James W. Ellington, trans., *Ethical Principles*, 2nd. ed. (Indianapolis: Hackett Publishing, 1999), 14. This is a paraphrase of one of the several formulations of the categorical imperative articulated by Kant, but it suffices for our purposes.

about who is due whatever is being fought over. We may hear an adult gripe about his boss or his job, and realize that a claim is being made as to what the person is or is not due. Occasionally people say things like, "no one deserves that." In fact, the U.S. Constitution claims that no one deserves "cruel and unusual punishment." Determining what exactly constitutes such punishment would require closer scrutiny in a chapter on, say, the death penalty. But what is important here is that all these claims are framed in the language of what one is due or deserves.

It seems we have a rather ingrained sense of evaluating situations in light of what people deserve, or what is their due. Where does this come from? As another indication of how intimately justice is tied to morality as a whole, this question harkens us back to the first chapter's discussion of why be moral? Is our grasp of what is due others simply a reflection of some basic understanding among people in civil society, conditioned in us from the earliest age, in order to protect ourselves from suffering at the hands of those who attempt to do what it is we all want to do, namely, get whatever we want? If so, then cries of "he deserved it!" or "mine!" are indignant recognitions that someone among us is violating the rules. Glaucon would be right that being just is not what is best for us, but a second best compromise given our selfish ways.

Against this view, the dominant strain of the Western tradition has consistently affirmed that being just is actually what is natural to us. This is a tricky term that requires our close attention since it is used in so many ways. Sometimes people call something natural because it is so common. In this sense we might say, "it's only natural to tell a lie." We mean it happens all the time. Sometimes we call something natural because it is effortless or feels right to us. Again, we might say someone is a natural-born liar because he does it so effortlessly. The third sense of natural refers to what happens when things are functioning well for someone. So we say it is natural to eat right and exercise. Eating right and exercising is natural in the third sense even if it does not happen a lot, or is not effortless. Sometimes things are natural in all three senses. We say, "it is natural to love your child" because it is what someone who is being a good parent does (third sense) and hopefully it is both common (first sense) and effortless (second sense). However, sometimes we say something is natural in a way that we do not mean all three senses. Drinking excessively may be natural to an alcoholic in the second sense (it is effortless), but not in the third sense (as in what is best for him), and hopefully not the first sense.

The dominant strain of the Western tradition has always claimed that it is natural for us to be just. This is meant primarily in the third sense. It would be nice if it were true in the first two senses, but sadly it generally is not. At first glance this claim seems odd even in the third sense. Why is it that maintaining right relations with others is what is best for me? How is it natural for us to give others their due when we seek our own happiness? Was Glaucon right that concern for others is solely an imposition on us? As in chapter 1, we are once again facing a question that has to do with the very origin of justice and morality.

Thinkers before and since have long recognized Aristotle's famous claim that we are "social animals."[5] In other words, the things we do to flourish and live a good life are done with others. Another way to put this is that we humans are interdependent.[6] Think of the varying commitments in your life that are important. I would venture to say that every single one of them demands that you rely on others. It is true of your families, friends, and romantic relationships. It is true of universities and companies and hospitals. It is true of churches and nations. In each of these cases, you share with others some common project, be it the nurturing of a family with a spouse, education with other university community members, or common defense with fellow countrymen. Even more basically, the language that structures our thoughts and enables us to communicate is passed on to us by others. The goods we need to live are provided with the help of others. As one contemporary philosopher argues, the very identities we develop in life are deeply shaped by our interactions with other people.[7] So when Aristotle says we are social animals, he does not just mean that there are other creatures around us who are the same as us. He means that how we live, and indeed who we are, is deeply shaped by our interactions with others.

If this is the case—and I would certainly agree that it is—then it is simply erroneous to think of giving others their due as somehow rivaling our own ability to live a good life. Being in right relationship with others, in other words being just, is constitutive of living a good life. Socrates was right in chapter 1! As one contemporary theologian writes:

> Recall that each person seeks happiness in accordance with what she considers herself to be; the just person considers herself to be a participant in a just community—even if that community exists only as an ideal in her own mind. Hence for her there can be no conflict between justice and happiness because she would undermine and destroy her own identity.[8]

Justice is simply the habit of acting in a manner that nourishes right relations with others, and these relations are essential to our identities and thus essential to living a good life.

5. See Aristotle's *Politics*, in *The Basic Works of Aristotle*, ed. Richard McKean (New York: Random House, 1941), i.2, 1127–1316

6. For an excellent analysis of this interdependence, including how it engenders virtues, see Alasdair MacIntyre's *Dependent Rational Animals* (Chicago: Open Court, 1999).

7. For an excellent and exhaustive inquiry into these questions of identity, see Charles Taylor's *Sources of the Self: The Making of the Modern Identity* (Cambridge: Cambridge University Press, 1994).

8. Jean Porter, *Nature as Reason: A Thomistic Theory of the Natural Law* (Grand Rapids: Eerdmans, 2005), 218.

One traditional way of describing this reciprocal relationship of individual and group flourishing is through use of the term "common good." The *Catechism* relies on the Vatican II document *Gaudium et spes* to define the common good as "the sum total of social conditions which allow people, either as groups or as individuals, to reach their fulfillment more fully and more easily."[9] Any level of human community (family, institution, state, etc.) possesses some common good. Communities are said to be just—and persons who are part of communities are said to be just—to the extent that they contribute to well-ordered relations that allow the corporate entity, or community, to flourish. Of course, as the *Catechism* makes clear, the common good presupposes respect for the individual persons that constitute the community, and so forms of collectivism that purport to serve the corporate whole at the expense of individual members actually violate the common good. In short, the social nature of the human person means that individual human happiness is inextricable from the common good of varying levels of human community.

We are now encroaching on topics more fully addressed in the second half of this book. We have started here to make big-picture claims about what society and the individual person are all about. Such judgments are inevitable in speaking about the cardinal virtues. Just as Glaucon's view of morality only works if people are ultimately self-centered individuals who face the burden of having to live in society with other people, the view of justice presented here as maintaining and restoring the common good only works if it is true that people really do flourish only in interdependent relationships at varying levels (peers, families, local communities, nations, etc.). The fact that articulating some understanding of justice requires that one at least implicitly take a stand on these deeper questions is one reason why theories of justice are so contested in modern thought. That need not concern us just yet. It is enough to move on having explained why a dominant strain of the Western tradition has always claimed that being just is natural to us, and having recognized that this claims rests on some assumptions about the nature of the person and society that are not shared by everyone. Before moving on to a particular arena of justice, some words on the prevalence of rules of justice are in order.

The Pervasiveness of Rules for Justice

As noted by C. S. Lewis in the brief treatment of justice given in chapter 3, the virtue justice may lead us to think immediately of courts, police, and

9. *Catechism of the Catholic Church*, 2nd ed. (Vatican City: Libreria Editrice Vaticana, 1997), 1906, citing *Gaudium et spes* 26§1. The *Catechism* (1905–12) quotes the early second century *Epistle of Barnabas* 4.10 as an early reference to the notion of the common good, and provides three essential conditions of the common good. For a helpful contemporary treatment of the common good, see David Hollenbach's *The Common Good and Christian Ethics* (New York: Cambridge Press, 2002).

jails. In short, we think of criminal justice, or more broadly civil justice. This is one crucial arena for justice. Since justice concerns right relations between members of some corporate entity, civil justice at the national, state, or local level is an obvious arena where the virtue justice is lived out. But the virtue justice applies to many more arenas than this. It applies whenever there are people living as a group and relating to each other as members of that group. So, for instance, there is justice, or injustice, in how a company or corporation is run. Justice governs right relationships between those who live and work at universities. Justice governs how people who are members of a club interact. Justice is the virtue that governs how sports are played, and how players or teams in professional sports do what they do. Justice governs how peer groups function, and how family members interact. Whenever there are relations among members of some corporate entity, there is a possibility of well-ordered relations (*ius*), and justice is the virtue that inclines people to contribute to these well-ordered relations.

Though *ius* describes a state of affairs where things are well-ordered, and the way they were meant to be, this state of affairs should not be understood in a staid, static, stiff manner. Well-ordered corporate entities are dynamic and organic. Nonetheless, such dynamic groups operate under sets of rules to guide and sustain their flourishing. Consider just one arena for right relations among members: the family. We all know from our experiences of families that family life is anything but static and staid. People are always on the go. Parents are trying to juggle work and family commitments. Children are off to school and other activities, such as sports and music lessons. With all this there are shared times for church, visiting family, and even vacationing together. Add to this domestic chores, family crises and sickness, and it is a wonder people in families sleep! So even in a well-functioning family where there is *ius*, or right relations, that order is still dynamic, surprising, and at times even downright hectic!

Yet even in the hecticness there are rules (spoken or unspoken) that govern how the family lives. There are set times when people are expected to be together, as for dinner each evening or for weekly visits to a grandparent, or for Thanksgiving. There are shared expectations about who does what chores around the house. Parents have different systems for getting children to school, helping with homework, overseeing extracurricular activities, and so on. There are understandings about which items (clothing, toys, the family car) are shared and used in common, and which items are not. Many rules are particular to specific families: for instance, each Wednesday everyone is expected to be home for a family game night. Some rules apply to all families: there can be no physical or emotional abuse, dishonesty, or stealing from one another if a family is to function well. But in all families there are rules that govern common life and hopefully enable the family to flourish.

Note that in accordance with the morality-of-happiness perspective endorsed in this book, these rules are not obligations externally imposed on members of the family (though at times doing our chores, or driving a family member to their appointment may feel like that!). Following the rules is not the end goal. The goal is right relations between family members, so that each member can flourish and live well. Following the rules means participating in that flourishing.

One important function of rules of justice in any group is to guide how members of the group respond to violations of justice. *Ius* is dynamic and organic, but its suppleness is not unlimited. In other words, there are indeed actions that harm right relations among group members. The virtue justice also guides people to respond appropriately when someone acts in a manner that harms right relations among the group. Right order (understood in the dynamic sense described above) can be disturbed, and when it is it needs to be restored. For instance, what should happen when a child steals from a sibling or lies to a parent? What happens when one parent is not carrying his or her load around the house, or when a parent is neglecting the family in favor of work? As noted in chapter 5, it takes prudence to see rightly when there are indeed violations of justice, and whether those violations are serious or not. With such prudence, the virtue justice inclines one to respond well to injustices in the family. There are of course rules governing how justice may be restored well. Children may be punished, but there should not be vindictive anger, and never abuse. A parent may change his or her ways and make it up to the family, but token gestures (like buying a new family toy, or a gift for a spouse) without genuine recognition of wrongdoing or any commitment to change do not really rectify, or make right, the injustice.

All of these rules serve justice in the family by maintaining right relations or restoring them when violated. Though we have mainly spoken here of the family, there are of course many other arenas where justice is important, namely, wherever there are people functioning in relation to each other as a group. You could easily identify similar rules for maintaining and restoring justice in companies, universities, nations, and churches.

We can better understand these rules of justice at all levels, from families and peer groups to national and international law, by looking briefly at Aquinas's definition of law. Though he has in mind civil law, what he says is easily applied more broadly to rules that govern other corporate entities. According to him, law is a dictate of reason, made by a legitimate authority and properly promulgated, that serves the common good.[10] Consider four key elements of this definition. First, he says a law is a dictate of reason. For our purposes we can simply say that there must be specific content to the rule. It must be

---

10. See Thomas Aquinas, *Summa Theologiae*, English Dominican trans. (New York: Benziger, 1948), I–II 90,4.

clear exactly what one's chores are, or what constitutes plagiarism at a university, or what constitutes speeding in this state or city. Second, a law must be made by the proper authority. So parents decide what is best for children, or the CEO or board of trustees sets company policy, or legislators decide speed limits. Third, a law must be properly promulgated, or made known. Parents must convey the rules to their children. Students must be told what is expected of them so they can be graded fairly. Speed limits and other laws must be posted or somehow made known so that people can follow the law. Fourth and finally, a law must be directed to the common good of the group under consideration. In other words, rules help sustain and protect the group to which they apply.

Of course, this definition of law does not enable us to neatly settle all disputed issues of justice. Sometimes what is debated is whether or not one of these features is present in a law or act of justice at hand. Students who say their uncited use of a webpage as a research source is not a case of plagiarism are basically saying the rule defining is not specific enough. Debates over whether the U.S. invasion of Iraq in 2003 was justified often turn on whether or not the U.S. had the authority to address injustice in the way it did, or if only the United Nations would have that legitimate authority. When you tell a police officer that the speed limit was not posted and so you couldn't know you were speeding, you are basically saying the law was not properly promulgated. Finally, when people debate the justice of, say, affirmative action, they are often trying to determine whether such a policy will indeed serve the common good or not.

It is clearly true that not every law or rule of justice (formal or informal) meets all these criteria. One need not even think of the extreme cases of Nazism or Jim Crow laws to see that some rules intended to support the common good actually corrupt it. Other group rules can be actually harmful in less drastic ways. Nonetheless, the point of a rule is to sustain and restore right relations in the group to which it applies. When a law or rule meets Aquinas's four criteria, it does exactly that.

The point of these introductory comments on justice in general is to expand our notion of justice in several ways. Justice is not simply about the courts or law. It is about all right relations between people. There is justice or injustice whenever there are people working together. Often formally (as in laws), but at least as often informally there are rules that both sustain right relations and restore them when violated. When these rules are indeed just they are not external impositions on group members (even though they may be experienced as such), but rather constitutive of living a good life in particular communities. Since living in such communities is part of what it means to be human, justice is called natural. The next section explores these claims in the arena of international relations, and more specifically the waging of war.

Waging War Justly?

The purpose of this second section is to explore how the vision of justice described in section one plays out with some specific question of justice. The following discussion explores how just judgments can be made by people in responding to people who disrupt the order of justice (*ius*) by acting unjustly. Even more specifically, though many of the claims made in this section are relevant for other arenas of justice, the focus here is on how nations may be described as just or unjust in decisions about whether or not to wage war, and if so, how. As will be clear, this is no simple matter of taking a general definition of justice as offered in the previous section and mechanistically applying it to a given situation in order to be just. Things are more complicated than that. Yet this is not to say it is impossible to determine and then act out what is just in messy real-life situations. This section's reflection is intended to assist people to do exactly that.

The first part addresses the question of whether or not judgments of justice can accurately be made. This is a crucial question, since it seems that nations so commonly see things in ways that support their own interests over that of other nations. This fact makes us rightly wonder if accurate judgments of justice are possible, or if they should be avoided altogether. The second part explores different ways that people have understood how to respond to acts of injustice at the international level. The final two parts adjudicate debates between people who have different answers to the question: can it ever be just to intentionally kill people to restore the order of justice?

Can We Make Just Rules, or Any True Judgments, about Morality and Warfare?

If actions concerning justice, or relations between individuals and groups, are rule-governed activities as described at the end of the previous section, then waging war is no exception. This observation often strikes people as odd. They may recall the famous quip that "war is hell" and assume that what happens during war (like what happens in Vegas) is outside of or immune to the type of moral analysis to which we subject the rest of our lives and activities, perhaps because it is so horrible. The horror of war is not contested here. Nor is the fact that extreme situations, such as the systematic elimination of an ethnic group, may indeed call for extreme measures, such as purposely killing thousands of perpetrators of the injustice. But note that these claims are rules themselves: under certain such conditions, normal moral rules do not apply; or, when circumstances are extreme then such rules can be changed.

The claim that war is a rule-governed activity is true both in a weaker, less interesting sense and in a stronger, more interesting one. As for the former, even war waged under the guiding principle of "win at all costs" is following some sort of rule. As noted below, this is what is meant by total war. It is a rule in the descriptive sense explained in chapter 1, since it is a principle guiding a nation's actions in warfare.

Yet war may be called a rule-governed activity in a narrower, more interesting sense as well. Even if deceitful or self-deluded, nations generally justify their actions in terms of justice. In other words, they claim they are acting justly when accused of acting otherwise. Consider the response of the U.S. government to cries of injustice when American precision bombs destroy civilian targets. The response is generally that the action was unintended and, while tragic, justified given the current engagement. (Whether and when this is an adequate response will be explored in chapter 8.) For now, note simply that the U.S. response was not, "Yeah, so what?" but rather a retort that there was no injustice done. Both sides are committed to arguing in terms of justice. Similarly, if you were educated in the southern part of the United States, you may have heard what is commonly called the Civil War called the "war of northern aggression." This name carries with it the claim that the South was a victim of injustice. Whether that is true or not, the point is that each side claims to have justice in its corner.

This is a perfect example of the traditional claim that the virtue of justice has a real mean rather than a rational mean. If we were talking about what constitutes virtuous eating, it may indeed be possible to claim that two different perspectives are both rational and thus virtuous. But with justice this cannot be so. Though justice obviously has various instantiations through different times and cultures, what constitutes justice in a specific relationship between people cannot be defined differently precisely because it concerns their relationship. For example, although both sides may believe their own cause to be just, it cannot be that the Civil War was both a just war to achieve justice and an unjustified war of aggression.

At this point a complaint is usually lodged by students and readers. Who is to say what really is just? Maybe the U.S. precision bombing was unjustified. Or maybe the Civil War was an unjust war by the North. The wisdom of this complaint is the absolutely accurate recognition that particular loyalties shape how we see the conflicts we are in, and shape what we think is just. This occurs on familial, neighborhood, racial, national, and international levels. Americans generally think the United States is right, for instance. But recognizing this is very different from taking a step further and claiming that labels of injustice are not really true or false, but simply expressions of what the accuser himself sees and wants. If we take this latter step, and thus give up on moral realism by claiming that we can never accurately identify things as just or unjust, we ought to beware the ramifications of that position. Giving up on moral realism means that certain seemingly obvious atrocities (child abuse, rape, genocide, racial violence, slavery) are not truly offenses against justice—it is just how we look at it.

Presumably, none of us wants to claim that child abuse or rape is not really wrong. But we are also acutely aware of how often our judgments of what is truly right or wrong can favor ourselves. Where does that leave us? We should certainly subject our own actions and opinions to scrutiny, recognizing that our particular communities (friends, families, racial groups, and nations) shape how we see the world around us, and what we recognize to be just or unjust. We must beware the common human tendency to see things in ways that favor us in defiance of reality. But as was noted in an earlier chapter on the sub-virtue *memoria*, the response to skewed perceptions of reality is not abandoning the endeavor of trying to see truthfully the world around us, an abdication which is surely undesirable and arguably impossible. Rather, we must try to be more prudent, and work on the often difficult task of seeing more clearly what truly is and is not just, giving explanations for our judgments, and debating them with those who disagree, to get at moral truthful judgments and so be able to prudently pursue true justice.

This is hard work, and will entail errors, errors that in many realms of justice may tragically cost lives. But if what you are seeking in moral theology is some way to ensure from the outset that your judgments about justice will be definitively immune from error, you are seeking in vain. However, this is far from saying it is impossible for us to make accurate judgments of justice. Much of what follows on the just-war tradition is simply the collective wisdom of an ongoing tradition as to what exactly such judgments are concerning waging war.

Spectrum of Responses to Injustice: Just War and Pacifism in Perspective

Even if we can make judgments about what constitutes genuine injustice (although we must be very attentive to error and ethnocentric judgments), questions remain. What are the best ways to respond, individually and collectively, to acts of injustice by nations of people? Is the use of violence ever justified, and, if so, are there any moral limitations to its use? The purpose of this subsection is simply to lay out a spectrum of possible responses to injustice that apply to the international level. (They also apply more broadly—as the use of Martin Luther King Jr.'s life will indicate—but that is not the focus here.) Here we simply present the spectrum with a basic explanation of how the various positions differ.[11] The task of substantiating and adjudicating the different positions is taken up later in this chapter.

11. The following discussion on a spectrum of responses to injustice is indebted to the work of James Childress. For a helpful brief account of his treatment of these issues, and even a chart similar to that used here, see James Childress, "Niebuhr's Realistic-Pragmatic Approach to War and 'the Nuclear Dilemma,'" in Richard Harries, ed. *Reinhold Niebuhr and the Issues of Our Time* (Grand Rapids: Eerdmans, 1986), 122–56.

Pacifism	nonresistance
Pacifism	nonviolent resistance
Just War	limited violent resistance (discrimination and proportionality)
Just War	limited violent resistance (proportionality alone)
Total War	unlimited violent resistance

Starting from the bottom of the figure, *total-war* advocates claim that there are no moral limitations on the use of force in warfare. It is summed up in the phrase, "win at all costs." Given the horror of war, it is foolish and naïve to think that people will allow moral considerations to influence their actions, especially when such influence will likely mean putting one's self in greater danger by refraining from fighting a war, or from using a weapon that will protect one's self. Note that in the broad descriptive sense, the total-war position does indeed follow a rule. But since the rule is "win at all costs," there are no resources available to limit how violence is used to protect or pursue a nation's interests. For reasons that will be clear in the next few paragraphs, people who explicitly advocate total war are actually few in number, since even the most violent aggressors tend to justify their actions with a warped vision of justice. Whether some nations live out this view, despite rhetoric to the contrary, is of course another question.

At the top end of the figure are the *pacifists*. This term loosely refers to those who are unwilling to use violent force in rectifying injustice. The term pacifist is rejected by some as too vague, partly because it includes importantly different groups. For instance, some pacifists adopt a stance of *nonresistance*. Trusting that God's providence suffices to establish justice without human intervention, and/or fearful that human sinfulness and myopia render attempts to establish justice actually as unjust as what is targeted, these people not only reject the use of violence to address injustice, but also refuse to resist evildoers. They are guided by the well-known injunction of Christ to "turn the other cheek" (Matt. 5:39).

Also included among pacifists are *nonviolent resisters*. These people are pacifists due to their refusal to use violent means to rectify injustice. But they are quite willing to make judgments as to what constitutes injustice, and then stand up against such injustice using means that do not include violence. Thus, they resist, but nonviolently. Famous nonviolent resisters include Mahatma Gandhi and Martin Luther King Jr.

Continuing down the figure, we come across two different sorts of just-war advocates. The *just-war* perspective refers to those who are willing to employ violent means to fight injustice. Though unlike pacifists,due to their willingness to use deadly force, they are like pacifists in that their goal is to secure and maintain peace, or the presence of *ius*. That goal makes them different from total-war advocates (since the just-war goal is a truly just and peaceful state of affairs rather than simply establishing whatever state of affairs is desired). It therefore limits the occasions and ways they will use force, limits beyond the simple total-war adage, "win at all costs."

What limitations are held distinguishes two types of just-war theorists, and leads us into the more specific criteria of just-war theory. Some just-war theorists claim that proportionality alone limits the virtuous use of force to redress injustice. Use of violent force is deemed "proportional" (or proportionate) when the damage caused by one's use of force is not above and beyond the force needed to restore a just and peaceful state of affairs.[12] Other just-war theorists agree that the use of force must be proportionate, but add discrimination as another limit to the virtuous use of force. Discrimination here, unlike the way we often use that word, is a good thing to do. Also called noncombatant immunity, *discrimination* refers to the claim that in order for the use of force to be just, one must discriminate between combatants and noncombatants, and never intentionally kill the latter. This will be a crucial argument in the examination, in chapter 8, of the debate over dropping the atomic bomb in World War II.

Adjudicating Just War and Pacifism in the Catholic Tradition

One question that people normally ask at this point is the extent to which the different positions on the spectrum described in the last section are determined by one's religious convictions. Though this is primarily a question for the second half of the book, the question of the compatibility of justice and the use of violence offers helpful insights into this question. Consider the example of Martin Luther King Jr. who focused his work for justice on the national level, but whose thought helpfully illuminates nonviolent resistance in general. King was a Protestant minister, and anyone who has read his work knows how deeply and pervasively his faith shaped his own mission to pursue racial justice in the United States. His recognition of the advocate's need to purify himself, and his insistence on love of the enemy and the necessity of forgiveness, are deeply rooted in his faith.

Yet at same time other reasons for his refusing to employ force are not at all related to distinctive Christian beliefs. He speaks of the effectiveness of nonviolence in demonstrating the brutality of the aggressor's injustice, and of the greater potential for lasting peace when change is secured through

12. Those familiar with twentieth century debates in Catholic moral theology will notice that the term used here is quite similar to the term "proportionalism." Proportionality is simply an assessment of whether the good achieved outweighs the bad. Proportionalism describes an approach to moral theology whereby actions are judged permissible or not based upon the proportionality of their consequences. All recognize that assessments of proportionality are important for moral theology. Proportionalism is an approach based on the claim that assessments of proportionality alone exhaust moral analysis. One need not be a proportionalist to recognize the importance of judgments of proportionality.

nonviolent means. These claims are not dependent on religious faith, and indeed there were many of non-Christian or no faith who walked by King's side in his pursuit of justice. The reason why people with differing theological commitments can agree on such issues is because cardinal virtues like justice concern innerworldly activities that are accessible to unaided reason. Just as you needn't be a Christian to be a good judge, in principle you needn't be Christian to see truthfully how to face injustice most virtuously. That said, theological commitments do indeed shape one's response, as is seen in the Catholic tradition on pacifism and just war.

One recent authoritative document on Catholic teaching on war and peace is the U.S. bishops letter entitled "The Harvest of Justice is Sown in Peace."[13] Here the bishops lay out Catholic teaching on war and peace in an accessible manner. They begin by noting that any authentically Christian response to injustice always aims toward the reestablishment of genuine peace. Though they do not use the term, we know they are referring not simply to the absence of conflict, but to *ius* understood as the proper order of things. In other words, any response to the actions of another (in this case nation) must be undertaken with the goal of restoring right relationship, which of course is based on what each party is due. This may seem obvious, but note that it eliminates any claim of the total-war perspective to be Christian. It is conceivable that some political theorists could adopt and follow the position that every nation should simply seek to secure what it regards as its own best interests, resulting in a social order constituted by a balance of competing self-interested parties. This may actually occur in international politics. But the U.S. bishops note that such a view of the use of force is incompatible with Christianity, where justice dictates that actions in response to injustice must aim at restoring a truly just state of affairs.

So according to the U.S. bishops, the total-war response is both always immoral and also incompatible with Christianity. What of the pacifist and just war responses? Are these compatible with Christianity? Recognizing that there have been virtuous Christians throughout history who have held each of these positions, the bishops claim that both pacifism and just war can be moral responses to large-scale injustice that are compatible with the Christian tradition: "The Christian tradition possesses two ways to address conflict: nonviolence and just war."[14] The bishops try to affirm both approaches as virtuous ways to restore justice by claiming:

13. This document was released as a commemoration of the ten-year anniversary of another U.S. bishops letter on war and peace, *The Challenge of Peace: God's Promise and Our Response* (Pastoral Letter, 1983).

14. National Conference of Catholic Bishops. *The Harvest of Justice is Sown in Peace: A Reflection of the National Conference of Catholic Bishops on the Tenth Anniversary of the Challenge of Peace, November 17, 1993* (Washington, DC: United States Catholic Conference, 1994), pt. I, sec. B.

Our conference's approach, as outlined in *The Challenge of Peace*, can be summarized in this way:

1. In situations of conflict, our constant commitment ought to be, as far as possible, to strive for justice through nonviolent means.
2. But, when sustained attempts at nonviolent action fail to protect the innocent against fundamental injustice, then legitimate political authorities are permitted as a last resort to employ limited force to rescue the innocent and establish justice.[15]

They deem it possible to affirm both approaches because both approaches "share the common goal: to diminish violence in this world."[16] It seems more accurate to say that both pacifism and the just-war perspective share the common goal of maintaining and restoring *ius*, or peace, in the world; but it is true that they share a common goal.

These two approaches, of course, employ significantly different means toward that common goal. In fact, they employ mutually exclusive means. The bishops suggest trying nonviolent means first, but are then willing to use violence in a manner governed by just-war principles. Their position, however, is not a combination of the two approaches, as they suggest, but rather *is* the just war approach, which (as seen below) affirms is it best to resolve injustices through nonviolent means first. The pacifist position does not simply try to avoid the use of force. It prohibits it as an absolute norm. Therefore, any approach—such as the bishops'—which is open to using violence even as a last resort is ultimately incompatible with an approach that sees the use of such violence as a violation of an absolute norm.

The U.S. bishops therefore seem to adopt a clear just-war position despite wanting to affirm the compatibility of pacifism with the Christian tradition. What really seems to be happening here is that the bishops are trying to let rival approaches within the same Christian tradition stand, which is a wise thing to do in the absence of compelling arguments that only one of these, rather than the other, is actually compatible with justice. But in affirming both of these approaches it is best not to suggest they are compatible on the use of violence when in actuality they are not.

Recall also the above claim that pacifism and just war are umbrella terms including different strains of thought. Do the bishops mean to affirm all strands of pacifism and just-war thinking? The answer is no. Consider pacifism first. If by pacifism is meant simply an unwillingness to fight because of cowardice, or because of disregard for injustice in the world, then this sort of pacifism is incompatible with Christianity. The bishops claim that the "Christian has

15. Ibid.
16. Ibid.

no choice but to defend peace. . . . This is an inalienable obligation. It is the how of defending peace which offers moral options."[17] Lack of commitment to justice in the world is not an option for the Christian.

More controversially, nonresistance is arguably also incompatible with Christianity, despite the common source of this position in Christ's own instruction to "turn the other cheek." If the Christian has an obligation to defend peace, presumably that means resisting those who violate the order of justice, even if simply by lovingly confronting them on their actions in the hope that they will change (see Matt. 18:15–17). One wonders if the nonresistance advocate would be willing to participate in any of the rules noted in the first section of this chapter for restoring justice at any level: punishing children, confronting boorish behavior in friends, arresting criminals, and so on. If so, then they are indeed willing to resist. If not, it is hard to imagine how this is compatible with seeking justice and defending peace, which are obligatory for the Christian. When the bishops affirm pacifism they are clearly in support of the nonviolent resistance of the sort practiced by Gandhi or King.

What of the just war tradition? Do the U.S. bishops approve any sort of just-war theory that includes some room for limiting force for moral reasons? Again, the answer is no. Recall from above that there are two dominant strains of the just-war tradition: limiting violence on the ground of proportionality alone, or on the grounds of both proportionality and discrimination (or noncombatant immunity). Both approaches aim toward a truly just peace, but are willing to employ different means to achieve it. To understand the difference between the two, consider the following question: what if by intentionally killing several hundred civilians we could end a war sooner and save thousands? People who limit the use of violence in a just war by proportionality alone are willing to intentionally kill innocent noncombatants if such action can help restore justice in a proportionate manner (i.e., by saving more lives in the long run). Yet the U.S. bishops firmly endorse noncombatant immunity as a requirement for just-war theory in their letter. The prohibition of intentional killing of innocent persons is perhaps the most foundational absolute moral norm in Christianity. (As noted in chapter 8, it also informs most secular versions of just-war theory.) It may seem "override-able" for the greater good. But, as St. Paul says, one must not "do evil that good may result" (Rom. 3:8). More detail will be offered on this in chapter 8, but it should be clear here that according to the U.S. bishops, only the just-war position that limits violence by both proportionality and discrimination (noncombatant immunity) is compatible with Christianity.

Therefore, there are two approaches to restoring justice on the international arena that are compatible with the Christian tradition according to the U.S. bishops: nonviolent resistance pacifism, and just-war theory, including

17. Ibid. Here the U.S. bishops cite *The Challenge of Peace*, 73.

both proportionality and noncombatant immunity. The following section will examine arguments for and against these two positions to complete our preparation for the test case to come in chapter 8.

Adjudicating the Debate between Just War and Nonviolent Resistance

Debate continues among advocates of each of these two more specific versions of pacifism and just-war theory who claim that the other approach is actually not most just, and/or is incompatible with Christianity.[18] Note again that though one's faith commitments are indeed relevant for this debate (as evidenced by the reference to St. Paul in the previous part), since we are debating an innerworldly activity, we should not expect such debate to be settled on theological claims alone. Hence, much of the following will proceed on natural-law grounds.

Since just-war advocates recognize that nonviolent resistance may at certain times constitute a just response to injustice, the question is not which one of these is always unjust. The key question may be phrased in two ways depending on one's stance: a) from the just-war side, can the refusal of nonviolent resisters to ever employ violence be at certain times a failure to be just by refusing to defend peace with available means; or, b) from the nonviolent resistance side, is the use of violence always unjust?

First, let us consider the question from the side of the nonviolent resistance school of pacifism. Two main pacifist arguments are offered here against just-war advocates. First, proponents of nonviolent resistance claim that the just-war approach to restoring peace and justice simply does not work. Though his work was primarily on a national level in the United States, the work of Martin Luther King Jr., is instructive on this point.[19] King's argument for nonviolence focuses on its effectiveness in restoring *ius*, or peaceful right relations, for two reasons. First, it helps prevent the victim's hatred of the one committing the injustice. If right relations are to be restored, they will presumably include the rectified former perpetrator of injustice. A refusal to employ violence helps the nonviolent resister continue to see the aggressor as someone with dignity, with whom one can be restored into right relationship. Well, you might say, that assumes the aggression will stop. What if it does not? King would retort that the second reason for the greater effectiveness of nonviolence is its impact

18. In this part, pacifism is understood more specifically to refer to nonviolent resistance, and just-war advocates are understood to be those who limit the use of violence by both proportionality and discrimination/noncombatant immunity.

19. For a brief and helpful synopsis of King's thought on nonviolence, see both his "Pilgrimage to Nonviolence," in his *Strength to Love* (Minneapolis: Augsburg, 1981), 146–54, and his December 10, 1964, Nobel Peace Prize acceptance speech, "The Quest for Peace and Justice," at http://nobelprize.org/nobel_prizes/peace/laureates/1964/king-lecture.html.

on the aggressor himself. The method of nonviolence so stirs the conscience of the aggressor that it awakens in him a realization of his injustice. If this sounds unrealistic, recall this is what seems to have happened as a result of both King's nonviolent resistance in the U.S., and Gandhi's nonviolent resistance of the British in India. Indeed, it seems odd to employ a means (lethal violence) that is antithetical to what one claims to be trying to establish (peace). Though King would have to acknowledge that there is no guarantee of the success of nonviolence, surely the same is true of the use of force. In fact, it seems that places which are subdued by violence are all too often marked by an illusory peace where the defeated merely wait for a better opportunity to exert themselves.

A second and related reason that King could offer for employing nonviolence, and indeed which is commonly offered by pacifists today, is that the just-war criteria simply do not actually work in eliminating or mitigating the use of force. Everyone thinks that their cause is just and that they are the victims of injustice. So, even when just-war advocates offer criteria that have to be met in order to use force virtuously, pacifists wonder if these criteria are ever actually followed. Has just-war theory ever actually limited the use of force, as it claims? Some pacifists suggest that if just-war advocates ever actually refused to use force, due to their theory, it might have more credibility. But despite claims to the contrary, in the opinion of some pacifists just-war proponents seem to live out total war while hiding under a cloak of just war.

Just-war advocates obviously see things differently. They would argue that throughout the history of the just-war tradition, reliable criteria have been developed to determine when it is indeed virtuous to wage war. Augustine was the first to famously list criteria for the just waging of war, and Christian and non-Christian thinkers alike since then have sought to list the conditions that would have to apply for someone to use violence justly to restore peace. One set of these criteria is given by the U.S. bishops in their document.[20]

There actually are two lists. One contains the conditions that must be met for a nation to enter armed conflict in the first place. These conditions are collectively referred to as *ius ad bellum*, or "being just in going to war:"

1. *Just Cause:* force may be used only to correct a grave, public evil, i.e., aggression or massive violation of the basic rights of whole populations;
2. *Comparative Justice:* while there may be rights and wrongs on all sides of a conflict, to override the presumption against the use of force the injustice suffered by one party must significantly outweigh that suffered by the other;

20. *The Harvest of Justice is Sown in Peace*, pt. I, sec. B, no. 2.

Introducing Moral Theology

3. *Legitimate Authority:* only duly constituted public authorities may use deadly force or wage war;
4. *Right Intention:* force may be used only in a truly just cause and solely for that purpose;
5. *Probability of Success:* arms may not be used in a futile cause or in a case where disproportionate measures are required to achieve success;
6. *Proportionality:* the overall destruction expected from the use of force must be outweighed by the good to be achieved;
7. *Last Resort:* force may be used only after all peaceful alternatives have been seriously tried and exhausted. [21]

If all of these conditions apply, a nation is justified in going to war. Of course, simply knowing the conditions does not eliminate debate over whether or not they actually apply in a certain historical situation. People may question a nation's right intention, as when some claimed that the real reason for the United States to lead the 1991 war against Iraq was to secure oil. Similarly, there are debates over the role of the United Nations concerning legitimate authority, or whether the recent war in Iraq violated the last-resort condition. So it is true that prudence, individual and communal, is required in order to make such judgments rightly. But this simply means nations must deliberate carefully, not that these conditions can never actually exist.

Just-war theory also includes a set of conditions that must apply in order for a nation already engaged in armed conflict to use violent means virtuously. These criteria are called *ius in bello*, or "being just in fighting a war." There are three:

1. *Noncombatant Immunity:* civilians may not be the object of direct attack, and military personnel must take due care to avoid and minimize indirect harm to civilians;
2. *Proportionality:* in the conduct of hostilities, efforts must be made to attain military objectives with no more force than is militarily necessary and to avoid disproportionate collateral damage to civilian life and property;
3. *Right Intention:* even in the midst of conflict, the aim of political and military leaders must be peace with justice, so that acts of vengeance and indiscriminate violence, whether by individuals, military units or governments, are forbidden. [22]

Given the separate sets of criteria, it is conceivable according to just-war theory that a nation could go to war justly but not fight that war justly. In fact, the

21. Ibid.
22. Ibid.

debate in chapter 8 over dropping the atomic bomb at Hiroshima is about precisely this claim. It is quite feasible to argue that this act violated *ius in bello,* even though the United States was fighting a just war.

Just-war advocates would respond to pacifists that these criteria can guide and indeed have guided nations' actions. They might argue that President George H. W. Bush demonstrated adherence to the right intention criterion of *ius ad bellum* when he did not occupy Iraq in 1991, but rather simply liberated Kuwait. Had his intention really been seizing Iraqi oil supplies, he would have occupied the nation or at least its oil fields. Just-war advocates could point to American use of smart-bomb technology to limit civilian (noncombatant) casualties even when larger scale bombs could ensure the destruction of the intended target. Of course, just-war advocates do not claim that national leaders must look up the appropriate just-war principle and call it by name in order to act in accordance with just-war theory. Rather, their claim is that a nation acts justly when its actions are consonant with those principles, even if they are not explicitly referring to them.

Therefore, in response to the pacifist charge that just-war theory is in reality indistinguishable from total war, just-war advocates can offer specific criteria for waging war justly, and point to real occasions when these criteria were lived out, even if not explicitly referenced. As for the claim that pacifism is more effective, just-war proponents would not only disagree, but also claim that nonviolence eliminates a crucial tool for restoring justice: war. Reminiscent of the U.S. bishops, who seem to adopt a just-war perspective even while purporting to endorse nonviolent pacifism, just-war advocates can endorse all of the claims of nonviolent resistance pacifism save one: the refusal to ever use violence. Surely nonviolence is often the best and most effective way to restore justice. God willing, no one wants to go to war casually. But against pacifism, the just-war advocate asks, what if all the conditions of *ius ad bellum* apply? Assuming they do, then and only then is war a virtuous—indeed the virtuous—way to restore justice. In this same situation (say perhaps, when the Germans invaded Poland in 1939), the pacifist refuses to defend the innocent and reestablish peace through warfare. And this, contends the just-war advocate, constitutes a failure against the Christian—indeed human—obligation to defend peace and restore justice.

One final arena for the debate over whether the use of violence is ever compatible with the just restoration of peace concerns the place of violence (understood as at least potentially lethal force) in the broader category of coercion (understood as acting against someone's will). Notice that the nonviolent resister does not refuse to employ coercion in the name of justice. These pacifists generally agree that parents should reprimand their children, friends can and should confront misbehaving friends, and police should arrest criminals, all for the sake of justice. Sanctions, boycotts, reprimands, and the like are all forms of coercion, since they seek to redirect the actions of aggressors even if against their wills. Indeed if they did not, they would not be effective. Presumably the pacifist would say that such coercion is in reality not true harm at all. It is perceived as harm by the perpetrator, but since the person is acting unjustly, restraining them from continuing their unjust action not only restores *ius* for the sake of the common good, but also restores the perpetrator herself to justice, which is for her own good even if she does not recognize it at the time.

If coercion can be for the good of all, including the perpetrator against whom it is targeted, why the unwillingness among nonviolent resisters to employ coercion that is lethal (assuming last resort and the other conditions are met)? (We say "lethal" and not even physical or violent coercion since surely incarcerating criminals is coercion in these senses, and not prohibited by the nonviolent resister.) This is a challenging question to both the just-war advocate and the pacifist. On the one hand, the just-war advocate has to argue that the death of the aggressor (assuming all just-war criteria are met) actually serves the common good, even though it means this individual (or all those individuals killed) will no longer be able to participate in that common good because they are dead. This is a very strong judgment, but just-war theorists must acknowledge that this is precisely what they are claiming when saying that waging war is virtuous.

On the other hand, pacifists have to explain why they are willing to employ coercive methods in some situations like life imprisonment (presumably in cases of true guilt), but yet will not allow for lethal coercion. Why will they draw that line? What principle distinguishes for them the allowance of coercion to serve justice in some cases, but not in others? One obvious answer is that being dead is significantly different than being restrained or incarcerated. True enough. But even this line is hard to maintain. For instance, is it permissible to arm jail guards with lethal force? What about police officers? How would the commitment to nonviolence look in these situations, assuming nonviolent resisters are not interested in dispensing with criminal justice?

This point is raised both to remind the just-war advocate of the seriousness of the claim that one can indeed kill for peace and justice, and to press the nonviolent resisters to specify exactly how and why they would draw their lines as to what constitutes just and unjust coercion, since they are apparently open to coercion in some cases.

This draws to a close this second section of the chapter. It is certainly easier to talk vaguely about justice and rules of justice. But when concrete rules for real-life situations must be determined and will indeed result in suffering for those involved, no matter which course is taken, debates over justice become more difficult and heated. The main task of this section has been to enter into the debate over whether or not the use of lethal force is ever compatible with justice as understood in the manner depicted in the first section.

Concluding Thoughts

The twofold purpose of this chapter is to explore the cardinal virtue of justice in more depth, and to engage in debates about how specific rules of justice are determined in some particular arena of justice, in this case the waging of war. As should be clear at this point, an accurate view of justice in general, and even a knowledge of specific norms like the just-war criteria, does not neatly settle all debate on matters of justice. But it does provide a platform on which to argue these challenging questions. Rather than simply saying, "this war is morally wrong," or "this way of fighting is morally permissible," specific norms (like those of the just-war tradition) enable one to specify exactly what is found virtuous or objectionable.

Sometimes debate will be over what rules justly govern an activity, such as responding to injustice. The previous section's adjudication of debate between pacifists and just-war advocates is one such example. So too is the question, particularly relevant for chapter 8, of whether noncombatant immunity is a necessary component of fighting justly, or whether proportionality alone renders use of force in warfare just. Sometimes debate will be over whether or not conditions exist that fit some rule that is accepted by all in the debate. In other words, two people may agree that there must be just cause to go to war justly, but disagree over whether a preemptive strike violates that condition or not. Or both may agree with the rule of non-combatant immunity, but disagree over who counts as a combatant, or whether certain acts (like targeting power grids) are directed against the military or civilians. In sum, learning what moral theology has to contribute to debates over waging war does not immediately and neatly settle all disputed questions, though it does give them further clarity, which will hopefully enable us to settle them more justly.

In any case, it should be abundantly clear at this point how important prudence is for acting justly. It is prudence that enables us to see rightly, so as to act rightly. It is prudence that enables us then to make accurate determinations of whether intentionally killing civilians actually subverts any justice secured in doing so, or whether last resort has actually been met in a case at hand. It is difficult to imagine where making right judgments about innerworldly activities is more important, since such judgments literally mean the lives and deaths of people. Our consciences must be properly formed to make such judgments well. One way the discipline of moral theology, and moral education more broadly (as in McCabe's sense from chapter 5), can be especially helpful is in forming people's consciences well, so as to make truly just judgments about these matters.

Study Questions

1. Define justice. Be sure to use and define the terms *ius* and *suum cuique*. What problems does this definition raise?

2. Explain what is meant by the claim that it is "natural" for us to be just.

3. Give some examples of different arenas in life where there can be justice or injustice. Give examples of rules (formal or informal) that preserve that justice. Include some examples of rules that help restore justice when it has been violated.

4. List Aquinas's four characteristics of a law. Give an example for some rule of justice, and explain whether or not it displays each characteristic.

5. Given that people tend to see things in ways that favor themselves (as individuals, families, racial groups, nations, etc.), is it possible to make accurate judgments of justice? Explain why or why not.

6. List and define the spectrum of responses given in this chapter for how nations can respond to violations of justice. Where would you place yourself and why?

7. What positions on that spectrum are compatible with the Catholic faith and why?

8. Define *ius in bello* and *ius ad bellum* and list the conditions for each.

9. Why is prudence and the formation of conscience so important in matters of justice? Give an example in your answer.

Terms to Know

justice, *ius*, *suum cuique*, common good, total war, just war, pacifism, nonresistance, nonviolent resistance, proportionality, discrimination or noncombatant immunity

Questions for Further Reflection

1. Think of some examples from your peer groups of rules that maintain justice, and restore justice once it has been violated. Use Aquinas's four characteristics of law to explain whether they are good rules or not.

2. Think of some concrete practices that enable people to make more truthful (prudent) determinations of what is just, despite the common tendency to see things in a manner that benefits ourselves.

3. Take a position on whether or not the use of lethal violence is ever compatible with justice in general, and Christianity in particular. What is the best argument against your position, and how do you address it?

4. Do you agree with the position of this chapter that nonresistance is contrary to justice for Christians? Explain why or why not. Do the same for the claim of this chapter that a just-war position that limits violence only by proportionality is contrary to justice for Christians.

5. Pick some contemporary situation having to do with the use of force and use the arguments of this chapter to substantiate your position on the issue.
6. Find a discussion of a war-related issue in some periodical and demonstrate how the distinctions and arguments in this chapter could clarify, correct, or be corrected by the article.
7. How relevant are the second section's arguments on waging war for other activities such as policing or the use of economic sanctions?

Further Reading

Aquinas is, unsurprisingly, the driving force behind this chapter's treatment of the virtue justice. See in particular his "Treatise on Justice," II–II 57–122 in his *Summa Theologiae.* Josef Pieper's *The Four Cardinal Virtues* has a helpful overview of Aquinas's thought on justice, as do the articles on justice by Jean Porter and Martin Rhonheimer in Stephen J. Pope's (ed.) *The Ethics of Aquinas*. The *Catechism of the Catholic Church* also contains a helpful overview of social justice (1877–1948). As for just-war material, the literature on this topic is voluminous. An excellent secular approach to just-war theory is Michael Walzer's classic, *Just and Unjust Wars* (New York: Basic Books, 1992). Other excellent overviews which attend to Christianity include: Richard B. Miller's *Interpretations of Conflict: Ethics, Pacifism, and the Just War Tradition*; Lisa Sowle Cahill's *Love Your Enemies: Discipleship, Pacifism, and Just War Theory*; and Oliver O'Donovan's *The Just War Revisited*.

8

Using the Atom Bomb
in World War II

Test Case Two

Few events in American history inspire as much pride as World War II.[1] Movies like *Saving Private Ryan* depict the tremendous sacrifices that American soldiers made in this war, and the powerful sense of purpose that guided those involved. Recently books like *The Greatest Generation* chronicle not only the heroic acts of those who fought for us in World War II, but also argue that such bravery must be understood in the context of a generation of people who were truly virtuous in their love of country, grasp of justice, and willingness to sacrifice. Many families proudly tell stories of their own members' contributions and sacrifices in World War II. In my own family, we repeatedly recount the story of my maternal grandfather driving a landing craft to the beaches of Normandy on D-Day, and joining Patton's army in the race across Europe after the successful invasion.

For many—myself included—World War II serves as a model, or paradigm, of the just war. Nazis were ravaging Europe and exterminating people by the

---

1. I would like to thank Dr. James Halstead of DePaul University for his generous and invaluable help on this chapter. Dr. Halstead regularly takes students to Hiroshima, and knows this issue as well as anyone. Though his conclusions differ from my own, this chapter would not have been possible without him.

millions. Japan was building an empire in East Asia that included the brutal subjugation of conquered peoples. Concentration camps and Hitler on the one side, Pearl Harbor on the other. What could be more just? It is easy in this context not to question any actions of the United States. It is understandable in the context of the horror of war in general, and of this war in particular, to regard any moral analysis of the actions of war as an ivory-tower academic luxury secured by precisely the actions of those willing to get things done. Moral analysis may appear to be Monday-morning quarterbacking, where in the safety and knowledge of hindsight we make judgments to which it is not reasonable to hold people in the heat of battle.

This hesitance is especially present among people with regard to analyzing the United States' decision to use atomic bombs to attack Japan at war's end. In the context of a just war, it is difficult for many to consider whether an act that clearly hastened the end of the war was not morally justified. Given the horrible loss of life at places like Iwo Jima and Okinawa, anything that could halt such carnage seems best. Individual families tell stories about how the bomb impacted their lives. In my own family, my other grandfather, who could not serve in battle due to a physical problem, was taught Japanese by the military in Hawaii, and was slated to be among the first wave of troops as an interpreter should the U.S. invade Japan. Given the projected casualty rates for such an invasion, members of my family commonly claim that without the atom bomb we would not be here, as my grandfather would most likely have been killed. For many reasons such as these, people are understandably hesitant to subject to moral analysis the decision to drop the atom bomb.

But we must resist the urge to avoid moral analysis for two reasons. First, decisions need to be made in these trying circumstances, and no matter what decision is made it will observe some rule, even if the rule applied is simply win a just war in whatever way protects as many of one's own as possible. (Note that this already includes a limit on the use of force, since it must occur in a just war.) As explained in chapter 7, war is a rule-governed activity. The refusal to reflectively subject our decisions to analysis is often an implicit decision to do whatever we want, or at least what is seen as necessary at the time to achieve a virtuous goal, without concern for the ways that force should be limited. True, it is difficult to do this sort of thinking at the time of the conflict. But it is not impossible, as evidenced by the classic essay by John Ford, SJ, "The Morality of Obliteration Bombing," where he subjected the United States' policy of obliteration bombing in Germany in 1944 to moral scrutiny as it was happening.[2] Furthermore, even after-the-fact analysis, when done with proper consideration of how things were at the time of the act, can pre-

2. See John Ford, SJ, "The Morality of Obliteration Bombing," *Theological Studies* 5 (1944): 259–309. This classic article on a very practical just-war issue was enormously influential on this chapter.

sumably aid our decision making in such situations in the future. Obtaining a more accurate view of the past, so as to direct our future action, may be the most important reason for this analysis.

Second, recall that from the morality-of-happiness perspective endorsed in this book, moral reflection about the use of force is not primarily a matter of adjudicating where and how restrictive rules apply or not. Deliberately following a policy like noncombatant immunity may indeed entail tough decisions about limiting how force is used on occasion. But those limitations should be understood in the context of the larger endeavor of restoring and preserving justice. Though they may be experienced as obligations limiting the use of force, they are most rightly understood as the best, even most effective, way to achieve the stated goal of restoring true justice. How this is so will be explained below.

Unsurprisingly, much of the terminology in the questions driving this chapter's sections comes from the *ius in bello* part of the just-war theory explained in chapter 7. The chapter proceeds as follows. The first section has two goals. It will simultaneously offer a rudimentary sketch of the situation in the summer of 1945, when the United States made the decision to drop the first atom bomb on Hiroshima, and examine whether or not those conditions justify the use of the atomic bomb according to the just-war criterion of proportionality. (Though much of what is examined in this essay obviously applies to Nagasaki, the focus will be on the initial decision whether to use the atom bomb or not, and the first use of the bomb occurred at Hiroshima.) The caveat stated in the first test-case chapter is repeated here, namely, that reading this chapter should be supplemented by other texts that will provide more data about the case under consideration. The second section of the chapter explores whether noncombatant immunity (or discrimination) even applies to Japan in the summer of 1945. The third section defines and employs a classic tool in moral theology—the doctrine of double effect—to scrutinize the intention behind dropping the atom bomb and determine whether noncombatant immunity, assuming it did indeed apply to Japan in 1945, was violated or not by dropping the atom bomb.

The Context for the United States Decision to Use Atomic Bombs: The Question of Proportionality

The criterion of proportionality in discussions of *ius in bello* is an attempt to ensure that only the force which is necessary to restore justice is employed in a just war. So, whether or not the use of the atomic bomb was a proportional use of force depends on the situation at the time. It is difficult to describe a situation objectively and then morally evaluate it. One's description of a situation is often shot through with evaluations. For instance, deciding what facts to present, and the order in which to present them, reflects one's position on how to best act in a situation. This makes sense, since how we see things indicates how to act rightly. People who disagree on how to act often see things differently.

Yet despite how intricately related the tasks of description and evaluation are, it is not the case that we have no ways to adjudicate who sees a situation more accurately. For instance, not all facts of the situation in the summer of 1945 are contested. Furthermore, claims about the situation that are contested can be substantiated in better or worse ways by careful examination of the historical data we have. In other words, despite the recognition that how we see things is not simply a matter of opening our eyes, there are indeed more or less accurate ways to describe the situation in which the decision was made to drop the atomic bomb on Hiroshima. Here is yet another indicator of the moral importance of prudence and seeing things rightly.

This section seeks to achieve two goals at once: first, to describe the context for the decision to drop the atom bomb on Hiroshima in the summer of 1945, and second, to evaluate that decision in the terms of proportionality. In recognition that it is not possible to give a complete and objective account of the facts of the situation in which the decision to drop the bomb was made, and then subject those facts to moral scrutiny, the two tasks of description and evaluation of proportionality are treated together here. Being no historian myself, the research of historians, often accessed through the research of moralists writing on this topic, is relied on here for describing the situation in 1945. This section will note the uncontested claims about the situation, and recognize where there are competing accounts of what that situation was. An evaluation of proportionality will be offered based on what is understood here to be the best account of that situation. Unsurprisingly, we will find that differences in evaluations of proportionality often result from different assessments of what exactly the situation was.

By the summer of 1945 the tide of World War II had clearly turned. The European theater had ended in May 1945. In the Pacific, the Americans were steadily defeating the Japanese on islands the Japanese had captured during and before the war. It is also clear that these battles were happening at tremendous cost to both sides, American and Japanese. To give some indication of the human cost of this fighting, one author reports that in 1945 Allied casualties were approximately 7,000 per week.[3] Note this does not even include Japanese casualties, which would surely be comparable, or even worse.[4]

Invasion plans for Japan were already well under way. Preparatory bombardment had begun by July of 1945, and the anticipated beginning of a full-scale invasion was November 1945. No one contests that planning for such an invasion was underway, or that it would have resulted in an enormous

---

3. See Paul Fussell, "Thank God for The Atomic Bomb," in *Thank God for the Atomic Bomb and Other Essays,* ed. Paul Fussell (New York: Ballantine Books, 1990), 18.

4. This is obviously not to discount the importance of Japanese casualties. But American casualty figures are given here since only those are found in the sources cited here.

loss of both American and Japanese lives. The most commonly cited figure for anticipated American casualties alone to fully secure Japan was one million people.[5] Another author reports that approximately 760,000 American soldiers were to be sent to the southern Japanese island of Kyushu to initiate the invasion. Given the 35 percent casualty rate suffered by American forces in invading Okinawa, this phase of the invasion alone could reasonably be expected to result in over 250,000 American casualties.[6]

The standard justification given for the use of the bomb at Hiroshima was that Japan was unwilling to surrender without being defeated militarily, and the only alternative to the use of the bomb was a full-scale invasion of Japan. The argument continues by saying that as horrific as killing 100,000 people at Hiroshima was, it actually saved lives.[7] If using the atomic bomb brought the Japanese to surrender, as the Japanese in fact did, then despite the horrible devastation it wrought, things would have been worse for both sides had it not been dropped. Therefore, granting the context of a just war, the use of the atomic bomb in this particular situation was justified since it helped restore the order of justice in a proportional manner. It not only achieved U.S. victory in a just war, but did so in a manner whereby less lives were lost than had an invasion been necessary. (The question of which lives were lost is taken up in the following section.)

The most common way this standard justification for the atomic bomb is attacked on grounds of proportionality is in its assumption that the only options available to the United States in early August 1945 were full-scale invasion or using the atom bomb. There are reasons to suspect that this is not true. First of all, by this point in the war the Soviet Union had joined the United States in the war on Japan. Soviet forces had soundly defeated Japanese forces on the mainland of East Asia.[8] Given the formidable forces surrounding the Japanese in early August of 1945, it is reasonable to claim that they might well have surrendered without a full-scale invasion.

Others retort that the samurai culture so ingrained in the Japanese mentality precluded any such dishonorable surrender, and that the Japanese as a people were committed to fight to the last man, woman, and child, with whatever weapon was available, to resist any invading forces.[9] It is of course impossible to know with certainty what the Japanese response would have been.

---

5. See, for instance, Fussell, 15.

6. See Charles Landesman, "Rawls on Hiroshima: An Inquiry into the Morality of the Use of Atomic Weapons in August 1945," *Philosophical Forum* 34, no. 1 (2003): 25.

7. This 100,00 figure is taken from Douglas Lackey, "Why Hiroshima Was Immoral: A Response to Landesman," *Philosophical Forum* 34, no. 1 (2003): 39.

8. For a helpful and brief article that argues against the use of the atomic bomb solely on the grounds of proportionality, see Douglas Lackey, "Why Hiroshima Was Immoral: a Response to Landesman."

9. See Fussell, "Thank God for The Atomic Bomb," 16–17, for an argument like this. See also Landesman, "Rawls on Hiroshima," 23–24, for his borrowing of the phrase "samurai culture" from John Rawls.

Two other options to end the war are often suggested. First, Japan could have been blockaded rather than invaded. One author suggests that given Allied exhaustion at the conclusion of the war in the European theater, there was hesitance on the part of the Americans for such a drawn-out strategy. There was also the hope on the part of the Japanese that Allied resolve would crumble, and peace could be negotiated on terms for more favorable than any which included, for instance, occupation.[10] Whatever the merit of this decision, it seems clear that the United States military in the summer of 1945 was preparing for an invasion of Japan, and not simply a blockade.

Mention of peace negotiations raises the second suggested option to secure Japanese surrender without invasion or atom bomb. It is uncontested that negotiations for peace had been underway between the United States and Japan throughout 1945. As noted above, it was clear by 1945 that the United States would win the war in some way or other. Apparently the main sticking point in these negotiations was the insistence on the part of the Japanese that their emperor be given immunity rather than be prosecuted, should the Japanese surrender. For its part, the United States insisted that the Japanese surrender be unconditional. This difference halted peace negotiations between the nations. Yet immediately after the second atomic bomb was dropped on Nagasaki, the United States accepted a peace agreement with Japan that included precisely the protection and immunity for the emperor that the Japanese had earlier sought. Some wonder why this term was acceptable after the bomb if it was unacceptable before the bomb.[11] The reason that this is an argument of proportionality is that it suggests the United States could have restored the order of justice without recourse to the bomb that killed 100,000 in Hiroshima.

Though these are the main arguments advanced in debates over the proportionality of the use of the atomic bomb, other points have been raised. Some supporters of the use of the bomb at Hiroshima claim that the bomb had a shock effect that not only made the Japanese desire surrender, but also made the United States more inclined to grant the emperor immunity. Some opponents contest whether such a shock was really needed to reach a peace agreement before the atomic bomb that was like the one reached after the bomb. Other opponents grant the need for such a shock, but claim it could have been delivered by dropping the bomb in a more desolate area of Japan first.[12] Perhaps these latter people think that had Japan not surrendered after such a display of power, the bombing would have been justified based on proportionality.

Note that all of these arguments concern proportionality. They all assume that winning the war was a just goal for the United States, and that the United States was morally justified in pursuing that goal, but only in a way that used no more

10. See Landesman, "Rawls on Hiroshima," 23.
11. See Lackey, "Why Hiroshima Was Immoral," 4–41.
12. Ibid., 41.

than that force necessary to achieve the goal. As noted in the previous chapter's discussion of different versions of just-war thinking, attending to proportionality is essential in any just-war argument. Making determinations of proportionality relies on the most accurate assessment of the situation possible. In other words, it relies on prudence. Based upon the assessment of the situation presented in this section, it is my position that the use of the atomic bomb can be justified if one examines solely the proportionality of its effects. In other words, if the whole of the question of the morality of the atom bomb were determined by whether or not it ultimately saved more lives, then its use was justified, and virtuous in accordance with the criterion of proportionality. Of course, this can only be the end of a moral analysis of the bomb if one adopts a "just-war proportionality alone" approach to just war reasoning. Yet, as argued in that chapter, there are other essential elements of just-war theory to attend to, particularly concerning noncombatant immunity. It is to these that we now turn.

Noncombatant Immunity in a Militarized Culture

Having addressed proportionality and acknowledged that the atom bomb could be justified if examining solely the proportionality of its destructive effects, there are two criteria of *ius in bello* that remain: noncombatant immunity and intention. Recall that an act of war must satisfy all three criteria in order to be virtuous. These last two criteria are both addressed in the following section. But before we can do that, we must ask a prior question: were there noncombatants in Hiroshima, Japan in the summer of 1945?

This may sound like an odd question. Surely in Hiroshima there were babies, and elderly, and invalid people who could not count as combatants in any conventional sense of the term. Of course this was true. But those who are more familiar with the Japanese people and culture in 1945 describe a society that was thoroughly militarized.[13] They describe a nation of one heart with the military, and so proud and protective of their nation that they would fight to the very last person to defend it against, say, an invasion. Indeed, policies were in place to enable people who would normally be described as noncombatants, such as children, elderly, and others on the home front, to help defend the nation against any invaders. Those knowledgeable with this culture at the time describe a militarized mentality that blurs, and perhaps obliterates, any clean distinction between combatants and noncombatants.

In order to thus determine whether or not there were noncombatants in Japan in 1945, we must examine the basis of this *ius in bello* criterion. What

13. This is what is meant by Landesman's citation of Rawls on the Japanese samurai culture. For a powerful description of this mentality, see Fussell, "Thank God for The Atomic Bomb," 26–27. There he cites one U.S. military intelligence officer as proclaiming publicly, "there are no civilians in Japan" (27).

is the rationale behind noncombatant immunity? One of the foundational principles of Christian and non-Christian approaches to just war alike is that innocent people must never be intentionally killed.[14] Why? The purpose of the use of force is to restore *ius*, a truly just peace. One of the defining features of such a state of affairs is the protection of innocent life. So the violation of that principle in the attempt to restore *ius* does not just open one to charges of intellectual inconsistency or moral hypocrisy. It is actually counterproductive to the very state that one seeks to establish.

Now this does not mean that no persons can be targeted for attack in warfare. It means no persons can be targeted who are innocent of the aggression which has triggered the just war. Just-war theory rests on the assumption that the order of justice is under attack by those who violate it. These aggressors are not innocent, and sacrifice their immunity to attack (granting all the conditions of *ius ad bellum* are met). Therefore, attacking only those determined to be guilty of, rather than innocent of, aggression is fundamental to just-war theory. The combatant/noncombatant distinction is precisely the attempt to determine who is guilty and who is innocent. Those who actively participate in the armed aggression of a nation are considered combatants. Those who do not are labeled noncombatants and are, according to just-war theory, not to be intentionally attacked.

There are several challenges to this basic explanation. First, the ascription of guilt or innocence is a corporate rather than an individual one. Determining a person's guilt in some individual act of aggression or crime (theft, murder, etc.) may require an investigation, but it is relatively straightforward. We look at the act performed, search for a motive (intent) on the part of the accused, and make a determination. On the corporate level of, say, a nation, this is far more complicated than individual criminal cases, since the guilt is corporate and individuals may have stronger or weaker ties to the corporate mentality and aggression. Therefore, in affording the status of combatant or noncombatant, it is impossible to look at individual attitudes or intentionality. Rather, the determination is made based upon what actions different civilians perform. People engaging in actions that are more directly tied to the corporate aggression (soldiers, base staff, munitions workers, etc.) are considered combatants, while others not so directly connected by their actions to the nation's aggression are considered off-limits. Of course, this could mean there exist people, for whatever reason, unable to fight who hate the enemy, would love to fight,

14. Recall this criterion of *ius in bello* from the U.S. bishops document, "The Harvest of Justice Is Sown in Peace," examined in chapter 7. For an example of a just-war theorist who holds this criterion while not writing from an explicitly Christian perspective, see Michael Walzer's response to Fussell in the essay "An Exchange of Views," in *Thank God for the Atomic Bomb and Other Essays*, ed. Paul Fussell (New York: Ballantine Books, 1988), 23–28. See also his important work on just-war theory entitled *Just and Unjust Wars*, 3rd ed. (New York: Basic Books, 2006).

and support the nation's aggression, but who are actually noncombatants. Conversely, there could be soldiers on the front lines who are drafted, hate the nation's cause and perhaps even its leaders, but who are combatants due to their status as soldiers. This is a clear tragedy of war, in that determinations of one's status as combatant may neglect individual circumstances that could otherwise affect that determination. Yet granting that aggressors may be justly resisted, it is difficult to see how this could be otherwise.

The second problem with noncombatant immunity concerns the difficulty of determining what sorts of activities are integral to a nation's aggression to grant the person who does them combatant status. In other words, what actions are "combative enough" to make one count as a combatant? Some authors note how this is particularly the case with modern warfare, where civilian contractors, power-grid employees, and scientists doing weapons research are all examples of people whose work is crucial for a nation's ability to wage war, even if these people are not soldiers in the traditional sense. So who count as combatants?

Clearly, soldiers in fighting units are combatants. People who do non-combat related work (custodial, food service, etc.) on bases are also generally considered legitimate targets, since they so directly support combat. We could say the same of mechanics working on the weapons of war, or even those civilians who work in munitions plants where arms are built. It is easy to see how quickly the lines determining who is a combatant expand. Some have concluded from this that really all citizens in a nation are rightly considered combatants. After all, doctors heal people who later fight. Farmers grow food that feeds the troops, and cobblers make shoes they wear to battle. Children write letters of support to their parent soldiers, and eventually grow into soldiers themselves. Particularly if we include moral support as a contribution to the war effort, it is difficult to see who would not count as a combatant. Given the myriad ways that citizens contribute to a nation's war-making efforts, it is difficult to determine who exactly counts as a noncombatant.

But despite the difficulties posed by having to draw such lines, many just-war theorists insist that draw such lines we must.[15] It is not the case, as is often nostalgically suggested, that premodern warfare made it easy to delineate combatants from noncombatants. Many of the war supporters identified in the last paragraph clearly existed in premodern warfare: farmers, cobblers, children, and moral supporters. These people did make indirect contributions to a nation's war efforts, but were nonetheless deemed noncombatants. It is certainly true that modern styles of warfare make these determinations more difficult: soldiers are often not uniformed and hide among civilians; research and development people seem to be direct contributors; and civilian contractors and pilots may

15. For a fine example of this line of thinking, see Ford, "The Morality of Obliteration Bombing."

be called upon to directly assist soldiers. These examples may reveal occasions where noncombatant immunity lines need to be redrawn to recognize that there are new forms of activity that directly contribute to the war effort. But what must not be sacrificed is the burden of explaining why those who are targeted are implicated directly in the nation's aggression. To do otherwise would be to subvert the very justice that one claims to attempt to restore in warfare.

What is the relevance of this issue for the specific issue of whether or not there were noncombatants in Hiroshima in the summer of 1945? Many people cite the militarized culture of Japan in this time period as a reason for claiming that the entire nation's people were combatants. This is a dangerous error. It makes some sort of internal attitude the feature that determines whether or not one is a combatant or not. When we see anti-American portrayals in 1945 Japan, and hear stories of pledges by civilians to defend their nation with every last drop of their blood, it is understandable to wonder whether these people should be afforded the protection of noncombatants. It is especially understandable when some have suffered at the hands of soldiers who demonstrated this same attitude with vicious intensity. Nonetheless, it is people's actions, and more specifically how directly people's actions are related to a nation's war making, that should determine their status as combatants or not. Of course, should such civilians pick up arms and indeed fight, this status has changed, but only because the actions have changed. The same applies to children who will one day fight. Though this is obviously true, they have not fought yet. When they do cross the line and participate in the military, they are legitimate targets.

Americans who are wounded by terrorism, especially after the events of September 11, 2001, should be particularly wary of arguments that obliterate any distinction between combatants and noncombatants. Nations or non-national peoples may differ, and have differed, as to when there is just cause to use force against another people. But one way to assess the justice claims of people's willingness to use force is to examine their willingness to kill the innocent. This willingness surely belies one's supposedly just cause.

In the absence of noncombatant immunity, any person in a targeted nation is a legitimate target, including people who participate in a capitalist system by working in the World Trade Center, or who are simply American citizens on board an airplane. This is not at all to say that terrorists who kill such people have a just cause. That is a separate question. But terrorists clearly violate noncombatant immunity understood in any conventional sense. We should be wary of how we expect noncombatant immunity to be respected among our enemies when we consider whether to respect it ourselves, or how stingily we will grant its protection.

Several conclusions can be culled from this section. First, noncombatant immunity is an essential component of fighting a just war. As noted in chapter 7 and in the previous section of this chapter, there are just-war theorists who limit the use of force by proportionality alone. Yet that position is rejected here. Refusing to intentionally kill innocent noncombatants is necessary if one genuinely seeks to restore a just peace that would of course be characterized by protection of innocent life. To kill the innocent to protect the innocent is logically inconsistent, hypocritical, and counterproductive. Therefore, it is argued here that acknowledgement of noncombatant immunity must be part of any virtuous war-making.

The second conclusion concerns Hiroshima directly. Even if one grant that noncombatant immunity must be respected, one could argue that there were no noncombatants in Hiroshima in 1945. This position is also rejected here. Given the corporate nature of warfare, determinations of guilt or innocence which underlie designation as a combatant or noncombatant must be based on a person's particular activity, and the extent to which the activity directly contributes not simply to the war-makers (in terms of their health, stomachs, or moral support) but to their war-making activity. Munitions workers, pilots who shuttle soldiers to battle, and civilian contractors who erect an invading military's barracks may all be legitimate targets. But even with this recognition, surely a great majority of a nation's non-fighting persons remain noncombatants.

Efforts to redefine all a nation's inhabitants as combatants should be seen for what they are: a self-protective and deluded way to justify the desire to kill the innocent among the enemy, despite an unstated recognition that the innocent should not be intentionally killed. Americans do well to remember our justified outrage when our enemies make just such self-deluding claims.

Noncombatant Immunity and the Principle of Double Effect

The previous section offered two conclusions. First, noncombatants should be granted immunity in warfare. Second, though changing conditions of contemporary warfare warrant the rethinking of who is afforded this protection, the protection should not be practically eliminated by such a broad understanding of what constitutes a contribution to war-making that nearly every person among the enemy is a legitimate target. Based on these claims, it is further concluded here that noncombatant immunity should have been respected by the United States in 1945, and it should have been understood in a reasonable manner such that a significant portion of the population of Hiroshima, indeed a majority of the population, were understood as noncombatants.

Given these conclusions, it would seem that the atomic bombing of Hiroshima was a clear violation of *ius in bello*. But we are actually unable to make that determination just yet. Even those who respect noncombatant immunity, and respect it in a manner that recognizes that many people are actually noncombatants, may be justified in purposely engaging in war-making activities that tragically kill substantial numbers of noncombatants. How can this be? And is Hiroshima an example where this is the case? To determine these answers, we must define the traditional *doctrine of double effect* and then apply it to the dropping of the atomic bomb.

In every war noncombatants are killed. If "not killing noncombatants" were required to wage war justly, no war would be just. (Indeed, this is one reason why some insist that nonviolent resistance is the only virtuous response to aggression.) So what does noncombatant immunity mean if it does not mean "do not kill any noncombatants?" If you review every use of the term noncombatant immunity thus far in this book, you will see that it is defined as not intentionally killing noncombatants. Is it possible to kill people unintentionally? The answer to this question invokes the principle of double effect.

In moral theology there has always been a distinction between what effects we cause with our actions, and what we intend by our actions. Both are morally relevant, and we may even be praiseworthy or blameworthy for both, but these are not the same. Consider some examples to make this point. First, a silly example. My wife was often sick and tired when she was pregnant. Yet what sense would it make if someone said to me, "your wife intended to be sick"? This is not true. It is true that she intended to get pregnant. It is also true that she knew ahead of time that being pregnant generally entails being extra sick and tired at times. But though being sick and tired was a foreseen consequence of her becoming pregnant, it would not be accurate to say that she intended to be sick and tired. What's the difference being intending something, and choosing something with foreseen consequences? Recall from chapter 2 that intentions are action-guiding. They are why we do what we do, and thus give meaning to our actions. They not only explain our actions but also shape our very selves. Who we become is in large part determined by what we intend.

If my wife were to have gotten pregnant to become sick and tired, she would shape herself to be a very different sort of person (perhaps an attention-seeking person, or a masochistic person) than if she intended to have a child with her husband and to endure the side-effect consequences she knew were entailed with being pregnant, like getting sick. So it should be clear that what we intend and what we foresee as consequences are indeed importantly different. Consider some more morally relevant examples. You can break up with your boyfriend or girlfriend, even though you know it will hurt him or her, either because you believe that is truly best for you both, since the relationship has no future, or because you intend to hurt him or her. These are two very different acts. It is possible to intend to end a relationship knowing it will hurt the person, but still not intend to hurt the person.

As one final example, consider a professor who fails a student, even while knowing that the student will be kicked off her sports team due to the failure. Would it be accurate to say the professor intended to get the student kicked off her team? Perhaps, if that is what drove the professor to give the failing grade. That would be a very different sort of act than if the professor gave the grade because it is what the student truly deserved, even if the professor knew the athlete would be kicked off a team.

Sometimes our actions have effects that extend beyond those we seek in intending the action. We often call these side effects. They may be foreseen, but they are not intended because they are not what is driving the action. (If they were, they would be intentions.) Of course, one can be blameworthy for unintended side effects. For instance, if you drive under the influence of alcohol and—God forbid—kill someone with your car, you did not likely intend to kill someone. But you should have foreseen the effects of driving under the influence, and so you are still guilty of a crime. It is not murder, which is intentional, but it is manslaughter. In fact, our legal system, with its various ways of holding people responsible for acts (murder one, murder two, manslaughter, etc.) recognizes the varying ways we can intend acts or do acts with foreseen—or foreseeable—consequences.

How can we determine if we are morally justified in proceeding with an action that has both good and bad effects (hence double effect), such as becoming pregnant, or breaking up with a significant other, or driving under the influence? The doctrine of double effect is used in precisely such situations to determine whether an act with double effect is virtuous or not. In order for any such act to be virtuous, it must pass all three conditions of the doctrine of double effect:

1. The intention must be good.
2. The bad effect cannot be the means to the good effect.
3. Proportionality: The good gained must outweigh the evil effect.[16]

If you think this sounds arcane, or overly academic, I would suggest that this sort of reasoning actually happens all the time, even if we do not use this terminology or name it "double effect." It is precisely this sort of thinking that would explain why it could be virtuous for my wife to get pregnant, or a professor to give an athlete a grade that will get her kicked off her team, but why it is not virtuous to drive under the influence.

This sort of thinking is also done all the time, even in warfare. Assume the United States is in an armed conflict that is a just war. A bomb goes awry and strikes a hospital or school, killing dozens of innocent noncombatants. The American response is never, "too bad!" or "we think it is good to kill

16. Most formulations of the doctrine of double effect include one more criterion, and place it first. It is "the object of the act chosen must be good or indifferent." However, that condition is omitted here because it seems to beg the question. The doctrine of double effect helps us determine whether the object is good or indifferent. If we already know it is bad, there is no reason to proceed with considering whether or not to do it! Furthermore, I know of no action that fails solely this first (omitted) criterion of the doctrine of double effect without failing at least one of the other three. Hence, that omitted first criterion is at the very least superfluous.

noncombatants." Rather, the response is that it was not intended. The intention was to hit a military target. We cite statistics to show how the vast majority of our weapons did just that, showing that we really were not intending to kill civilians. Of course, any time a bomb is dropped the military knows there is a chance that unintended side effects will occur, namely, innocent people will be killed. This is often called "collateral damage." It is the bad effect which goes along with the good effect of waging a just war. It of course could be avoided. Not dropping a bomb would result in no civilian deaths (good effect), but it also would not use an available method to fight a just war, thus threatening the possibility of restoring justice (bad effect). What should one do when there are good and bad effects that follow, no matter what one chooses? That is precisely what the doctrine of double effect helps one ascertain.

As an example of using the principle, let us apply it to the case of bombing military targets in a city in a just war. In such cases there will most likely be collateral damage. Can one use such bombs in a virtuous manner? First, we must ask if there is a good intention. Since we are assuming a just war here, and assuming we can show through the results of other weapons that killing noncombatants is not the goal (intent) of the use of the weapon, then the first condition is met. The intention, or purpose driving the particular action, is destroying a military target. Second, are the bad effects the means, or path, to the good effects? The good effect intended here is the destruction of military targets. Not only is the death of noncombatants not the path to such success, but given the political costs of such deaths, it is clearly not desired in itself. The second condition is passed.

The third condition generally poses the biggest problem. Are the deaths of dozens of noncombatants acceptable losses, given the value of the objective sought in the particular strike? What if it were hundreds? Thousands? This depends on many factors. What is the objective targeted? How likely are civilian casualties? What alternative methods, or times, of attacking the target are available? The assumption in each of these questions is that one is trying to minimize the unintended deaths while maximizing the likelihood of achieving the objective. Presumably there are some objectives that warrant the risk of great loss. (The question of who risks the loss is often key.) And presumably there are some atrocities that are so awful one must never risk them. All of these are questions of proportionality.

Let us use the principle of double effect to evaluate the bombing at Hiroshima. The common argument in support of the bombing runs something like this. The atom bomb had good and bad effects. The good effect was an earlier end of the war and the resulting saving of hundreds of thousands of lives. The bad effect was the tragic deaths of 100,000 Japanese. These numbers make the bombing proportionate (criterion three). After all, if the bomb were not dropped, the 100,000 from Hiroshima would have been saved (good effect), but hundreds of thousands of other Japanese and Americans would have been killed (bad effect). Thus, reminiscent of the first section of the chapter, the atomic bombing of Hiroshima can be justified on the grounds of proportionality.

As for intention, the argument continues, it was not the civilian deaths (which were in fact terrible but proportionate side effects) that were intended, but rather the destruction of military installations in Hiroshima that was sought. That good intention, combined with the proportional reasoning justifying the bomb as ultimately saving lives, renders the act permissible under double effect.

This reasoning, however, is seriously deficient as it regards the first two conditions of double effect. What is the exact intention of dropping the atom bomb on Hiroshima? Note first that this standard justification is at least accurate in not naming "ending the war more quickly" as the intention behind dropping the bomb. That may indeed have been the ultimate goal. But recall an intention is a goal that drives a particular action. And winning the war does not suffice to describe this act. Some stated intention is needed to describe what particular act (in this case, dropping an atom bomb) one is doing to win the war. And so the above rationale claims the intended target was killing military personnel. As an example of this stated intention, see how one author, in response to a critic's claim that this was not truly the intent of the atom bomb, writes:

> I think Walzer's not right when he says: "Though there were soldiers in Hiroshima, they were not the targets of the attack (or else we would have attacked a military base)." But Hiroshima was a military base, the headquarters of the Japanese Second Army, and soldiers were the [intended] target of the attack: we dropped the bomb accurately on the corner of their parade ground and killed thousands of them.[17]

If this reasoning were accurate, that soldiers were the intended target, then the first criterion of double effect could be passed, and this act could be justified at least on that criterion.

This is actually a question of fact. What was the intent of dropping the atomic bomb? It is hard to deny that the intent was destroying the city and its inhabitants, the majority of whom were noncombatants. If the goal were really to destroy a military base, the United States already had the technology (short of an atomic bomb) to achieve such a goal. It would hardly justify the mammoth commitment of intellectual and financial resources, given to the Manhattan Project (as the development project to make the atom bomb was called). No, the purpose of an atom bomb is to destroy a city, and not discriminate between combatants and noncombatants. It may be the case that thousands of soldiers were killed. But if that were the true intention, then other methods would have

17. See Paul Fussell's portion of the essay "An Exchange of Views."

been employed to achieve it. The intention was clearly the destruction of a city, for the further purpose of demoralizing a people into surrender. If you hold a "just-war proportionality alone" position, this makes perfect sense. But if you think it immoral to intentionally kill civilians (as the previously cited author must think in order to justify the act in the way he did), then this act fails the first criterion of double effect with its bad intention.

It seems clear that the immediate intention of dropping the atomic bomb was to destroy the city and all its inhabitants, including noncombatants, to secure a further goal of ending war more quickly and saving lives. This leads us to the second criterion of double effect, and reveals why dropping the atom bomb also fails that condition. The terrible suffering inflicted on the civilian population was not a side effect in achieving the further goal of ending the war more quickly. It was the path, or means, to that goal. In other words, the war was only going to end more quickly if the bomb inflicted such suffering on the Japanese population that the nation's leadership decided it must stop the war. This is what happened. If targeting military personnel were truly the intent, not only could this have been achieved with already available means (as noted above), but it also would not have ended the war as quickly as the atom bomb did. The atom bomb only worked to end the war so quickly by killing so many civilians. And the doctrine of double effect's second criterion states that this must not be the case.

The third criterion of double effect, proportionality, was addressed in the first section of this chapter. I believe that the atom bomb could be justified if examined solely in terms of proportionality. This obviously reveals just how crucial the just war tenet of noncombatant immunity is for analyzing the morality of the atom bomb at Hiroshima. Note that the doctrine of double effect, according to which the use of the atom bomb was not justified, is unable to establish the grounds for noncombatant immunity. That was done in the second section of this chapter. In other words, if you do not think purposely killing innocent people is wrong, the application of the doctrine of double effect will look different than it does in this section. The doctrine of double effect is not a magic formula that immediately and convincingly determines the morality of any act. It is rather a reliable principle that helps people sort out what acts are justified when there are good and bad effects no matter what one does. In the case of the atomic bomb, it is only helpful in replying to those people, like the author quoted in this section, who at least implicitly recognize that intentionally killing the innocent is wrong.

Concluding Thoughts

We can now summarize the conclusions of the preceding questions. First, a standard feature of examining just-war issues is proportionality. In other words, the evil caused by either entering a war (*ius ad bellum*) or, as in the case of Hiroshima, waging a just war (*ius in bello*) must not outweigh the good caused by those acts. Since deliberations of proportionality by definition involve projecting things like casualties, alternative paths of action not taken, and different enemy responses, these deliberations are subject to criticism on these assumptions. This is seen in Hiroshima when opponents ask things like, "need there have been an invasion?" or "would an earlier offer of immunity to the emperor have made the bomb unnecessary?" These are reasonable questions. Nonetheless, the position is taken here that as horrible as it was, dropping the bomb on Hiroshima can be justified as proportional when we consider how quickly it ended the war and what we could have reasonably expected to happen otherwise.

For those supporters of just-war theory based on proportionality alone (as outlined in chapter 7), this is really the end of the moral analysis. The atomic bomb was justified. However, the analysis is not complete for those who support just war theory based on both proportionality and noncombatant immunity. For reasons explained in chapter 7, and seen again here, the U.S. bishops endorse only the latter just-war theory, and the consistent witness of the Christian tradition is that the intentional killing of innocent person (i.e., noncombatants) is gravely wrong and never justified. Unsurprisingly, given that Christians regard this as a natural law moral norm, many non-Christian thinkers also adopt this view of just war.[18] So further questions remain: were there noncombatants in Hiroshima in 1945? If so, were they intentionally killed when the bomb was dropped?

As for the first question, the argument is made here that it is essential, even given the challenges posed by modern warfare, to maintain a sharp distinction between combatants and noncombatants. The very notion of combatant is based on a determination of guilt, though in the case of war it is a corporate assessment of guilt. The way individuals are implicated in the corporate acts of a nation is by their actions, not their attitudes. Furthermore, determinations of whether an individual's actions can be considered part of a nation's aggression should not be established merely by some sort of causal relationship between someone's act and some ultimate assistance to a nation's military. If this were the case, surely such causal relationships could be established between military activities and almost anyone— medical staff, town bread-makers, grandparents writing letters, and even children who are simply growing up. This would destroy any conventional use of the term combatant. It suggests the person deliberating may be trying to justify precisely an act against noncombatants. Of course there are tough cases in determining noncombatant status. But if the tough cases are those just mentioned, surely there are no clear noncombatants.

18. See, for example, Michael Walzer, *Just and Unjust Wars* (New York: Basic Books, 1992).

Finally, granting that there are indeed a significant number of noncombatants in cities like Hiroshima, the last question to answer is whether or not the atomic bomb was an act of intentionally killing these noncombatants, or whether it may be justified by the principle of double effect. Granting that the criterion of proportionality is met, the dropping of the atomic bomb still fails the doctrine of double effect's second and even first conditions. The second condition is breached when we acknowledge that the ultimate goal of ending the war quickly was sought by the means or path of killing noncombatants. Even the first criterion is breached if we look at the nature of the weapon developed and the manner of its use, both of which clearly show the intention to be the destruction of a city without any discrimination between combatants and noncombatants.

It is with some trepidation that I come to this conclusion, realizing the ramifications of it for my countrymen, and even for the family reasons I mentioned in introductory section of this chapter. I should note that the primary goal here is not assigning blame, a task that would require the sort of analysis offered here and a consideration of things like duress and the formation of conscience (to determine, for example, whether there was invincible ignorance). Nor is the main goal here to determine whether dropping the bomb was some sort of cosmic or religious no-no, or artificially imposed restraint. The main goal here is to determine whether the act of using atomic bombs at the end of World War II best served the goal of restoring a just peace, or *ius*, which is certainly the goal of any just war. Despite the fact that precisely such a peace ensued, we rightly ask ourselves if that just peace was attained *by* dropping the atomic bomb, or whether the just peace ensued despite an act which may have ended armed conflict sooner, but which actually was not consonant with the generally otherwise just actions of the United States in a just war.

From this perspective, the rule of noncombatant immunity is not some artificial or externally imposed restriction on the actions of a corporate body (like a nation) seeking to restore and guard justice. It is a necessary requirement of those acts if the goal is truly to restore a just peace. Though it may seem like some odd rule about noncombatant immunity is the only thing keeping the atom bomb from being just, the claim here is that that noncombatant immunity is not some odd or random rule, but constitutive of pursuing *ius* justly (which is purposely redundant!). You may be able to stop a child's bad behavior by an occasional brutal beating, but we rightly wonder whether such beatings corrupt not only the peace that ensues, but also the very characters of both the parent and child. The same is true of intentionally killing those who are to be protected by the very peace we are trying to establish.

In World War II, and certainly before and since, the United States generally observes noncombatant immunity, and rightly so. This should make us question anomalies like the atom bomb at Hiroshima (and obliteration bombing in Germany) even more. We should also beware the dire ramifications of deciding that noncombatant status is to be observed, except in drastic situations when one's very way of life is threatened, a possible justification for events like the atom bomb.[19] Some today perceive precisely such a threat to their people, and respond to that perceived injustice by targeting innocent persons to kill. The United States suffered dearly at the hands of such people recently. What is most blatantly unjust about terrorism is the targeting of civilians, an *ius in bello* issue. We may also claim that the overall cause of these enemies is unjust, and it may well be. But surely the justice of their cause is further corrupted, if not eliminated, by intentionally killing innocents. And surely peoples of all nations would be better off if what governed their responses to perceived injustices were not only the conditions of *ius ad bellum* (which may indeed be contested), but also the conditions of *ius in bello,* including noncombatant immunity. The United States would do well to consider if the peace it pursues is one where noncombatant immunity can be suspended at times, and if we as a nation are willing to suffer at the hands of others who would similarly suspend this crucial portion of just-war theory.

Of course, a commitment to stand fast in observance of rules such as noncombatant immunity may entail more suffering before right relations are reestablished by means which are not antithetical to that peace. Living virtuously, even from a morality-of-happiness perspective, can entail great cost and suffering in our present condition. Acting in a manner constitutive of right relations renders one vulnerable to others who do not observe the same rules. Nowhere is this more evident than in questions of warfare, where the immediate cost of observing rules such as noncombatant immunity may imperil the lives of soldiers charged with defending the common good. Yet the difficulties posed by living virtuously are not limited to warfare. In fact, they are present in everyday life. And so it is fitting to turn now to the last of the cardinal virtues, fortitude, which deals precisely with facing difficulties and enduring suffering well.

Study Questions

1. According to the discussion of the situation in the summer of 1945, would you agree with this chapter's claim that dropping the bomb was a proportionate use of force? Why? What conditions or factors do you think most morally relevant?

2. Why are there noncombatants in war? On what basis is noncombatant immunity determined?

19. For more on this position, research John Rawls's extreme-crisis exception. His discussion of it in the context of Hiroshima can be found in "Fifty Years After Hiroshima," in his *Collected Papers*, ed. Samuel Freeman (Cambridge, MA: Harvard University Press, 1999) 565–72.

3. Define the principle of double effect and give its conditions. Use it on an easy case to show how it works.
4. Does the bombing at Hiroshima pass or fail the doctrine of double effect? Explain your answer.

Terms to Know

doctrine of double effect (including its conditions), noncombatant immunity, proportionality

Questions for Further Reflection

1. Based on your position, how would you defeat or strengthen the argument of the first section?
2. How would you determine who counts as a noncombatant? Give some tough cases and say whether the person would be a legitimate target or not.
3. Do you think it is ever justifiable to intentionally kill noncombatants? Why or why not?
4. What difference, if any, is there between the terms enemy and noncombatant?

Further Reading

The most influential writing on this chapter is easily John Ford's essay cited above, "The Morality of Obliteration Bombing." Though written in 1944, and thus obviously not addressing the atom bomb, it is a model of clear moral analysis, and also addresses an issue that is very closely related to the dropping of the atomic bomb. It rewards close reading.

The literature on World War II in general, the development of the bomb, and the delivery and aftermath of the bomb is literally immense. The most formative pieces on this chapter include the exchange between Paul Fussell and Michael Walzer in the collection of essays entitled *Thank God for the Atomic Bomb and Other Essays*, and the exchange between Charles Landesman and Douglas Lackey in the 2003 volume of *Philosophical Forum*.

9

THE VIRTUE OF FORTITUDE
AND THE UNITY OF THE VIRTUES

Life is hard. There is an important insight in this simple truism. What difficulties you face, how big they are, and how well you face them all vary. But it is a universal feature of human life that you will face difficulty. Facing difficulty is an innerworldly activity that is encountered by all persons of whatever time period or culture. Therefore, the ability to face difficulties well is essential to a good life. The cardinal virtue fortitude is, most simply put, a habit that enables you to face difficulties well.

The purpose of this chapter is to define and explain the cardinal virtue of fortitude. Most people have a ready grasp of the basic meaning of this virtue. The first section will explore in more detail the different components, assumptions, and characteristics of this virtue. In order to do so it will focus on more obvious, extraordinary examples of fortitude, such as laying down one's life. But then the second section of this chapter applies the lessons of the first section to everyday occasions for fortitude. It will become clear that this virtue is not simply for extraordinary occasions, but rather is needed on a daily basis. It will also become clear how this virtue is needed for the exercise of the other cardinal virtues, a claim we ran across once already, with prudence. Thus the second section concludes with a brief explanation of a classical claim in morality called the unity of the virtues, which is a fitting way to conclude the last chapter in this book's first half on the cardinal virtues.

Fortitude: A Close Analysis

This section explores in depth the cardinal virtue fortitude. Fortitude is synonymous with bravery and courage. *Fortitude* is most basically defined as the virtue that enables one to face obstacles or difficulties well. The brave person is not swayed by trials and tribulations from her pursuit or grasp of goodness. So fortitude may also be defined as the ability to suffer hardship well, whether the hardship is bodily or otherwise. Any time you have called someone brave, or tried yourself to be more courageous, you have been dealing with the virtue fortitude. The terms fortitude, bravery, and courage (and their adjective forms) will be used interchangeably in this chapter.

Though you certainly have a basic grasp of what fortitude is, the virtue is more complex than you might expect, and rewards deeper inquiry. This first section will explore several interesting facets of this cardinal virtue, including different models of fortitude, assumptions implicit in praising fortitude, its essential parts, and its relationship to suffering, fear, prudence, and justice.

Rival Models of Fortitude

As will be explored in more depth in the second section of this chapter, there are countless occasions for fortitude in everyday life. But in order to more easily examine the characteristics, acts, and assumptions of fortitude, the focus in this first section will be on the model act, or best example, of fortitude. What is that model act? Since fortitude is the ability to face difficulties, or suffer hardship, well, and since death is the ultimate human hardship, the willingness to lay down one's life in pursuit of the good has always been seen as the model act of fortitude. For the Greeks and Romans, the ultimate act of fortitude was the willingness to lay down one's life on the battlefield in service to the *polis* or republic. What made this the exemplary act of fortitude was both the magnitude of the hardship suffered (death), and the magnitude of the good that the hardship is suffered for, namely, the common good of one's country. The greater the hardship and the greater the cause, the greater the act of fortitude. So, for these ancient peoples the willingness to suffer death for one's countrymen was the ultimate act of fortitude.

In the Christian tradition, fortitude is praised as highly as in non-Christian cultures. But the Christian understanding of the model of fortitude is different due to the different Christian view of what is most important in life. Though Christians can surely praise the bravery of the soldier in a just war, for Christians it is the martyr, not the soldier on the battlefield, who is the model of fortitude. A *martyr* is someone who is killed for his faith. The classic examples of Christian martyrs are those in the early church (St. Peter, St. Paul, St. Perpetua, St. Felicity, and thousands of others) who were killed for their faith. The martyr, like the soldier, is willing to make the ultimate sacrifice, namely, her life. Yet the cause for which the martyr lays down her life is God, who is more excellent than one's country. Such a willingness to die for the sake of the ultimate truth is seen even in Socrates, who lays down his life in adherence to the truth, even in defiance of the countrymen.[1] Here we have a foretaste of the Christian recognition of martyrdom over even death on a battlefield as exemplary of fortitude. But of course Christian martyrs do not lay down their lives for a philosophical notion of truth, but rather for the personal God who became flesh in Jesus Christ, with whom the martyr is united in his suffering. This discussion of Christian fortitude anticipates the second half of this book, which focuses not only on the distinctively Christian theological virtues, but also the transformation of even the cardinal virtues in light of Christian faith.[2] For now it suffices to note that in praising fortitude one must attend both to the hardship faced and to the cause for which one faces it.

Implicit Assumptions in Praising Fortitude

Before examining further the causes for which one is brave, it is worth noting two assumptions that we make when praising fortitude. First, the brave person is by definition vulnerable. He has something to lose. If this were not the case, there would be no difficulty to face, and no possibility of hardship. To consider an example from the movies, Superman is not properly called brave. Given that bullets bounce off him and he is indestructible to villains, we may praise Superman's pursuit of justice, but not his fortitude. I was recently reminded by a student that even Superman is vulnerable in the presence of kryptonite, and so perhaps we can call him brave. Fair enough. Nonetheless, the point should be clear that for us non-super people, it is our vulnerability that makes fortitude even a possibility.

Second, the brave person assumes that what she does matters. In other words, if the brave person thought that no matter what she did, it would all turn out fine in the end, then presumably she would not place herself in harm's way, or take a stand that would involve personal cost. Why bother if it ultimately does not matter in the end?

Therefore when we praise someone as brave we are assuming two things. First, the brave person is vulnerable because he can suffer. Second, the good that the brave person seeks or maintains is not guaranteed or assured. It requires sacrifice to be reached or maintained. These two presuppositions are quite evident in the life of Martin Luther King Jr., whose life is relatively well known among us today. King is an outstanding modern example of fortitude, so his life will be used repeatedly as an example of fortitude in this chapter.

---

1. For more on non-Christian examples of laying down one's life in service to the truth, see John Paul II's *Veritatis Splendor* (Encyclical Letter, 1993), 94.

2. This argument about the transformation of the cardinal virtues in light of faith is made extensively in chapter 16.

King was clearly vulnerable. He and his followers suffered taunts, jeers, and broader threats to their reputations. They endured jail sentences and physical abuse, even at the hands of authorities. King obviously made the ultimate sacrifice in his pursuit of social justice when he was killed for his work. These hardships of varying kinds and degrees make it clear that King was vulnerable. Those who have read King's work also know that he was quite aware of what he was suffering, and even of the possibility of his own death. Yet he was willing to endure these hardships due to the importance of his cause, and his belief that the cause would not necessarily "win out" without such sacrifice. If King thought racial equality would certainly be achieved in this nation no matter what, then his actions would be foolish. Thus his actions reveal his belief that his cause, while important and true, would not necessarily win out without sacrifice by people committed to the cause.

Fortitude: Praising Suffering?

Though the Western tradition has been consistent in its praise of people who are willing to lay down their lives, what is being praised here is not injury, hardship, or suffering in itself. As Augustine once said, it is "not the injury, but the cause, that makes martyrs."[3] The point, which is relevant for all brave people, is that suffering is not good in itself. The truly brave person appreciates the goodness of whatever she is willing to sacrifice, be it her reputation, her health, or even her life. These goods are not dismissed casually. Yet the brave person is willing to forfeit these goods, and thus suffer harm, only for the sake of pursuing or guarding something even greater.

Therefore, what exactly is being praised in the courageous is his dogged pursuit and grasp of the most important goods in life (faith, social justice, fellow citizens, etc.), even in the face of losing important but lesser goods (such as one's health, reputation, or even life). It is not the suffering itself that is praised. In fact, if we learned that a brave person actually escaped unharmed, we would not cease to praise his fortitude, and we would even be relieved that he did not suffer injury. It may seem that we more commonly do praise those who actually have suffered and/or died, but this is likely due to the fact that fortitude is most obvious in these people, since the harm they suffered for the sake of their goal is most obvious. It is possible to wonder if someone who did not actually suffer great loss would have been willing to do so had that opportunity arose. Of course, they may indeed have been so willing. But there is no doubt that those who do suffer and/or die are so willing. The point here is that what is praised in the brave is not their loss but their willingness to suffer hardship in seeking or guarding some important good;

3. See St. Augustine's *Enarrationes in Psalmos* 34,13, cited in Josef Pieper, *The Four Cardinal Virtues* (Notre Dame, IN: University of Notre Dame Press, 1966), 125.

and this is true even though we may in fact more often praise those who do end up suffering.

For precisely this reason—that it is not suffering itself that is praised when we acknowledge the brave—the virtuous person does not seek to lay down her life. She is willing to lay down her life, but it is not what she seeks. If the primary goal, or intention, were to lay down her life, this would be a careless disrespect for life's preciousness. But for the martyr or soldier, the primary goal is to seek or protect something even more precious that warrants being willing to lay down her life, should that occasion arise. One twentieth-century thinker tells the powerful story of how early church leaders positively forbid Christians to report themselves to the Roman authorities to be martyred.[4] Why not, if becoming a martyr is the greatest act of fortitude? Because martyrdom was never to be sought, only endured if thrust upon one. In fact, saints such as Ambrose and Augustine taught that should someone seek martyrdom (presumably to glorify themselves as heroic and faithful—see the importance of intention yet again!), then the Lord who provides the gift of strength for those who endure martyrdom would actually withdraw that gift of strength, presumably leading the would-be martyr to wither.

The Necessity of Prudence and Justice for Fortitude

This treatment of fortitude has repeatedly insisted that the brave person has an accurate grasp of the relative importance of different goods in life (faith, country, health, reputation, etc.). This enables him to judge rightly when lesser goods are to be sacrificed for greater goods. For this reason, the virtue of prudence is essential for the courageous person. Recall that the virtue of prudence enables one to see things rightly so as to act well, and that one of its functions is to enable one to grasp rightly the relative importance of different things in one's life. The brave person therefore needs prudence to be able to accurately assess what goods are more or less important.

Consider an obvious (and tragically true-to-life) example to illustrate the necessity of prudence. Two teenage boys are driving their respective automobiles toward each other at high speed, playing a game of chicken. If fortitude were simply the willingness to lay down one's life, this would be a fine example of courage. But, of course, most people would see this as a stupid and potentially tragic game. There are no true goods at stake here that justify such a dangerous activity. Of course, the young men might see things differently, judging either that their reputation among friends and their bravado are indeed quite important, or that they won't really lose their lives. Both would be errors of judgment, and examples of imprudence. Even when a genuine good is at stake, a person must be prudent to exercise true fortitude. The soldier who rashly

4. Ibid., 118–19.

storms a machine gun nest over hundreds of yards of open ground, with no chance to overcome the enemy, may fight for an important cause and be well-intentioned. But prudence is needed to know when and how to fight, as well as what is truly worth fighting for.

The notion of what is truly worth fighting for raises a hotly contested issue: the relationship between fortitude and justice. Ambrose famously said, "Fortitude without justice is a lever of evil."[5] Fortitude has traditionally only been considered true fortitude when it is just. In other words, those who pursue injustice simply cannot be truly brave, even though they are willing to suffer hardship for their cause. For example, a thief may risk life or limb while committing crime. But though this is a willingness to suffer while facing difficulties, it is not true fortitude, since it is for the sake of injustice.

This is a challenging claim because it means someone must not only think what they are willing to suffer for is truly good, but it must actually be truly good in order for the person to be rightly called brave. Given contemporary world events, the question can be worded this way: can a suicide bomber who lays down his life killing civilians at a bus stop, or by destroying a building, be called "brave?" Clearly there is a willingness to lay down one's life. But is this enough? Some people may try to get around this difficult question by answering that as long as the person sincerely believes he is pursuing a truly just cause through truly just means, the person may then be called just. Here our analysis of conscience from chapter 5 helps. This person is acting on what we would call an erroneous conscience. He really believes he is acting rightly, but he is not. Let us even say that the person is invincibly ignorant. In other words, he could not have known better, and so he is not blameworthy for his ignorance. But is he truly brave?

It may be tempting to say he is. And clearly there are some similarities to true bravery here. Most obviously, there is a willingness to sacrifice, and even a willingness to do so in what is understood, wrongly, to be a just manner. But recall from above what is actually being praised in recognizing fortitude. It is not the suffering, or even willingness to suffer, but rather that for which one is willing to suffer. The unjust person may be deluded and may even be invincibly ignorant. But to praise him would necessarily mean praising that for which he acts and the way in which he does it. And given the case laid out here, such praising we must not do.

Of course, this means that many debates over the possibility of fortitude in suicide bombers, kamikaze pilots, and American soldiers in Iraq will really be debates over whether those conflicts are just, a topic explored in the previous and following chapters. That is a separate debate. The claim here is simply that a willingness to lay down one's life, even in a selfless manner, does not necessarily constitute fortitude, since fortitude relies on justice to truly be

5. Ibid., 125.

a virtue. This claim points us to the concluding lines of this chapter on the unity of the virtues.

Fortitude and Fear

Before proceeding to examine how fortitude is needed in everyday life, two further points on this virtue are necessary. First, does the brave person experience fear? Recall the discussion in chapter 4 on the nature of emotions, and how they are judgments of a certain sort. It other words, their very arousal indicates that a person perceives, often unconsciously, that a certain state of affairs exists around him. For instance, experiencing fear means something. It means the fearful person perceives himself in a situation where he is threatened, experiences certain associated bodily changes (racing heartbeat, sweaty palms, etc.), and is inclined to flee the perceived threat. Should a brave person experience this emotion of fear?

Given the above claims about the vulnerability of the brave person, and the genuine goodness of what may be lost, it is completely reasonable for a brave person to experience fear. Further still, if a person who is truly in a situation where he is threatened does not experience fear, it would indicate a failure to accurately perceive the situation and thus a failure of prudently seeing things rightly. Aquinas calls such a person foolhardy, and claims this foolhardiness is a vice actually opposed to fortitude. *Foolhardiness* looks like fortitude because one is willing to continue to pursue some good even in the face of difficulty. But the problem here is that this is done without an adequate realization of the danger present, or an adequate appreciation for the value of the goods (health, life, reputation, etc.) that may be lost. The brave person experiences fear precisely because he understands the value of what is threatened, and the reality of the danger at hand.

Of course, saying the brave person experiences fear does not mean he flees in cowardice. The emotion of fear entails an inclination to flee. But that inclination can be resisted, and indeed it should be if a greater good is at risk that is worth fighting for. The brave person may, and indeed should, experience fear. But he does not act on that fear and flee. He overcomes the fear so as to face the difficulties at hand, being willing to suffer in doing so. Not so with the coward. *Cowardice* is another vice opposed to fortitude. Like the brave person (and unlike the foolhardy person), the coward does realize the value of what may be lost, and the magnitude of the present danger. But unlike the brave person the coward does not stand fast and endure in the face of the threat. The coward cuts and runs in the face of difficulty.

Consider Martin Luther King Jr. to better understand the place of fear in the brave person's life. Was King ever scared? I would submit that if he never experienced fear for his life, then he was a less virtuous person. King knew his life was in danger; he knew he and his family had received bomb threats;

and he knew that he and his followers would suffer in their pursuit of justice. If that impending suffering did not arouse fear, then King would not have accurately assessed his situation, and the value of his life. He would have been foolhardy, and not brave. Of course, given his prudence in other areas of life, I can only assume he did indeed accurately assess both the threat and the value of what was threatened. If so, he did indeed experience fear, but unlike the coward he stood fast in pursuit of an even greater good. King's life provides a fine example of how virtue lies in the mean: neither foolhardiness, nor cowardice, but rather fortitude.

The Two Main Parts of Fortitude

One last consideration for this section concerns the odd claim of Aquinas that there are two main parts of being courageous, of having the virtue fortitude. Though the brave person may exhibit only one of these at a time, she must be willing and able to do both to be truly brave. Explaining these will help us further understand fortitude, and lead us into the next section on its application to more everyday examples.

One of the two parts of fortitude is *attack*, the part of fortitude in which the difficulty at hand is faced well by seeking to eliminate or remove it. The difficulty at hand poses a hardship by threatening certain goods a person has or is seeking. The person with fortitude acts to remove that threat. This resonates with our common vision of fortitude as something a soldier has. The brave person recognizes a threat to something precious, such as one's nation and countrymen. She thus fights that threat to protect what is threatened. The soldier clearly does this with an invading enemy. Consider also the firefighter entering a burning building. She sees the threat to life and, if she is truly brave, experiences fear. But she also refuses to let that fear debilitate her as she enters the building to fight off the fire and eliminate the threat to people's lives. These are classic examples of attack.[6]

The other part of fortitude is *endurance*. Aquinas describes endurance as "standing immovably in the midst of dangers."[7] Endurance is hanging in there in the face of hardship. It is not weak passivity. To the contrary, it is a resilient clutching to what is precious even when it is threatened and one is suffering. It is truly a part of fortitude because it is prudently and justly facing a difficulty well. On certain occasions it is either impossible or imprudent to

6. Note there is an important place for prudence here. If lives are threatened, or the fire may spread to devour a neighborhood, entering the building and putting her life on the line may well be brave. But if the fire were in an isolated empty building that was already damaged beyond repair, entering the building and risking her life to extinguish the flames would be imprudent and thus foolhardy. Better to let it burn itself out.

7. Thomas Aquinas, *Summa Theologiae*, English Dominican trans. (New York: Benziger, 1948), II–II 123,6.

attack the cause of difficulty, and so one simply endures without letting one's spirit be broken. An obvious example of endurance would be the prisoner of war who maintains resolve despite captivity and abuse.

Endurance seems less obviously a part of fortitude to us than attack. But Aquinas actually claims that endurance, not attack, is the primary part of fortitude, mainly because it is more difficult than attack. He offers three reasons for this claim. First, attack implies that one has at least the possibility of overcoming the difficulty, while endurance implies a stronger threat that can only be endured. Second, one who endures already experiences the difficulty directly, whereas one who attacks may be acting to prevent suffering to come. Finally, endurance implies greater duration of time, whereas attack may consist of punctuated actions. We could add that when the time and possibility of attack are gone, it is still possible to endure. For all these reasons, endurance is the primary of the two main parts of fortitude.

The following example of both attack and endurance should help further illuminate both parts, demonstrate the primacy of endurance, and lead us into the final section of the chapter on fortitude in everyday life. Consider a patient diagnosed with life-threatening cancer. This is clearly an occasion for fortitude, since he faces a great difficulty and has the opportunity to suffer this hardship well or poorly. He is vulnerable and has something to lose. His health and chance of survival depend in no small part on how he will respond to his diagnosis, so how he acts does indeed matter. He is quite afraid, but does not let it debilitate him. With the help of others, he prudently understands his situation accurately and makes good decisions.

The patient begins by learning all about his disease in order to fight it as best he can. This is a classic example of attack. The cancer threatens his life and he seeks to eliminate that threat. He educates himself, exercises, eats well, and receives treatment. Of course, at moments when he is not reading, exercising, or seeing doctors he must endure. Though the ultimate injury, death, may be avoidable, in a very real sense suffering is already present. In the quiet moments especially, he must endure and not let his spirit be crushed. Thus bravery in this situation requires acts of both attack and endurance.

Eventually, however, it may become clear that though he has fought the good fight, the cancer has significantly advanced to the terminal stage and will soon take his life. Further treatment will no longer help. The time for attack has passed. And yet endurance remains. We sometimes speak of the terminally ill being brave in their facing of death, and this seems odd given the more militant models of fortitude that are forefront on our minds. But the story of this patient perfectly reveals how fortitude is not only for soldiers, and why Aquinas is correct that endurance is the primary part of fortitude. The patient bravely faces his impending death. Perhaps there is strengthening of family bonds or needed reconciliation. There may be spiritual and/or sacramental preparation. There is certainly a refusal to let the impending enemy of death destroy what goods in life there are still available. Eventually the person passes from this life having exemplified fortitude to the end.

A helpful way to end this section on fortitude (and especially its two parts) is with the famous Serenity Prayer of Alcoholics Anonymous, both because it is so widely known from speaking to our experience, and because it perfectly exemplifies points made here, such as fortitude's need for prudence and its two parts. The prayer is:

> God, grant me
> The serenity to accept the things I cannot change,
> Courage to change the things I can, and
> Wisdom to know the difference.

It is fitting that this prayer is treated under the virtue fortitude, since the condition of having alcoholism is certainly a hardship. It is also fitting that we seek God's help—"God, grant me . . ."—on such occasions (but that is a topic for the second half of this book). Look carefully at what is asked here, and with some minor changes in terminology you will see summarized some key points of this section. The serenity to accept the things I cannot change is the same as endurance. There are certain hardships in the alcoholic's life (and in all our lives) that cannot be eliminated or removed. Thus we must endure them. Serenity is stability in the face of hardship, which keeps one's spirit from being crushed. It is endurance, the primary act of fortitude that is fittingly placed at the start of this prayer.

The prayer then asks for "courage to change the things I can [change]." The prayer employs the term courage (synonymous with fortitude) for effecting change, and this is certainly a crucial part of fortitude. It is one of the two parts: attack. In asking to change what can be changed, presumably to remove the hardship at hand, the person is asking for assistance in attack. Finally, the prayer asks for the "wisdom to know the difference." We might add "practical" to wisdom, and then clearly see that the person praying is asking for prudence. He is asking for the help to see things clearly, so as to be able to act rightly. He wants to accurately differentiate what can be changed so as to act accordingly with attack, and what cannot be changed so as to act accordingly with endurance. Without prudence a person cannot have fortitude, and thus the prayer fittingly ends with a plea for this charioteer of the virtues. In sum, the Serenity Prayer is a prayer for fortitude, which illuminates both parts of fortitude and the necessity of prudence for this virtue.

Everyday Fortitude and the Unity of the Virtues

The examples of the cancer patient and the alcoholic extend our notion of fortitude beyond the martyr's execution site or the soldier's battlefield.

Nonetheless, the difficulties faced here are still enormous. In most cases, the hardship faced is death itself. As noted at the start of the chapter, the ability to face death well is indeed the model act of fortitude. But there are far more ordinary and everyday occasions for fortitude. They are worth reflecting on here, lest one think that fortitude is only for extraordinary moments, and only a rare possibility in life.

A Broader Understanding of Fortitude

The difficulties and hardships that are faced in life are many, and can be minor as well as major. Consider one of the classic sub-virtues of fortitude, *patience*. Aquinas claims the patient person does not become overcome with sorrow while facing difficulties. One modern moralist elaborates on this and says that "to be patient means to preserve cheerfulness and serenity of mind in spite of injuries that result from the realization of the good."[8] Patience is a type of endurance.[9] Patience is evident in even the littlest things in life, like waiting in line at the store. While pursuing the simple good of obtaining needed things for her family, a mother may face difficulties in having that goal hindered by a long line, or a less-than-competent salesperson. The patient person bears this in stride, not letting her cheerfulness and serenity of mind be overcome by, for instance, making rude comments, becoming irritable, or doing something rash. This is obviously a minute example of facing difficulties well. But the patient person is prudent enough to see that the difficulty at hand is miniscule, and is not troubled inordinately. The impatient person, on the other hand, may become irritable, try to cut in line, or lash out at those around him. He has not faced this difficulty well.

We have now gone from the extraordinary to the most ordinary and everyday. There are many occasions for fortitude in between, where the difficulty faced is far more serious than having to wait a few extra minutes in line, but still not be life-threatening. During exams a student may face great difficulty and stress. But the brave student will step up and prudently study hard (attack), while also not being overcome by the stress (endurance). A lack of fortitude could be seen in this situation in countless ways: simply staying in bed to avoid the stress, unjustly stealing notes to make studying easily, imprudently trying to re-read everything to prepare for the exam, and so on. Some anxiety or fear will indeed be felt by the courageous student in exam period, but he will not be overcome by it.

8. Pieper, *The Four Cardinal Virtues,* 129.
9. Pieper notes (129–30) that while patience is important, it is only a sub-virtue of fortitude, since fortitude includes both endurance and attack. And while the brave person is always patient when need be, the patient person may or may not be virtuous in knowing how and when to attack.

Numerous other difficulties come to mind that can be faced well or poorly. Asking a question in class can be an occasion for fortitude, if one fears looking silly. It may take bravery to talk to a professor about a contested grade. A job search is a stressful process that poses difficulties to be faced well. An athlete in training must be willing to endure hardship to excel in a sport. Being a virtuous family member surely calls for fortitude, since family life is difficult at times. One needs patience to endure another's annoying characteristics or even intentionally harmful acts. Endurance is needed, as no family is perfect, but attack is needed too, since at times disagreements must be addressed head-on, and people must be lovingly confronted with their harmful acts.

Confronting friends can be a particularly difficult challenge that calls for courage. Telling someone they drank too much to drive is difficult, but also prudent and just. Standing up for someone in the face of peer pressure can be very brave, particularly in the teenage years. Dating relationships, too, are ripe with occasions for fortitude. Being faithful, attentive, and lending an ear may all be experienced as difficult at times, but are all needed for a relationship to grow. On the other hand, at times a relationship may have run its course, and the brave thing to do would be to end it, even though it is difficult and may seem easier to just keep the *status quo*.

Basically any situation where one experiences difficulty is an occasion for fortitude. One broad arena for this virtue should be mentioned last: fortitude is needed for progress in the virtuous life. Recall the discussion of habits and developing virtuous desires in chapters 3 and 4. When one has a bad habit, acting badly feels natural. A vice, rather than a virtue, has become second nature to the person. Performing good acts for good reasons, to overcome a vice and develop a virtue, is difficult. But trying to remove sources of temptation so as to act positively (attack), and standing fast even when one is tempted to do otherwise (endurance), are occasions to display fortitude. Development in the virtuous life would be impossible without fortitude. In fact, Theresa of Avila is reported to have said "an imperfect human being needs more fortitude to pursue the way of perfection than suddenly to become a martyr."[10] Here we are reminded again of Aquinas's claim that endurance is the primary act of fortitude. In sum, fortitude is a crucial part of living a virtuous life, even for those of us who will never be called to literally lay down our lives in service to our nations or to our faith.

The Unity of the Virtues

Repeatedly throughout this chapter the connection has been made between fortitude and some other cardinal virtue , a connection that works both ways, so to speak. On the one hand, true fortitude requires the presence of the other

10. Ibid., 137.

cardinal virtues. We noted earlier how prudence and justice are required. The same may be said of temperance. If one is immoderately attracted to certain sensible goods, it will be impossible to face difficulties well, since those difficulties will include the sacrifice of those very sensible pleasures one is too attached to.

On the other hand, fortitude is needed in order to fully possess the other three cardinal virtues. This point was just made with regard to temperance. Becoming free of an overreliance on sensible pleasures will entail refusing to partake in those pleasures, and that is difficult. Fortitude enables us to stick with it. In this chapter we repeatedly referred to Martin Luther King, Jr., and his fortitude in pursuing racial equality. If he was not brave, he would not have been able to be so just. This is true of every occasion for justice in our lives, even in cases far less extreme than King's. Finally, we certainly need fortitude to be prudent. That may sound odd. But recall that seeing things rightly in order to act well entails such things as remembering things accurately, and being docile in listening to mentors. To the extent that these are difficult (and no one likes hearing what they do not want to hear even if it is—or especially if it is!—true), fortitude is necessary.

Therefore it should be clear that in order to have one of the four cardinal virtues fully, one must have the other three as well. The virtues are organically interconnected. This basic claim is common throughout the Western moral tradition, in Christian and non-Christian thinkers alike. It is called the *unity of the virtues*. The claim is not that there really is only one virtue. The claim is that there is such interconnectedness among the four cardinal virtues that full possession of any one cardinal virtue requires possession of the others.[11]

Concluding Thoughts

Fortitude is a virtue that seems easy to grasp once we realize it is the same as bravery and courage. Yet a closer analysis of its parts, its assumptions, its model acts, and its relationship to other virtues reveals what a rich cardinal virtue this is. It also reveals how necessary it is for ordinary life, as well as extraordinary situations. Because life is difficult, fortitude essential for living a good life. To the extent that this chapter helps you better understand the nature of fortitude, it is hoped you will be better able to live it out.

Life in general is hard, but the good life, which is the moral life, can be particularly hard at times. Pope John Paul II's encyclical on moral theology, *Veritatis Splendor*, with its concluding reflection on martyrdom, demonstrates the crucial importance of fortitude for living the virtuous life. He claims that

---

11. This seemingly straightforward claim is actually articulated in importantly different ways throughout the Western tradition. For a helpful overviews of different ways it is expressed in classical ethical thought, see Julia Annas's *Morality of Happiness* (New York: Oxford University Press, 1995), 66–84.

the martyr (a term derived for the Greek word for "witness") witnesses to the truth by refusing to participate in evil despite the genuine goodness of what may be lost by (life, health, etc.), and the suffering entailed in, such witness. Though this is most obvious in the example of those who literally lay down their lives, John Paul recognizes few are called to this. Yet there are countless little deaths (which do not feel so little when experienced) by people who are steadfast in the virtuous life, even in the most ordinary circumstances.[12] By giving such witness, virtuous people proclaim more loudly than words the beauty of the good life. They know and live the truth, and it sets them free.

Study Questions

1. Define fortitude. What are model acts of fortitude, and what does a people's model of fortitude reveal about what they hold most important?
2. Does the Christian martyr want to die? Why or why not? Why is the brave person willing to suffer?
3. Why is it essential that fortitude be connected to prudence and justice?
4. Are the brave ones fearless? Why or why not?
5. What are the two basic parts of fortitude? Which is the primary one and why?
6. What does patience have to do with fortitude?
7. Give three examples from everyday life that require fortitude, and say how each illustrates some claim about fortitude made in the first section of the chapter.
8. Explain what is meant by the unity of the virtues. Give an example of this claim.

Terms to Know

fortitude, martyr, foolhardiness, cowardice, attack, endurance, unity of the virtues

Questions for Further Reflection

1. What is at stake in the debate over whether people who are willing to lay down their lives for an unjust cause that they think is just are truly brave? Where do you stand on that question?

12. In ways discussed in the second half of this book, Christianity has always understood all these deaths as connected to the cross of Jesus Christ.

2. According to chapter 4, we can habituate our emotional responses. So if a person was fully virtuous, why can't the person get to the point of feeling no fear on occasions when it is indeed virtuous to fight. In other words, is the presence of fear a sign that one is not fully brave or virtuous?

3. The classical thesis of the unity of the virtues seems circular. It seems one must have every other virtue in order to fully have a particular cardinal virtue. But those other ones cannot be fully possessed unless the virtue one seeks is fully had! Does this mean there is no true unity of the virtues? If so, what of the seeming reliance of each virtue on the others? If not, then how to avoid this circularity?

4. Having read this chapter on fortitude, how might it apply to the discussions of war and peace in the previous two chapters. Can a nonviolent resister be brave? How? How can a just-war advocate be brave, with regard to both attack and endurance?

Further Reading

In his *Summa Theologiae* II–II 123–40, Aquinas devotes a treatise to the virtue of fortitude. Josef Pieper's *The Four Cardinal Virtues* is an outstanding explication of Aquinas and was crucial for this chapter. R. E. Houser's chapter on courage in Stephen Pope's (ed.) *Ethics of Aquinas* is also a helpful analysis of fortitude. For a superb example of relating Thomistic thought on fortitude to the social sciences in the context of examining a contemporary issue, see Craig Stephen Titus's *Resilience and the Virtue of Fortitude*. Finally, see also the concluding section of John Paul II's *Veritatis Splendor* on martyrdom, along with his *Salvifici Dolores* on human suffering.

10

A TRANSITION

Actions, Practices, and Big-Picture Beliefs
about the Way Things Are

It may seem odd at this point to call this book one of moral theology. After all, there has been little discussion so far of God, Jesus Christ, the church, and other central theological topics. Chapter 1 explored whether religious people are more likely to hold a morality of obligation or happiness. Chapter 3 noted the existence of the theological virtues, and even hinted, at the end, that the specific actions constitutive of cardinal virtues may be shaped by religious commitments. There was also some discussion in chapters 7 and 9 of the ways that Christians understand justice and fortitude differently from others. But it is safe to say that so far the majority of this book has not been focused on how people of a particular religious tradition like Christianity live out the virtues. Having completed so much analysis of the cardinal virtues, it may seem as if religious beliefs are irrelevant to how one lives out the cardinal virtues. Leaving that impression on the reader would be a drastic mistake.

The second half of this book seeks to rectify this inattention to the importance of theological beliefs for the moral life. Why wait until now to make this argument? As noted in the introduction, there is a reason for this order of presentation. The cardinal virtues concern innerworldly activities that are engaged by people of whatever religious persuasion. Therefore they can be discussed intelligibly without solely relying on arguments particular to one religious tradition, such as claims made in the Bible. Particularly since its audience includes people of various religious beliefs, this book emphasizes that determining the most virtuous way to, say, wage war or drink alcohol is not simply a matter of sorting through different religious beliefs. One serious error that people can make concerning different positions on moral issues is that they are driven simply by different religious beliefs. (Observe in the newspapers how an anti-abortion stance is described, often derisively, as held by "religious" groups.) Yet as innerworldly activities, these issues entail questions and claims that are accessible to people of any or no religious conviction. When does human life begin? Does the use of lethal force impede the reestablishment of justice, or at times aid it? Which, if any, uses of alcohol are compatible with and even foster human health and good relationships, and which uses impede such human happiness and flourishing? Questions such as these are not simply matters of religious belief. That is why the cardinal virtues are addressed first in this book, with less attention to the impact of religious beliefs on those issues.

That said, another serious error that people can make in determining how to best live out innerworldly activities is to assume that religious convictions do not matter for those activities. The assumption of such people is that there is no important difference in how people of different religious beliefs live out activities such as pursuing sensual pleasures, making practical decisions, having good relations with others, and facing difficulties well. This is not true. A main goal of this second half of the book is to explain not only what Christians believe, but also how it transforms their moral lives. Though living a virtuous life directed toward happiness is not solely dictated by one's religious beliefs, such beliefs are indeed important for that endeavor. This half of the book attempts to explain how this is so by examining those virtues distinctive to the Christian tradition, namely, the theological virtues of faith (chapter 11), hope (chapter 13) and love, or charity (chapter 15). It will also examine certain crucial features of the Christian story, namely sin (chapter 12), Jesus Christ (chapter 14), and grace (chapter 16). Chapter 16 in many ways represents the climax of this book, since its treatment of grace ends with an argument explaining how the discussion of the cardinal virtues in the first half of this book needs to be reexamined and augmented with the claims of the next six chapters in mind. Two particular issues are then examined to see how the claims of this half of the book play out: sex (chapter 17) and euthanasia (chapter 18).

The purpose of this chapter is to prepare for the second half of the book by explaining why and how it is that different religious belief commitments matter in living morally. *What difference do religious beliefs make in how I live out innerworldly activities that are accessible to and engaged in by people of any or no religious belief?* Though this question will only fully be answered after chapter 16, this chapter makes two important contributions toward that answer. The first section offers an example of how the theological beliefs of two very different schools of thought play out in different moral rules for a particular innerworldly activity, namely, sex. Since one of the views portrayed is Christianity, this section also offers a basic portrait of the Christian story to the reader. The second section then offers a more precise argument about why and how religious beliefs do indeed matter for how we do innerworldly activities.

The Moral Importance of Different Big-Picture Beliefs about the Way Things Are

One of main claims of this book is that living in accordance with reason—in other words living virtuously—requires a truthful grasp of the way things are around us. This is why the virtue of prudence is so important. To refer to an example from chapter 7, waging war justly requires an accurate judgment about whether or not a true injustice has been committed, or, in other words, whether or not there is indeed just cause. As discussed in chapter 8, it also requires an assessment of whether the methods used in warfare will indeed enable a nation to reestablish justice (*ius*), or whether those methods actually impede the reestablishment of right relations. In both cases, seeing rightly enables us to act rightly. So it is no surprise to claim that an accurate grasp of the way things are matters in determining how to live virtuously.

But prudence enables us to see rightly as it concerns the dynamics of innerworldly activities. In living out the cardinal virtues, what, if any, difference does it make to see rightly as it concerns what are casually called here "big picture," or ultimate questions. Is there a God? If so what is God like? Is Jesus Christ the Son of God? What happens after death? These questions are less obviously related to living out innerworldly activities. Does what you think is true regarding such questions matter for how you live morally? This section attempts to show how one's beliefs on these big- picture questions matter by offering two strikingly different answers to them, and explaining how these different big-picture views lead their adherents to different rules on how to live out one particular innerworldly activity, namely, having sex. In the course of this section, one of these views—Christianity—will be presented in summary fashion, since the perspective of this book is living virtuously in the context of Christian faith.

Lucretius's Epicurean Beliefs and Their Impact on Virtuous Sex

Lucretius was a Roman thinker in the first century BC who was an adherent of a school of thought known as Epicureanism, named after the Greek thinker Epicurus. In a work entitled *On the Order of Things*, Lucretius offers a synopsis of his big-picture beliefs, and goes on to discuss sexuality in a manner that makes it clear how those beliefs shape his understanding of how to live a virtuous sex life. It may seem random to choose this text when, presumably, many others could be chosen to make the same point. It is used here both because of my own experience using the text in class, and because of the particularly clear way it demonstrates the connection between his Epicurean beliefs and his rules for virtuous sex.[1]

As an Epicurean, Lucretius was an atomist. *Atomism* is the view that all of reality can be reduced to material things (atoms). In this it is akin to a common modern approach to such questions called materialism. The basic claim here is that there exists nothing beyond the matter of this life. There is no monotheistic god, in the sense understood by traditions such as Judaism or Christianity, where God creates and transcends the matter of the universe, as opposed to being made up of that matter. Nor is there a human soul, in the sense of something that can be distinguished from, or especially live on without, one's material body. Nor is there any afterlife for a person, given what happens to the matter of a person's body after death. Lucretius claims that surely the matter that composes our bodies today was part of some other person long ago. But just as we have no memory of that existence, since the chain of personal identity is broken in the decomposition of matter, so too can we say that we have no personal identity after death. We simply cease to exist.

This is obviously not the place for a thorough overview of Epicurean thought or the work of Lucretius. Yet some basic tenets of this school of thought—some of the big-picture beliefs—are identified here in order to explain how they give rise to a certain view of what it means to live virtuously, or live a good life. Needless to say, in such a system there is no discussion of living in accordance with God's guidance. Since there is no providential god, in the manner understood by monotheistic traditions, it would not be "living in accordance with reason" to act as if there were. What, then, should guide how we act? Three observations are offered here about Lucretius's morality that flow directly from his big-picture beliefs.

First, the entire moral life may be summed up by the injunction "to banish pain and also to spread out many pleasures for ourselves."[2] Since ultimately there is only matter, it makes perfect sense that the best life is "a body free from pain" and a "mind released from worry" so that one can be most free "for the enjoyment of pleasurable sensations."[3] Interestingly enough, this vision of morality (which, reminiscent of claims in chapter 1, is indeed a morality in the descriptive sense of the term) does not lead Lucretius to condone debauchery

1. For a helpful excerpt from Lucretius's whole text, and for the text referred to here, see Lucretius, "On the Order of Things," in *The Good Life,* ed. Charles Guignon (Indianapolis: Hackett Publishing, 1999), 42–52.
2. Ibid., 43.
3. Ibid.

or to say that one should live however one wants. The way to best achieve a pleasurable state is through tranquility and equanimity. Raucous bouts of pleasure-seeking spoil the tranquil state, which is ultimately more pleasurable. He even dismisses those who concern themselves with seeking money or status, since these concerns also ultimately disturb, more than support, a life of pleasurable sensations. Thus, how Lucretius recommends living out a life of pleasure is far from the "eat, drink, and be merry" stereotype we may have of the Epicurean school of thought.[4] In fact, some of his rules seem rather close to what, say, Christians would recommend, though for very different reasons. Those differing reasons do, however, at time leads to quite different rules or ways of living.

An example of such a difference is seen in the second observation on Lucretius's ethics. In this school of thought, where the whole universe consists of isolated bits of matter flying spontaneously through space in perpetual motion, it is unsurprising that there is no significant place in Lurcretius's thought for the common good in any strong sense of the term, understood as interdependent and shared happiness. To the contrary, he claims that it is the

> greatest joy of all to possess a quiet sanctuary, stoutly fortified by the teaching of the wise, and to gaze down from that elevation on others wandering aimlessly in search of a way of life, pitting their wits one against the other, disputing for precedence, struggling night and day with unstinted effort to scale the pinnacles of wealth and power. O joyless hearts of men! O minds without vision![5]

To call looking down on the misery of others the "greatest joy" clearly indicates that happiness for Lucretius is not something that is most perfectly shared with others. Though he admits that "not that anyone's afflictions are in themselves sources of delight," he does say that they help one "realize from what troubles you yourself are free," which is "joy indeed." Reminiscent of Glaucon's view of justice, here there is no understanding of justice (in the sense of right relations with others) as constitutive of one's own happiness. And surely that impacts both why and how one lives justly.

Third and finally, Lucretius claims that it is a fear of death that leads people to superstition (such as religious practice) and futile quests for longevity in wealth or status. "Some sacrifice life itself for the sake of statues and a title."[6] But in reality there is nothing to fear in death, not because it is overcome but rather because it is inevitable and final.

4. For an enormously helpful overview of different classical (Greek and Roman) schools of ethics, and a more nuanced depiction of the Epicurean school of thought, see Julia Annas, *The Morality of Happiness* (New York: Oxford University Press, 1999).
5. Guignon, *The Good Life*, 43.
6. Ibid., 45.

> Rest assured, therefore, that we have nothing to fear in death. One who no longer is cannot suffer, or differ in any way from one who has never been born, when once this mortal life has been usurped by death the immortal.

Nothingness and death, not life, are final for Lucretius,. Since the dead person simply does not exist—much as one did not exist before birth—then there is nothing to fear, since one does not exist to experience pain (or pleasure). This big-picture belief leads to some moral injunctions we could find in Christianity, such as: do not fear death; and, understand pursuits in this life such as wealth and status in the broader perspective that extends beyond this life. But, of course, that broader perspective radically differs from Christianity, since death and nothingness are final for Lucretius. This leads him to have no problem whatsoever with something like taking one's own life, should one's life be wracked with pain and leave one no longer able to enjoy pleasures.[7]

How do these basic observations of Lucretius's ethics play out in terms of sexuality? Rather than any extensive examination of Epicurean sexual ethics, a few observations from his text will suffice to illustrate the point of this section. First, sexual desire (which he calls Venus) is a basic and mechanistic human body response to a stimulus. In people this stimulus is the shape of another human body. Surely we would question this rather crude understanding today, particularly with questions about the origin of sexual orientation, and the ways attractiveness is shaped by societal convention. But more related to our purposes is the claim here that sexual desire is not inherently related to any human friendship or relationship. In fact, the only reason Venus is directed toward any particular person, according to Lucretius, is that it is appropriate for a response to be elicited toward the stimulus that provoked it.[8]

As for the relationship between sexual desire and romantic love, Lucretius claims getting involved in any way with the latter is a drastic mistake. Many foolishly let their sexual desire (Venus) lead them to become romantically attached (Eros) to the object of their sexual desire. This is foolish because the passion of romantic love is "storm-tossed," leading the one in love to "waves of delusion and incertitude."[9] Unlike sexual desire, which can be satisfied and pleasurable, romantic love cannot be satisfied and thus is always a path to unhappiness.

Given this view of sexuality, what rules does Lucretius suggest? First, in order to keep one's mind free from pain and worry, avoid romantic love at all costs. He even has practical guidance about how to do so, instructing his reader to concentrate on the faults of the beloved rather than his or her attractive attributes! Second, he counsels his audience (surely comprised of men) to "ejaculate the build-up of seed promiscuously and do not hold on to it—by clinging to

7. Ibid., 47.
8. Ibid., 49.
9. Ibid., 50.

it you assure yourself the certainty of heartsickness and pain."[10] Since sexual desire can lead one foolishly to romantic love, one is best off discharging that desire "promiscuously" rather than letting it build up. Lest one think that the delights of sex would be lacking something in the absence of romantic love, he claims to the contrary that "this pleasure [sex] is enjoyed in a purer form by the sane than the lovesick," and that in sex without romantic love "you are reaping the sort of profits that carry with them no penalty."[11]

A more detailed analysis of Epicurean sexual ethics might explore whether what is avoided here is simply overly passionate romantic love, what today we might call an infatuation or obsessiveness. But it suffices for our purposes to note that sexual desire for Lucretius is ultimately about securing pleasure without pain, and no mention is made of it as a human activity intended to bring people together. This is unsurprising given Lucretius's big-picture beliefs and the ethical approach they engender.

Before turning to the Christian story about the way things are, and the impact of that story on sexuality, it should be noted that the goal of Lucretius's ethics is indeed happiness, or "greatest joy." This quest leads to rules, and those rules are clearly shaped by his big-picture beliefs about the way things are, including his understanding of atomism, the ultimate relationship, or lack thereof, between human persons, and the content of human happiness as the "enjoyment of pleasurable sensations." Lucretius is quite clear that the good life is living in accordance with reason. People who fail to live such a life do not see accurately concerning things, such as the meaning of death.[12] They are "minds without vision." Thus, Lucretius would agree with a central claim of this book that it is in knowing the truth that we are set free. However, his vision of what that truth is differs radically from Christianity, to which we turn now. His different vision of the way things are concerning big-picture questions leads to a different understanding of how to live virtuously in general, including a different understanding of how to do particular innerworldly activities, like sex, virtuously.

The Christian Story of the Way Things Are and Its Impact on Sexuality

Given that this book is an examination of moral theology in the Christian (particularly Catholic) tradition, more attention will be devoted here to that vision of the way things are. Still, the presentation of Christian belief here is embarrassingly brief. Even so, some such presentation is needed, both to support the main claim of this chapter that big-picture beliefs shape moral rules concerning innerworldly practices, and to offer readers of varying back-

10. Ibid., 49.
11. Ibid., 50.
12. Ibid., 46.

grounds some basis for the following chapters' more detailed discussions of aspects of the Christian story.

How to summarize the Christian story? One helpful text for this purpose is the Irish bishops' pastoral statement entitled "Love is for Life." It is not only concise and well-written, but like this chapter it also seeks to show how the basic tenets of Christian belief shape how sex is done virtuously. After a brief look at their summary of the Christian story, we will look more closely at the relationship of that story to sexuality by examining the main movements in Christian salvation history.

The point of it all, according to the Irish bishops, can be summed up in one word: love. That word is the basis of the entire Christian story. More precisely, we could say that self-giving interpersonal communion is the point of it all. That is what is meant by love here. Love is the best word to describe who God's very self is. After all, the New Testament says that "God is love" (1 John 4:8). This is also what is meant by the Christian doctrine of the Trinity, a belief that can too often seem abstract and irrelevant for morality. But that is far from the case. Christians believe that God's very self is a communion of persons—Father, Son, and Holy Spirit—three persons united as one. Loving communion is therefore the very fiber of God's being, and thus the very basis for all reality which originates in God.

Since God's love is self-giving, God created everything as an expression of self-giving love. "Creation is God's love made visible to us. It was from love that He made the world. It is out of love that He continues to care for it. It is in love that God looks on all he has made."[13] And it is to an ultimate destiny of loving union with God that all persons are invited. Thus love is the origin, the sustenance, and the destiny of creation. It is best exemplified in the person of Jesus Christ, in whom the God who is love became a human person and lived out perfectly the self-giving love to which all of us are called.

Having mentioned this call, the centrality of love for humanity according to the Christian story should now be clear. Not only is humanity created out of love. Given a special place in all creation, as created in the image of God (*imago Dei*), humanity is specially equipped to participate in the love that characterizes God's very being, which spills out in all creation, and which characterizes the ultimate destiny to which humanity is called. That is why the greatest commandment is to love God and to love others (see Matt. 22:37–39; Mark 12:29–31; Luke 10:27). This is not some externally imposed obligation placed on humanity. It is rather an invitation for us to live the way we were created to live; in other words, it is a call to be who we are as *imago Dei*. It is also a foretaste of the fullness of life, which is complete loving union with God.

The Irish bishops rightly claim that all of Christian morality follows from these claims. Christian morality is not some arbitrary set of obligations

13. Irish Catholic Bishop's Conference, *Love is for Life* (Pastoral Letter, 1985), 16.

imposed on people to keep them from having too much fun. Rather, genuine moral rules are simply aids for humanity in living the most loving lives. In doing so, people live lives that conform to how they were built, so to speak, and thus experience true fulfillment and happiness. This is true of all inner-worldly activities, and not simply one's religious activities. The Irish bishops state plainly how it is true with regard to sexuality: "The Church's whole moral teaching about sex is above all the application to sexuality of God's greatest commandment to charity [i.e., love]."[14] The question to ask ourselves in any moral issue is how to live most genuinely loving lives. In doing so we are not merely obeying God's commandments, though we are doing that too; we are actually living in accordance with the reality of things, including our own natures, the point of all creation, our ultimate destiny, and even the very essence of God's own being.

Of course the rub, if you will, is determining what counts as genuinely loving. Much disagreement on particular moral issues occurs, not between opposing big-picture schools of thought like Lucretius vs. the Irish bishops, but between those who share, say, the view of the Irish bishops and yet debate whether or not a particular act (e.g., sex before marriage) constitutes an act of genuine self-giving love. In other words, common vision on the answers to big-picture questions does not guarantee common vision on whether or not particular activities are expressions of those big-picture beliefs. Nonetheless, commonality on such big-picture questions is still hugely significant. It provides people with a set of common beliefs to appeal to in determining whether a particular act is virtuous or not. In other words, if the Irish bishops are making an argument against sex outside of marriage, they need to know whether their audience includes people like Lucretius who do not accept the tenets of the Christian story, or whether it includes other Christians who do accept that story but disagree on how those big-picture claims are specified in the particular case at hand. There are different sources of disagreement at work in those two audiences.

Since we are now veering too close to the next section's more analytic examination of how different big-picture beliefs matter in shaping one's position on moral issues, let us first examine how the Christian story plays out with regard to sexuality. Rather than simply asking what constitutes genuinely loving sex, let us look more specifically at the Christian story of salvation history in order to see how sex fits into it. The three basic movements of Christian salvation history are *creation, sin, redemption*.

What do Christians believe about creation? As noted above God, who is love, created all things out of love, and created humanity in God's own image for a special destiny of friendship with God. It is worth pausing to note how radical this claim is. The God who is the origin of the entire universe is not

14. Ibid., 24.

simply a transcendent and powerful god in a distant and impersonal sense. God is indeed powerful and transcendent, but also immanent and personal. The union to which God invites all people is deeply interpersonal and self-giving. In fact, many great Christian thinkers echoing Jesus's words to his disciples (John 15:15: "I call you friends") have described the union with God (and to others in God) to which all are called as friendship. Hence when people live lives of personal, self-giving love they are living according to their created purpose.

What has this to do with sex? First of all, sexuality is a created part of our nature as human persons. Though certain erroneous interpretations of the book of Genesis have understood sex to enter the picture only after humanity's sin in Genesis 3, a closer look reveals that sex and marriage are present in humanity before sin (Gen. 2:24). Therefore, sex comes from God, and is good and beautiful. There is no reason to have shame with regard to nakedness and sexuality in themselves. Second, given that sex is a divinely created capacity given to humanity, it should be no surprise that its purpose is to express self-giving love. Sexual intercourse is a powerfully intimate expression of union in self-giving love, where two become "one flesh" (Gen. 2:24), and where humanity participates in God's own loving creativity by heeding the call to "be fertile and multiply" (Gen. 1:28). When sex is an expression of this deeply personal, self-giving love for which we were created, then it is virtuous.

Of course, this is not the whole of the Christian story. As a reading of Genesis 3 reveals, and as will be examined in far more detail in chapter 12, sin enters the picture contrary to God's plan. Despite being created for self-giving love, and being given the assistance to live lives of such love, which are indeed most fulfilling and satisfying, humanity lives not out of self-giving love but rather for ourselves. Out of pride we decide that we, not God, know what is truly best and life-giving for us. And so we turn away from the fullness of life that is offered to us. This is sin.

How is sin manifest in human sexuality? Any expression of sexuality that is not an occasion of personal self-giving love is a manifestation of human sinfulness. The sad reality of sin is seen in gender discrimination, dominance, manipulation, shame about sexuality, and any occasion where we do, intend, or desire sexual acts in a manner that uses other people for ourselves in defiance of the self-giving love to which we are all called, in our sex lives and beyond. When sex is used in this manner, the partners are warping sex into something other than the expression of fully self-giving love that it is created to express.

Thankfully, sin is not the end of the Christian story. Christians believe that all of human history is the story of God's reconciliation of humanity to himself. God initiates a restoration of right relationship. God does so through the law and the prophets of the Old Testament, through the ongoing presence of the Holy Spirit in the Church, and most perfectly in the life, death, and resurrection of Jesus Christ (discussed in chapter 14). In short, God's help (or "grace") helps to heal humanity in our sinfulness so that we can live the lives of self-giving love in communion with God and others that we were destined to live. This redemption occurs in this life, but it is only complete in the next, when the fullness of life in union with God can be experienced completely. The scriptures describe humanity's ultimate destiny as coming "to share in the divine nature, after escaping from the corruption that is in the world because of evil desire" (2 Pet. 1:4). That divine nature is of course interpersonal communion in self-giving love.

What does this have to do with sexuality? Though our sinfulness is quite evident in how we express our sexuality, with God's help it is indeed possible that the sexual expressions of our sinfulness—discrimination, domination, manipulation, and selfishness—can be overcome. In other words, we can be healed so that our sexuality can be an expression of the self-giving interpersonal love that it was meant to be. Though redemption is complete only in the next life, it is truly inaugurated in this life; hence in our sexuality, which is proper to this life, we can indeed know the transformation of redemption.

It should be clear at this point how radically different both the big-picture beliefs of the Irish bishops, and their more particular rules concerning sex, are from those of Lucretius. What is most important for this chapter is recognizing how each vision of the way things are concerning big-picture beliefs shapes the different specific rules they have concerning sexuality. It is not the case that big-picture beliefs are irrelevant for determining how to virtuously go about innerworldly activities. Explaining more precisely how and why this is so is the purpose of the second section of this chapter.

The Importance of Big-Picture Beliefs for Innerworldly Practices

Much as chapter 1 started with the *Ring of Gyges* story in order to distinguish a morality of happiness from a morality of obligation, this second half of the book begins with a contrast between Lucretius's and the Irish bishops' understanding of sex in the context of their big-picture beliefs. The goal here is to provide an example of how those beliefs matters in shaping how we do innerworldly activities. The purpose of this next section of the chapter is to examine in more detail exactly how and why those beliefs matter, a task that will only be truly complete by the end of chapter 16. While the task of the first half of the book was to look at the virtues—in particular the cardinal virtues—as a way both to expand the scope of discussions of morality beyond acts to persons, intentions, and desires, and to shift the emphasis of such discussions to happiness over obligation, this second half seeks to better understand the content of happiness through the lens of the Christian faith, and particularly the theological virtues. As noted at the outset of this chapter, it is a legitimate criticism to ask why this analysis does not follow chapter 2 and precede the discussion of cardinal virtues. But the cardinal virtues are examined first in this book to demonstrate how discussion of them invites— no, demands—attention to one's big-picture beliefs. Discussion of religious faith, or some such big-picture beliefs, far from being plopped on top of one's understanding of the cardinal virtues, shapes and in turn is shaped by one's practice of those virtues. This section will demonstrate how.

Two Errors on the Relation of Big-Picture Beliefs to Innerworldly Activities

It may help to identify two views on the moral importance of big-picture beliefs which this section will argue against. The first view grants that things like belief in God and an afterlife matter in how we act morally in this world. After all, people of religious faith such as Christians believe in a God who rewards the good and punishes the evil. In the next life, in particular, heaven or hell awaits each person based upon his or her actions. So believers presumably try and alter their behavior on earth in light of that impending judgment.

Though this is indeed an example of how big-picture beliefs shape how we do innerworldly activities, it is not the view espoused here. Not that the realities of God's judgment, or heaven or hell, are denied here; they are not. But on this view, the relationship between our actions and our final destiny is understood poorly. Our actions here in this life are only extrinsically related to our destiny in the next. It is as if God arbitrarily decides on a set of actions that must be performed here in order for us to get a reward later. Yet on this view there is no recognition that what God commands in this life is intrinsically related to our final destiny. Virtuous activity shapes us into the sorts of persons we will fully become (in ways that explode our imagination) in the next life, where there is fullness of life. Note that the above presentation of the Irish bishops' summation of Christianity and the impact of those beliefs on sexuality never once mentioned heaven or hell. Clearly it is not because they deny heaven or hell. Rather it is because they have a more intrinsic view of the relationship between Christian faith and having sex. Who God is, and how God made us to live, are prior to (and in fact the basis of) whatever ultimate destiny we will enjoy or suffer. In other words, the life of self-giving love and all its demands, to which God calls us in this life, is a foretaste of, an initial participation in, that fullness of life with which God rewards people in eternity. This point is explained in greater detail in chapter 13. It suffices here to note that the morality-of-obligation view, whereby our eternal destiny shapes our behavior simply because of the reward or punishment associated with our actions in this life, is not endorsed here. Though there is certainly a connection between how we live this life and our eternal destinies, the connection is stronger and more beautiful than supposed in this simplistic model. From a morality-of-happiness perspective, living the virtuous life here is constitutive of, and not simply an extrinsic means to, the happiness offered by God in eternal life.

A second target of this section is the mistaken view that only people of religious faith have big-picture beliefs that shape their actions on earth. After all, it seems, if you do not believe in God or judgment in an afterlife, then there is nothing there to shape how you act in this life! Hopefully the error of this view is obvious after the brief look at Lucretius's thought. Clearly Lucretius held beliefs about the nonexistence of God, human destiny (or lack thereof) after death, and the relationship among human persons in general. They are certainly not the beliefs held by Christians. But they are big-picture beliefs nonetheless. And they clearly shaped his understanding of how to live a good, virtuous life, as when he counsels people not to fear death, and to seek a life of enjoyment based on pleasurable sensations, and to enjoy sex without the trappings of romantic love. In the descriptive senses of the terms, Lucretius has beliefs, and he has a morality shaped by them. The question is not whether such beliefs are present. The real question is whether or not they are true, and so how accurately they shape one's moral practices.

Actions, Practices, and Big-Picture Beliefs

This book focuses on virtues rather than simply external acts because of the way that virtues, as habits with corresponding intentionality and desires, constitute changes in a person. A virtuous person—say, a temperate person—does not simply perform temperate acts; she is a temperate person. The main reason that she consistently performs temperate acts has everything to do with intentionality. She sees things correctly concerning sensual pleasures, and intends to and desires to act in accordance with that accurate grasp of sensual pleasures. So she acts well consistently, for the right reasons, and with pleasure and promptness, largely because she has an accurate grasp of the way things are and purposely acts—even desires—accordingly. In fact, she knows that acting so is constitutive of genuine human happiness.

Thus the virtuous person sees rightly the goals to be pursued, and pursues them. Of course goals, or intentions, exist on a variety of levels. Some are very immediate and short term. Others are more central to a whole life and longer term. Recall the discussion in chapter 2 of how the particular constellation of goals in a persons' life, and their relative importance, is what makes up a person's character. It is what makes him who he is. Furthermore, this constellation can be imagined as a sort of triangle, since one's higher goals not only take precedence over lower goals, but also shape the manner in which they are done.

We are now on the cusp of a richer understanding of how big-picture beliefs shape our innerworldly activities. The first half of this book argued that the virtuous life leads to genuine human happiness, or flourishing. But the content of happiness, if you will, is based upon one's big-picture beliefs. Recall how differently Lucretius and the Irish bishops see what constitutes happiness, and how they accordingly pursue innerworldly activities like sex in contrasting manners. Since our ultimate end—or what we are all about—shapes how more proximate goals or intentions are understood and pursued in our lives, it stands to reason that our big-picture beliefs, which are determinative of our ultimate end, shape how we understand the point or meaning of innerworldly practices, and thus our understanding of how to do them well. Recall from chapter 2 how our ultimate goal, and how it shapes all other goals, is what establishes our character. Now it should be clearer why this is so. For instance, if the Irish bishops are correct that God is love, that creation is a divine act of love, and that life in love is itself participation in the divine nature (2 Pet. 1:4), in the life of God who is love, then sex is most accurately understood as having a purpose in that overall plan. Therefore it is done well (virtuously) to the extent that it is an expression of the self-giving love that constitutes our ultimate end and complete happiness.

Most basically, we can say that our big-picture beliefs concerning the ultimate purpose or goal in life shape how we do things in this life, which are presumably understood as parts of the path to that goal. As noted above, this can be understood in a manner whereby the relation between the ultimate goal sought and the path to that goal are only extrinsically related. In other words, though the innerworldly activities are done for the sake of some further end (like reward in heaven), what constitutes the manner of doing those activities well is not shaped by the nature of the final end. Of course, there is still a vision of the final end operative here; in this case, God is an arbitrary lawgiver who demands and rewards obedience. If that is the most accurate and complete understanding of God we have, living that way makes sense. Yet the Irish bishops offer an example of doing innerworldly activities for the sake of one's final end of union with God, in a manner whereby the very shape of those activities is reflective of who God is, what we are called to be, and a taste of our final goal, In other words, they have a morality-of-happiness perspective in which following the rules is constitutive of, and not simply an extrinsically related path to, full human happiness.

The introduction of the term *practice* will help illustrate the formative impact of big-picture beliefs on innerworldly activities, and also enable us to see how the reverse is also true. Simply put, a practice is a way of doing something. It could be something simple, like changing a tire, or something rather complex, like dating or waging war. Since we human persons act intentionally, the way we go about doing things is only properly understood if we look at not only what we do but also why we do it. Furthermore, more complex and interesting practices include many levels of goals. We have more immediate goals, and more far-reaching goals. Though debates about, say, waging war may focus on more immediate actions such a dropping an atomic bomb, only a broader understanding of how that action is situated in the practice of waging war, and what the more far-reaching goals of war making are, will enable us to adequately analyze the particular action under examination. And since our more far-reaching goals are reflective of our big- picture beliefs in the manner described above, any thorough analysis of a practice like waging war will attend to those big-picture beliefs.

This is why it is important to analyze moral issues like sexuality or waging war by looking at how these innerworldly activities are practices. It makes us attentive to both immediate and more far-reaching goals. It enables us to understand the impact of one's community on those goals. And it enables us to see what big-picture beliefs must be held—consciously or unconsciously—by the participants in order to live out that sort of practice. For instance, if we spoke to Lucretius or had a friend who lived out sexuality in the manner recommended by him, then we could say, "For you to practice sexuality in this way means you must believe _____." Similarly, we could say to someone who practiced sex in the manner described by the Irish bishops, "For you to practice sexuality in this way means you must believe _____." Analysis of how innerworldly activities are practiced is only complete with attention to the specific big-picture beliefs that underlie and shape the practice.

There is another important consequence of this understanding of the relationship between big-picture beliefs and our practices of innerworldly activities. Though our practices are indeed reflective of the big-picture beliefs we hold, it is also the case that our practices are formative of those beliefs. People do not first come to some fully developed understanding of God and ultimate happiness and then act accordingly in the world. Instead, people are shaped by those around them (families, churches, etc.) to act in the world in a certain way, which then propels them toward big- picture beliefs that correspond to those practices. Thus, our practices not only reflect, but also help form, our big-picture beliefs. This claim leads us directly to the virtue faith, which is the topic for the next chapter.

Concluding Thoughts

The purpose of this chapter has been to exemplify and explain how big- picture beliefs matter in determining how to most virtuously practice innerworldly activities. Exactly what ramifications this has for the source and content of the cardinal virtues—which concern innerworldly activities—is spelled out in chapter 16, after a more thorough engagement with other central features of the Christian story and the three theological virtues of faith, hope, and love. Given the importance of big-picture beliefs for how we practice innerworldly activities, the problem with the two errors mentioned at the beginning of this chapter (as opposed to this section) should now be clearer.

One of those errors is the view that since innerworldly activities are practiced by people whatever their big-picture beliefs, then those beliefs must not matter for innerworldly practices. Demonstrating why this view is false has been the primary task of this chapter. In fact, the structure of this book could be mistakenly taken to imply that innerworldly activities may be practiced without any relation to big-picture beliefs. This is not true. It is true that people of very different big-picture beliefs all practice some vision of the cardinal virtues. At times what they do may even be quite similar. But at times what is understood to constitute the content of a cardinal virtue is quite different, and the impact of different big-picture beliefs on how innerworldly activities are practiced helps explain many such differences. We may see, for instance, that debate about the use of the atomic bomb entails difference over what constitutes proper relations between human persons. These differences may in turn reflect different big-picture beliefs.

But we should avoid letting an emphasis on this point lead us to fall into the other error mentioned at the outset of this chapter. It is not the case that all disagreements over innerworldly practices are simply about differences in big-picture beliefs. Not every debate over waging war or sexuality is simply a theological debate. The fact that these practices concern innerworldly activities does mean the activity can in principle be examined with integrity free of reference to supernatural destiny. Much can be learned and debated without further reference to big-picture beliefs. Indeed, much debate occurs between people who hold similar theological commitments, and yet disagree over how or whether an innerworldly practice can best reflect those commitments. We saw this clearly with the U.S. bishops' claim that both nonviolent resistance and just-war theory have been understood to be expressions of Christian justice. However, though not all debate is ultimately about rival big-picture claims, failing to attend to how such claims shape our innerworldly practices is always problematic. The following chapter explores the virtue of faith whereby people hold their big-picture beliefs.

Study Questions

1. The outset of this chapter mentions two errors that people are prone to when addressing the importance of big-picture beliefs. What are they? According to the conclusion of the chapter, why are both wrong?
2. Describe three big-picture beliefs held by Lucretius. Explain how they shape the way he says sex is practiced virtuously.
3. How do the Irish bishops summarize the Christian story? Be sure to describe both the prominent role of love in that story, and the three movements of salvation history.

4. Give two rules for sexuality that the Irish bishops would endorse, and show how they flow from their big-picture beliefs.
5. The beginning of section two describes two errors (different from those at the outset of the chapter) on how big-picture beliefs might be said to shape our practices. What are they? Why does this chapter claim each is wrong?
6. What is a practice? Explain how human practices are reflective of the fact that we act intentionally for goals on a host of different levels.
7. Explain why big-picture beliefs shape our innerworldly practices, being sure to use the terms (in whatever order): final end, intention, virtue, happiness, the way things are.

Terms to Know

atomism, creation, sin, redemption, practice

Questions for Further Reflection

1. Give some examples of big-picture beliefs beyond those mentioned here. How would you define a big-picture, or ultimate, belief?
2. Take some hotly contested ethical issue, and try to determine the sources of disagreement between two particular positions. Are they at the level of big-picture beliefs or not? If so how? If not, what is the source of disagreement?
3. Think of your own practices in some area, such as dating. Name several rules you live by in this area, and try to identify what you think the activity means by saying, "For me to (for instance) date this way, I must think dating means _____." Then note to what extent your understanding of the activity (such as dating) is shaped by and reflective of your big-picture beliefs.

Further Reading

A helpful collection of texts from over two thousand years of great thinkers on the question of what constitutes the good life is Charles Guignon's *The Good Life*. A more difficult and thorough treatment of particularly classical ethics and some of their concomitant big-picture beliefs is Julia Annas's *The Morality of Happiness*. There are many basic overviews of the Christian story. The *Catechism of the Catholic Church* is lengthy and dry but comprehensive. I have also found C. S. Lewis's *Mere Christianity* and Robert Barron's *The Strangest Way* to be very helpful on this topic. Basic summations of the story of salvation history can be found directly in scripture, such as in Acts 2 and 6. St. Augustine offers long and short versions in his manual *On Catechizing the Unlearned*. Genesis 1–3 seems invaluable for presenting basic Christian big-picture beliefs. Finally, Pope Benedict XVI's *Deus Caritas Est* offers a synopsis of love as central to the Christian story, as does the Irish bishops' *Love Is for Life*, relied on heavily in this chapter.

11

THE VIRTUE OF FAITH

Answering Big-Picture Questions

The previous chapter sought to establish the moral importance of our big-picture beliefs, and offered a basic outline of those beliefs for Christians. The next obvious topic for this book concerns how we obtain those beliefs. Faith is the virtue that enables us to believe well concerning the answers to big-picture questions. The first half of this chapter relies on Pope John Paul II's encyclical *Fides et Ratio* (*Faith and Reason*) to explain the dynamics of how and why people believe in general, and believe the answers to big-picture questions in particular. This is a human thing to do and present in all people, of any or no religious tradition.

By explaining this, John Paul prepares us perfectly for the second half of this chapter, which looks at the Christian way of believing. There we find that though the dynamics of how people believe are present in all people, the content of what different people believe is importantly different. Furthermore, the dynamics of how people believe are then transformed in light of what people believe in. In sum, Christian faith is in some ways very much like, and in other ways importantly different than, other ways of believing in answering the big-picture questions. Given that the rest of this book in large part explores the difference that Christian faith makes in how we live our lives, this chapter on the content and dynamics of Christian faith is foundational for the rest of the book.

Believing in Answers to Big-Picture Questions: A Human Thing to Do

John Paul II's 1999 encyclical *Fides et Ratio* relies on a straightforward quote from Aristotle to make the claim that "all humans desire to know," and what we seek to know is the truth about the "way things are."[1] The document supports this with an observation from Augustine: "I have met many who wanted to deceive, but none who wanted to be deceived" (25).[2] Human beings are the sorts of creatures who "seek the truth" (28). John Paul notes that this concerns not only theoretical matters, such as scientific research. It also concerns practical matters. In a quote that is an apt synopsis of this book, John Paul says:

> No less important than research in the theoretical field is research in the practical field—by which I mean the search for truth which looks to the good which is to be performed. In acting ethically, according to a free and rightly tuned will, the human person sets foot upon the path to happiness and moves towards perfection. Here too it is a question of truth. (25)

There are different sorts of knowledge, or truth, needed to live well. There is the knowledge of the dynamics of innerworldly activities and decisions, which is the domain of prudence. Yet there is also the knowledge about big-picture or, as *Fides et Ratio* says, ultimate questions which similarly have practical import in shaping how innerworldly activities are done. Such questions include: what is the meaning of life? What happens after death? Is there a god, and if so what is god like? Particularly given the reality of human suffering in our own lives and all around us, and given the inevitability of our death, John Paul claims:

> Each of us has both the desire and the duty to know the truth of our own destiny. We want to know if death will be the definitive end of our life or if there is something beyond—if it is possible to hope for an after-life or not. (26)

Our answers to questions such as these will guide how we live our lives, and we want our answers to be true.

Note the breadth of John Paul's claim here. He is not saying that only Christians, or only philosophers, long for the answers to ultimate questions. He is saying that all people, in whatever time or place, do so.

> No one can avoid this questioning, neither the philosopher nor the ordinary person. . . . People seek an absolute which might give to all their searching a

---

1. *Fides et Ratio* (Encyclical Letter, 1998), 25. The citation from Aristotle is given as *Metaphysics* I,1. Further references to *Fides et Ratio* will be given parenthetically by paragraph number.

2. The reference to Augustine is given as *Confessions* X.23.33.

meaning and an answer—something ultimate, which might serve as the ground of all things. In other words, they seek a final explanation, a supreme value, which refers to nothing beyond itself and which puts an end to all questioning. . . . Whether we admit it or not, there comes for everyone the moment when personal existence must be anchored to a truth recognized as final. (27)

This is clearly present in different philosophical schools of thought throughout history, as seen with regard to Lucretius in the previous chapter. But it is also present in all people who, consciously or not, live out their lives in a manner reflective of our answers to big-picture questions. Our answers are embedded in our "personal convictions and experiences, in traditions of family and culture" (27). And so:

All men and women, as I have noted, are in some sense philosophers and have their own philosophical conceptions with which they direct their lives. In one way or other, they shape a comprehensive vision and an answer to the question of life's meaning; and in the light of this they interpret their own life's course and regulate their behavior. (30)

With the previous chapter, these passages should confirm both the moral importance of big-picture questions, and the longing for and indeed necessity of addressing these questions in all our lives. Yet if all persons are therefore built to seek the truth, and if the truth is able to be known (as *Fides et Ratio* clearly affirms it is), then why is there any uncertainty or disagreement regarding the ultimate questions in life, as there most surely is? Why can't we just open our eyes and see the way things are in answer to the ultimate questions in life? In fact, humans should be uniquely equipped to know the truth of such things. Reason, or intellect, is the human capacity to know and understand the truth. Through human reasoning we can not only know what is directly seen, but also what is inferred, deduced, and construed from what we can see.

Fides et Ratio recognizes that the truthful answers to these questions are not always so transparent and offers two reasons to explain this: the "natural limitation of reason and the inconstancy of the heart often obscure and distort a person's search" (28; cf. 22, 43). The human heart can be inconstant simply due to a welter of other concerns, and/or because our sinfulness distracts us from seeking and finding the truth that sets us free. Furthermore, the sorts of answers sought here are literally metaphysical, and thus unable to be verified with more empirical methods that so often provide us with clarity and certainty. In fact, as seen in the following section, Christians claim the truthful answers to these questions transcend even nonempirical metaphysical inquiry. This natural limitation of reason is described by St. Paul when he claims that at present we "see indistinctly" and "know partially" (1 Cor. 13:12), and that "we walk by faith not by sight" (2 Cor. 5:7; cf. Rom. 8:25). For these reasons, despite the universal presence in humanity of the longing for answers to these questions, we simultaneously lack the knowledge of clear sight in answering them.

So what is one to do? If all persons long for the answers to ultimate questions, and yet the truth of those answers is not so transparent, how is one to live? The problem is more serious than it may initially sound. After all, it may seem as if you can just simply avoid answering these questions and get on with it. That way the lack of clear sight that marks their answers would not be a problem—simply do not answer! But this is not possible. After all, the way we live our lives speaks our answers to these questions. Consciously or not, explicitly stated or not, our "personal convictions and experiences, . . . [our] traditions of family and culture" are shot through, if you will, with our answers to these questions (27). This was precisely the point of the last chapter. Our practices of sexuality, waging war, grieving for the dead, and so on all speak our answers to big-picture questions. So even if you were to try to avoid consciously thinking about these big-questions, how you live your life would still reveal your answers. So how can you come to the answers?

Simply put, we believe. Aquinas describes an act of belief as clinging to something as true even in the absence of the certitude of clear sight.[3] He claims that some things in life we know because when we encounter them, or once we learn them, our reason understands them completely. We see clearly and realize the truth of the matter just by looking at what is at hand. Once we learn basic math functions, we understand the truth of things in this way. But it also happens with practical matters. A good mechanic can listen to an engine, or open the hood, and know immediately—see clearly—what is wrong with the engine based on extensive experience and knowledge of engines. Of course, errors in such matters are still possible. But in these cases there is no need to believe since we see, or at least are able to see, the truth of the matter at hand clearly.

But Aquinas recognizes there are many occasions where we may affirm things to be true without seeing clearly, without having a high degree of certitude. For instance, we may doubt or suspect something to be true. These words indicate we have a guess, if you will, as to what is true but do not know it, or see clearly. Sometimes we are a little more sure as to what is true, but still not totally sure, as in an opinion.

Where does belief fit into this? To believe is to cling to something as surely true, much in the way you do when you see clearly the truth of the matter at hand. Yet when we believe, it is not the matter at hand that is so clear or obvious that compels us to see something as surely true. Things we believe in do not lend themselves to such complete and clear knowledge. But then why,

---

3. For the following analysis of faith as the virtue of believing well, see Aquinas, *Summa Theologiae*, English Dominican trans. (New York: Benziger, 1948), II–II 1–16, esp. 1, 2, and 4. He relies on Heb. 11:1 for his basic definition of faith: "faith is the realization of what is hoped for, the evidence of things not seen."

you may ask, do we believe them as surely true? Perhaps we should only have doubts or opinions about such matters. We believe some things in life as surely true because something moves, or persuades, us to see it that way, even if it is not the matter at hand. Consider some simple examples of this.

How many people are there in the United States today? You have probably learned some number that jumped into your head at the sight of this question—say, 250 million. Yet how do you know? Have you counted? No, you rely on certain individuals who are charged with conducting the census every ten years. In fact, you believe them when they tell you. This is not to say there is no right answer, or that your belief is blind. There are good reasons to believe census takers. But in the end you believe them and do not personally verify that there are 250 million people in the United States. In fact, given the amount of information we rely on in life we believe people all the time. We believe scientists who conduct research, and people who make maps, or people with local knowledge when we are traveling and ask for directions. As John Paul says,

> There are in the life of a human being many more truths which are simply believed than truths which are acquired by way of personal verification. Who, for instance, could assess critically the countless scientific findings upon which modern life is based? (31)

Believing things to be true, even when we cannot personal verify them, or see the answer clearly from just the matter at hand, is a very human thing to do. It is for this reason that John Paul defines the human being not only as "one who seeks the truth," but also "one who lives by belief" (28 and 31, respectively).

Certain things in life are believed as a matter of efficiency. It may be possible to verify them on our own using our capacity to reason, but there is simply no point in verifying all the information we need when we live in community with others who can and have done so. There are other sorts of things which are believed to be true not simply as a short cut, but rather because they are the sorts of things that elude, or rather transcend, personal empirical verification. Who are my genuine friends? Will this work be satisfying to me? Will my girlfriend or boyfriend be a good spouse? These are questions that can be answered truly or falsely. But they are not the sort of questions that are verifiable by simply using more reasoning. This is not to say there is no data available to reason about. There is often plenty. But even after considering the data at hand, we do not know for sure if we are seeing things truthfully. Nonetheless, we must decide. We must believe and act accordingly. Actually, it seems that most of the important questions in life are precisely like this; namely, they are open to reasonable consideration, and yet ultimately elude the knowledge of clear sight and thus invite us to believe and act accordingly.

What, then, impels us to believe one way or the other even in the absence of a sure knowledge of the matter at hand? After all, recall that to believe is to cling firmly to something as true, and not simply to have an opinion or suspicion. What moves or persuades us to cling firmly? In the end, we believe primarily because of people we find compelling. We trust our friends because we love them and want to do so, even though we do not know for sure that they will never betray us. We embark on a career or vocation because someone or some people who do that work are appealing to us, and/or we have been led by other people to imagine ourselves as people who would be good at, and happy in, that calling. We believe in our spouses not because the evidence of their love and character is verifiable beyond doubt. Rather we consider available evidence but ultimately believe in the person. We believe people, and that leads us to affirm many important things in life as surely true.

Doesn't this mean we can get hurt, that we can be misled? Sadly, yes. In our friendships, vocations, marriages, and elsewhere we can believe in people and see things accordingly, and yet those people can be wrong, and perhaps even manipulative. This is why a whole web of family and friendships is so important in our lives, to give us support and broader perspective on each of our commitments. Good friends and family can indeed help us sniff out those relationships and endeavors where we are mistaken or misled. But even such a healthy network is no guarantee. Nonetheless, the only alternative is to avoid any commitment, to not believe. Or, more accurately, this is to believe that no one is trustworthy! But of course that is not only an empty life, but also equally inaccurate if it is the case that some are trustworthy. It is evident here how belief can actually enable us to reason more accurately, if what we believe in is true. Our beliefs can grow out of our reasoning about a question (since we should not believe in things that defy our reasoning), and yet once we believe that belief can then enable us to do further accurate reasoning based upon accurate beliefs. After all, the goal in answering important questions in life is not to not believe; it is to answer them truthfully. If that requires belief, then belief is the path to see things more truthfully, which then enables us to further truthful reasoning. Thus there is no way out of belief; the only question is, what do we believe in? Whom we do believe?

How we answer big-picture, ultimate questions in life is precisely like this. Questions such as whether there is a god and what god is like, what the meaning of life is, what happens after death, and so on—all these are certainly open to reasoned analysis. We consider evidence, keep an eye out for contradictions and inconsistencies, and consider ramifications of the positions we hold. In short, we use our reasoning. It is important to affirm that matters of belief, including religious belief, are not resistant to reasonable analysis. The human person may be one who lives by belief, but the person is also one who uses reason to consider the truth of things. But on some important questions our reason comes up short. We cannot know completely, or see clearly, the truth of the matter at hand. And so we believe that Jesus Christ is God, or that he is not. (Different people around Jesus in his life took each of these paths.) We believe that life goes on after death, or that it does not. There are reasons to affirm or deny these claims for sure. But reasoning will not get us all the way to an answer. So one must believe an answer, and a truthful answer will presumably best account for the evidence at hand.

Two observations regarding answers to big picture questions can be made from what was said above. First, this is not simply or even primarily an abstract intellectual exercise. It is a communal, embodied, and practical endeavor. As John Paul says

> Human beings are not made to live alone. They are born into a family and in a family they grow, eventually entering society through their activity. From birth, therefore, they are immersed in traditions which give them not only a language and a cultural formation but also a range of truths in which they believe almost instinctively. (31)

The answers to the big-picture questions one obtains almost instinctively come not primarily from formal education, although that certainly helps too, but from the myriad of everyday practices one grows into in life. Recall from chapter 5 on prudence that the ability to see and decide needs formation to be done well (prudently), and that this formation comes largely in a communal context by seeing how our parents relate, how people are treated in our household and communities, and how pleasures are pursued.

The same is true of beliefs concerning big-picture questions. They are generally formed in people over time in what Cardinal Newman famously called a "muddy and bloody process."[4] What we say before meals, how we mourn the dead, whether and how we observe the Sabbath—growing up and living in all these practices is what shapes our big-picture beliefs. Note that if the argument of chapter 10 is true, big-picture beliefs are obtained not just in how we soak in the explicitly religious, or nonreligious, practices around us, like going or not going to church, or saying grace, or not saying it. Those beliefs are reflected in how we live out innerworldly practices, like sharing our resources, reconciling after arguments, talking about other people, and so on. So our big-picture beliefs are also obtained through these not explicitly religious practices. They are obtained in trust of the people who nurture us in these practices.

Of course, this is not to say that such beliefs are simply inserted into us, and never taken on as our own. Sadly, it can be the case that people unreflectively stick with whatever vision of the way things are given them, perhaps to please, or out of fear of their parents, or just because it is easier. But

---

4. See Robert Barron, *The Strangest Way: Walking the Christian Path* (New York: Orbis, 2002), 28.

part of growing into maturity is reflectively making the worldview one has been given one's own, or altering it slightly, or radically, based upon other experiences. This is one area where formal study—especially theology and philosophy—can help. As C. S. Lewis aptly puts it, "If you do not listen to theology, that will not mean that you have no ideas about God. It will mean that you have a lot of wrong ones—bad, muddled, out of date ideas."[5] Yet the assimilation can also be informal, as when we discuss such matters with friends, read books that interest us, or listen to a preacher or speaker who moves us. Though such reflection and growth cannot guarantee the complete accuracy of our big-picture beliefs, it can certainly help broaden our perspective and ward off errors.

Second, though it should be clear by now that belief goes beyond, but is not hostile to or dismissive of, reason, the big-picture questions in whose answers we must believe (one way or the other) are such that it is unsurprising if questioning and uncertainty persist. Belief enables us to cling to some answers as true, often with great certitude based upon the person whom we believe. But at times, due to the nature of these questions as ultimate, we will cling to our answers even as further questioning and even uncertainty persist. The presence of questioning or uncertainty at times does not mean one does not believe. Of course, should there be only uncertainty and no clinging, and particularly should there be no reflection of particular big-picture beliefs in our activities, then it is no longer accurate to say we believe in that way. But particularly in challenging times, periods of questioning and uncertainty over our beliefs do not signify the loss of those beliefs. Especially at this point, we have taken this chapter's analysis of believing, as a human thing to do, right to the point of needing to specify exactly what one believes, and how the content of our belief shapes the dynamics of our belief.

The Theological Virtue Faith

The main point of the previous section was to use John Paul II's encyclical letter *Fides et Ratio* to explain how believing in general, and believing in answers to big-picture questions in particular, is the sort of thing that human persons are built to do. It should be clear that belief is not simply—or even primarily—an abstract theoretical exercise. It certainly is an intellectual activity, since we can examine and understand the content of our beliefs in order to profess them, change them, and teach them. But the most important way to assess, profess, and teach our beliefs is through living them our in our practices. The famous words of St. Francis illustrate well where our beliefs should be most manifest: "preach the gospel at all times; use words if necessary."

5. C. S. Lewis, *Mere Christianity* (San Francisco: HarperSanFrancisco, 2001), 155.

What Do You Believe? Fides Qua *vs.* Fides Quae

Mention of the gospel reminds us that what has not been done yet in this chapter is talk about Christian faith, or indeed the content of what anyone believes. What does Christian faith have to do with the previous section's discussion of belief? In short, Christian faith is simply one way of believing. Believing is a human activity. When it is done consistently it is a habit. So we can have a habit of believing in our friends or spouses. We also have habits of believing in answers to big-picture questions. Some people—recall Lucretius—consistently believe that the God of the Israelites whom Jesus Christ called Father does not exist, or that there is no destiny of union with any such god after death. That is a habit of believing, one that is manifest in Epicurean practices. Of course, Christians believe in an entirely different set of answers to big-picture questions. Both of these ways of believing are habits.

We know that a virtue is a good habit, and vice a bad habit. What constitutes a good habit with regard to believing answers to big-picture questions? Since the goal of belief is to grasp the truth, a good habit is believing the accurate, or truthful, answers to those questions. Thus, though there are many different habits of believing answers to big-picture questions, it is not possible to say that both Lucretius and Christians believe well when they affirm opposite things about the way things are. Only one, or neither, can be right, where the content of their faiths is directly contradictory. The term faith can be most basically understood as virtuous believing, the good habit of believing true answers to big-picture questions. There may be many types of habits for believing, but to the extent that they are importantly different they cannot all constitute virtuous believing.

Note that the term faith is used in two ways in this chapter. In one sense, it refers to a habit by which we believe answers to big-picture questions. One has a good habit of believing (i.e., the virtue faith) when one believes the true answers to those questions. Here the term refers to the habit one possesses. A second meaning of faith refers to the answers themselves. People may ask you, "what is his or her faith?" and you might reply, "he is a Muslim" or "she is Christian," or "he is Jewish," or "she is an atheist." All of these answers refer to the content of what the person believes in. In short, faith can be understood either as the habit by which we believe answers to big-picture questions (traditionally called *fides qua*, or "faith by which" we believe), or as the content of what we believe, the actual answers to those questions (traditionally called *fides quae*, or "faith which" we believe).

The entire first section of this chapter has been a discussion of *fides qua*, or the faith by which we believe. The point there was to show that human beings are believing persons about many things in life, but especially about the answers to big-picture questions. In a more general and descriptive sense, everyone has some sort of faith, if faith is meant simply as any habit of believing answers to such questions. Not only people of different religious traditions, but even atheists like Lucretius have faith in this sense of a habit of consistent belief.

But so far there has been almost no discussion of *fides quae*, or what people believe in. The last chapter offered a contrast between two faiths in the *fides quae* sense: Christianity and Epicureanism. But so far this chapter, relying on *Fides et Ratio*, has simply described the human dynamic of believing, or *fides qua*. This is done intentionally both by John Paul II, and here in this chapter. The point of starting with *fides qua* is to demonstrate that believing in answers to big-picture questions is a human thing to do, and not simply something done by Christians. All persons, of any or no religious tradition, believe in the *fides qua* sense, as seen not only in what they consciously and explicitly profess, but also in how they live out their lives.

That said, the content of what is believed, *fides quae*, matters enormously. In fact, attending to the content of faith impacts the dynamics of how one believes, the *fides qua*. In this chapter on faith, we are exposed for the first time to a main theme of the second half of the book. The theme is summed up in the famous phrase, "grace perfects nature," a phrase explained more fully in chapter 16.[6] For now, suffice it to say that Christian faith not only responds to and satisfies natural human longings, like the longing to believe, but also transcends and transforms them. Explaining how this is the case with regard to believing is the task of the remainder of this chapter. We will see how what Christians believe in (*fides quae*) transforms the dynamics of how Christians believe (*fides qua*).

What Christians Believe and Its Transformation of How They Believe

The task of this section is neither a comprehensive explanation, nor a defense, of what it is that Christians believe. Enough will have to be said about the content of Christian faith (the *fides quae*) in order to explain how that impacts the virtue faith by which Christians believe what they do (*fides qua*). The rest of this chapter explores how believing looks different for Christians based on the content of what we believe. That will prepare us for the rest of the book, which explores how Christian faith shapes how we live by permeating all areas of our lives.

Turning back to Pope John Paul II's *Fides et Ratio*, we can see both how Christian faith satisfies natural human questioning and proclivity for belief, and yet also supernaturally transcends that natural human longing. John Paul has already established the general human dynamics of belief to which Christian faith responds:

> It is the nature of the human being to seek the truth. This search looks not only to the attainment of truths which are partial, empirical or scientific; nor

---

6. See Aquinas, *Summa Theologiae*, I.1,8 ad. 2: "*cum enim gratia non tollat naturam sed perficiat.*"

is it only in individual acts of decision-making that people seek the true good. Their search looks towards an *ultimate* truth which would explain the meaning of life. And it is therefore a search which can reach its end only in reaching the absolute. Thanks to the inherent capacities of thought, man is able to encounter and recognize a truth of this kind. Such a truth—vital and necessary as it is for life—is attained not only by way of reason but also through trusting acquiescence to other persons who can guarantee the authenticity and certainty of the truth itself. There is no doubt that the capacity to entrust oneself and one's life to another person and the decision to do so are among the most significant and expressive human acts. It must not be forgotten that reason too needs to be sustained in all its searching by trusting dialogue and sincere friendship. . . . Men and women are on a journey of discovery which is humanly unstoppable— a search for the truth and a search for a person to whom they might entrust themselves. (33)[7]

This long quotation is a perfect summary of the first section of this chapter. It is also a perfect preparation, as John Paul intends, for understanding how it is that Christian faith satisfies and transcends the natural human longing to understand, in belief and in community with others, ultimate truths about the way things are.

Christian faith is the virtuous and truthful expression of this longing. With humanity poised to know the truth in the manner described in the above quotation, John Paul claims that Christian faith fulfills that longing, both in its answers to the ultimate questions, and especially in the ultimately trustworthy person of Jesus Christ:

Christian faith comes to meet them, offering the concrete possibility of reaching the goal which they seek. Moving beyond the stage of simple believing, Christian faith immerses human beings in the order of grace, which enables them to share in the mystery of Christ, which in turn offers them a true and coherent knowledge of the Triune God. In Jesus Christ, who is the Truth, faith recognizes the ultimate appeal to humanity, an appeal made in order that what we experience as desire and nostalgia may come to its fulfillment. (33)

Christian faith satisfies what human persons long for by nature: to know the truthful answers to big-picture questions based on trust in some reliable person. Yet Christian faith opens humanity up to a knowledge of God and a human destiny that far transcend what humanity could know through the "simple believing" that is proper to human nature. Thus, Christian faith satisfies the nature of the human person as one who lives by belief, and yet offers

7. Note the word "ultimate" (emphasis added) is used here instead of "ulterior," which is found in the official English translation of the document. Based upon the original Latin text (*Eius perscrutatio in ulteriorem intenditur veritatem quae sensum vitae dilucidare posit*) the English term "ultimate" seems more accurate.

answers which the person could never arrive at on his or her own. Then how do Christians have faith?

In short, Christian faith (as both *fides qua* and *fides quae*) is a gift given to persons. Christian faith (*fides qua*) enables the believer to know that the answer to his or her questions about the ultimate source and ground of all being (*fides quae*) is not an abstract formula, but rather the personal God of love, the triune communion of persons that is Father, Son, and Holy Spirit. As stated in the last chapter, the God who is love created all out of love, and created human persons with unique capacity (*imago Dei*) for loving union with God in interpersonal communion. For reasons explained in chapter 14, the God of love became a human person, Jesus Christ. The content of Christian faith (*fides quae*) is this story about who God is, how God relates to humanity, what destiny God calls us to, and how God is most perfectly known in the person of Jesus Christ.

Jesus Christ is not only the focal point of Christian faith, in the *fides quae* sense; Jesus Christ is the path to Christian faith in the *fides qua* sense. Jesus says, "I am the way the truth and the life. No one comes to the Father except through me" (John 14:6). All Christian faith derives ultimately from an encounter with this person, who is found ultimately trustworthy and thus who leads us to faith. Recall that we are moved to believe things in life through trust in a person. Christian belief comes from trust in Christ. From the disciples who walked with Jesus in the Holy Land, to followers today who encounter the living Christ in the church as the Body of Christ, all Christian faith comes from Jesus Christ. In Jesus Christ we encounter that perfect communion of God and humanity to which all persons are called. Humanity from the beginning has been called to a destiny—a supernatural destiny—of union with God, which is made perfectly visible in the ultimate sacrament, or symbol, of God's presence with us: Jesus Christ. This is eternal life, most properly understood not simply as life without end (eternal) but as life without any limitation, sometimes translated as the fullness of life. It is complete happiness, fulfillment. Indeed, Christian faith as knowledge of these truths (*fides qua*) is actually a foretaste of our supernatural destiny of eternal life in union with God, since knowledge of who God is constitutes a sort of union with God, although it is not complete in this life).[8]

See how far we have gone in just paragraphs from the human quest described in the first section. That quest has been answered, but in a manner far transcending humanity's unaided capacities. And so we see how the content of what Christians believe (*fides quae*) shapes the habit by which they believe (*fides qua*). Consider several distinctive features of the virtue of Christian faith that follow based upon the content of what Christians believe to be true.

8. See *Catechism of the Catholic Church* 163. It references Aquinas, *Summa Theologiae*, II–II 4,1, as well as St. Basil the Great's *On the Holy Spirit* 15, 36.

First, faith is personal. The Christian virtue faith is not the conclusion of some abstract reasoning process. One can, of course, reason about one's faith. But the origin of Christian faith is a personal relationship with Jesus Christ. Note that personal here refers to interpersonal communion, and not primarily to an individual relationship with Christ. Though a person of faith is surely in relationship to Christ as an individual, that relationship always has a communal context. Faith is obtained in community with others, and the destiny to which we are called, as illuminated by faith, is a thoroughly communal one. The church in this life, and communion of saints in the next, are simply names for this community. Thus both the destiny known in Christian faith (*fides quae*), and the way in which that faith is obtained and held (*fides qua*), are rooted in loving interpersonal communion.

Second, this relationship is initiated by God. We know what we know in faith only because God has revealed Himself to us, most perfectly in Christ Jesus, but also in a multitude of other avenues including the Old Testament, our consciences, and creation all around us. Faith is a gift. We know this through the stories of God's generous gifts of faith to people throughout salvation history.[9] We also know it must be a gift because what is given exceeds our unaided human capacities. Beliefs in the Trinity, in the full humanity and divinity of Jesus Christ, and in the resurrection of the body (explored in chapter 13) are all beyond what we could understand on our own. Thus faith is only possible through God's assistance (called grace, and explored in more detail in chapter 16).

Third, though faith transcends our unaided capacities and originates from God as a gift, that is not at all to say faith it not truly our own. Faith in the sense of *fides qua* is the virtue by which we believe truthful answers to ultimate questions. A virtue is a quality of a person, a part of that person. And so one's faith is truly one's own. It is not possible without God's help, and it is born and nurtured in community with others. But it is truly one's own in that it is a change in us whereby our intellect and will know the truth about the God who is. In fact, because the virtue faith is one's own, God does not give faith against the will of the believer. Here is yet another example in the Christian story of how God respects and satisfies human nature, yet ultimately elevates and transcends it. Faith is part of us and our own, but when given it transforms us and makes us more than we could be on our own.

Fourth, and to come full circle back to John Paul's description of faith as the answer to a natural human longing, the knowledge of faith does not defy or leave unaffected human reasoning. It completes and elevates human reasoning. As John Paul says:

9. The *Catechism of the Catholic Church*, 2nd ed. (Vatican City: Libreria Editrice Vaticana, 1997), 145–49, mentions two exemplars of faith, Abraham and Mary.

[St.] Thomas had the great merit of giving pride of place to the harmony which exists between faith and reason. Both the light of reason and the light of faith come from God, he argued; hence there can be no contradiction between them. . . . More radically, Thomas recognized that nature, philosophy's proper concern, could contribute to the understanding of divine Revelation. Faith therefore has no fear of reason, but seeks it out and has trust in it. Just as grace builds on nature and brings it to fulfillment, so faith builds upon and perfects reason. Illumined by faith, reason is set free from the fragility and limitations deriving from the disobedience of sin and finds the strength required to rise to the knowledge of the Triune God. . . . Faith is in a sense an "exercise of thought"; and human reason is neither annulled nor debased in assenting to the contents of faith, which are in any case attained by way of free and informed choice. (43)

Faith and reason have been compared to two wings of a bird which work together in support of the human person's quest for truth. Both are needed, and they complement rather than rival one another.

This truth [of faith], which God reveals to us in Jesus Christ, is not opposed to the truths which philosophy perceives. On the contrary, the two modes of knowledge lead to truth in all its fullness. . . . It is the one and the same God who establishes and guarantees the intelligibility and reasonableness of the natural order of things upon which scientists confidently depend, and who reveals himself as the Father of our Lord Jesus Christ. This unity of truth, natural and revealed, is embodied in a living and personal way in Christ. (34)

This complementary relationship between faith and reason is not at all surprising once we recall that the God who is known in faith is the God who created us with the capacity to reason. And thus this final observation on faith and reason is the perfect way to conclude this section, the purpose of which has been to show how Christian faith, in terms of what we believe (*fides quae*), not only satisfies the natural human longing for truth but also elevates and transforms that capacity to believe (*fides qua*). Just as "faith liberates reason in so far as it allows reason to attain correctly what it seeks to know and to place it within the ultimate order of things, in which everything acquires true meaning" (20), Christian faith satisfies, transforms, and elevates the nature of the human person as one who believes.

Concluding Thoughts, with a Definition

Though a chapter conclusion should generally not be the place to offer new material, it may help here to state some straightforward definition of faith that assimilates the arguments made in this chapter. Faith can refer to the content of what is believed (*fides quae*), as when we hear, "Do you believe the Catholic faith?" or "Even an atheist has faith in some sense!" But in this book structured on the virtues, it is the other sense of faith, the habit of believing answers to big-picture questions (*fides qua*), that is meant when we list together faith, hope, and love as theological virtues.

It can be said that everyone has some sort of faith, both in content and in manner of believing. After all, explicitly or not, consciously or not, everyone lives out some set of answers to the big-picture questions in life. This is true of people of different, or no, religions. And everyone develops some sort of habit of believing in those answers. But, of course, to the extent that the term faith means not just a habit, but a virtue, then it only properly refers to people who believe true answers about big-picture questions, and who believe those things well.

It is this more precise sense of the word that is meant by the theological virtue faith that is grouped with hope and love. The theological virtue *faith* may be defined as the virtue by which we believe in true things about God and God's relationship to humanity. Faith is properly called a theological virtue since, as you recall from chapter 3, theological virtues concern God directly. Even though faith shapes all our activities in life, what is believed in faith concerns God's very self, and how God has related to humanity. Furthermore, because faith concerns God's very self, it satisfies, yet transcends and elevates, our natural human capacities. Therefore it is possible only with God's assistance, called grace. We see already how importantly different the theological virtue faith as Christians understand it is from the broader sense of faith understood, say, by Epicureans like Lucretius. It would make no sense for Lucretius to say that the habit he has of believing answers to big-picture questions is a gift, a fruit of personal relationship initiated by God. Here we see typified how one's *fides quae* impacts one's *fides qua*. We also see why only believing Christians have the theological virtue of faith.

This sounds offensive to some people. How in this day and age can we dare say that only one group of people (in this case a religious group) can be right? Isn't this being judgmental? More on judgmentalism will follow in chapter 17, but we can say here that the nature of big-picture questions is such that opposing view points cannot both be right. There is a god or there is not. Jesus Christ is the Son of God or he is not. There is a destiny of union with God and others after death, or there is not. The answers to these questions are not true or false based upon what we believe. The answers are what they are, and we seek to believe truthfully. Particularly given the way faith is lived out in our innerworldly practices, this surely raises complicated questions about how and why people have faith in the Christian sense or not: need faith be creedally professed? Are people who lack faith to blame for that lack? If the Christian story is true, what does God have in store for people who are not Christian?

These are important questions, but questions for another book. Suffice it to say two things here. First, the *Catechism of the Catholic Church* recognizes that though Christians know through revelation that baptism and the sacraments are a path to eternal life, God is not limited in his action to his sacraments.[10] In other words, God can bring people to full union with himself even outside the sacraments. What exactly this means as for who is saved, what is required, how that happens, and so on is one of the most difficult and divisive set of questions today in theology. Still, the point here is that Catholics do not today make the absolute claim that no one who is not a baptized Catholic can attain eternal life.

Second, the problem here is not simply one of religious people being exclusive. People of no matter what set of big-picture beliefs must think that those who hold contrary beliefs are wrong. If it is the case that one's answers to big-picture questions matter (as this chapter and the previous have sought to demonstrate), then to know the truth concerning such questions will set us free. Yet this is true of whatever set of answers is true. Note, this is exactly the claim of Lucretius as well as Christians. Presumably an atheist like Lucretius would think Christians are living in a manner reflective of an importantly distorted view of reality. He would think their ability to live a good life is hindered by this. If the truth matters in these questions, it is no use saying it does not matter just to avoid sounding offensive to those of a different or no faith tradition. And as for those who think any view of the big-picture questions is irrelevant for how we live, that is not a way to avoid disagreeing with folks like Christians or Epicureans; it is simply another position, and one that regards both Christians and Epicureans as deficient in important ways. Regardless of one's position, then, there is no way to avoid having a position, and doing so inherently means an at least implicit recognition that other positions are deficient in some important way.

So it suffices here to rest in the tension between affirming the importance of believing truthful answers to big-picture questions, and recognizing that from a Christian perspective we trust God is just and loving and thus somehow fair and inclusive. But to return to our definition of faith, for Christians the virtue faith is belief in true answers to ultimate questions, and the way it is obtained and expressed is reflective of the Christian understanding of who God is, how God relates to us in history, and how humanity is built with a capacity for faith and reason.

Study Questions

1. Why does John Paul II claim that all people, no matter what, if any, religious belief they hold, seek the answers to ultimate or big-picture questions?

10. *Catechism of the Catholic Church*, 1257.

2. Why, according to John Paul, are the answers to these questions elusive? Can, therefore, one avoid answering (even if not asking) these questions? Why or why not?

3. Describe the act of belief. Give two different reasons why it is necessary to believe certain things. Give an example of each from your own experience.

4. What role is there for other people in the ways we believe? In what ways are we vulnerable when we believe? How can we ensure we are not misled when we believe?

5. Describe the relationship between faith and reason. Are they the same thing? Mutually exclusive? Complementary? Explain.

6. Explain the difference between *fides qua* and *fides quae*.

7. How does faith in the *fides qua* look different in the context of the Christian story (*fides quae*)?

8. In what sense can everyone be said to have faith? Who has the theological virtue faith?

Terms to Know

to believe, *fides qua* vs. *fides quae*, faith in general, faith as a theological virtue

Questions for Further Reflection

1. John Paul II claims that people are built, if you will, to seek the truth. They are also built to believe as part of that quest. Is this true? What sorts of evidence would you offer to support or refute this view of humanity?

2. The chapter parallels belief in human relationships with belief on big-picture questions, such as Christian faith. In what ways are they similar? In what ways are they different?

3. Try and imagine how some non-Christian (religious or otherwise) would understand belief in ultimate questions. How would the *fides quae* impact the *fides qua*?

4. The conclusion of this chapter is the natural springboard from which to engage in study or discussion of the question of whether and how non-Christians can attain eternal life. Is eternal life possible for non-Christians, and if so, how? Is it possible to simultaneously claim that faith is morally important and that people who do not hold Christian faith can live most fully?

Further Reading

The foundational text for this chapter is obviously Pope John Paul II's *Fides et Ratio*. Also crucial is Aquinas's analysis of belief and faith in the *Summa Theologiae*, II–II 1–16. For a helpful overview of faith, see also the *Catechism of the Catholic Church* 26–184 (esp. 142–84). Robert Barron's *The Strangest Way* and C. S. Lewis's *Mere Christianity* have also been helpful in teaching these topics.

12

SIN

Corruption of Human Happiness

I n his wonderful book, *The Strangest Way: Walking the Christian Path*, Robert Barron has a chapter called "Knowing You're a Sinner."[1] He begins with a helpful question: why is it that saintly people seem to emphasize their sinfulness? You read that right. The great saints throughout history have always been quite clear in acknowledging their sinful brokenness. See St. Paul's letter to the Romans (7:13–25), where he poignantly acknowledges the perversity of his sinfulness. St. Augustine's *Confessions* is full of acknowledgment of his sinfulness. St. Thomas Aquinas spent the last few months of his life in a daze dismissing all the great theological work he had done as "mere straw," or insignificant compared to a powerful encounter with God he had late in life. St. Theresa of Avila begins her great spiritual classic *Interior Castle* insisting that she is a worthless servant of God. Perhaps you know holy people in your life who humbly acknowledge their own sinfulness.

Why do these greats of Christianity do this? Is this simply a matter of false humility? We see examples of that all the time, when people object to a compliment because it seems to embarrass them. They may note that another person was even more important for the success, or downplay the goodness of what

---

1. See Robert Barron, *The Strangest Way: Walking the Christian Path* (New York: Orbis, 2002).

was done. Sometimes this is a simple lack of comfort with being acknowledged. Sometimes it is a more pernicious—even if unconscious—invitation for further affirmation, compliment, and praise. Either way it is false humility because it is a denial or dismissal of something that is true, namely, that they truly did something good and special.

Are saints falsely humble, acknowledging their sinfulness out of awkwardness, or even to invite praise from others? In other words, when acknowledging their sinfulness, are saints seeing things wrongly? Barron thinks not. He suggests an alternate explanation, and uses a vivid metaphor to explain his answer. A resident of Chicago, Barron describes how in the winter snow you can drive around and have your windshield become caked over with road salt. The interesting thing is, however, that at night it is still possible to drive with such a windshield. Since you are in the dark, and looking out at lighted signs and car headlights, it is possible to navigate your way. But as anyone who has had such a windshield knows, in the morning it is a whole other story. In the sunlight, it is impossible to see out of the opaque windshield, and if you do not have windshield wiper fluid, you are in trouble.

What does this have to do with saints and sin? Barron observes that even when you are driving at night, the salt is there, and the windshield is opaque. Yet in the absence of strong light, you do not see it, and operate as if it is not there. This is impossible in the presence of strong light. The light illuminates the salt on the windshield, prompting you to act accordingly. You acknowledge it is there, and seek its removal. In Barron's analogy, all of us are cars, the salt stands for sin, and the light is God's presence. All of us are driving around with more or less caked-over windshields, an image for our present human condition in which we are all sinful, to one degree or another. It is precisely those people who are in the presence of God's truth and love who are able to see their sinfulness. In this analogy, the saints are people who drive in the daylight, and are thus more aware of how caked over their windshields are. They therefore act accordingly, which means confessing their sinfulness, asking for forgiveness, and seeking God's help to live holy, rather than sinful, lives. By contrast, many of us are like drivers at night, who think our windshields are just fine even though they are not. Occasionally we catch glimpses of our sinfulness, as when passing under street lights. But we rest content with driving in the dark, navigating as best we can. Not so with the saints, whose openness to God's brilliant presence enables God's light to illuminate their brokenness. The point of Barron's analogy is that while acknowledging their sinfulness, the saints are actually seeing things more, not less, accurately than the rest of us.

Why open this chapter on sin with this odd analogy? One of the main purposes of this chapter is to emphasize the reality of human sinfulness, which is too often overlooked. Continuing this point will be the purpose of the first section below. The second section attempts to define sin more precisely through an analysis of the definition of sin provided in the *Catechism of the Catholic Church*, followed by reflections on the theme of pride and the story of Genesis 3. The third section provides even more detail on the nature of sin, through two ways of categorizing different sins. Finally, having emphasized, defined, and probed in depth the reality of sin, the final section properly contextualizes this chapter's focus on sin within Christianity as a whole, where sin is far from the end of the story.

The Pervasiveness of Sin

Let's begin this section on the pervasiveness of human sinfulness with a startling claim about the Christian story: if you do not think something is radically wrong with our world, and indeed yourself, then Christianity is not for you. The life, death, and resurrection of Jesus Christ only make sense if we acknowledge that something is fundamentally wrong with humanity and with each of us individually. In ways described further in chapter 14, Jesus Christ is understood by Christians to save all people from something. If there were nothing fundamentally wrong with people, there would be nothing to save us from! It is sin, and the effects of sin, that is wrong with the world and with ourselves.

Recognition of human sinfulness is everywhere in the gospels. The first words spoken at the time of Jesus's public ministry in each of the three synoptic gospels—Matthew, Mark, and Luke—are "Repent! The kingdom of God is at hand!" (Matt. 3:2; Mark 1:4; Luke 3:3). Yes, Jesus Christ has come to inaugurate God's kingdom. But the first word, "repent!" makes it clear that his coming is in response to something wrong that needs changing. In the story of the Pharisee and the tax collector, Jesus praises not the seemingly law-abiding Pharisee, but rather the humble tax collector who acknowledges his own sinfulness (Luke 18:9–14). Jesus surprises us in another story by extolling not the seemingly upright Pharisee, but the sinful woman who anoints Christ's feet, bathes them with her tears, and dries them with her hair (Luke 7:36–50). The claim that Christ came to redeem us from sin is all over the New Testament. In story after story Christ praises those who acknowledge their need for forgiveness.

Sin is a central theme in the Christian story. Therefore the saints, whose lives are understood primarily in the terms of that story, are acutely aware of their sinfulness. An old friend who is a priest once related a story to me about his encounter with a woman at a wedding. Seeing a priest, she asked him why Catholics are so explicit in recognizing their sinfulness. "You Catholics are too concerned with sin and repentance," she said. "In my church we just try to be good people." His response reflects the importance of sin in the Christian story. "Oh what a terrible burden," he replied, "Our church is a church of sinners."

This is not of course to say that saints do not try to be good people. One need only look at saintly lives to know this is not the case. It simply means that people who truthfully see their own condition, and that of humanity in general, recognize the sad reality of sin in their lives. Saints are not free from all sin. They feel deeply the presence of sin in their lives, and not merely as some abstract observation. Yet they have the humility to walk with a group of redeemed sinners, which is the people of God, the church.

There are two common errors concerning the recognition of our sinfulness that warrant attention here. The first is simply its denial, or better, the assumption that things are really not that bad. This is exemplified in self-help approaches that simply emphasize the goodness of the person. Consider the title of the renowned 1970s book, *I'm OK, You're OK*. From the perspective of the Christian story seen in previous chapters, it is indeed the case that creation is fundamentally good. But this is not the whole story. The Christian tradition also reminds us of the reality of sin. In an important sense, I'm *not* OK, and you are *not* OK. There is something broken that needs fixing. Furthermore, this fixing is not simply some sprucing up around the edges or fine tuning that all of us recognize we could use. We might say to ourselves, "Sure, I should call my family more, try to be more generous to those in need, and take better care of myself. But in general I'm doing pretty good!" Though this perspective may display the recognition of a need for some changes in one's life, it fails to grasp the perniciousness of our sinfulness in intent and magnitude.

A second error concerning the recognition of our sinfulness is found in those who point the finger at people who call themselves faithful or religious, and yet fail to live fully virtuous lives. It is true that people of faith still sin. It is even more scandalous that religious people can use their faith or good acts to pridefully lord it over others. This dynamic is examined in a later section of this chapter. Yet despite the fact that this charge of hypocrisy can be accurate, note how it often serves to deflect attention away from the accuser's own life and sinfulness, as if to say, "Why should I bother critically examining my own life when even so-called religious people are sinners?" The latter may indeed be the case. But whether it renders the accuser any less sinful is another question indeed.

The basic opening claim of this chapter is that sin is a reality among us. If we see things rightly, we will recognize this fact more clearly. In fact, unless we do it will be impossible to find freedom from the trappings of sin. The purpose of this recognition is not despair, some old-fashioned guilt trip, or worse, a false humility that actually egotistically seeks further affirmation. As the final section of this chapter notes, the Christian cannot reflect on sin without immediately recognizing that the gift of forgiveness is available. But in order to truly appreciate the need for and gratuitousness of that gift, we need to, in Barron's words, "smell the stench and taste the acidity of sin."[2]

2. Ibid., 76.

Defining Sin

In order to "smell the stench and taste the acidity" of sin, it is necessary to explain more clearly exactly what sin is. The *Catechism* defines sin as an

> offense against reason, truth, and right conscience; it is a failure in genuine love for God and neighbor caused by a perverse attachment to certain goods. It wounds the nature of man and injures human solidarity.[3]

The purpose of this section is to reflect more deeply on this powerful definition, and then examine further the reality of sin through a look at the central sin of pride in the classic text on the first sin (Gen. 3).

The *Catechism* definition importantly begins with the claim that sin is an offense against "reason, truth, and right conscience." Since our reason is how we grasp what is true, and since conscience is a (hopefully true) judgment about the rightness or wrongness of an act, the fact that sin is an offense against all three of these terms is no surprise. Acting sinfully truly harms ourselves and others. If something is rightly called a sin, it is not simply a taboo, a no-no that one must avoid, simply because the rules say so. We are reminded yet again here of a morality of happiness vs. a morality of obligation.

Sinful action impedes our ability to live truly happy lives. It manifests a false estimation of how to live a good life. The *Catechism* goes on to explain this by saying that sin is "caused by a perverse attachment to certain goods." Reminiscent of the second chapter on intention, and the different ways we prioritize things in our lives, sin is an occasion of improperly ordering our goals by placing imagined or lesser goods above true and more important goods. In other words, we are perversely attached to lesser goods. For instance, there is nothing wrong with wanting others to think well of us. But when we do good acts simply so that others think well of us, we place a lesser good (our reputation) above a greater good (service to others). This is a false valuing of what is truly important, and actions resulting from it are sinful. Similarly, there is nothing inherently wrong with drinking alcohol. But as chapter 6 discussed, we can place too much priority on the real importance of drinking, such that we are perversely attached to this lesser good and neglect or devalue other more important goods.

Thus, sinful acts are wrong not because they constitute disobedience to some arbitrary rules, but because acting sinfully truly impedes our happiness and thus harms ourselves and others, and offends God. In chapter 7, on justice, we explored how an individual's flourishing is inextricably bound to others' flourishing through the notion of the common good. This is why

---

3. *Catechism of the Catholic Church*, 2nd ed. (Vatican City: Libreria Editrice Vaticana, 1997), 1849.

sin "wounds the nature of man and injures human solidarity."[4] Acts that harm the good of others genuinely wound one's own nature. They thwart the ability of people to flourish in common, and reflect and further ingrain a false estimation on the part of a person about the dignity of other persons and one's own connection to others. Note that the same connection between individual and communal flourishing can be found in the opposite direction. Just as individual sins always reverberate and have impacts on others, so too do social structures of sin corrupt individual lives. We are increasingly aware that the adjective "sinful" can describe social entities as well as individuals. Whether it be an institution such as slavery, pervasive intemperate drinking practices at a university, or economic structures that systemically debilitate the lives of the poor, the reality of sin always entails individual sinfulness, but also often pervades more widespread social structures.

Conversely, even acts that seem victimless injure human solidarity. We commonly hear people say, "What is the problem if no one is getting hurt?" Yet if the act is truly harmful to an individual, it does hurt others by extension. And again, an act that reflects and further ingrains a false estimation of the way things are ultimately does hurt others in subjecting them to that false estimation. Consider the example of pornography. People commonly say, "How is looking at pornography in private hurting others?" Even if we were to neglect the fact that supporting pornography, even on the internet, does indeed bolster and perpetuate an industry that dehumanizes people (even willing participants, let alone others), viewing pornography leads one to falsely see others as objects of one's own sexual desires rather than as people with dignity who are not simply instruments for one's own sexual pleasure. Ingraining that false way of seeing things not only harms one's self by obstructing right action, which relies on seeing rightly, but also ultimately impacts others who are seen falsely and treated accordingly. To put it simply, sin is not simply a no-no but is rather falsity. It is genuinely harmful, and that is why it is bad. If the true precedes the good, falsity leads to sin.

A word is in order on the *Catechism's* claim, immediately following the definition given above, that "sin is an offense against God."[5] This may seem like an odd claim, implying that God is in need of our recognition, and somehow slighted and angry at our failing to acknowledge and obey his rules. But this morality-of-obligation perspective reveals a poor understanding of both morality and God. Sin is an offense against God, because God out of great love for us guides us to live according to the truth, which sets us free. Consider a simple analogy to explain this. A parent is trying to help a child who really wants to learn to ride a bike. Each time the parent tells the child what to do, and tries to run alongside the child on the bike to help, the

4. Ibid.
5. Ibid., 1850.

child insists on doing things his own way and continually falls. This is an "offense" to the parent, not because the parent is trying to lord it over the child and be recognized, but because the parent wants the child to do well, to flourish, and is trying to help the child do so. But even though the parent clearly knows better, the child will not listen,

In the analogy, God is like the parent, and each of us is like the child, who thinks he does things better his own way. Like the parent, God wants what is truly best for us and even knows best what that is. But we so often fail to heed God's guidance, however it is received. In doing so we explicitly or at least implicitly say that we do not believe it is there for our own good. This is offensive in reflecting a lack of trust in God. It even explicitly, or at least implicitly, questions God's sovereignty. When we sin we decide that it is we who really know what is truly best for us and others, or we recognize that something is generally not best for us and others but really OK for us in this particular situation.

Hence sin is offensive to God, not in the same way that we might be offended by someone's comment at a social event, but rather by implying God is not truly loving and sovereign. Of course, Christians think that what we believe about God in faith is true. So saying sin is an offense against God is really the same as saying sin is an offense against reason and truth. But the recognition of sin as a questioning of God's goodness and sovereignty points toward another consistent claim in the Christian tradition, one that will help explain the concept of sin. In some shape or form, pride is at the root of all human sin. Understanding what this particular sin is—and is not—will help illuminate the concept of sin as a whole.

Pride: Root of All Sin

The term "pride" has a distinct meaning in moral theology that is not what we often mean when we use the term in everyday life. As used here pride is roughly synonymous with vanity. Simply put, *pride* is selfishness, or putting ourselves first. There are obvious examples of this, as when people take what belongs to others out of concern only for themselves, and not those who are wronged. But the pride that is the root of all sin goes deeper. It is a fixation on one's own life and desires. Indeed it is seeing all of reality out there through the warped lens of "what does this have to do with me?" When we are inattentive to the needs of those around us because they do not seem to immediately impact us, we are prideful. When we find ourselves reading any situation through its ultimate impact on ourselves, we are prideful. Being prideful entails seeing things not as they truly are, but how they would be with ourselves at the center. For the prideful person, all the world is a stage, and he is the star of the show. In fact pride is self-centeredness, in the sense that the prideful person sees things and acts as if he is indeed at the center of all things.

Given this definition of pride as self-centeredness, it should be clear that the pride described here as the root of all sin is not the pride we refer to when we say we are proud of a loved one's accomplishment, or proud to be a member of some group. C. S. Lewis calls this sentiment "warm-hearted appreciation," and notes that it is far from the central vice of pride, since it takes pleasure in the accomplishments of others.[6] Of course, should one begin to be proud of, say, one's child in a manner that leads one to see one's self as better than others and as the reason for the child's success, one is coming far closer to the sin of pride.

Indeed, it is even possible to say one is proud of one's self in a manner that does not refer to the central sin of pride described here. Lewis calls this sense of pride "pleasure in being praised."[7] Again, if we derive such pleasure from being praised by the right people for the right things, we are far from the vice of pride. After all, the very recognition that there are others we admire for their grasp of what is truly good and life-giving is itself a recognition that we are not the stars of the show. But if this pleasure in praise becomes simple delight in one's self, devoid of any sense in which our accomplishments are also gifts due to our reliance on others and God, then we are veering sharply toward pride.

Finally, nor is it pride when we recognize our rightful, truthful place in the world. A common feminist critique of the claim that pride is at the root of all sin counters that pride is exactly what some people—especially abused, neglected, or otherwise disenfranchised people—need in this world. As victims they need to assert themselves! But note that a just and accurate recognition of one's proper place in the world, including asserting one's self when that place is not recognized, is not the sin of pride, since it is neither self-centered nor inaccurate. The sin of pride is always both of these.

For prideful people, their triangle of priorities and goals in life ultimately has themselves at the top. They therefore act accordingly and subvert what should be more important goals to their own interests. Of course, the proud person can love his family, keep a job, and even go to church. But each of these is done with one's self as the ultimate purpose. How does being a good family member help me? What does this job do for me? What does going to church do for me? Since the prideful person is doing such activities in an ultimately self-serving manner, the person may on occasion do the right thing, but when push comes to shove what he does will always be ultimately self-serving. This self-centeredness is why Lewis calls pride an essentially competitive vice. If one sees one's self as the top of the triangle or center of all things, obviously no one else can occupy that territory. The prideful person is thus easily threatened. As Lewis notes, the prideful person does not just see herself as smart or good-looking or rich, but as smarter or better-looking, or richer than those

---

6. See C. S. Lewis, *Mere Christianity* (San Francisco: HarperSanFrancisco, 2001), 127.
7. Ibid., 125.

around her. There is room for only one at the top, and so the prideful do not look happily on the successes of others.

Nor are the prideful able to truly know God. Lewis calls pride the "anti-God state of Mind."[8] In the Christian story, God is of course the source, goal, and sustenance of all that is. God, not any human person, is the center of the story.

> In God you come up against something which is in every respect immediately superior to yourself. Unless you know God as that—and, therefore, know yourself as nothing in comparison—you do not know God at all. *As long as you are proud you cannot know God.* A proud man is always looking down on things and people; and, of course, as long as you are looking down, you cannot see something that is above you.[9]

If a person is prideful enough to think it is all ultimately about himself, he obviously does not think it is all ultimately about God, which it is. Therefore pride is actually incompatible with genuine religious faith.

One of the ironies noted by Lewis, as well as others who have written on pride, is that pride is all too commonly found in seemingly religious people. How can this be? Anything that is beautiful and true can also unfortunately enable those who possess it to think that they are better than others, that it is due to their own importance that they are in the know. The Pharisee in Luke perfectly, and tragically, articulates prideful religiosity: "O God, I thank you that I am not like the rest of humanity—greedy, dishonest, adulterous—or even like this tax collector. I fast twice a week, and I pay tithes on my whole income" (Luke 18:11–12). Here is a seemingly religious man who is even doing good deeds. But they are done to exalt himself, and they establish his superiority over others such as the tax collector who, of course, Jesus says was the one who walked away justified. In reality this Pharisee is not truly religious, but simply performing religious actions. This is not of course true of all who call themselves religious. In fact, recall from this chapter's opening how the great figures of the Christian story do just the opposite of this Pharisee. But sadly pride does infect all potential great human activities, including religion. Of course, people who are prideful about religion corrupt the supposed source of their superiority and reveal themselves for what they are: self-centered rather than God-centered.

Sin and Genesis 3

This is why sin, which in some way always contains pride, is an offense against God. Though the prideful surely do not consciously think of themselves this way,

8. Ibid., 122.
9. Ibid., 124 (emphasis added).

the sin of pride, as an attempt to make one's self the top of the triangle, is in effect the attempt to make one's self into God. Nowhere is this more clear than in the famous Genesis 3 account of humanity's first sin. This text is so rich that any brief discussion of it seems paltry. But for our purposes we can focus on what it is that tempts the man and woman. In the story, the serpent is the metaphorical representation of the fact that we people are often tempted to do that which we know is not best. When the serpent questions the woman, she knows full well what she should and should not do. Why, then, do the man and woman sin?

Note the cleverness of the serpent, and how temptation works in leading people to sin. After hearing the woman explain that they are not to eat of the fruit lest they die, the serpent responds by saying, "You certainly will not die! No, God knows well that the moment you eat of it your eyes will be opened and *you will be like gods* who know what is good and what is bad" (Gen. 3:4–5, emphasis added). Sounds appealing! Not only appealing, but even upright. After all, wouldn't it be nice to have our eyes opened so as to know what is good and what is bad? Far from sinful, this seems like rather useful information to have to live a good life.

But note two key parts of this passage. First, the serpent clearly implies that God is guarding something from the man and woman. The serpent introduces distrust between God and God's beloved creatures, man and woman. Though God's rules are clearly presented in the Genesis text as the way to have life, even life in right relationship with God, the serpent suggests that is not really the reason for the rules. "Maybe God does not want what is best for you, man and woman, and maybe you can have that anyway!" Adam and Eve begin to question whether the morality God gave them is truly one of happiness, or perhaps, as the serpent suggests, really just an obligation imposed on them that actually limits their full happiness.

Second, note the key phrase of the serpent: "you will be like gods who know what is good and what is bad." What does this mean? The serpent cannot just mean by this that they will know what is good and bad; Eve demonstrates that they already know what they should and should not do when she lays out the rules God gave them before the serpent makes this tempting offer of becoming like gods. By saying, "you will be like gods," the serpent is offering them something they do not already have. The man and woman already know, but do not determine themselves, what is good and bad. And when they think they know what is good, it may not be, and their knowing it to be good does not make it such. In other words, man and woman are creatures, not gods. Yet in this powerful story the man and woman let themselves be deluded into thinking they are not mere creatures. Why live in accordance with the way things are, when perhaps we can decide how things are in accordance with our wishes! It is as if they say, "maybe we can become like gods. We could decide for ourselves the way things are, and thus what is truly good and bad. That way we can live as *we* want, not as God wants."

This perfectly exemplifies the sin of pride, the root of all sin. Pride is doing what we want, under the assumption that it is we who really know what is right and wrong. How we see things—or better how we want to see things—is how they really are. We are like gods, not only knowing but determining what is good and bad. If this sounds dramatic, think of all the little rationalizations we devise to justify (in other words, make right) our acts as good, when our very tone and justification betrays that we know full well the truth. Whether it is the rationalization that cheating on this test is not really bad given all the pressure I'm under, or the assumption that "yes, that is normally wrong, but in *my* case. . .," pride is the assumption that it is we who know what truly is right and wrong.

Thus the story of the first sin in Genesis 3 is a powerful depiction of how we succumb to pride, and are tempted to see things as we want to and act accordingly, rather than humbly respond to how things really are and order our desires and goals accordingly. We know, of course, how the Genesis 3 story ends. When the Lord confronts the man and woman about their actions, everyone blames someone else: the man blames the woman, and the woman blames the serpent. What an accurate account of what happens when we sin; it is surely not our fault! By the end of the story, the man and woman have indeed obtained some knowledge they did not have before: they now know shame.

Worse yet, they have alienated themselves from their source of true life. They sought to exalt themselves to become like gods, and end up degrading themselves and sacrificing the happiness that had been bestowed upon them. In a supreme irony, the prideful person longs for an imagined happiness and ends up sacrificing what was readily available to him as a free gift from God. Thus the prideful person actually acts in a manner corruptive of his true happiness.

Differentiating Sins

One of the best ways to understand something better is to categorize its various instantiations. So, for instance, this entire book is structured mainly by the four cardinal and three theological virtues. The assumption is that it is easier to know how to live virtuously if one can better understand what exactly is meant by virtue in its different forms. Well, the same may be said of sin. We can better understand sin by learning some different ways that people of faith have categorized sin throughout the Christian tradition. This section explores two traditional ways to categorize sin.

Mortal and Venial Sin

The first way sins may be differentiated is by their degree. In other words, how serious is the sin? The traditional distinction here is *mortal* vs. *venial* sin. It is the nature of sin that it harms our relationships. It harms first and foremost our relationship with God, since it is God who invites us to fullness of life, in relationship with God and others. When we sin we reject that invitation. Hence any sin, including those against other people, is an offense against God, as noted above. Of course our sins also harm our relationships with others, even those sins that do not involve direct action against to others. But sin is first and foremost a blow to our relationship with God.

The terms "mortal" and "venial" describe how serious that blow is. Mortal sin ruptures our relationship with God. Venial sin strains our relationship with God. Consider two analogies. First, you hurt your knee playing sports. You can simply strain your muscles or tendons, or you could rupture or tear them. Now both are bad; you want neither of them. But it is more difficult to repair the rupture since there has been a severing of something that should be connected. Mortal sins sever our relationship with God, while venial sins strain a muscle. For a second example, consider ways you may harm a relationship with a friend. First, you could fail to celebrate with her some important event, or forget to call her when you said you would. Second, you could betray your friend by talking behind her back, or by going out with her boyfriend. Now, both of these are bad. Yet the first are examples of a strain on the relationship. The relationship itself has not been attacked or severed. The second examples are direct attacks on the relationship. Betrayal is diametrically opposed to ongoing friendship. In the analogy, the first examples of harm to a friendship are of the venial type, while the second would be mortal.

The term "mortal" means deadly or lethal. In other words, mortal sin spells the death of a relationship. Note two things about the death of relationship caused by mortal sin. First, as both of the above analogies should make clear, a mortal sin severs a relationship. But that is not the same as saying there can be no reconciliation. Some people wrongly assume that mortal sin cannot be forgiven. This is false. The task required to restore a severed relationship is great, for sure. But with God all things are possible. Second, the severance originates from our side of the relationship, not God's. In mortal sin, we decisively reject fullness of life in relationship with God and others. A relationship is a two-way street, and so despite the fact that God's love and offer of forgiveness is always there, mortal sin constitutes an obstinate rejection of that offer from our side.

What makes a sin mortal rather than venial? The *Catechism of the Catholic Church* summarizes the traditional criteria nicely. There must be a grave matter, full consent, and full knowledge.[10] In other words, what is done must be serious (grave matter). It must be done knowingly, and not out of ignorance or accidentally (full knowledge). Finally, it must be done consensually, and not against one's will or under duress (full consent). It is natural for people

10. *Catechism of the Catholic Church*, 1857.

learning about mortal sin to immediately wonder whether some area of their lives constitutes mortal sin. In a common caricature of the Roman Catholic tradition, Catholics find themselves in and out of mortal sin regularly, committing acts and repenting of them in the confessional. In reaction against this, some have explained the conditions of mortal sin in such a way that it is almost impossible to imagine anything constituting mortal sin save some direct rejection of God and God's love. This is surely an error on the other extreme. It is true, however, given that two of the three conditions of mortal sin concern not the act committed, but the interior state of the one committing it, that identifying something as a mortal sin requires a pastoral sensitivity to the particular person and situation. This is not to say there are no mortal sins—far from it. But the task here is to identify the conditions that render sin mortal rather than listing some set of acts that in and of themselves always constitute mortal sin.

The Seven Deadly (Not Mortal) Sins

There is a second way of categorizing sins that can help us understand better the presence of sin in our lives. Whether it be from reading Dante's *Purgatorio*, or from a Brad Pitt/Morgan Freeman movie, most people have heard of the seven deadly sins. The seven deadly sins are differentiated not by their degree of seriousness, but rather by the type of activity (object) constituted by the sin. Before explaining each of the seven, a word is in order on the confusing name of the deadly sins. Some people hear these seven sins called "deadly" and immediately, and understandably, assume they are the same as mortal sins. This is not the case. The Latin name for seven deadly sins is the capital sins. They are called such, most famously by St. Gregory the Great, because these seven sins are the source of other sins. Each of these deadly sins may indeed be mortal—if there is grave matter, full knowledge, and full consent. But each may also be venial, if any of those three conditions are lacking. So beware when speaking of the seven deadly sins that they may be, but are not necessarily, mortal sins. The seven deadly sins are: pride, envy, anger, sloth, greed, gluttony, and lust. Space prohibits an extensive examination of each of these seven deadly sins. The remainder of this section will briefly define each of them, and suggest ways they may be more common in our lives than we imagine.[11]

This first deadly sin is *pride*. It was discussed extensively in the previous section, since it is commonly referred to as the root of all sin. There is an element of pride in all sin, something that is not true of the other deadly sins. The second deadly sin is envy. *Envy* is basically delight in the misfortune of others, and sadness in the good fortune of others. It is similar to jealousy but

---

11. The following material is indebted to Robert Barron's superb discussion of the seven deadly sins in his book, *The Strangest Way*.

importantly different. The jealous person wants something he has does not have, or guards something that is perceived as threatened. But the jealousy ceases once the object is obtained or is held securely. Not so with the envious person. Even if the envious person already has good grades, he does not want his friend to have them and is, perhaps secretly, pained when his friend does get good grades. Even if an envious person has no interest in a friend's girlfriend, he is (secretly?) pleased when they break up. Again, note that it is not the lack of a particular object that makes one envious—that is jealousy. Someone could be jealous of a friend's good grades, but that ceases when one starts to get one's own good grades. Yet the envious person acts as if another's happiness somehow diminishes him, and another's misfortune somehow elevates him. Sadly, it seems all the more common with people who share more in common to us, or who are closer to us.

Who could be so callous? With a moment's reflection it should be clear how prevalent this sin is. Grades and relationships have already been mentioned. We could add jobs or financial status. When a group of people (like seniors in college) are on a job search, the questioning and reporting of successful and unsuccessful job applications is often fraught with envious response, even when people are not applying for the same jobs. The same is true regarding financial status. Even when another's success or failure has no bearing on our own, it is all too easy and common to be threatened by another's successes or relish their struggles. This dynamic is seen in parents discussing and comparing their children. People pridefully extol the successes of their own children (as if it reflects mainly on them) and enviously listen to delight in the weaknesses, and lament the successes of, others' children. Many more examples could be offered, but the pervasive sin that is envy should now be more clear.

The third deadly sin is anger. In general, *anger* is an emotion aroused by the perception of an injustice, and accompanied by a desire to right that perceived injustice. As an emotion, anger is a God-given human capacity that is not inherently sinful. In fact, as is clear from chapter 4 on habituating the emotions, well-ordered anger can become an important aid to living a virtuous life. (This is why some distinguish the sin of anger by the term "wrath.") But of course, we are all too familiar with the myriad of ways that anger can be disordered, or sinful. For instance, we all too often pridefully think that something constitutes an injustice against us when it really does not. Perhaps it was unintentional, or actually an act of justice, even if not what we would prefer. Furthermore, people can overreact in anger, and seek vindication in ways that are brutal or excessive. People explode too intensely, or stew too long, in anger, even where there is a legitimate cause of anger. All of these constitute occasions of sinful anger, which damage right relationship (justice) between people. Anger is an enormous impediment to reconciliation or forgiveness, which is simply the restoration of right relationship.

The fourth deadly sin is *sloth*. This term may prompt the image of a couch potato lounging lazily rather than doing anything productive. It is true that the slothful person may be a couch potato. But the deadly sin of sloth most properly refers to spiritual laziness. The slothful are inattentive to the higher things in life, particularly their relationship with God. Ironically, the slothful are sometimes the busiest people. The same people who populate the treadmills of the world's gyms, in the frantic attempt to schedule exercise throughout their busy days, may be the same ones who simply do not have the time to attend to their spiritual needs. The college student who is so overbooked with genuinely good activities, but who lives frantically moving from meeting to class to library without a moment's time to pause and reflect on what it all means, is another example. The slothful are not necessarily physically lazy; they are spiritually lazy. For whatever reason—lack of time or interest, perhaps—the slothful never get around to prayer, the sacraments, or any communal worship. They may even be too busy to speak reflectively with friends about where things are going in their lives, and how they understand their path in the context of the big picture. Note that not only may the slothful be busy, they may also be busy doing genuinely good—even churchy—activities. Robert Barron cites the moving story of Chicago's Cardinal Bernadin, who realized at one point as a cardinal that he had been so consumed with the tasks of his position that he had been systemically neglecting his prayer life.[12] For him it took a commitment to wake one hour earlier each day, to pray to be rid of the sloth that had marked his life.

The fifth deadly sin is *greed*. Greed is the inordinate desire for, and attachment to, material goods. Material things are obviously not bad in themselves. In fact, it is appropriate to seek material goods to support us and others in seeking to live a good life. But the greedy person confuses ends and means by over-prioritizing material things, such that they are not merely helpful supports in our lives, but the goal to which we aspire. The greedy person becomes too attached to material goods, and ironically they begin to own him rather than the other way around. There are obvious examples of greed in our materialistic and super-financially-conscious society. Yet perhaps a focus on extreme examples can hide the more everyday and equally pernicious ways that greed infects our lives. To what extent do I let a concern for money shape how I judge others, whether friend or stranger? To what extent am I conscious of name brands on cars, clothes, or other items, and make judgments or act accordingly? How generous am I with my resources, and how accurately do I judge what I really need vs. what is surplus and thus can be shared more freely? All of these questions help us determine the extent to which greed is present in our lives.

12. Ibid., 86–87.

The sixth deadly sin is *gluttony*. Gluttony is an inordinate desire for and an attachment to eating and drinking. A common image of the glutton is French King Louis XIV, seated at a lavish table covered in delicious food and drink, drumstick in one hand and goblet of wine in the other. Yet again, this obvious example of excess with regard to food and drink may mask the more ubiquitous ways we are too attached to our palate. Given chapter 6, it should be all too clear that an over-prioritization of, and indulging in, alcohol is a particularly common manifestation of gluttony in our society. We could also ask to what extent our desires for excellent food and drink drive us to actions that we cannot afford, given the cost in money or health or time. Food and drink are most obviously things that are good in themselves, and can be central components of family time, companionship, and social justice. Yet when the focus on food and drink begins to eclipse the goods they are meant to support, gluttony is present.

The seventh and final sin is *lust*. Lust is an inordinate desire for, or engagement in, sexual activity. Again, we have a sin that concerns an activity that is not in itself sinful. As will be discussed in far greater detail in chapter 17, sex is a beautiful gift from God. Though some people may hear lust and think of all sex as dirty, this is not the Christian view, even if Christians past or present may have contributed to this perception. Like anger, greed, or gluttony, the sin of lust entails using a good thing (in this case, sex) in a manner that defies the purpose of the thing. Material things are supposed to support us in our quest to live a good life, but the greedy become entrapped by them, and are inhibited on that quest. Anger is supposed to aid us in pursuing justice, but for those with the sin of anger it actually impedes right relations with others. The gluttonous use what is meant to support their health and companionship in a manner that impedes both. So, too, with the lustful. They use what is meant to bond people together and engender new life in a manner that is contrary to those two goals. Note that we are not simply talking about sexual intercourse here. Pornography and sexually objectifying those around us corrupt our ability to use the gift of sexuality for it proper purpose. Even in marriage lust is a common sin. Anytime sex becomes a prideful way to serve and pleasure one's self, rather than give one's self away lovingly, lust is present.

The main point of this section has been to offer different categorizations of sin in order to better understand how it is present in our lives. Given this section, and the earlier one on the pervasiveness of sin in our lives, it may be easy to despair at this point, and wonder if one's life is awash in sinfulness, such that one cannot escape. If this thought has crossed your mind, this chapter has served one of its goals: to convince you of the bitter reality of sin in our lives. But the Christian tradition is clear that the story does not end with sin. So we are only now ready to look past this focus on our sinfulness to the Christian message of hope and redemption.

Sin: Not the End of the Story for Christians

This chapter's first section was on the pervasiveness of sin in our lives. Before that, the introduction examined how even the holiest people of the Christian tradition are acutely aware of the presence and power of sin in their lives. At this point, it may appear as if there is no cause for hope. But this is importantly not the case. After all, note that it is those people who are most alive in the power of God's love—the saints—who are so vividly aware of their sinfulness. What does this tell us?

One point made earlier is reaffirmed here: without an adequate recognition of the prevalence of sin in the world, the Christian story makes no sense. There can only be salvation if there is something we need saving from. That said, we are now ready to begin exploring the other half of this claim: no genuinely Christian reflection on the reality of sin can even begin without the at least implicit recognition that the power of sin over the world has been shattered by the life, death, and resurrection of Jesus Christ. Indeed, the moment one begins to reflect accurately on sin, the saving power of God is already present, illuminating the ways we are estranged from God in our lives, always for the purpose of reuniting us with the true purpose of our lives: life-giving loving union with God.

Indeed, even in the very ancient text (Gen. 3), where we read the story of humanity's first sin, Christians have always found a theological reference to God's saving action in Christ. In response to the first sin, God reveals punishments for all involved. Turning first to the serpent, the Lord says: "I will put enmity between you and the woman, and between your offspring and hers; He will strike at your head, while you strike at his heel" (Gen. 3:15). Christians have interpreted this as a reference to Christ (her offspring) who will come to destroy the power of sin and darkness over humanity ("He will strike at your head"). Thus, amazingly, even at the very first moments of humanity's sinful rejection of God, God's plan to restore humanity to right relationship with God through Christ is underway. For the Christian, there is no recognition of sin without the presence of the very grace of God that takes away that sin.

Thus there are actually two extremes people can err on when reflecting on human sinfulness. As noted earlier in this chapter, one error is an inadequate recognition of the reality of sin in our lives. An emphasis on God's love and salvation, without simultaneous recognition of our need for such redemption due to sin, results in an overconfidence in humanity and a naiveté with regard to our brokenness. Though usually not intentional or explicit, it entails a lack of respect and gratitude for God, since such a person assumes that God cannot or will not reconcile people who are indeed truly sinful; plus it fails to appreciate the generosity and magnitude of God's saving forgiveness.

The other error is a fixation on human (or one's own) sinfulness without adequate recognition that God is indeed present to us in our brokenness, and offers us, individually and communally, a path out of that desolation and into the fullness of life called salvation. This failure leads to despair or terror at God's judgment. Though usually not intentional or explicit, it entails a lack of confidence in God's love and power, since such a person thinks God has either no interest or ability to restore people from the damage wrought by sin.

Concluding Thoughts

This chapter has now come full circle, back to sin in the context of the holiness of the saints described in the first paragraph. After all, it is only through the light of God's presence that we can see clearly the depth of our sinful brokenness. It is also that same light that reveals God's saving forgiveness to lift us out of that decrepit state. Besides defining sin and explaining its different types, the purpose of this chapter has been not only identifying the reality and pervasiveness of human sinfulness, but also recognizing that in order even to grasp this reality and its pervasiveness, God's saving grace is already at work. Sin is a crucial part of the Christian story. But thankfully, it is not the first, or last, word in that story. The following chapters on hope, incarnation, love, and grace all help explain how it is that sin is not the last word.

Having begun with some insight on sin from Robert Barron, it is fitting to conclude on a similar note. One of the most helpful contributions of Barron's book is that it not only identifies central themes of the Christian story, but it also identifies practices by which one lives in recognition of these themes. Reminiscent of practices and big-picture claims about the way things are (chapter 10), Barron in effect says, "If you think this is true you will live it out by . . ."

How does he do so with regard to sin? First, he notes that Christians confess their sins. Whether it be in the confessional or in other contexts, living out the Christian way always entails explicit recognition of our sinfulness. Again, we are reminded of the saints at the start of this chapter. Second, Christians tell the truth about their sin. They refuse to let themselves be blinded either by prideful ways of seeing their own lives, or by a cowardly refusal to lovingly confront those near to them about the ways they are separating themselves from a truly good life. Finally, in a theme that will be crucial throughout the rest of this book, Christians forgive others even as they have been forgiven. Forgiveness is far from ignorance or some passive forgetfulness of past wrongs. It is rather the radical practice of bearing with and moving toward others in their wrongs in order to restore right relationship. If sin is a strain or severing of right relationship, forgiveness is simply the restoration of that right relationship. To foreshadow the next four chapters, forgiveness is what we hope for, what Christ accomplishes, what Christian love does, and what grace empowers us to do. Forgiveness as the restoration of what is damaged by sin is arguably the central theme of the Christian life.

Study Questions

1. According to Robert Barron, why is it that holy people are actually more aware of their sinfulness? Use his winter windshield analogy to explain.
2. Why is the reality of sin such a crucial part of the Christian story?
3. Why, and in what ways, do people neglect the reality of their sinfulness?
4. Define sin. What does it mean to say sin offends God? Why are all sins ultimately offenses against God?
5. Define pride. Why is it the root of all sin? Why is it essentially competitive, and the anti-God state of mind?
6. How does the Genesis 3 story illuminate pride? What is the meaning of the phrase, "become like gods?"
7. Define mortal and venial sin, and give the conditions that make a sin mortal.
8. List and define the seven deadly sins. Explain the difference between mortal and deadly sin.
9. Why is sin importantly not the end of the story for Christians?

Terms to Know

sin, pride, mortal sin, venial sin, envy, anger, sloth, greed, gluttony, lust

Questions for Further Reflection

1. The claim here is that sin is a central feature of the Christian story. How might one not believe in sin? What alternate explanations could be offered for what Christians explain by sin? How might a Christian respond to such an alternate explanation?
2. Are there any truly private sins? Why or why not?
3. Give an example of how some everyday sin you encounter is tainted by pride.
4. Go through the seven deadly sins and give an example of how you might encounter each one in your own experience.
5. Barron offers some concrete ways that people live differently if they know they are sinners. Pick one or two more ways that such knowledge should shape how one lives and describe why.

Further Reading

The two most formative works on this chapter are those that my students have read on this topic in the past. First, C. S. Lewis's *Mere Christianity* not only has the best discussion of pride I have seen, but also most accurately describes the role of sin in the Christian story as a whole. Second, Robert Barron's *The Strangest Way* contains an extraordinarily helpful reflection on human sin, including an in-depth look at the seven deadly sins through an analysis of Dante's *Purgatorio* (which would be rewarding reading in conjunction with this chapter). In addition, Michael Himes's *Doing the Truth in Love* contains a brief and powerful reflection on sin through the theme of creatureliness. Finally, for a quite in-depth (and Thomistic) analysis of sin, see Josef Pieper's short book entitled *The Concept of Sin*.

13

THE VIRTUE OF HOPE

Eternity in this Life and the Next

"You made us for you, and our hearts are restless until they rest in you."

St. Augustine, *Confessions*, I.1

It is fitting to examine the virtue of hope after chapters on faith and sin. Hope concerns our ultimate destiny, and Christian faith does indeed entail beliefs about human destiny beyond this life. In fact, heaven is perhaps the belief most popularly associated with Christians (ironically, more than faith in Christ). Virtuous belief in (faith) and yearning for (hope) union with God beyond this life are indeed crucial components of a good life here on earth, according to the Christian story. As for sin, the main reason why we need the virtue hope to keep us properly oriented toward our final destiny is due to the separation from God caused by sin. It is through hope that we cling to union with God as possible, despite our sinfulness. Of course, it is through Jesus Christ that such separation is overcome, and so salvation, in the sense of reconciliation between God and humanity, is addressed more fully in the following chapter. But the previous chapters on faith and sin make hope the fitting topic to address next. Hope is a virtue for persons of faith who believe that God invites us to union with God, but who also realize that such union right now is far from complete.

The purpose of this chapter is twofold. The first section defines and describes the second of the three theological virtues, hope. As will be seen, hope is a virtue for this life which also concerns things of the next life. Thus, the second task of this chapter is to say a bit more about that destiny in the next life. Christians are guilty of some very simplistic notions and images of that destiny, which may be fine for children, but which should be understood in a more complete way for those who are able. The second half of this chapter will examine the traditional doctrines of heaven, hell, and purgatory, and also examine how the Christian tradition has understood death itself, which is the path to these states.

Hope: Virtue for the Wayfarer

In order to properly understand the virtue of hope, it is necessary to explain the human condition that occasions hope. In other words, what state of affairs marks our condition in this life that makes hope a good habit to have? The first part of this section relies on the thought of several contemporary thinkers to describe our condition. In order to better understand hope, which is a virtuous response to this condition, the next part explains some poor responses to that situation. The third and final part of this section then defines and explains hope. It will be clear there how hope both orients us toward our complete fulfillment in the next life, yet also enables us to live more virtuously in this life by attending to our final destiny.

The Human Condition that Occasions Hope

Who needs hope? According to the Christian story, it seems that one can already know (faith) and love (charity/love) God in this life. Why the need for hope? Several contemporary authors take up this question and offer helpful images to explain the human situation that occasions hope. Acknowledging his debt to St. Augustine, Michael Himes claims that human beings are fundamentally restless.[1] We always hunger for more, and never seem to be fully satisfied. Note that we are not yet making a judgment about whether that longing for more is properly directed—that will come below. The simple claim here is that human persons never do sit back in this life and say, "there is nothing more to do, or nothing further I could enjoy." Even when we think of people who just seem to sit back and relax, we find they actually continue to pursue things. They eat and drink; they continue to nourish their relationships with others; they seek to enjoy things like leisurely activities. And even those of us who live satisfying and rewarding lives would have to admit that our lives are not

---

1. See Michael Himes, *Doing the Truth in Love: Conversations about God, Relationships, and Service* (New York: Paulist, 1995).

complete. We long to be closer to others, to work on important life projects, to continue to improve ourselves, to understand more. Furthermore, we yearn for a world without the brokenness found all around us: poverty, injustice, sickness, suffering, and sin. And when things may be going well, even then we sense that and live as if all is not as it could be or should be. Unlike animals, who are without reason and will and cannot consciously understand this state and react to it, we humans are aware of our restlessness and can respond in better or worse ways, as we will see.

One twentieth-century thinker follows Aquinas in describing the human person in this life as a wayfarer.[2] This archaic English term may be better understood by a look at the Latin term it represents: "*status viatoris*." The human person exists in a state of being "on the way." There are two claims implied in this description. First, the person is not yet where she is destined to be. Thus, at least some of the good about that final destination is lacking in the current state. That does not mean, of course, that there is nothing good about the current state. But one is not yet complete or totally fulfilled in the current state.

Second, even in the current state, where one is not yet at the final destination, there is nonetheless some knowledge, even if incomplete, of what being at that destination would entail. After all, to realize one's self as on the way implies some goal which, even if not understood fully, must be understood enough for one to know that one is not already there. The term to describe one who is already there, by the way, is *status comprehensoris*. The person in this state has arrived. She has reached the goal. Here is where the analogy to a journey breaks down. On human journeys in this life, reaching a destination does not fulfill a person completely, to the extent of quelling all restlessness and fully satisfying one in all ways possible. But this is indeed what marks the *status comprehensoris*.

Christians believe that the *status comprehensioris* describes the person who has inherited eternal life in union with God. At this point, the reliance of hope on faith should be clear. We run into a classic big-picture question here: what is the destiny or purpose of human life? If you think there is none, then the human state of affairs described here is simply one of absurdity, a cosmic joke where conscious humanity can somehow understand and yearn for more, and yet find that yearning perpetually unfulfilled, and indeed unable to ever be completely fulfilled. Christians believe, however, that this natural human longing for completion, for fulfillment, is a natural consequence of the fact that humanity was indeed created for a purpose. That ultimate purpose is fullness

---

2. For these terms, Pieper relies primarily on Aquinas's discussion of whether Christ was both a wayfarer (*viator*) and having arrived (to use a colloquial translation of *comprehensor*). See *Summa Theologiae*, English Dominican trans. (New York: Benziger, 1948), III 15,10. Pieper relies on these terms in his wonderful monograph on hope, published with the treatises on faith and love as *Faith, Hope, and Love* (Notre Dame: University of Notre Dame Press, 1966).

of life—complete happiness—in union with the God of Life. The specific shape of this destiny transcends what humans are capable of understanding, let alone achieving on their own (hence it is a super-natural destiny). Yet we do naturally long for it inchoately, since our human nature is a creation of the God with whom we are destined for union.[3] We are now anticipating the last part of this section on hope. But note here that one needn't be Christian to affirm the point of this part, namely, that human persons exist in a state of restlessness, or longing for more. Even twentieth- century atheist existentialists like Jean Paul Satre and Albert Camus recognized this condition.

But is earthly life really so incomplete? Or better, even when earthly life seems relatively fulfilling, is there really something greater compared to which it pales in comparison? This may seem like an overly pessimistic view of life. C. S. Lewis appeals to a common experience to explain what is meant by this claim.

> The longings which arise in us when we first fall in love, or first think of some foreign country, or first take up some subject that excites us, are longings which no marriage, no travel, no learning, can really satisfy. I am not now speaking of what would ordinarily be called unsuccessful marriages, or holidays, or learned careers. I am speaking of the best possible ones. There was something we grasped at, in the first moment of longing, which just fades away in reality. I think everyone knows what I mean. The wife may be a good wife, the hotels and scenery may have been excellent, and chemistry may be a very interesting job; but something has evaded us.[4]

What is that "something we grasped at" that always evades us in this life? Presumably, Lewis means the complete satisfaction of all our longings. No relationship, trip, or job can offer that. In our world, marred by the sin described in chapter 12, this is certain. Our endeavors in this world are fraught with life's tribulations.[5] As Lewis notes, even the beautiful and fulfilling things in our lives and world are not complete.

The troubling ramification of this observation is that the happiness that we all long for, and which this book consistently claims is the point of the moral life, is not immediately available to us. This is evidenced by our lack of satisfaction, or ongoing restlessness, even in the presence of genuinely good things for which we long. But the problem is not simply our seemingly unquenchable desire. It is a result of the brokenness, or at least finitude, of the

---

3. This is the traditional teaching on the natural desire for God in all human purposes. See *Catechism of the Catholic Church*, 2nd ed. (Vatican City: Libreria Editrice Vaticana, 1997), 27–30.

4. C. S. Lewis, *Mere Christianity* (San Francisco: HarperSanFrancisco, 2001), 135.

5. See Paul Wadell's *Becoming Friends: Worship, Justice, and the Practice of Christian Friendship* (Grand Rapids: Brazos, 2002), 130. Wadell's work on hope, along with that of Thomas, Pieper, Himes, and Lewis have been hugely influential for this discussion of hope.

things we long for in this life, and our own ability or inability to constantly long for the right things. Lewis is right. No spouse, job, or trip is perfect, and that is why we continue to grasp at what continually evades us. If this is our situation, how should we respond? Is there any real hope for us?

Poor Responses to the Human Situation that Occasions Hope

Before examining how one can respond virtuously to this situation, consider first some bad responses to this situation. The contemporary authors who vividly depict the human situation that occasions hope consistently describe two such poor responses. Michael Himes offers an anecdote that appeals to a culture such as ours, which is so enthralled with romantic love. As a priest, Himes frequently prepares couples for marriage. He describes the common experience of hearing a young spouse-to-be say something like, "she's all I need," or, "he's all I want!"[6] Himes seems stodgy and disillusioned about love when he replies

> That might work if he or she dies on the honeymoon, or if you do, but if the relationship lasts any longer than a very brief honeymoon, you will discover to your dismay that it hasn't worked. You will remain restless and hungry. You will find yourself ruefully admitting that he or she is not all you want. And, alas, this is the moment when many marriages hit enormous problems.[7]

Any person who has been married or in any serious relationship or friendship knows this from experience. Another person cannot possibly fulfill all our needs and desires.

Lewis describes this same experience and labels it, as a poor response to the occasion for hope, the "fool's way."[8] This person, when encountering the disappointment that the seemingly perfect job, relationship, or trip inevitably offers, concludes that the problem is the object he chose. Better find another job, spouse, or pastime. These people spend their lives continually jumping to the next best thing, and repeatedly becoming shocked and disappointed that even the next one still is not the real thing.

What is the problem with this response? Don't we all have to commit, or attach, ourselves to something(s) in life? One problem with the fool's way concerns what we choose to satisfy us and still our restlessness. Too often the things we pursue to fill the void and quench our hunger are pathetic substitutes for what we truly seek. We all know people who try and quell their restlessness with pleasures like alcohol, drugs, or sexual activity. For others it may be money, social status, popularity, or power. In these cases it is happiness and fulfillment

6. Himes, *Doing the Truth in Love*, 39.
7. Ibid.
8. See Lewis, *Mere Christianity*, 135–36.

that is sought, but poor candidates are chosen to fill that role. Another problem with the fool's way is not what is sought but how it is sought. Even when such people throw themselves completely into genuinely good things in life—such as a marriage, job, or some worthy cause—they are seeking complete satisfaction in something that is simply unable to fill that need.

Himes perfectly diagnoses this problem. What one is doing in these situations is, in effect, making something god that is not God. When most of us today read the first commandment—"thou shall have no other gods before me"—we may chuckle and be grateful that, unlike the Israelites in the desert, we enlightened moderns are not the least bit tempted to worship some golden statue as a god (see Exod. 32:3–6). True indeed. But that does not mean *idolatry*, in the proper sense of putting something before God, is not still a common and serious sin today. In fact, it is exactly the poor response that Himes and Lewis are describing here—the fool's way. For example, the person who thinks her lover will satisfy all her needs is basically making that lover into her god. After all, if the lover could so completely satisfy her, the woman would rightly make her lover the most important thing in her life. Nothing should come before him. To use the visual image in chapter 2 on intentionality, her lover would be the top of her triangle, more important than all other things in life, and her love of that person should govern all other things in her life. The same could be said of another person's job, or another's worthy cause.

You may ask, "what is wrong with that? Shouldn't a person make her spouse or job or worthy cause her number-one priority?" Certainly these things should be rather high on the triangle of the goals and purposes in one's life. But there are two problems with putting any of them at the very top. First, if something is the most important goal in one's life, nothing else governs or limits it. As one's ultimate goal in life, it controls all of one's pursuits in life. To use the example of a marriage being the most important thing in one's life, if your spouse were to ask you to do something contrary to the good of either you or your spouse, and thus the relationship, you would have to say yes. After all, that person is your "be-all-end-all" (or god) in life, and there are no resources other than that person's will by which you could say, "wait a second, that is not right!" (If this is starting to sound weird, it should.) You would need to be completely obedient to that person as your ultimate goal in life, under the assumption that this person will fully satisfy you. If that were not the case, then whatever basis you used to say, "Wait, this instead is actually better for us," would in fact be god, governing your relationship with your spouse. And of course this is what should happen. Even the best of spouses is not perfect—all-loving, all-knowing, all good.

The second reason that making another person one's be-all and end-all in life is foolish is that it simply does not fully satisfy one. Himes is right in his comment on the young married couple. Or as the scripture author says, "Put no trust in princes, in mere mortals powerless to save. . . . Happy are those whose hope is the Lord, their God" (Ps. 146:3–5; cf. 49:6). The first part of the greatest commandment, "love the Lord your God with all your heart, mind, and soul," is far from some externally imposed obligation that impedes our true happiness. It is actually the guard against our seeking to make something else the source of our complete fulfillment, when it—whatever it is—cannot deliver. Of course, we still have not explained why it is that God is the proper object of our hope, a task for later in this chapter.

The second poor response to the human situation that occasions hope is what Lewis calls the way of the "disillusioned sensible man."[9] This person has learned Himes's and Lewis's lesson, and knows that no relationship, job, or activity will fully satisfy him. In this he is wiser than the fool. However, he then concludes that therefore such satisfaction is simply impossible. Rather than seeking a new object to satisfy him, he stops seeking full satisfaction. So he is willing to settle for less in life. We might imagine this person having a mediocre relationship with his wife, but thinking, "well, that's life." He seeks a decent job and neighborhood for his family and figures you cannot seek much more in life. But, as Lewis notes, what if full satisfaction is available, even if not in this life? What has this person missed out on?

Nothing, one might reply. Complete fulfillment is only available in the next life, and that is still a possibility for even the disillusioned sensible man. But, of course, we must examine how the disillusioned sensible man's avowal that such satisfaction is not possible impacts how he lives his life in this world. Aquinas suggests two possibilities. The first he calls the sin of *presumption*. This is the sin of living as if no matter how one lives in this life, God will indeed welcome one to the union with him that, as seen below, constitutes complete fulfillment. Aquinas seems to have in mind here one who does believe in God and eternal happiness, but who does not let that belief shape his yearning and subsequent action in life. In other words, he seems to hold that God is the be-all and end-all, but assumes—really presumes—that union with God is assured, and thus he can live in this life as if other goals may take precedence over God. The disjuncture here should be obvious; this person claims to seek an ultimate goal in life, but it does not shape how other goals in this life are pursued. You cannot have your cake and eat it too by living as if destined for union with God, but acting in a sinful way that constitutes separation or alienation from God. The second section of this chapter explores further the relationship between our actions in this life and our destiny in the next.

The more likely stance of the disillusioned sensible man is the belief that the eternal happiness that union with God constitutes is not truly available. This is called *despair*. Perhaps such a person thinks there is no God, or that God cannot offer such fulfillment. Or perhaps he thinks his own sinfulness and the broken condition of the world makes such fulfillment impossible even

9. Ibid.

for God to make happen. In any case, there is a lack of faith in God's existence, God's power, and/or God's mercy. It is a sad reality that many people
go through life without thinking full satisfaction, the complete joy that marks
union with God, is possible. Such people can act cheerful and friendly. They
may function well. Yet

> they have abandoned any sense of life as promising and are reluctant to believe
> any talk of a human being's vocation to find peace and fulfillment in God. For
> reasons we cannot always understand, and in ways of which they may hardly
> be aware, they anticipate each day the "non-fulfillment of hope."[10]

This non-fulfillment of hope, or despair, is actually a foretaste of hell, a topic
addressed below. Aquinas claims such despair commonly flows from the deadly
sin of sloth, a spiritual sadness and laziness that also reflects the belief that
fulfillment is not possible.[11] Thus, the second poor response to the human
condition that occasions the virtue of hope is the disillusioned sensible man,
manifest in either presumption or despair.

The Theological Virtue of Hope

So what, then, is the virtuous response to this situation? The virtue hope.
Interestingly enough, each of the contemporary authors we have been treating
claims in his discussion of hope that the very restlessness that occasions hope
can actually be a gift. It seems odd to claim that a state of experiencing one's
own lack of complete fulfillment can be a good thing. Yet that is what they
claim. Why? It is a good thing if it is true that we are not completely fulfilled
in this life and can nonetheless be truly fulfilled. Because then the restlessness
is a reminder to keep our gaze fixed toward that which will indeed truly satisfy
us completely. And if such a destiny is truly available, as the Christian faith
contends, than any reminder of that destiny before its realization is exactly
what is needed to keep our eyes on the prize. As Himes says, our restlessness
is what drives us to God, if we attend faithfully to the restlessness.

The virtue of hope inclines one to yearn for union with God as one's true
destiny, and the source of complete fulfillment. As noted above, it succeeds
faith, since it is only by faith that one is even aware of the possibility of such
fulfillment in God. It also engenders love, since it is through longing for God
as our source of fulfillment that we cling in genuine friendship to God and
God's creatures, who share in this fellowship. Like faith and love, hope is a
theological virtue in that it concerns God directly, since it inclines us to seek
union with the God we are destined for, even when that full union is not yet

---

10. Wadell, *Becoming Friends*, 132. For the phrase, "non-fulfillment of hope," Wadell relies
on Pieper, *Faith, Hope, and Love*, 113.

11. See Thomas Aquinas, *Summa Theologiae*, II–II 20,4.

evidently present. Like the other theological virtues, hope is possible only through grace, since the nature of that destiny is beyond our unaided comprehension, and therefore remaining fixed on it as our ultimate goal requires divine assistance.

Despite the fact that the fulfillment hope seeks is not available in this life, hope is truly a virtue that leads us to act well even now. How does hope shape a person in this life who has this good habit? First, it sustains the wayfarer while on the way. In this state of longing marked by restlessness, it is all too easy to become like the fool who seeks happiness in counterfeit goods, or who seeks complete happiness from things that are genuinely good but cannot fully satisfy us. In times of doubt, in times of death and tragedy, in times of vicious injustice, in recognition of our own sinfulness, it is all too easy to become like the disillusioned sensible man and fall into despair by giving up on the possibility of complete happiness. In the tribulations of this life, it is difficult to keep our eye on the prize and steadfastly yearn for union with God as our complete fulfillment. In this state of "not yet," our separation from that for which we hope is difficult, and it is hope that sustains us. In fact, in this sense hope is similar to the cardinal virtue fortitude, since it enables us to face difficulties well. Yet unlike fortitude, hope is a theological virtue, fixing us on God directly, and is possible only through God's grace.

Second, despite its focus on a destiny not available in this life, hope does enable us to seek the goods of this life more truthfully. It is often wondered whether Christian belief in the afterlife leads to a lack of appreciation for the goods of this life, and neglect of the injustices that harm them. Sadly, there have been Christians throughout history whose focus on the next life has indeed led to a neglect of the real presence of God's kingdom in this life. Yet in actuality, neglect of this world is incompatible with true hope.

Lewis claims that throughout history, it is the Christians who thought the most of the next life who were most able to effectively transform this life for the better. Martin Luther King Jr. again serves a good example here. No one who has read his writings can doubt that his work for social justice flowed directly from his faith in and hope for God's kingdom. How could this be? Hope's foretaste of the true fulfillment that ultimately satisfies us most effectively illuminates the ways in this life that such fulfillment is not yet present. Furthermore, hope's steadfast clinging in trust that the realization of this destiny is a real possibility actually generates movement toward that goal, even though full realization is not possible here. Finally, when the good things of this world are understood in proper relationship to their ultimate destiny, that destiny further dignifies those goods and leads us to more fully cherish them—though of course not as gods, or our be-all and end-all. More on how this happens is seen in chapter 15 on love, which inclines one not only to love God in God's very self, but also to love all things for the sake of God.

A final word is in order concerning hope's relationship to truth. Sometimes when people hear Christians express hope in union with God after death, they refrain from judgment but seem to assume that this is a nice sentiment that simply helps Christians get through the trials of this life. Hope is seen as a crutch, veiling the harsh reality that no such fulfillment actually exists. It must be said here that Christian hope is not an idle fantasy to make us feel better when times are hard. The Christian claim is that such a destiny is true. If it is not our faith is in vain and, reminiscent of what Paul says regarding the resurrection of the body, we are the most pitiful people there are (1 Cor. 15:19). Simply put, hope is not a virtue because it makes us feel better. It may make people feel better, but that is because it is true. If what Christians hope for is not true, then hope is pathetic self-deception. Of course, the Christian story states exactly the opposite. And in that story, despair is not simply a downer—it is actually false.

The Christian Tradition and Life after Death

It should now be obvious why a discussion of hope leads naturally to reflection on last things, or life after death. So far we have simply discussed union with God in the next life, and described it as complete fulfillment. That is actually a good start, and the point where we will pick up this discussion of last things. But more needs to be said on the destiny for which Christians hope. This will then lead to an examination of the familiar terms heaven, hell, and purgatory. It will even require some refection on the meaning of death itself, and what it means to rise from the dead. The purpose of this second half of the chapter, however, is not an exhaustive look at the Christian tradition's teaching on the afterlife. Most of what is described here can be found in the *Catechism of the Catholic Church*.[12] The point of this discussion is simply to say enough about the Christian tradition's teaching on last things to make a discussion of hope intelligible.

There is also an ulterior motive here. Another goal of this section is to offer a vision of the afterlife that is one step further in sophistication than that which most Christians are able to articulate. Many of us have vague and simplistic notions of heaven and hell, constituted by images such as halos, harps, pitchforks, or fire. Perhaps we are content to rest in those images, since this is a topic where it is particularly obvious that we do not see things with

---

12. See *Catechism of the Catholic Church*, 988–1065. For another helpful introductory text to these questions, see Romano Guardini's *Eternal Life: What You Need to Know About Death, Judgment, and Life Everlasting* (Manchester, NH: Sophia Institute Press, 1989). By far the most helpful book in my teaching this material has been C. S. Lewis's allegory called *The Great Divorce*, an imaginary ride to heaven that demonstrates, in narrative form, many of the Christian traditions claims about the afterlife.

clear sight, to recall the language of chapter 11. But through some clear thinking and the guidance of revelation, we can avoid the more simplistic notions
of the afterlife that often prompt people to regard Christians as people who
delude themselves with fanciful hope and childish imagery.

Nunc Dimittis and Union with God as Fullness of Life

There is a beautiful story in the beginning of Luke where Mary and Joseph
present the infant Jesus in the temple (Luke 2:22–38). The holy family is greeted
in the temple by a man named Simeon, who had been told in a dream that
he would not die before seeing the Messiah of the Lord. On the day when he
meets Jesus, he knows right away this promise had been kept. He lifts up the
baby in his arms and exclaims, "Now Master, you may dismiss [in Latin, *nunc
dimittis*] your servant in peace, according to your word, for my eyes have seen
your salvation!"[13] Simeon had been promised to witness God's decisive act in
history, and having witnessed it, he cries, "you may now dismiss your servant
in peace!" He in effect says, "my life is complete; all that I have longed for has
been fulfilled, so there is nothing further to seek with my life."

Simeon's cry is a grateful response to the Lord's fulfillment of a promise
that he would not die before seeing the Savior. Now that he had, he could die
in peace. Yet the story is offered here for that beautiful phrase, *nunc dimittis*.
Think for a moment about what would prompt you to utter Simeon's cry. What
would satisfy all your desires? What state of affairs would have to exist in order
for you to say, "That's it! I've arrived. I'm complete." The answer to this question
is exactly that for which Christians hope. It is what they call *heaven*, eternal
life, the fullness of life, union with God, or seeing God face to face.

Christians have all sorts of images to represent this state. C. S. Lewis claims
people traditionally speak of gold because gold is precious and endures. They
speak of harps because, for many, music is something in this life that "suggests
ecstasy and infinity."[14] They speak of crowns to suggest the splendor and joy
of union with God. The book of Revelation is full of such images. But all
of these are images, images that suggest something true about that state but
which, of course, are ultimately inadequate.

In the context of this work on moral theology we can explain these images
further. Eternal life is not just life like we experience now but longer in duration. It is fullness of life, which includes greater duration, but much more.
It is life without the restlessness that marks our current state, not because
we cease to value complete fulfillment but because it has been achieved. All
the limitations that mark this life—sin, ignorance, death, finitude, injustice,
and the like—are gone in that state, and thus there is nothing more to long

---

13. Luke 2:29–30. The Vulgate Latin reads: "*nunc dimittis servum tuum Domine secundum
verbum tuum in pace quia viderunt oculi mei salutare tuum.*"

14. C. S. Lewis, *Mere Christianity*, 137.

for. In fact, longings that are not even possible without guidance from God are fulfilled. These longings are given in the theological virtue of hope. And because that for which we long in this life can actually be achieved in the next, hope ultimately passes away. There will come a point when no virtue of hope is necessary, since what we hope for is actually present. The same is true of faith. Faith is belief in things unseen, and will no longer be necessary once we see God face to face.

Of course, though it is helpful to understand union with God as the fulfillment of all our desires, one must be careful not to make our desires the basis for our understanding of eternal life. Union with God (which is eternal life) is the fulfillment of all our desires, and more, because such a state is true happiness, not because God wants to satisfy any or every desire we might have. What is offered to humanity in union with God is true fulfillment, and not fulfillment on one's own terms. Thus, only our true and holy desires are fulfilled, even surpassed. For instance, we commonly hear people say they long to be with departed loved ones in the next life. It is a true and holy desire to be united with others in love. Such a longing will be fulfilled, and the communion with others enjoyed in the next life even surpasses the loving union we can experience or even imagine here. (Christians call this belief the communion of saints.[15]) We long to be free in the next life of our brokenness here: ignorance, sickness, sin, and so on. That longing is indeed fulfilled and surpassed since it is a truthful and holy longing.

This understanding of eternal life as fullness of life means that even life on this side of death can be more or less full. If living most fully is the having and attaining of good, truthful, and holy desires, then we could even say that people are more or less alive while living this life. When Christ said he came that we might have life, and have it more abundantly (John 10:10), he of course was referring to the way he made possible full union with God, something known only after death. But life on earth can also be lived more or less fully. Though we commonly think of life as part of a binary function— you are alive or dead—life is also a qualitative state. Indeed, the virtuous life is a fuller life. That is why it leads to happiness. Full happiness (fullness of life) may only be achievable beyond the grave, when there will be no more suffering, sin, and death. But life can be more or less full, or happy, even on this side of the grave.

Judgment and Hell

Saying that not all longings are satisfied, or that life can be more or less full, obviously implies judgment made among specific goals. And this raises a topic that is very uncomfortable to modern ears, that there is a final judgment,

---

15. See *Catechism of the Catholic Church*, 946–53.

leading some to be thrown into hell. A more careful look at hell both intensifies and ameliorates this teaching. If heaven as fullness of life is rightly understood as union with God, then *hell* is best understood as definitive separation from God. How does this happen?

Though this is different from some other Christian traditions, the Catholic faith clearly states that "God predestines no one to hell."[16] By default, then, the teaching must be that one chooses hell. How could this be? In his fascinating book *The Great Divorce*, C. S. Lewis beautifully describes the tragedy of how such a choice is possible. Most of the characters in his story choose hell. But none of them says, "I want to suffer and be in hell." Rather, all of them, in varying ways, decide that they want their desires to be fulfilled on their own terms. One wants to be with his spouse in heaven, but only if he can continue to be the petty, self-pitying spouse he was on earth. One mother wants to be with her son who died before her, but only if she can have him on her own obsessive terms. One man is shocked to find a great sinner in heaven, and claims he will go no place where his own ethical decency is not recognized and rewarded. None of these characters say, "I want hell." But they each want things—often otherwise good things—on their own terms. We are reminded here of the discussion in chapter 12 of how pride works. These people want their desires fulfilled in manners that are ultimately false and destructive, of themselves and others. Thus, in wanting their warped desires fulfilled, they do not want their truly satisfying desires fulfilled. Though they do not word it that way, they "want hell." The Lord will not—cannot—make what these people want to be truly satisfying. Thus, in the end they are given what they want, but what they want is hell.

Each of the above characters has a set of purposes or desires—a triangle representing their character—that does not conform to the way things really are. Certain lower goods are pursued above higher goods. Since the good earthly goals (spousal love, motherly love, ethical decency) that are pursued are not properly governed by a love of God, they are corrupted and actually lead one away from God. Ultimately, they become self-serving rather than truly loving. Thus, each character manifests the pride of insisting that their grasp of what is important in the world is truly the way things are. They are corrupted by that false vision, and become the sorts of people for whom true self-giving love (of spouse, child, one's self, etc.) is not possible.

In this state, brought about and ingrained by their own sinfulness, they are judged. It is indeed God who judges, in that God is source and sustainer of the standard of truth by which a life is deemed essentially loving or self-centered, more or less full. But it is the individual choices that lead to God's judgment. The beauty of Lewis's book is demonstrating that hell is really possible. But hell as a definitive judgment is actually just the finalization (or

16. *Catechism of the Catholic Church*, 1037.

fossilization, or solidification) of the hellish life the damned person chooses for himself on earth.

Judgment can be understood in two different ways. Too often it is understood as only extrinsically related to actions in this life. If we do good, we get the reward of heaven. If we do bad, we get punished with hell. In this view, the life lived here and one's ultimate destiny are only extrinsically, even arbitrarily, related. For example, a popularized version of Muslim belief in the afterlife states that a martyr for the faith is rewarded with many virgins in paradise. If this were an accurate statement of Muslim belief, it would be an odd sort of god who would reward his followers with something prohibited them in this life.[17] If promiscuous sex is not living in accordance with the fullness of life here, why would it be offered by God in the next life? Another example of this inadequate view of judgment is the way many believers, especially Christians, imagine final judgment as some sort of handing down of a decision, much like learning if one has passed or failed a test. In this view everyone wants heaven, but some get hell. Lewis disagrees; everyone may want happiness, but people may or may not desire true happiness. Desiring true happiness is heavenly; desiring happiness on our own terms, whatever they may be, is hellish.

On another view of judgment, the one espoused by Lewis and the bulk of the Christian tradition, sin in this life is living less fully and is thus a foretaste of hell. Virtue is living more fully and thus is a foretaste of heaven. Judgment is simply the extension of a trajectory that one has voluntarily lived during one's life. The question is whether one lives in this life as if one wants union with God, and therefore lives out that desire in all one's relationships or endeavors, or whether one wants to live out life on one's own terms. In the end, *everyone gets what they want.*

Catholic Teaching on Purgatory

One part of the tradition on heaven, hell, and judgment that is held by Catholic but not Protestant Christians is the doctrine of *purgatory*. The above presentation of heaven and hell has prepared the reader for an understanding of this teaching, which is ultimately rooted in scripture and in the Christian practice of praying for the dead devoid of the legalism that often stirs reaction against the teaching.[18]

Heaven and hell are presented above as definitive union with or separation from God. The union or separation is begun in this life, but becomes definitive at some point in heaven or hell. At which point is examined in the following section on the meaning of death. For now, note that there

---

17. I do not know enough about Islamic faith to know whether or not this is actually the case. The claim here is simply about popularized, and hopefully inaccurate, thought on Islam and the afterlife.

18. See 2 Macc 12:46. See also 1 Cor. 3:15; 15:29; and 1 Pet. 1:7.

is a problem with a view of heaven and hell as radically continuous with this life. The benefit of such a view is that heaven and hell are seen less as external impositions than as reifications, or as finalizations of a trajectory set by the person herself. The problem is that this implies that only people who are sinless will be welcomed into full union with God. Perhaps we can imagine people who consistently separate themselves from God in this life, since even the good they do may be self-serving or done out of obligation. Hell seems to accurately describe such a life. But does or can anyone live "heaven on earth"?

Yes and no. Yes, in the sense that union with God can indeed be experienced in this life, through God's grace, in a life of holiness and virtue. Yet in another sense, no. No one experiences union with God fully here (hence the need for hope), and the things that block that full union with God here are not just suffered by us, but are often perpetrated by us. The sin that is perpetrated by us does shape who we are, so for us to be united with God definitively, any remaining sin must be purged from us. And recall from chapter 12 that even the great saints recognize they are not sinless. Purgatory is simply this purging, in preparation for full union with God.

Consider two images of purgatory. In a more legalistic one, which fails to see our earthly actions as intrinsically related to our final destiny, purgatory is like a temporary jail sentence, where we put in time to pay our debt to God, and then are released into heaven. Though there are elements of truth here, what is completely lacking is a sense of the change in a person required for union with God.

Consider another image. Have you ever had the experience of falling in love and feeling completely unworthy of the beloved? Or meeting a truly holy person and feeling woefully inadequate in her presence, as if she could see through you and view all your sinfulness? In the presence of truth and goodness, such feelings of inadequacy are common. And reminiscent of Robert Barron's reflection on knowing you are a sinner, they are accurate. Well, imagine the experience of standing in the presence of the Lord, the source of truth and goodness. It must be excruciating to see God's beauty and goodness, and simultaneously be aware of all the ways, great and small, that we turned away from God to do things on our own terms. Imagine that through God's grace and forgiveness, and the prayers of others, such an encounter could radically transform the parts of our persons that had become habituated into vices and turned us away from God. This process would be painful, in that it would entail letting go of parts of our lives to which we clung in opposition to loving God and others. C. S. Lewis describes such an encounter splendidly in *The Great Divorce*.[19] But such an encounter would be both a necessary and painful purging, and ultimately an occasion for joyful healing and transformation

19. See *The Great Divorce*, (San Francisco: HarperSanFrancisco, 2001), 106–15.

with God's help, in order to unite us with God.[20] This is the essence of the Catholic teaching on purgatory.

The Meanings—Yes, Plural—of Death

Discussion of purgatory, and all the above topics, leads naturally to reflection on the meanings of death. When, after all, do all these things happen? After we die, of course. But it is actually more complicated than that. After all, the previous parts explained the important continuity between our final destinies and our lives in this world. Consider some further challenging questions. When does definitive judgment happen? If it is when someone dies, why do we pray for the dead? When does the resurrection of the body (a topic addressed below) occur? If after death, are those who have passed already risen? With resurrected bodies? What, then, is interred in graves? What did Jesus mean when he said, "I am the living bread that came down from heaven; whoever eats this bread will live forever" (John 6:51)? Are people who die thus excluded from eternal life?

It may sound odd to speak of death as having more than one meaning, but this is done purposely here. As important as those discussions are, what is meant here is not a contemporary bioethical debate over when some persons are rightly labeled "dead." The Christians tradition speaks of death in several ways, and it is important to have a sense of these in order to better understand the topics above, and the challenging teaching on the resurrection of the body examined below. What is common to both meanings of death in the Christian tradition is that they do not signify an end, but rather a disintegration, or radical loss of purpose. Death occurs when things are separated that should not be separated—there is disintegration. Or better, things die when they are radically separated from their proper orientation or purpose.

One meaning of death is precisely what most of us think of when we hear this term. Death is a separation of soul and body. It occurs when whatever vivifies our bodies—whether you call it "soul," or "spirit," or "life force," or whatever—is no longer present making our bodies alive. When we see a dead body, perhaps at a wake or viewing, we know something is missing. The person whom we love is not fully there, even as we stand before a body. In fact, we even have a special name for the body at this point—corpse—to indicate its separation from the soul.

Death in this sense is bad. Though we were made with mortal bodies, it was not God's plan that we should die in this way. People were made to live, and persons are body and soul. Thus, Christians have always understood death as a result of sin. This should not, of course, be taken in a crude sense,

---

20. There are important parallels between the teaching on purgatory and the Catholic understanding of sacramental confession. Both involve a painful, yet ultimately joyful and life-giving, transformation or purging.

to mean that the death of a particular individual at a certain time is some indication of sinfulness. Rather, the claim that death is a result of sin is simply the claim that death was not in God's plan for humanity—it is not the way things were meant to be.

However, this is not to say that God cannot bring anything good out of death. To the contrary, the resurrection of Christ reveals to us that God has conquered death, and that due to God's power and mercy new life can come from death. More on that will follow below. But before discussing in what sense people are said to rise, consider a second meaning of death. Death can also refer to the soul's estrangement from God. This death is also a radical loss of purpose, since the soul was meant to be in union with God. It is death in this sense that Jesus refers to when he says, "I am the living bread that came down from heaven; whoever eats this bread will live forever" (John 6:51). Clearly people who have shared in the eucharist (to which Jesus refers) have died in the first sense described above. But in the sense of life as union with God, we can see in what sense they never die. Conversely, there are people who are alive around us that may be dead in this sense, by living lives estranged from God. Recall from chapter 12 that mortal sin is precisely such a state. This again is a reference to life as a qualitative measure. People can be more or less alive. Death of the soul occurs when ever one is definitely separated from God.

Thus, the Christian tradition has two meanings for death. Death can mean the separation of body and soul that we normally think of when we say someone has died. But it can also mean a person's estrangement from God. Both deaths are abominations, in that they defy God's plan. Yet whereas the first can have what the *Catechism* calls a positive meaning, which God in mercy makes use of to bring new life, death in the second sense is in no way good.

Rising from the Dead

When many people think of rising from the dead, they think of a more general notion of the afterlife. In other words, they think of how souls or spirits live on without their bodies. The *Catechism* affirms this belief. If death in the first sense is a separation of body and soul, then after this death the immortal soul lives on. How the soul lives on depends importantly on how one lived during one's earthly life. If one lives an earthly life in union with God, that union continues in the afterlife. Of course, the opposite is also true. The Christian scriptures are clear that living lives of social justice is crucial for determining how one lives on after death. (See esp. Luke 16:19–31; also Matt. 25:31–46.) But this meaning of rising from the dead is actually not the primary one for Christians. The creedal affirmation of the "resurrection of the dead" is a far more astonishing claim than merely the belief that life continues for the immaterial soul after its separation from the body.

What is the resurrection of the dead? Christians have affirmed from the very beginning of the church that at some final definitive point in history—on the last day, or at the second coming of Christ—all persons will rise and be reunited with their bodies. That's right. Despite the corruption that obviously occurs to earthly bodies after death, the Christian claim is that at the end of time all people will rise from the dead, body and soul. Note that this is a communal event, rather than something that happens individually to people when they die. Before examining the basis for this astonishing claim, it should be noted that this resurrection is not the same for everyone. When that happens, God's judgment is final, and the good are raised to everlasting glory in an incorruptible bodily state. The evil are judged definitively as well, and eternally separated from God. This last day of judgment is thus a wondrous ground of all hope for those who live in union with God and long for that union to be complete. It is also the notorious and final "second death" spoken of in Revelation for those who estrange themselves from God (Rev. 2:11). Second death is definitive separation of a soul from God for eternity.

Why do Christians believe in a bodily resurrection? It seems challenging enough for people to believe that life continues after the horror of death. Why affirm a bodily resurrection? After all, this belief engenders a host of theological questions, such as, what are incorruptible bodies? How can such a body truly be mine if I am dead for many years? What manifestation of one's body is one reunited with on the last day: a child's body? an adult body? my body at the time of death? Furthermore, what bodily weaknesses or disabilities exist on the last day? Since people are raised with glorified bodies, are those bodies marked by the same individual faults that we possess in this life?

This is not the first Christian claim to defy belief. Recall from the Gospel according to John the response of many of Jesus's followers when Jesus told them to eat his body and drink his blood in order to have eternal life—they returned to their former way of life and no longer accompanied Jesus (John 6:41–66). Similarly, St. Paul clearly acknowledges that Christian faith in the bodily resurrection is difficult, and that many preach against it. Yet he insists that this belief is central. For if the dead are not raised, then Christ was not raised. And if Christ was not raised bodily from the dead, then we Christians "are the most pitiable people of all" (1 Cor. 15:19). Why is this belief so central? There are two reasons.

The first, and most important, reason is mentioned by Paul. Christian belief in the resurrection is not simply some intellectual position arrived at by logic. It is God's saving action that Christians witness and proclaim. How is it witnessed? First and foremost in Christ Jesus. It is because Christ rose from the dead that Christians affirm the resurrection of the dead. And as all four gospels make clear in varying ways, the risen Christ was not a ghost. He was risen in a body. True, his glorified body was not like yours and mine. His friends initially do not recognize him; he appears and disappears suddenly. But nonetheless he is no ghost. He eats with his disciples. They touch him, most famously St. Thomas, who puts his fingers in Christ's hands and his hand in Christ's side (John 20:24–28). And even though his friends do not recognize him immediately, they always do eventually recognize him as their friend and Lord Jesus. In other words, it is Jesus, body and all, and not someone else— not some ghost—who is resurrected from the dead.

This is the most important reason why Christians affirm a bodily resurrection. It is a stumbling block to many. If someone were making this up, it would certainly be more readily believable to claim a merely spiritual afterlife. But again, Christians are witnesses to what God does in Christ, not determiners of it. Of course, unsurprisingly, given the Christian affirmation of the complementarity of faith and reason, this doctrine received by faith also makes sense. After all, we read in the first chapters of Genesis, God created man and woman, body and soul, and called this creation "very good." Therefore people are body and soul, rather than just souls. Bodies are good, and an essential part of who we are. If it is truly and fully we who are resurrected from the dead, it only makes sense that this resurrection be a bodily one. This is another, albeit secondary, reason why Christians affirm the bodily resurrection.

Concluding Thoughts

We have now come full circle to answer the question that was raised at the start of this chapter: if human persons are restless, longing creatures, what exactly is it we are longing for? We started to answer this question from the perspective of our own longings and we basically said "we are longing for all of our longings to be satisfied." We saw that there are better and worse ways to respond to this state of restlessness. Two common errors, called by Lewis the "fool's way" and the "way of the disillusioned sensible man," entail seeking fulfillment in things which cannot offer it, or giving up on the possible of complete fulfillment, respectively. It is the theological virtue of hope that inclines us to keep our eye on the prize and keep longing for union with God, fully available only in the next life, as our true destiny and complete happiness. We also saw not only how the person of hope remains steadily fixed on a destiny beyond this life, but also how this virtue enables one to fully appreciate, yet not idolize, the goods of this life. Though a theological virtue, a life of grace marked by hope entails a transformed stance with regard to innerworldly goods, a topic explained more fully in chapter 16.

The second half of this chapter appealed to reason and especially Christian revelation to learn more about the content, if you will, of Christian hope. Though people quite commonly associate Christianity with a belief in heaven, they far too often have no mature idea of what exactly Christian belief about life after death entails. Two points about that teaching should be kept in mind. First, there is important continuity between how one lives in this life and one's destiny in the next. In one sense this is obvious: everyone knows Christians believe you go to heaven or hell based upon how you live on earth. Yet hopefully this chapter has presented an understanding of God's judgment as something far richer than some externally imposed or arbitrary grade that one receives at the end of life, all the while waiting in trepidation to see if one passed or not. Rather, judgment is more properly understood as a finalization, or solidification, of a way of living that one has already been shaped into during one's whole earthly life. In line with Lewis's view on final judgment, in the end everyone gets what they want. The interesting question is whether or not what we want in this life is the genuine complete fulfillment that is indeed available to us.

Second, what the Christian tradition teaches actually happens after death is both less impenetrable and yet far more extraordinary than is commonly assumed. On the one hand, this is a topic that exceeds the perfection of clear sight, so we cannot clearly see what happens after death without the assistance of revelation. But we can certainly say more about it than we can talk about people in white sheets playing harps! We can talk about death as a separation of body and soul, of union or separation from God. And we can talk about the communal nature of what happens after death (the resurrection of the dead).

The Christian tradition teaches that the afterlife is far more than some wispy spiritual state. There is ultimately a bodily resurrection on the last day, final judgment, and a new creation which is begun in this life in the grace of baptism, but completed only at the second coming of Christ, a fulfilled destiny for which "all creation is groaning" (Rom. 8:22). Though there are solid reasons why this teaching makes sense, it far exceeds our unaided capacities and, as Paul recognized from the first century of Christianity, it poses a stumbling block for many. It is in this sense that Christian belief about the afterlife is far more extraordinary that is commonly assumed. And when we recall how dimly we see now, as if through a glass, then we may wonder even further about the ways this destiny must transcend even the extraordinary things we are only able to fleetingly imagine in this life.

Study Questions

1. Describe the human situation that occasions hope.
2. This chapter presents two poor responses to the human situation that occasions hope. Name and describe each. Why is each one a poor response?
3. Define the virtue hope. Why is it a theological virtue? Why is it only possible with God's grace?

4. What does having hope have to do with how we live in this life?
5. Define heaven, hell, and purgatory. Describe two ways these terms can be understood: in a manner that is only extrinsically related to our lives on earth, and a manner that is intimately connected to our lives on earth.
6. What two meanings do Christians have for death? When does one die in each sense?
7. What does it mean to rise from the dead? What role does one's body play in one's life after death?

Terms to Know

restlessness, Lewis's "fool's way," idolatry, Lewis's "disillusioned sensible man," presumption, despair, hope, heaven, hell, "everyone gets what they want," purgatory, death, second death, resurrection of the body

Questions for Further Reflection

1. Hope is a theological virtue that requires God's grace. How, then, to explain people who are not Christians, but do not seem to fall into either trap of the fool's way or the disillusioned sensible man? In other words, can people live in hope without believing in God and union with God in the next life?
2. In what ways is hope similar to the fool's way? In what ways is it similar to the disillusioned sensible man's way? Yet how is it importantly different from each, and how could you determine in real life whether one had the virtue hope or was slipping into one of these two errors?
3. What are some of the concrete ways that people are led to have hope, rather than fall into despair or the fool's way? What experiences lead people to either affirm or deny the possibility of true fulfillment?
4. What are some examples of being more or less fully alive in this life?
5. One question Lewis addresses in *The Great Divorce* is whether or not the communion of saints in heaven can truly be full if even one person is estranged from God and that communion for eternity. In other words, if sharing in the divine nature is living fully in self-giving love that is God, how can such a person be happy if one whom they presumably love is separated from God from eternity?
6. What experience from life can be cited as "mini-purgatories" and help make that teaching more accessible to us?
7. To what extent can nonrational creatures (such as animals) participate in eternal union with God?
8. What difference does the claim that eternal life is outside of time—

and not merely an extended period of time—make for understanding the resurrection of the body and its relationship to bodily death?

Further Reading

Three authors have been particularly influential on this chapter due to their accessible descriptions of hope: C. S. Lewis's *Mere Christianity*, Michael Himes's *Doing the Truth in Love*, and Paul Wadell's *Becoming Friends*. For more exhaustive inquiry into this virtue, see Thomas Aquinas's treatise on hope (*Summa Theologiae* II–II 17–22) and two more contemporary Thomists, Josef Pieper (*Faith, Hope, and Love*) and Romanus Cessario, OP ("The Virtue of Hope," in Stephen J. Pope, ed. *Ethics of Aquinas*). As for the second section's discussion of life after death, the most clear and concise synopsis of Christian teaching is found in the *Catechism of the Catholic Church* 988–1065. The classic scriptural text on resurrection, besides the four gospel accounts, is St. Paul's 1 Cor. 15. St. Augustine's work on death (in *City of God* IX) has also been influential on this chapter. Two comprehensive but relatively accessible overviews of the Christian tradition on last things are Joseph Ratzinger's (now Pope Benedict XVI) *Eschatology: Death and Eternal Life,* and Romano Guardini's *The Last Things: Concerning Death, Purification After Death, Resurrection, Judgment and Eternity*. C. S. Lewis's *The Great Divorce* is a superb resource for presenting Christian teaching on hope and life after death in narrative form. Finally, Pope Benedict XVI released an encyclical on hope entitled *Spe Salvi* as this book was going to print.

14

JESUS CHRIST

Incarnation and Life in Christ

Having reached the midpoint of this second half of the book, it may be helpful to take stock of where we have gone so far, and where we have left to go in that second half. After a chapter that both illustrated the importance of big-picture beliefs for innerworldly practices, and offered a summary picture of Christian big-picture beliefs, we launched into chapters on the theological virtues and particular elements of that Christian story. Chapter 11 on faith relied on *Fides et Ratio* to demonstrate how believing in answers to big-picture questions is the sort of thing human persons do, and explored how Christian faith as a theological virtue is a distinctive way of believing, based upon a Christian understanding of the way things are. Chapter 12 explained the important role that sin plays in the Christian story, and further examined the nature of human sin. Chapter 13 explained why the theological virtue hope is crucial given our human situation, and offered a brief synopsis of what the nature of the destiny it is that we hope for, namely, union with God in complete happiness.

Notice that so far we have presented the content of Christian faith and the nature of Christian hope. In other words, it should be more evident both why we are here, and where we are called to by God. We also saw how sin, as alienation from God, keeps us from that destiny. Sin is a main reason why what we are destined for is at present only a hope, rather than a present reality. Yet to this point there has been no attention given to how we get to our destiny from our broken sinful condition. We have explained the hole, or problem, we are in, and where we are called to. But there has been no discussion of any ladder to get out of the hole, or bridge to get us from this state to the next. This chapter begins that task, one that will continue over the following two chapters as well.

This bridge, if you will, is Jesus Christ. It is fitting to have a chapter on Jesus at the center of this half of the book, since Christ is literally the center of the Christian life. It is through Christ that we have the faith we have, that we are aware of the depth of our sinfulness, and have any hope of full union with God. It is also Christ who lifts us out of the depth of our brokenness and vivifies us to live virtuous lives centered on God, or, as St. Paul says, to "live in Christ" (e.g., Gal. 2:20, Rom. 8:2). Thus this chapter, which has two sections, explores the starring role of Jesus Christ in the Christian story. . The first examines the theological question of what God accomplishes in Jesus Christ. The second attends more directly to moral theology and explores what God's work in Christ has to do with how particular people live their lives today. It should go without saying, but will be said anyway, that writing a single chapter on who Christ is and how we live in Christ is akin to answering the question who are you? in one sentence. Interesting and accurate things can be said, for sure, but they will be far from the whole picture. The same can be said of this chapter.

God's Saving Action in Jesus Christ

It is tempting to begin this first half of the chapter by examining a question posed repeatedly in the gospels by Jesus: "who do you say that I am?" But in order to emphasize the moral importance of that question, such discussion is reserved for the second section below. Instead, this first section explores what God has accomplished through sending his Son Jesus Christ, and how Christ accomplished it. First, we will state succinctly the hole, or problem, that we people had gotten ourselves into that necessitated God's action in Christ.[1] Second, we will examine what God becoming man in the incarnation achieved in response to that hole. Finally, the last part of this section will address the challenging but essential Christian claim that Christ "died for our sins" (1 Cor. 15:3).

1. It is C. S. Lewis who uses the term "hole" for the human situation of sin in his *Mere Christianity* (San Francisco: HarperSanFrancisco, 2001), a book that has influenced this chapter enormously. Of course, Lewis himself purports to be simply presenting the basics of the Christian story in his book (hence "mere" Christianity) and so this material is readily found elsewhere. For another succinct and penetrating exposition of the claims of this section, see the *Catechism of the Catholic Church*, 2nd ed. (Vatican City: Libreria Editrice Vaticana, 1997), 456–63, 595–623, 651–58.

The Hole We Had Gotten Ourselves Into

This brief part will simply repeat and slightly expand a claim made in chapter 12 on sin: the Christian story of God's decisive action in Jesus Christ only makes sense if you have an adequate understanding of human sin. There can be no salvation if there is nothing we need saving from! The consistent witness of the Christian tradition is that God sent his only son in order to free people from sin, to reconcile them to himself. It is sin that alienates people from God, and thus sin which must be overcome in order to reunite, or reconcile, humanity and God into right relationship. Without an adequate understanding of this alienating sin, it is impossible to understand God's saving action in Christ to overcome that alienation.

Sin is not simply something that happens to people, something that we fall into. It is something that we perpetrate. Our sinfulness is a stance we voluntarily adopt. It is a stance of resistance against God. Lewis describes sinful humanity as rebels who need to lay down our weapons.[2] The Christian claim about human sin is not simply that it is imperfection, or that there is room for improvement in all of us. Who could contest that? The claim, you recall, is that we tend to pridefully put ourselves first. As Lewis says, we "set up on our own as if we had created ourselves," we try to be our own masters and we "invent some sort of happiness for ourselves outside of God" on our own terms.[3] Even though people may not consciously understand their sinfulness as active resistance to God's love and sovereignty, this element of pride is always at least implicitly present in our sin.

What is required for right relations to be reestablished with God, Lewis explains, is not simply some subtle change in direction in our lives. To continue the rebel analogy, it is not simply a change in how we fight or whom we target. It is a radical surrender, a laying down of our weapons. It is "unlearning all the self-conceit and self-will we have been training ourselves into [as a human race] for thousands of years."[4] This is what it means to repent, which you recall from chapter 12 is the first word spoken in the synoptic gospels when the kingdom of God is announced at the time of Jesus's public ministry. Repentance is hard. It is a sort of death of an old self. In fact, given the sorts of persons that rebels like us have become, repentance is not even a feasible option for us without help. As Lewis explains,

> It needs a good man to repent. And here comes the catch. Only a bad person needs to repent: only a good person *can* repent perfectly. The worse you are the more you need it and the less you can do it. The only person who could do it perfectly would be a perfect person—and he would not need it.[5]

2. See Lewis, *Mere Christianity*, 56–57.
3. Ibid., 49 (pronouns have been altered to the first person plural).
4. Ibid., 57.
5. Ibid. (emphasis added).

We now see why Lewis entitles this chapter in his book "The Perfect Penitent." We are also ready to explain how God responded to humanity's situation of being in the state of obstinate resistance to God.

The Incarnation: God's Loving Response to Humanity's Sin

The term *incarnation* derives from Latin and literally means coming "into flesh." The *Catechism* calls the incarnation the "distinctive sign of Christian faith."[6] It is the belief that the ever-living and transcendent God became a human person in Jesus of Nazareth. Why this is the central event in the history of humanity, according to Christians, should be clear from Lewis's depiction above of the hole we had gotten ourselves into. Prideful humanity had alienated ourselves from God, and needed to repent in order to be back in union with God, a union for which we are destined, and which is our complete fulfillment and happiness. However, the very pride that necessitated repentance also made such repentance impossible for us on our own. A perfect penitent was needed (who would not, ironically, actually need to repent for himself) to live out what we could not. And so God becomes a man in Jesus. He lives a life in perfect loving obedience to God his Father in order to reestablish right relationship between humanity and God (in other words to "save" or "redeem" humanity). "For our sake he [the Father] made him [Jesus the son] to be sin who did not know sin, so that we might become the righteousness of God in him" (2 Cor. 5:21). This is what Christians mean when they profess together the Nicene Creed (the classic summation of their faith stated by Christians for centuries): "*For us men and for our salvation,* he [the Son] came down from heaven; by the power of the Holy Spirit he was born of the Virgin Mary and became man."

What did the incarnation of God's only begotten son as the human person Jesus accomplish? Before examining this question, we should note Lewis's distinction between believing what God accomplished in Christ, and understanding how what God accomplished in Christ works. The former is necessary for Christian faith. The latter is not. Lewis uses a helpful example to illustrate the difference.[7] When you are hungry, you know you need to eat, and that if you eat you will be satiated. Eating when you are hungry is necessary to live. It is not necessary, however, to understand why it is that eating satiates our hunger. Lewis observes that we now have a theory about how food provides vitamins for our nourishment. Long before people understood what vitamins were, however, they ate and sustained themselves. Even today there are plenty of people who have never heard the term "vitamin" and do just fine! What is necessary is to eat. Of course, understanding how eating sustains us may enable us to eat more healthily, and so such knowledge can be useful. But it is not necessary in order to actually live well.

6. *Catechism of the Catholic Church*, 463.
7. See Lewis, *Mere Christianity*, 54–55.

Lewis says the same is true of understanding the theology of the incarnation. Christians have always professed, even before the words of the Nicene Creed were formulated in the fourth century, that for us and our salvation the son of God came down from heaven. He died for our sins and reconciled us to God in fullness of life. Affirming that this happened is fundamental to Christian faith. Understanding how and why it worked to save humanity, however, is not. Nonetheless, understanding this further may help us in living our lives in response to it, so we turn to that task here.

The *Catechism of the Catholic Church* offers four reasons why "the Word became flesh" in Jesus Christ (John 1:14).[8] The four are actually mutually affirming; in other words, they are four different claims about the same event, each of which on closer examination actually entails the others. Listing them may help us better understand the incarnation. First, the "Word became flesh for us *in order to save us by reconciling us with God.*" Jesus is the "Lamb of God," who "takes away the sins of the world" (John 1:29). Jesus takes away human sin by overcoming humanity's alienation from God, and that is what reconciles us with God. Second, the "Word became flesh *so that thus we might know God's love.*" God's saving act in the incarnation is the perfect revelation of God's love for us, since "God so loved the world that he sent his only Son, that we might not perish but have eternal life" (John 3:16). Indeed, the fact that God became a person to save us reveals that God loved us first, reaching out to reconcile us to himself even though we were obstinate in sin (Rom. 5:5–12; 1 John 4:19). Third, the "Word became flesh *to be our model of holiness.*" Christ not only taught this love—"love one another as I have loved you"(John 15:12)—but more importantly lived out this love most perfectly in his sacrificial death for humanity—"no greater love has man than this, than to lay down his life for his friends"(John 15:13). Finally, the "Word became flesh to make us *'partakers of the divine nature'* [2 Pet. 1:4]." In other words, God became a person to enable human persons to know the fullness of life that only God (who is love) lives to the fullest. As the early church fathers were fond of saying, God became man so that men might become gods.[9]

The irony in this last claim should be clear. The origin of human sinfulness is a prideful striving to become like gods. Yet fullness of life in union with God, understood radically as a very partaking in God's nature, is exactly what God has been leading us to all along. Thus, on the one hand we pridefully exalt ourselves to become like gods, seeking happiness on our own terms, while actually alienating ourselves from God and the very happiness we truly seek. On the other hand, God sends his only son who "humbled himself," "being born in the likeness of men," "obediently accepting death, death on

8. See *Catechism of the Catholic Church*, 456–60. The four reasons given here appear in 457–60, (italics original).

9. See Ibid., 460, for a sampling of quotations from Irenaeus, Athanasius, and Augustine on this point.

a cross" (Phil. 2:6ff.), precisely to make us "partakers in the divine nature" (2 Pet. 1:4), which is the fullness of life tasted in this life and known fully in the next. In sin we work against the very happiness and fulfillment we seek. In the incarnation God makes what we seek possible through the self-giving love that constitutes fullness of life.

Thus, in the incarnation God accomplishes something. God becoming man in Jesus Christ is essential in enabling humanity to once again be able to live in right relationship with God, a relationship we had spurned in our pride and were unable to restore on our own. Christ restores it. Through living in Christ, humanity is once again able to live in the self-giving love that constitutes fullness of life in union with God. All humanity, conscious of Christ or not, has been impacted by this event.

Christ Died for Our Sins

Christians may notice something important missing from the above discussion of the necessity of the incarnation for God's salvation of humanity. Though everything said there is affirmed as true, Christians do not just think that God accomplished salvation, or reconciliation, between himself and humanity by becoming a human person in Jesus Christ. The further claim is made that Christ died for our sins. There is a clear sense in scripture and tradition not only that right relationship has been restored (reconciliation), but also that some price was paid by Christ's sacrificial death. It is impossible to overestimate how central a claim this is for Christian faith. As Lewis states

> The central Christian belief is that Christ's death has somehow put us right with God and given us a fresh start. . . . We are told that Christ was killed for us, that His death has washed out our sins, and that by dying He disabled death itself. That is the formula. That is Christianity.[10]

No discussion of God's salvation of humanity in Christ can fail to attend to this central Christian claim. But what does it mean?

First, note what it does not mean. Christians do not believe that God the Father is some vindictive bully who has to hurt or punish someone, and if humanity is going to get off the hook—well then—someone else will just have to pay. Christ's suffering and death for our sins should not be understood in this crude sense of scapegoating, as if Christ stepped in to take the punishment that God would not withhold from someone.

Though this affirmation of faith is always challenging to understand, a far richer understanding of it is available through the notion of *sacrifice*.[11] A

---

10. Lewis, *Mere Christianity*, 54–55.

11. For a helpful discussion of this difficult discussion of Christ's death being an atonement for our sins, see Richard John Neuhaus's *Death on a Friday Afternoon: Meditations on the Last*

sacrifice occurs when someone gives up something for another. As it concerns God, a sacrifice is an act of worship by a creature (like a person) to the Creator. It testifies to the truth of the proper relationship between humanity and God, namely, that God is God and we are his creatures. Such an act makes amends for breaks or strains in that relationship by putting it back on track. From this perspective, Christ's death for us was a sacrifice putting humanity back on the track of right relationship with God. By becoming a real human person in Jesus Christ, the Son of God took on creatureliness. Being a creature should mean dying to one's self, being perfectly obedient to the Father, and being willing to lays down one's own life. Because Jesus Christ was fully human, he was called to live this out. Because he was also fully divine, Jesus Christ was able to live this out.

You may wonder why a sacrificial death was necessary. Couldn't Jesus have been fully obedient and restored our relationship with God without having to actually die? But Christ's death was not some price that needed to be paid in addition to restoring right relationship. Repentance is simply dying to one's old self in turning toward God and, in doing so, ironically finding one's true self. Death to one's wayward self is simply what going back to God is like.[12] Jesus Christ was fully human; in fact, he was the perfect exemplar of what it means to be truly human. Thus, even though he was without sin and not in need of repentance, as representative, if you will, of the human race he who was without sin gave himself up in the most perfect and complete obedience to the Father, "humbly accepting even death, death on a cross" (Phil. 2:8). Jesus's death was the perfect and complete act of sacrifice, a testimony to the right relationship between humanity and God. This act was vindicated in his resurrection, where God the Father raises up the Son, revealing that sin and death no longer have hold over him and, by extension, his fellow humanity for whom he died. It is for this reason that Christians affirm that Christ's death definitively changed humanity's relationship with God by reestablishing right relationship between God and humanity, or saving humanity from the hole we had gotten ourselves into.

As Lewis noted, understanding how this works theologically is ultimately far less important than affirming in faith that it happened. This mystery does not defy—it transcends—our full understanding and hence requires faith in the manner discussed in chapter 11. It should now be clear why Christians believe Jesus Christ is far more than simply a great moral teacher. He was that, and his injunctions on forgiveness, love of others, and the like are powerfully true rules for us in how to live our own lives. That said, Christians worship Jesus Christ as God incarnate, and celebrate and remember (especially in the

---

Words of Jesus from the Cross (New York: Basic Books, 2001), 187–228. Neuhaus's text was formative for this treatment of sacrifice.

12. See Lewis, *Mere Christianity*, 57.

eucharist) how his life, death, and resurrection effectuated a change in human history that goes beyond whether or not individual persons follow his moral guidelines.

Living in Christ

At this point one might wonder what any of this has to do with moral theology. After all, aren't we talking about things stated in the Nicene Creed that Christians hold to be true, like that Jesus is the Son of God sent to save humanity? What has this to do with how we should act, especially if Jesus Christ's moral guidance is not the central reason why Christians follow him? Well, if one of the central claims of this book is true, namely, that living virtuously is living in accordance with how things really are, then it makes all the difference whether or not one has an accurate grasp of how things are. If the claims made in the first section of this chapter are true, then what ramifications are there for how we live? Answering that question is the task of this second section of the chapter.

Who Do You Say That I Am?

One of the more haunting questions that appears repeatedly throughout the gospels is when Jesus asks, "who do you say that I am?"[13] Why haunting? The question is far from an abstract one. Notice, Jesus does not say "who am I?" which presumably one could answer distantly and nonchalantly. He asks, "Who do *you* say that I am?" How you answer this question will not only indicate something about Jesus, but also something about you. The wording of the question makes it clear that who you say Jesus is demands a response. As Lewis puts it while making a point described below (that Jesus was not simply a great moral teacher):

> You must make your choice. Either this man was, and is, the Son of God: or else a madman or something worse. You can shut Him up for a fool, you can spit at Him and kill Him as a demon; or you can fall at His feet and call Him Lord and God.[14]

Who one claims Jesus is demands some decisive response.

Christology is the name for the study of who Jesus Christ is. The point of the previous paragraph is that studying who Jesus is should not merely be some theoretical and abstract exercise. It is simultaneously the study of discipleship, or what it means to follow Jesus. After all, who Jesus is dictates how we

---

13. See Mark 8:29; Matt. 16:15; Luke 9:20.
14. C. S. Lewis, *Mere Christianity*, 52.

respond. For example, if Jesus is indeed the Son of God, we should follow him. If he is not, we should not. More specifically, even if we grant that Jesus is the Son of God, we must further determine what that means. How Jesus reveals what it means to be in right relationship with God, what is means to live most fully, will dictate how we should follow Jesus.

The main purpose of Jesus asking his disciples in the gospels, "who do you say that I am?" is not merely to see if they believe him to be the Son of God, the messiah sent by God to deliver humanity. Jesus also asks this question to see what kind of messiah sent by God they believe him to be. Nowhere is this more evident than in the Gospel according to Mark. A close look at a crucial section of that gospel will help us see how Jesus instructs his disciples as to who he really is.[15]

This section of Mark (8:27–10:45) begins with our title question, as Jesus asks Peter, in particular, who he says Jesus is. Peter answers, "You are the Messiah" (in Matthew Peter adds, "the Son of the living God"), and Jesus confirms that this response is true. End of lesson, it would seem. Peter has accurately identified Jesus. And if Jesus is the Messiah, the Son of God, presumably this is all we need to know. However, then Jesus oddly instructs his disciples "not to tell anyone about him" (Mark 8:30). Why is this? It surely cannot be to keep Jesus a secret; the whole point of Jesus's ministry (and of Mark writing this gospel) is to proclaim the good news of what God has done in Jesus! What can explain this theme in the first half of Mark, often called the *Markan secret*, whereby Jesus instructs those who recognize him as the Son of God not to tell others who he is (1:34; 3:11–12; 8:30)?

Perhaps it is because knowing Jesus is the Son of God is not enough. It is an important start, and the first half of Mark (which ends at this passage) is largely the story of Jesus's disciples coming to learn this about him. But that is only half the story. The next half concerns what sort of messiah Jesus is. Or better, if Jesus is the Son of God and thus we can learn truly who God is by looking at Jesus, what does Jesus reveal about who God is? This is also necessary to know in order to truly follow Jesus. And in Mark the fact that the disciples still have some learning to do at the time of Peter's response could not be more evident.

Notice that the two chapters following Peter's right answer concerning Jesus are rather repetitive. This section of Mark basically contains three similar claims by Jesus, followed by three similar responses by the disciples, followed again by three similar responses by Jesus. There are other important stories in these two chapters, for sure. In fact, here one finds the story of the rich young

---

15. The following discussion of Mark 8:27–10:45 is heavily indebted to Werner Kelber's *Mark's Story of Jesus* (Philadelphia: Fortress, 1979), 43–56, a text I have enjoyed teaching for years. Kelber does an outstanding textual analysis of this part of Mark. He actually focuses on Mark 8:22–10:52 to include healing stories at the beginning and end of this section, but those are not addressed here.

man asking Jesus how to inherit eternal life, a crucial story for moral theology, and one examined closely in chapter 2 on freedom. But the basic structure of this part of the gospel is a threefold pattern repeated three times. What is Mark trying to accomplish here with this obviously intentional structure?

Immediately after Peter's correct answer, Jesus informs his disciples that he will suffer and be rejected, be killed, and rise after three days (Mark 8:31). Jesus repeats this claim two more times in the ensuing chapters (9:31; 10:33–34). Why is such repetition necessary? Because though the disciples know Jesus to be the Messiah, they clearly do not get it fully. They do not understand what this entails, namely, that Jesus will lay down his life for others. This lack of understanding is evidenced by their reaction to each of these predictions.

After the first prediction, Peter rebukes Jesus. The term "rebuke," according to biblical scholars, is no mere admonition. Thus far in Mark it had been used only toward an unclean spirit (1:25). Think of how amazing Peter's rebuke is. Just lines earlier Peter had accurately identified Jesus as the Messiah. Now he is telling Jesus that what Jesus thinks that means is all wrong. The brazen absurdity! In response, Jesus rebukes Peter with the famous, "Get behind me Satan! You are thinking not as God does, but as human beings do" (8:33). Here we see in Peter the perfect portrayal of how the disciples in general both get it (that Jesus is indeed the Messiah) and yet do not get it (in terms of what sort of messiah Jesus is). Peter thinks as broken human beings do, and not as God does, which is why Jesus has repeatedly insisted that others stay quiet about who he is (the Markan secret). Though they have part of the picture, they are missing important parts, without which they would only be spreading an inaccurate view of who Jesus is.

Who is he *really*, then? Or what understanding of who the Messiah is reflects how God thinks rather than how people think? In the very next lines Jesus goes on to say that "whoever wishes to come after me must deny himself, take up his cross, and follow me. Whoever wishes to save his life will lose it, but whoever loses his life for my sake and that of the gospel will save it" (8:34–35). The disciples were clearly not expecting that sort of messiah! Peter rebuked Jesus for saying he would suffer and die. (Interestingly, Jesus also says he'll rise again, which we would think the disciples would take note of—this is a rather radical claim! But it goes right over their heads.) After Jesus's second prediction of his suffering, death and rising, the disciples "did not understand the saying, and they were afraid to question him" (9:32). In fact, they then go on to argue who among them is the greatest (9:33–34)! Clearly they understand Christ's lordship to be one of worldly power and glory; they are still warped by the very sin and pride that Christ comes to overcome.

After Jesus's third prediction of his suffering and death, James and John have the nerve to ask, "Teacher, we want you to do whatever we ask of you" (10:35). Is this for real? Here they are talking to the Messiah, and they only want to receive him on their own terms? It gets better. Their request is to sit on his left and right once Jesus enters into his (they must think "earthly") glory. Jesus is saying he will suffer and die, and James and John, much like the other disciples, are only concerned with status and positions of power, much as a volunteer on a politician's campaign might ask for a cabinet position if the candidate wins. The other disciples are indignant at this, but one has the impression it is because they too would want such positions, and not because of the foolishness of the request. In each of these three responses to Jesus's prediction of his suffering and death, the disciples show that they indeed do not fully get it; in other words, they do not understand the sort of messiah that Jesus is.

But Christ the teacher instructs them each time. After enjoining them to take up their crosses and follow him after the first prediction, Jesus corrects them after the second prediction (when they were afraid, and still arguing over who is greatest) by saying, "If anyone wishes to be first, he shall be the last of all and servant of all" (9:35). After the third prediction and James and John's self-interested request, Jesus replies

> Whoever wishes to be great among you will be your servant; whoever wishes to be first among you will be the slave of all. For the Son of Man did not come to be served, but to serve and to give his life as a ransom for many. (10:43–45)

In these three responses to the disciples' misunderstanding of what sort of messiah he is, Jesus states clearly what his lordship is all about, how God thinks, and what truly following Jesus (rather than some false and worldly image of Jesus) means. Christ came to take up his cross, serve others, and lay down his life for them. Anyone who wishes to follow him must do the same.

Some may read this scathing portrayal of the disciples and think it must not be an accurate portrayal of them. Yet we must keep in mind that it is clearly not Mark's intent to besmirch the disciples' reputations. After all, any audience who would be reading or hearing this text (written a generation after Jesus's life) would know full well what happened to the twelve apostles. Peter went on to be crucified as Christ was, though upside down. In fact, all the apostles who witness the resurrection of Christ (except John) were martyred. And anyone who hears James and John's request from a perspective after the resurrection might chuckle at what they ask for, to sit at Jesus's left and right. There were three, not one, crosses on the hill at Golgotha when Jesus was crucified. Being at Jesus's right and left is not exactly what these two had in mind. They are indeed granted to drink of the cup of suffering from which Jesus drinks (10:39; cf. Luke 22:42), and in James's case this includes martyrdom. We need not fret about protecting the disciples' reputations from Mark. Instead, we must recall who the real target of Mark's passage is: we, the readers, the hearers. The disciples eventually learned the lesson of who Jesus really is after encountering the risen Christ, and they followed him accordingly. That part of the story is over. How we will respond, however, remains to be seen. The real target here is us. "Who do *you* say that I am?"

Thus, by proclaiming who we think Jesus is, we simultaneously state what it means to follow Jesus. If Jesus is God's only begotten son, the path to fullness of life in union with God, then how the incarnate word of God lived as the human person Jesus is the clearest sign of what it means for us human persons to live as God's children. Jesus makes it abundantly clear what sort of messiah he is: a suffering servant who lays down his life for others in love. He is the opposite of, and antidote to, that anti-God state known as pride and sin. And if one calls him "lord" and understands truly who he is, then we can only respond by taking up our crosses, serving others, and following him even to the point of laying down our lives in love.

Living/Participating in the Incarnation Today

The basic message of the previous section seems rather innocuous: love and serve other people because that is what Jesus did. You probably did not need to read a chapter in a book to tell you that! Of course, living it out is another story. If people genuinely tried to live this out the world would be a much different place. But just to be sure that what needs to be lived out is clear, this part of the chapter relies on two examples of such loving, selfless service to further illuminate what is means to live the incarnation today; what it means, in other words, to live as God's sons and daughters in a manner most perfectly exemplified by the Son of God, Jesus Christ.[16]

The central claim of this chapter is that Jesus is God's definitive response to human brokenness and sinfulness. Note that God conceivably could have responded otherwise. He could have ignored humanity. Or he could have snapped his fingers, if you will, to just make all the sin go away. But neither was his response. "God so loved the world that he sent his only Son, that all who believe might have life eternal (John 3:16)." Out of love God acted definitively to save humanity from its sin, not simply by making it go away, but by entering into our broken condition, healing it, and enabling humanity to live more fully. That is what the incarnation and Christ's death accomplished. Unsurprisingly, we see in Christ's own life the exact same approach toward people in their brokenness and sinfulness. Whether it be people with physical disabilities, people with unclean spirits, or simply people captive to their own sinfulness, Jesus repeatedly encounters them in such states, loves them, serves them, and enables them to live more fully. He does not dismiss or avoid the poor, the sick, or sinners. He encounters them where they are and seeks to give them a richer life. And this is exactly what is expected of his followers.

---

16. For more on this theme of living the incarnation today as a basis for Christian spirituality, see Ronald Rolheiser's *The Holy Longing* (New York: Doubleday, 1999), 73–81.

In the classic Matthew 25:31–45 passage, Jesus speaks most directly about the final judgment. "When the Son of Man comes in glory" (that is, the Second Coming) he will assemble all nations before him and separate them as a shepherd separates sheep and goats, the sheep to eternal reward and the goats to eternal punishment. What determines whether or not one is a sheep (which is what you definitely want to be in this story)? The sheep fed the hungry, gave drink to the thirsty, clothed the naked, sheltered the homeless, visited those in prison, and took care of the sick. This passage is, of course, the basis for the Catholic tradition's seven *corporal works of mercy*.[17] In this extraordinary passage we have from Christ's own mouth what is necessary to attain eternal life, which, as we know from chapter 13 means life in full union with God.

This may seem to be no surprise. Sure, we are supposed to be good people and do nice things like these. Yet the messiness of what it means to actually live the works of mercy is easily misunderstood. This is not naïve idealism, or some sentimental idealization of what it means to help those in need. Robert Barron tells a classic story of Dorothy Day, an early twentieth- century American woman who was tireless in her service to the poor and hungry. Reportedly she would tell young idealistic volunteers who arrived with romantic visions of helping poor people at her soup kitchen in New York City's Bowery, "there are two things you need to know about poor people: they are ungrateful, and they smell."[18] Her point was not to insult the poor, which should be obvious once one knows she devoted her life in service to those in need. Her point was that living the works of mercy is not the stuff of Hallmark cards. It is difficult and messy business. It means encountering those in need in their brokenness, entering into their situation just as Christ entered ours. It then means laying down our lives in service to them, in order that they may have life more fully. Obviously in our time this rarely means literally dying. But laying down our lives can be just as difficult for us—and just as life-giving for those served—when we let go of our own safe distance, comfortable presuppositions, and self-protectiveness to actually put our lives in service to others in a manner that is guided by what is genuinely best for those served. This means even when doing so is uncomfortable for us, and when others smell. It means even when others are ungrateful (or perhaps sinful in some glaring way), we still encounter them where they are (just as Christ loved us first) and serve them.

Note that though direct service to those who are not well-known to us is an obvious and necessary way to live out the works of mercy, these works of love certainly apply to those closer to us. A parent can sacrifice her own desires to

17. The seventh traditional corporal work of mercy is to bury the dead. There are also seven spiritual works of mercy: teach the ignorant, counsel the doubtful, correct sinners, bear wrongs patiently, forgive wrongs willingly, to comfort the afflicted, and to pray for the living and dead.

18. See Robert Barron, *The Strangest Way: Walking the Christian Path* (New York: Orbis, 2003), 152.

put the needs of her family (say, feed the hungry, clothe the naked) first and thus live in Christ. One can "lay down one's life" in service to a sick friend by putting his needs (even when he smells, and is ungrateful) first. Anyone who has had a loved one lose someone close to them knows that the work of mercy—to "bury the dead"—means far more than putting a body in the ground. It means bearing with a grieving one in her pain, supporting her in her time of weakness, and doing what is needed for her to live most fully even when it means sacrificing one's own desires, even when she may be ungrateful or difficult. In all these ways, and countless more, we can live in Christ by participating in the incarnation, where God reached out most personally to those in need, joined them in their suffering, and laid down his life to give others life. When we do these things, then we are truly living in Christ through the works of mercy.

Consider a second helpful way to understand how to live out the self-giving love of Christ. In an insightful article on this topic entitled "Wholesomeness, Holiness, and Hairspray," M. Cathleen Kaveny, like Robert Barron, tries to dislodge from our heads more idealistic or wholesome understandings of what it means to follow Christ.[19] Too often, she says, we think following Christ means being wholesome, by which she means tidy and orderly. In wholesome lives there are no addictions, no debilitating disabilities, no pregnancies out of wedlock, no ravaging diseases, no vicious arguments, no messiness. Of course, there is nothing inherently wrong with a life marked by none of these. (Indeed, full union with God in the next life will include none of them.) But wholesomeness becomes a problem when one begins to seek orderly appearances rather than what is truly life-giving to those in need. When we hide our disabled children, ignore blatant problems that are corroding our family life, send away pregnant teenagers, fail to face the real weakness and suffering of those who are sick, then we have made *wholesomeness* more important to us than true *holiness*. True holiness, exemplified in Christ, reaches out to people in their messy brokenness and sinfulness, always to serve them and enable them to live more fully. When things are indeed orderly—when our parents genuinely love each other, when people live chastely, or when we are fully healthy—the holy person is grateful. But never does a wholesome concern for orderly appearances lead the holy person to fail to see or avoid serving where there is brokenness, be it sinful or otherwise.

Kaveny's main point is that what people frequently describe as "Christian values" is really wholesomeness. It is too often a thin veneer of tidiness masking the real brokenness so prevalent among us in our current condition. Jesus Christ was not concerned with wholesomeness. He ate with prostitutes, tax collectors, and sinners. He touched the blind, the hemorrhaging, and dead. He

---

19. See M. Cathleen Kaveny, "Wholesomeness, Holiness, and Hairspray," *America*, March 3, 2003, 15–18.

endured a bloody, unjust death out of love for his own in the world whom he loved. Of course, this is not to say any of these states are good in themselves; indeed, Christ came to free us from them. But he did so by reaching out to us in these states (rather than ignoring us or the wretched states we actually are in), so as to genuinely bring us healing, reconciliation, and fullness of life. When we do the same to those around us—loved ones or strangers—then we, too, are living in Christ.

Concluding Thoughts

The purpose of this chapter has been to describe what God has accomplished in Christ, and then to explain what difference that makes for how people who follow Christ live their own lives. It may seem at this point that these two issues are unrelated. In fact they have everything to do with each other. There are two common errors to avoid in understanding how the incarnation and Christ's life, death, and resurrection impact how we live our lives. Looking at these will help us understand the proper relationship between the two issues.

The first error is thinking of Christ primarily as a great person, even our lord, who both gave us moral teachings to follow and even provided a model of how to live them out. In this view, we could not be saved without Jesus Christ. But salvation, in terms of our being back on track in our relationship with God, is accomplished when we follow him.

The reason this is inadequate is summed up in an expression that was a favorite of late twentieth-century theologian John Howard Yoder: *noster agnus vicit*! It is Latin for "our Lamb has conquered!" The lamb, of course, is Jesus Christ, and what is conquered is sin and death. But the crucial part of the expression for our purposes is the past tense of "conquered." The righting of the relationship between humanity and God is already done. We do not save ourselves. The hard work of salvation has already been accomplished in Jesus Christ, and his death and resurrection not only occurred; it definitively changed things for humanity, regardless of whether or not one follows His moral teachings.

There is an opposite and yet equally erroneous way to understand how the incarnation and the way we live are related. It is perfectly seen in the movie *Dead Man Walking*, where death-row inmate Matthew Poncelet assures his counselor, Sr. Helen Prejean, that she need not worry about him. "I know Jesus died for my sins, and is going to welcome me in heaven when I die," he tells her. She sternly corrects him by telling him that salvation is not some magic trick that simply happens to us. We need to respond and participate in it. Though the hard work has already been accomplished in Christ, salvation is not simply a clearing of the slate between us and God; it is also a transformation that enables us to be partakers in the divine nature. The train that is humanity has been put back on the right track in its journey toward union with God. But we must allow ourselves to be taken aboard that train in order to reach the destiny described in the previous chapter on hope and eternal life.

This is what life in Christ is: being taken up in the reconciliation between God and humanity achieved by Jesus Christ. When we follow Christ in the ways described in the second section of this chapter, we are not accomplishing the work of salvation, but rather: a) acknowledging Christ the lord who accomplished our salvation, and, b) living in accordance with how he accomplished it. For Christians Jesus Christ is the central event in human history. Though this event definitively changed things, this event is not only backward looking. Nor is living in Christ simply a matter of looking to Jesus as a role model or teacher. As chapter 16 on grace explains, God's action is ongoing through Christ to help us live as sons and daughters of God. In the second section of this chapter, we have started to see how we can live in Christ with God's help. The next chapters on love and grace will continue to illuminate that life in Christ.

Study Questions

1. What hole had humanity gotten itself into that necessitated the incarnation? Why couldn't we get out on our own?
2. Define incarnation and give several reasons why it happened.
3. Why do Christians believe Jesus died for our sins?
4. Why is Jesus's question, "who do you say that I am?" more than some abstract intellectual exercise?
5. How do the disciples demonstrate their lack of full understanding of who Jesus is? Give three examples.
6. What sort of messiah does Jesus say he is? Give three examples.
7. List the (corporal) works of mercy and state where they come from. How are they an example of living in Christ?
8. What is the difference between true holiness and what Kaveny calls "wholesomeness"? When is wholesomeness bad? How can true holiness be unwholesome?
9. The concluding section describes two opposite and equally erroneous understandings of salvation in Christ. Describe each and state why each is erroneous.

Terms to Know

incarnation, sacrifice, christology, Markan secret, (corporal) works of mercy, wholesomeness vs. holiness, *noster agnus vicit!*

Questions for Further Reflection

1. How would you respond to someone who asked, quite simply, why Christians think Jesus Christ was so important?
2. If someone told you their central idea of Christian faith was asking, "what would Jesus do?" what could you tell them so as to help them avoid the error of seeing Christ simply as a great moral teacher?
3. Werner Kelber says: "It is sometimes claimed that religion is a case of an escape from the realities of life, a denial of the brutalities of suffering and of our common destiny of death. Whoever makes such claims must not be familiar with the texts of the New Testament" (*Mark's Story of Jesus*, 51). He was referring explicitly to the text discussed here from Mark (8:27–10:45). Why does he think that text disproves that view of religion? Do you agree or disagree?

Further Reading

The most helpful resources in teaching the contents of this chapter have been the portions of the following works cited here: the Gospel according to Mark, *Catechism of the Catholic Church*, C. S. Lewis's *Mere Christianity*, Werner Kelber's *Mark's Story of Jesus*, Robert Barron's *The Strangest Way*, M. Cathleen Kaveny's "Wholesomeness, Holiness, and Hairspray," and Richard John Neuhaus's *Death on a Friday Afternoon: Meditations on the Last Words of Jesus from the Cross*. As always, the work of Thomas Aquinas (esp. *Summa Theologiae* III) is an important foundation for this chapter.

15

THE VIRTUE OF CHARITY

The Form of the Christian Life

It is fitting that this chapter on charity, or Christian love, immediately follows one on Jesus Christ. Love is the sum of the Christian story, and that story is centered on the person of Jesus Christ, who perfectly reveals to us the God who is love, and who lives out a life of self-giving love here among us. For Christians, love is first and foremost a person, Jesus. Yet that person invites us to live lives of self-giving love, and participate in the reconciliation, or restored relationship, between God and humanity. It is the virtue of charity that enables us to live out lives of self-giving love.

Charity is the crux of the Christian life. After his classic and beautiful description of love ("Love is patient, love is kind . . ."), St. Paul lists the three theological virtues and tells us that "faith, hope, love remain, these three, but the greatest of these is love" (1 Cor. 13:13). Love alone remains when, in the next life, we see God face to face. It is love that perfects all our actions and points them toward their ultimate destiny of union with God. And it is living a life of love that constitutes the very participation in the divine nature that is begun in this life and complete in the next (2 Pet. 1:4). Love is indeed the point of the Christian story in general, and the lives of Christians in particular.

This chapter cannot hope to do justice to a topic of this central importance. And it certainly fails to adequately depict the beautiful adventure that is a life of Christian love. In fact, for the particulars of living that love, the previous chapter's discussion, of how activities like the works of mercy constitute living in imitation of Christ, offers more detail than this chapter. The more modest goals of this chapter are threefold. The first section defines charity. Though charity may be defined as love, that overused word is not adequate to explain what charity means. The first section explains the sort of love charity is, and how it is directed to both God and neighbor. The second section briefly explains what human capacities are exercised in charity. In particular, it delineates the roles of the will and the emotions. The third section examines the impact of charity on natural loves such as friendships, family relationships, and the like. This third section delineates the ways that love in a Christian sense is distinctive, but also the ways that charity is intimately related to human loves that are not essentially charity. We again run into the claim here that "grace perfects nature," and are left prepared for the thorough examination of that theme in the following chapter on grace.

Defining Christian Love: Friendship with God and Others

Defining love is one of the most elusive tasks for moral theology. Just think of all the different ways we use the word "love" in our language. We love types of food or sunsets. We love a certain actor or a band. We love our families, our friends, our spouses or those we date. Christians are even told they must love the enemy! What common definition could ever describe all these loves? Part of the problem is the English language. We use one word to describe things for which other languages use several words. A fine example of looking at different types of love from this perspective is C. S. Lewis's short book *The Four Loves*, where he sorts out different types of love using the Greek words *storge* (affection), *eros* (romantic love), *philia* (friendship), and *agape* (charity, or Christian love).[1] Another text that explores the different types of love and their relation is Pope Benedict XVI's encyclical *Deus caritas est* ("God is love").

We even see this tendency to differentiate types of love in English. For instance, the name of this chapter includes the term "charity," rather than "love." When most people hear the term charity, they may think of giving help to those in need (what is traditionally called almsgiving). It is understandable that this usage has developed, since presumably if you love people in a Christian sense you will help those who are in need. But the English word "charity" is originally rooted in the Latin term *caritas*, which is the name for love in a distinctively Christian sense (the Greek *agape*).

OK, so charity means love in a Christian sense. But that is no definition. In fact, it may cause more problems than it solves, since it may seem that

1. C. S. Lewis, *The Four Loves* (San Diego: Harcourt, 1991).

charity (which will be used in this chapter synonymously with Christian love) is altogether different from, even opposed to, other loves such as friendship and romantic love. Yet that's not true. The relationship between charity and other loves is discussed below, but suffice it to say here that—unsurprisingly in this book—charity perfects, rather than destroys or leaves untouched, good natural loves like friendship, parental love, and romantic love.

So what is charity? The formal definition of *charity* is the theological virtue by which we love God for God's own sake, above all else, and all others in God. Simply put, it is the greatest commandment referred to by Christ in each of the synoptic Gospels: "You shall love the Lord your God with all your heart, and with all your soul, and with all your strength, and with all your mind; and your neighbor as yourself" (Luke 10:25–28; see also Matt. 22:35–40; Mark 12:28–31). Charity is loving God first, and all else in God. This is certainly a helpful starting point. But what does love of God look like? What does it have to do with loving others? These are the questions for this first section. We begin by appealing to the work of Aquinas, who saw friendship as the best way to understand charity. Charity is friendship with God. To understand what he meant, it is worth pausing to describe friendship in general.

Friendship in Aristotle

To better understand charity, Aquinas no doubt appeals to friendship because it is so prevalent and important in our lives. As Aristotle claims in describing human happiness, who can truly be called happy without good friends?![2] Yet friendship is still poorly understood and appreciated, both as to what it is and why it is so important to living a good life. Certainly moral theologians far too often ignore it.[3] But even in everyday life, despite how commonly we speak of and spend time with friends, true friendship is too rare, and we hear people say things like, "If you have one true friend over the course of your life you are fortunate." It is hoped that this very brief treatment of friendship will not only enable us to better grasp the following analysis of charity, but also further illuminate for the reader the nature of friendship and its importance for our lives.

Aristotle's writing on friendship in the *Nicomachean Ethics* is still one of the most extraordinary analyses of friendship ever written.[4] There Aristotle observes that there are three types of friendship. There is friendship based on

2. See Aristotle, *Nicomachean Ethics*, in *The Basic Works of Aristotle*. ed. Richard McKeon (New York: Random House, 1941), I.8. See also viii.1; ix.9.

3. There are important exceptions to this general neglect. Two that stand out are Gilbert Meilaender's *Friendship: a Study in Theological Ethics* (Notre Dame, IN: University of Notre Dame Press, 1981), and Paul Wadell's *Friendship and the Moral Life* (Notre Dame, IN: University of Notre Dame Press, 1989).

4. See Aristotle, *Nicomachean Ethics*, viii; ix.

utility, as when we are joined to someone else based upon a common cause. Friendships at work often start and remain of this type. There is real friendship here in that there is benevolence (good will) toward, beneficence (good acting) for, and a sense of unity with, the other person. But the friendship is based on the common task, and would likely dissipate without it.

The second type of friendship is based in pleasure. Again, there is benevolence, beneficence, and union with the other. But the basis of the friendship is some common pleasure, as when people get together to play or watch sports, or form a book club together. Whereas in the first type the friendship (of utility) is based on a common task, the second type of friendship (of pleasure) is based on a commonly enjoyed pleasure. Note that our different friendships can be of different types, and our friendship with one person can even have elements of different types. My wife has a workout partner with whom she enjoys walking. This is a friendship of pleasure, because they enjoy something in common. Yet there is a utility component there too, since both women help each other pursue the common task of exercising regularly. They keep each other on task, if you will.

There is nothing inherently wrong with these two types of friendship. Many relationships in our lives remain at these levels. They are still friendships, as long as there is benevolence toward, beneficence for, and a sense of union with the other. Yet Aristotle claims a third type of friendship, which is friendship in the fullest sense of the term. It is friendship based on goodness, or the virtue of the other. He does not primarily mean we should only be friends with virtuous people, although Aristotle clearly thinks such people are more attractive to us. This type of friendship, a friendship of goodness, is marked by one's recognition of, and desire to contribute to, the friend's goodness and virtue. In other words, in the third type of friendship each friend seeks the virtue and happiness of the other as, Aristotle famously says, "another self."[5] The focus is more on the friend than on the common task or pleasure. These friendships can contain elements of utility or pleasure, though they are not basic to it. And friendships of the first two types can certainly develop into friendships of virtue; indeed, most friendships in the third sense begin out of shared utility or pleasure. But with a friendship of goodness, the friend is appreciated as a person in his or her self, rather than as a partner in something immediately sought (like a pleasure or common goal). In this highest sense of friendship, the other's good is desired and sought as one desires one's own good.

Therefore, in full friendship we see, appreciate, and seek to contribute to the goodness in our friend. We see and treat our friend as another self. Note this includes, but is more than, simple goodwill. We can have goodwill toward others without friendship. In full friendship, we not only see the good in, and seek the good for, the other. There is also an element of enjoyment in being

5. Aristotle, *Nicomachean Ethics*, ix.9.

at rest with our friends. We simply wish to be with our friends, and enjoy our union with them, as an end in itself (rather than as simply something useful or a path to some pleasure). We see the goodness of our friends, appreciate it, and want to be with them due to it.

Friendship with God in Thomas Aquinas

An astute commentator on Aristotle, Aquinas immediately saw in the pre-Christian Greek's thought rich resources for understanding charity.[6] Of course, friendship with God is a deeply scriptural notion, emphasized in the Gospel according to John, but present also in the Old Testament (see Ws 7:14, 27). Even so, Aristotle's description of the highest form of friendship, friendship of goodness, is a perfect way to understand charity as love of God and others in God. Charity is loving God above all else, not arbitrarily but because God is goodness, and the source of all that is good.[7] Thus, it is fitting that we love God above all else. To recall the language of chapter 2, God alone is our be-all and end-all. There is no further good to seek above or beyond God. And thus charity is resting in, enjoying, God as supremely good, much as we would appreciate and enjoy a true friend.

It may seem odd to speak so casually of charity as friendship with God. After all, one of the basic claims of classical thinkers like Aristotle is that true friendship is something that exists between equals. We sense this with certain unequals in our lives. It is difficult to be friends with a boss. Parents and children can become friends when the children are adults, but even then children will generally report there is still no doubt their parents are different than their peer friends, and still very much their parents! Certainly our relationship with God is not one of equals—nothing could be further from the truth. How can Aquinas insist that charity is friendship with God?

Such friendship is possible only because God takes the initiative and makes it possible. That God is one who invites us to friendship is only known through the gift of faith. There is a sense that faith is prior to charity; we must first know God and what God is like in order to love God as he wishes.[8] It is through faith that we understand God made us in the *imago Dei*, called to and fulfilled by living lives of self-giving love in friendship with God and others. It is by faith that we understand that, by living such lives we participate in God's very own divine nature (2 Pet. 1:4) and are united in friendship with the God who is love (1 John 4:8). Knowing any of this is only possible in faith.

6. See Thomas Aquinas, *Summa Theologiae*, English Dominican trans. (New York: Benziger, 1948), II–II 23, esp. art. 1, 4, and 6.

7. As Catholics hear in the second eucharistic prayer: "Lord you are holy [i.e., good]. Indeed, you are the fountain of all that is holy [good]."

8. See Aquinas, *Summa Theologiae* I–II 62, esp. 62,4.

Knowing it most fully is possible only through Jesus Christ, "who, though he was in the form of God, did not regard equality with God something to be grasped. Rather, he emptied himself, taking the form of a slave, coming in human likeness" (Phil. 2:6–7). Jesus Christ is God become human, who reveals the Father ("whoever has seen me has seen the Father," John 14:9). Furthermore, friendship with God is not only something that must be known, but also lived (James 2:26). This, too, is possible only through Christ who (in ways described in the previous chapter and the next) reconciles humanity to God, to make this union in friendship not only a known possibility but also a lived reality. Therefore, charity is friendship with God made possible through Christ, through whom we know God most fully, and through whom we are reconciled to God so as to be able to be friends with God ("I have called you friends" John 15:15). Thus, living the life of charity is rightly called life in Christ (see Gal. 2:20), a phrase examined more closely in the following chapter on grace. But first a word is in order on what love of God has to do with love of others. After all, in this very chapter in John, where Jesus calls His disciples his friends, he repeatedly commands them to love one another. What does love of God have to do with love of others?

Charity as Friendship with Others

What the love of God which constitutes charity means should now be clearer. But recall that the definition of charity also includes the phrase, "and all else in God." It is the task of the third section to explain how exactly charity transforms what is loved in God. The task for this part is more modest. Why does charity have anything to do with loving others? After all, if charity is a theological virtue it concerns God directly. It seems the cardinal virtue justice should suffice in governing our relationships with each other. If charity is essentially love of God above all else, what has this to do with love of others?

Consider two ways to understand the relationship between love of God and love of neighbor. The first views love of neighbor as an obligation deriving from obedience to God. It is as if one thinks, "If I love God above all else, and God tells me to love my neighbor, I'll do it." In this view, there is no intrinsic connection between love of God and neighbor. We love the neighbor only because God commands it; in fact, if God did not command it we would not bother! It even seems conceivable that God could command otherwise.

But this is an inadequate understanding of the relationship between love of God and love of neighbor. Love of neighbor is not some additional or arbitrary obligation imposed on those of us who love God. Rather, as the biblical author says:

> If anyone says, "I love God," but hates his brother, he is a liar; for whoever does not love a brother whom he has seen cannot love God whom he has not seen.

This is the commandment we have from him: whoever loves God must also love his brother. (1 John 4:20–21, cf. 1 John 3:14–17; 4:7–12)

Why are people who hate their neighbor but claim to love God liars? This passage reminds us that we can see our neighbor but cannot see God (to recall chapter 11, on faith), and so the one who fails to love the neighbor who is seen cannot love God. The passage seems to imply that loving our neighbor is more tangible to us than loving God, and so if we cannot love the neighbor we are certainly unable to love God. Though there is something true to that, the connection between the two loves assumed here is even closer once we remember John's astounding claim that God is love.

The God who is loved above all else in charity is the triune God, a communion of persons in self-giving love who created all things out of love. All human persons are created to be in loving union with God in ultimate happiness. Despite sin and brokenness, true happiness through the self-giving love that is union with God can indeed be experienced in this life, even though it is complete only in the next. What such a life entails is made perfectly manifest and possible through Jesus Christ. Since God desires our happiness, God helps people to know and live out this life of charity. Therefore, being a friend of God in charity means appreciating who God is, and participating in God's plans to the fullest extent possible. It means living out, in our relationships with others, the self-giving love that is God's very own nature. Doing so is not an obligation derived from love of God. Nor are we simply using other people as ways to know the happiness of self-giving love offered by God. Rather, that love of others in charity is constitutive of life in union with the God who created all persons in the *imago Dei* for a common destiny of union with God and each other. Loving our fellow brothers and sisters in charity is participation in the life of God, and a taste of our ultimate destiny.

Consider an analogy from the family to help illuminate this intrinsic relation between love of God and love of neighbor. Any sibling knows that nothing makes a parent happier than when the siblings truly love one another. Good sons and daughters love their siblings. This can be done out of obligation (though it is then questionable as to whether it is indeed self-giving love). But it is best done not just because it pleases their parents, but because the sons and daughters trust that sibling love is the desire of their parents because it is truly good and life-giving for all involved. After all, what do parents want more than the genuine happiness of their children? Presumably, parents desire that their children love one another not simply for the parents' own enjoyment, but because it is what is most fulfilling for the siblings themselves. Similarly, we love our neighbors not simply out of obedience to God, but because we trust that the God who is love and who desires our complete happiness calls us to love others as constitutive of the very happiness to which all are called.[9] This is why Christ says to the disciples, "This is my commandment: love one another as I love you" (John 15:12). They are enjoined to heed his command and love one another not arbitrarily or out of sheer obedience, but rather "so that my joy may be in you and your joy may be complete" (John 15:11).

This integral relation between love of God and love of neighbor is best evidenced in the greatest-commandment passages from the synoptic Gospels. As countless homilists have noted, in these passages Christ is asked which is the greatest commandment. The question invites a single answer. But Jesus seems to give two answers: love God, and love your neighbor as yourself. Was Jesus pulling a fast one, giving two answers when one is sought? No, given what we know of God in faith, loving the God of love who created all out of love and who invites all people to union with him in love surely entails loving those brothers and sisters (i.e., all people) who are also called with us to be united to God in love. Though they are distinct enough to be mentioned separately, love of God and neighbor are so integrally related that they are fittingly given together as the greatest commandment.

In summary, the formal definition of charity should now be clearer. Charity is a theological virtue since it concerns God directly. It is best understood as friendship with God, where the goodness of God is not only seen but appreciated, cherished, and enjoyed. Reminiscent of, yet far transcending, how we are with an old friend, we cherish and just want to be with God. And since that friendship is not simply a one-on-one affair, but friendship with a God who invites all people to union with him, loving our fellow human beings is essential to the love of God that is charity. Of course, the full union with God and others for which we long is possible only in the next life. That is why hope is needed in this life. But the friendship with God that is charity can be tasted in this life, even while we hope for its full arrival in the next. And when it is complete in the next life, hope will pass away, and love will remain.

Charity: A Virtue of Emotion and/or Will?

Love is such a multi-textured word, as noted above, that it is easy to be misled as to what exactly is being commanded with Christian love, or charity. For instance, many of us hear love and immediately think of the affection we have toward friends or family, or the powerful feelings we have when we fall in love. Note that these are essentially emotional responses; the words "affection" and "feeling" recall to us chapter 4 on the passions. However, love is not, or should not be, simply an emotional response. If love were primarily a matter of how

---

9. Note that while we ideally do not love our neighbors simply out of obedience to God's command, if it is only fear of God's commands that leads us to do so in times of weakness, better that than to not love our neighbor at all!

we felt about others, it would be unreliable and inconsistent, since our feelings are not always expressive of what we know and will. It is certainly better to wish someone well and do good to them even when we do not feel like it. That is why it is so important that love is centrally an act of will; we can love even when we do not feel like it. Indeed, even in those relationships where we generally do have fond feelings for the other (friendships, family members, etc.), there are plenty of times when we do not feel that love, and nonetheless act lovingly toward them. As Lewis says, "Do not waste time bothering whether you 'love' [in the sense of affectionate feelings] your neighbor; act as if you did."[10] For these reasons it would be impossible, even nonsensical, for Christ to command us to love one another if love were essentially a feeling. No, love is an act of the will. Whether it be a family member, friend, spouse, or whomever, we love others when we wish them well, when we want them to be truly happy, even when we do not feel like it.

Saying charity is primarily an act of the will can make it sound cold and heartless. However, although love is not primarily an emotion, the emotions can indeed become important components of love. Indeed, it is crucial that human love involves our emotions, since our emotions are God-given gifts that grant our actions facility, or pleasure and promptness. The fact that the emotions can be shaped into good habits, and why it is important they are, recalls to us all the claims made in chapter 4. Though it is better to treat our neighbor well even when we do not feel like it, it is even better both to will and do good to our neighbor, and to desire to do so emotionally. Reminiscent of chapter 4, Lewis describes how our emotions can be shaped, or habituated, to be more in line with our reason and will:

> When you are behaving as if you loved someone [in the affectionate sense], you will presently come to love him. If you injure someone you dislike, you will find yourself disliking him more. If you do him a good turn, you will find yourself disliking him less.[11]

Our emotions are not fully under our control, for sure. And sometimes, try as we might, we still feel affectionate toward those who harm us, or we dislike those whom we will to love. Nevertheless, we can, to use Lewis's words again, "encourage our affections." In fact, he says we have a duty to do so, "not because this is itself the virtue of charity but because it is a help to it."[12]

It should be noted that what Lewis is doing here is distinguishing love as primarily an emotion from love as primarily a matter of will (that hopefully also includes our emotions). Our emotions are rich and beautiful facets of our lives. But for all of the reasons discussed in chapter 4, it is fitting for human persons

---

10. C. S. Lewis, *Mere Christianity* (San Francisco: HarperSanFrancisco, 2001), 131.
11. Ibid.
12. Ibid.

endowed with reason and will to have their emotions guided by those higher powers. Our reason and will help us respond emotionally to the way things really are. However, saying charity is in essence a willful love does not adequately distinguish it from other human loves such as friendship, familial love, and spousal love. Any of these loves are mainly acts of the will, unless they are mere passing fancies or infatuations. The same is certainly true of charity.

Thus, the virtue charity is based primarily in the will. Though this fact alone does not distinguish it from other mature natural loves, it is important to explain charity's relationship to the will and emotions here for three reasons. First, through many of the songs, movies, television shows, and so on we encounter today, love is portrayed primarily as emotional sentimentality. Love is indeed emotional, as explained here. But it is more than that. When speaking of charity as love, it is important to emphasize its rootedness in the human will. Second, since charity is an exercise of the human will, it is a love (like other loves, such as friendship) that is truly our own. It may be unique in being directed toward God and others in God, and in its requirement of God's grace to blossom in us. But as an expression of our wills, charity is indeed truly our own and not some state of being possessed from an outside force against our wills. Third and finally, though it is true that charity's basis in the human capacity of will does not in itself distinguish charity from other natural human loves such as friendship, it is important that charity shares that commonality with other loves, since it means charity can transform and perfect, rather than obliterate or leave untouched, natural love, such as family relationships, friendships, and the like. Though charity is a unique and ultimate form of love, it is not alien to human persons or unrelated to other forms of love. This point is essential for the following section on charity's relationship to other loves in life.

Charity and Loving "All Else in God"

Having defined charity as love of God, above all else, and all else in God, the question remains: what does loving all else in God look like? What difference does it make to have charity? What does friendship with God have to do with the rest of our lives? The short answer is, "everything." We have already seen that it drives us to love of neighbor. Explaining further facets of how charity permeates all else is the point of this section.

Particularly given the similarities between charity and other human ways of loving, what is distinctive about Christian love? A main concern of this section is examining what charity as a distinctive sort of love has to do with the many interpersonal loves in our lives. Is charity unrelated to these natural loves (such as family relations, romantic loves, etc.)? Does it eliminate and replace them? Reminiscent of this book's first mention of grace perfecting nature in chapter 11 on faith, and pointing ahead to the full discussion of that topic in the next chapter, we find here that Christian love neither eliminates nor leaves untouched other loves in our lives. With regard to both how we love, and what is loved, charity perfects natural love even as it transcends it.

Why Charity Changes Everything: Charity as the Form of the Virtues

When defining Christian love, it is not enough to say, as the last section did, that it is an act of will. First of all, there are loves other than charity that are acts of the will. Second, as we recall from chapter 2 on intention, free will (of which love is surely an act) is not simply an act of the will but also of the intellect. In other words, we do not just will or intend; we will or intend *something*, understood as such by our intellect, our reason. So it is not enough to say love is an act of the will. Will to what? Answering this question reveals what is distinctive about Christian love, and what charity as love of God above all has to do with everything else.

In *Mere Christianity*, Lewis answers this question when, in speaking of charity, he says we will the happiness of another just as we wish for our own (love your neighbor as yourself). This goodwill is the basis of love as an act of will. Love is willing the good of another, which is the other's happiness. Yet what is distinctive about Christian love? Simply put, it is what sort of happiness we wish for the other. Lewis adds that in charity we wish for another's happiness, "just because it is another self, made (like us) by God."[13] This is what makes Lewis's discussion not just one of any love in general, but one of charity. By claiming that charity is wishing another's happiness as someone made by God, Lewis makes it clear that charity seeks the good of the other in the broader perspective of Christian faith. As stated in *Fides et Ratio* from chapter 11, people seek the truthful answers to ultimate questions so that they can most fully pursue the true good in life—complete happiness. The person with the theological virtue charity wills the good of others in the context of the Christian story about the way things are.

As described above, but always worth repeating, the triune God who is a communion of persons in self-giving love created all things out of love. All persons are created to be in union with God in ultimate happiness. Despite sin and brokenness, true happiness through the self-giving love that is union with God can indeed be experienced in this life, even though it is complete only in the next. What such a life entails is made perfectly manifest and possible through Jesus Christ. Since God desires our happiness, he helps people to know and live out this life of charity. Thus, the "willing another's happiness" that is done in charity is not some vague sense of goodwill, but rather is done with a rich and complete understanding of what is truly good, in an ultimate

13. Ibid.

sense. The person who is given the gift of charity is able to love others most completely by loving all persons with the broadest perspective in mind.

This claim calls to mind one of the central claims of this book: acting rightly requires seeing rightly. Despite the famous Beatles' song, it is not true that "all you need is love." If love is seeking the good and happiness of another, doing so requires that we have a sense of what is the true good of the person we love, and how we can pursue it effectively. Having such a grasp gives a distinctive shape to how we love. This discussion recalls to us chapter 5, on prudence. Remember the example there of the woman who, with all the best intentions, tried to parent her children lovingly but ended up actually confusing and alienating them because she lacked the prudence to know when to be lenient and when to stand firm? Despite wishing the best for her children, she was unable to actually love them well in many ways, due to her lack of prudence. The knowledge that prudence gives regarding innerworldly activities (what children thrive on, what constitutes appropriate punishment, etc.) is needed to act well. In fact, in the next chapter on grace we explore further how charity and God's grace transform cardinal virtues such as prudence. For now it suffices to reaffirm that seeing rightly is needed to act rightly.

The same is true with regard to how we see concerning big-picture questions. Recall the moral importance of faith from chapter 11. Seeing rightly on these questions shapes how we act in this world. Charity is simply love of God and others that is shaped by faith's knowledge of the way things are given by faith. It is the love of God and of all things in the broadest, most accurate, perspective possible for us in this life, the perspective granted by faith, which completes our reason's ability to grasp how things really are. To recall a phrase from chapter 1, loving God above all else and all else in God is actually a life lived most completely "in accordance with reason," with reason understood to include faith's completion of reason.

Reminiscent of how prudence shapes the exercise of the other cardinal virtues, this broader perspective is enormously important in shaping exactly how love is lived out. It makes a concrete difference in how we love others. Charity leads to particular sorts of actions that direct people ultimately toward their supernatural destiny. What sorts of acts does charity lead one to do? As an example, consider Jesus's powerful farewell discourse in John just before his death. There Jesus speaks poignantly of love, friendship, and joy. To some it seems odd that in this context he keeps insisting the disciples follow his commandments:

If you love me, you will keep my commandments. (14:15)

Whoever has my commandments and observes them is the one who loves me. (14:21)

If you keep my commandments, you will remain in my love. (15:10; cf. 1 John 3:24)

Jesus is telling the disciples here what charity as love of God and all else in God looks like. The broader perspective grasped in faith and sought and enjoyed in charity makes a difference in how we act. That difference is specified in God's commandments.

In this way we know that we love the children of God when we love God and obey his commandments. For the love of God is this, that we keep his commandments. And his commandments are not burdensome. (1 John 5:2–3)

As this last passage makes clear, a life of love is constituted by living out the commandments, not as ends in themselves that are burdensome, but rather so that "our joy may be complete" (John 15:11).

The person with charity sees the big picture truthfully (faith), and based upon that perspective loves and enjoys God above else, and all else in God (charity). In short, this person sees and loves all things in accordance with the way things really are. As Augustine puts it:

Living a just and holy life requires one to be capable of an objective and impartial evaluation of things; to love things, that is to say, in the right order, so that you do not love what is not to be loved, or fail to love what is to be loved, or have a greater love for what is to be loved less, or an equal love for things that should be loved less or more, or a lesser or greater love for things that should be loved equally.[14]

Augustine is speaking here of what is classically called the order of love, or what we have described in this book as one's triangle of goals or loves in life. Only by having an accurate grasp of the way things are can we properly prioritize our loves in life. But what Augustine says also applies to any one particular love: only by having an accurate grasp of the way things are can we love any one person or thing properly: not too much, not too little, and in just the right manner. Otherwise we can, perhaps with all the best intentions, act in ways that impede rather than foster another person's, and our own, happiness.

In sum, having the virtue charity makes a concrete difference in how we live our lives, by inclining us to the sorts of actions that lead us and others to the ultimate destiny of union with God, which is true happiness. The commandments are a perfect example of such actions. This is why charity is traditionally called the *form of the virtues*. Charity gives shape to (or trans-forms) acts of all the virtues by directing them toward the ultimate goal of union with God. A person with charity loves all things in the proper perspective granted by

14. Augustine, *Teaching Christianity* (New York: New City Press, 1996), 118.

faith. Granted that proper perspective, charity then orders all our loves in life accordingly, so that each person in our lives is loved, and indeed all our lives' loves are prioritized, according to our charity, or friendship with the God of love who calls all people to union with him in love. Charity perfects acts of all the virtues by directing them, or whisking them along, toward a person's ultimate happiness in God. In the manner described in chapter 2, being directed toward that ultimate goal shapes how all other goals are sought and accomplished. In short, our friendship with the God who is known in faith shapes all we do by ordering it all to the ultimate goal of complete happiness, constituted by union with the God of love.

How does charity perfect, and serve as the form of, the theological virtues? In a certain sense, faith and hope are required in order to have charity. In order to love God in friendship, we must know who God is and understand him as the complete fulfillment for which we long. That said, charity perfects even these two theological virtues. For we seek union with God in hope as the fulfillment of all our desires. And in charity we seek unio with God who is appreciated and enjoyed in Himself rather than just as the fulfillment of our longings. And with charity we not only know true things about who God is, we also enjoy and seek to be fully united with God. Charity thus perfects faith and hope by completing their orientation toward God with a sense of enjoyment and friendship.

Charity also perfects the cardinal virtues. The cardinal virtues concern innerworldly practices that are accessible to unaided reason (i.e., reason without faith). Nonetheless, to be done virtuously, such activities must be understood truthfully. An accurate grasp of big-picture beliefs, such as that given in faith, does indeed impact (in the manner described in chapter 10) how we do innerworldly activities. More detail as to how this is so is given in the next chapter, on grace. But for now suffice it to say that for one with charity whose ultimate aim is friendship with God, and who loves all else in relation to God, doing the innerworldly activities of the cardinal virtues will be different—indeed, perfected—based upon that ultimate goal of friendship with God.

Some Distinctive Acts of Charity

So far, this analysis of how charity changes how we love all else may seem rather formal. In other words, it may be alluring to say, "OK, I see how the person with charity does everything in her life for the sake of God. But what concrete difference does that actually make in what she does?" Some answers are given in the previous section. For instance, the person with charity follows the commandments. Furthermore, given the claims in chapter 2 about how our ultimate goal in life shapes all we do, we should not underestimate the difference it makes to love all else for the sake of God. Even though it may not appear distinctive to the external observer (can't any person follow the commandments?), the love of the person with charity is indeed importantly different in meaning, even when the same acts are performed. Nonetheless, it may help illuminate the virtue charity to describe some acts that are indeed distinctive to it. Thus, the task of this section is to offer three examples of distinctive acts of charity.

The first example of how we live our lives differently with the theological virtue charity is through acts of worship. If charity is love of God above all else, and all else in God, then worshipping God together with others who recognize their call to union with God in friendship is one of the exemplary acts of charity. Indeed, the scriptures speak repeatedly of the heavenly hosts singing praises to God, in passages that depict in some way humanity's destiny of union with God. The book of Revelation is full of references to the holy ones of God gathered in songs of praise (4:8–11; 5:11–14; 7:9–12). And the birth of the Messiah, the one who reveals, exemplifies, and is the path to humanity's destiny of union with God, is announced by heavenly hosts singing, "Glory to God in the highest!" a clear prefiguring of what communal life in union with and praise of God is like (Luke 2:14). Joining together to worship God in union with each other, as we do at Mass, is a very foretaste of complete union with God, and thus a clear act of charity.

A second example concerns our love of others in God. Given that there are people who surely love others and know nothing about, or want nothing to do with, Christianity how does charity as loving others in God look different from love of others which is not charity? Charity is distinctive in its scope. Simply put, the person with the virtue of charity loves all persons, without exception. As Christ himself says, in the Sermon on the Mount, "if you love only those who love you, what recompense will you have?" (Matt. 5:46). This is perhaps best seen in the famous Good Samaritan parable (Luke 10:25–37). The riches this parable offers are inexhaustible. But the one point emphasized here is Jesus's direct answer to a scholar's question as to who is the "neighbor," in the greatest commandment's injunction to love your neighbor as yourself.

Jesus tells the classic story of a man who fell victim to robbers, was beaten, and left for dead on the side of the road. Two people, a priest and a Levite, each pass by the man without helping. The third passerby is a Samaritan, considered foreign and inferior by Jesus's people, the Jews. The Samaritan not only stops to help the man, but also brings him on his own animal to an inn to care for him. He leaves the next day after paying the innkeeper to continue the man's care. Interestingly enough, Jesus ends the parable by asking the scholar not who treated the victimized man as a neighbor, but rather who was neighbor to this man. We see here Jesus emphasizing the need for us to be active in loving our neighbor. But more central for our purpose is Jesus's point that we are called to love all persons as neighbors. The Samaritan shares no familial, national, or religious bonds with the victim. In other words, all the natural connections that normally engender our relationships are not present. But still, the message is quite clear—we are to love even strangers, those different from us, as our neighbors.

This reminds us of what C. S. Lewis said in his discussion of the relationship between charity as an act of will and the emotions, or affections:

> The difference between a Christian man and a worldly man is not that the worldly man has only affections and the Christian has only 'charity.' The worldly man treats certain people kindly because he 'likes' them: the Christian, trying to treat everyone kindly, finds himself liking more and more people as he goes on—including people he could not have imagined liking at the beginning.[15]

Besides his point about the emotions, Lewis clearly affirms here that the Christian is called to love everyone with charity. But why? For all the reasons explained earlier in the chapter on the intrinsic connection between love and God and love of neighbor, all other persons are created by the God of love, out of love, for a destiny of communion with him and all other persons in self-giving love. The basis of love of neighbor, which is both our common creation as *imago Dei*, and our common destiny of full union with God, applies to all persons. And thus it drives a love of all in this life. This is a love of concrete, embodied service, as perhaps best seen in Matthew 25, where Christ rewards with eternal life all those who have loved their neighbors with the corporal works of mercy. Indeed, all that was said in chapter 14 should be recalled here, namely, how life in Christ entails living out a self-giving love that reaches out to encounter people in their brokenness and loves them in embodied, often messy, ways such that new life comes from that engagement. But the point here is that charity as friendship with God and others in God extends to all others.

A third and final example of how charity makes a tangible difference in our lives is related to this last one. Christian love is distinctive in its emphasis on love of enemy and radical forgiveness. That charity includes love of enemy should be unsurprising, since it includes love of all. Indeed, love of enemy in particular is the focus of Christ's quotation about not only loving those who love us:

> I say to you, love your enemies, and pray for those who persecute you, that you may be children of your heavenly Father, for he makes his sun rise on the bad and the good, and causes rain to fall on the just and the unjust. (Matt. 5:44–45)

Love of all, including enemies, is understood as a way to love like God the Father, who loves all persons good and evil. Yet especially given the discussion in chapter 13 of final judgment and separation from God, it is quite understandable to press further concerning love of enemy, and ask what exactly this

15. C. S. Lewis, *Mere Christianity*, 131.

entails. Does love of enemy mean everyone should be loved, no matter what they do? If so, does that mean someone with charity has no interest in what the neighbor does? Answering these questions leads us to the radical practice of Christian love known as forgiveness.

In another famous gospel passage, Peter asks Jesus how many times the neighbor who sins against Peter must be forgiven. Could it be as many as seven times? Jesus replies by saying, "Not seven times, but seventy-seven times" (Matt. 18:22). Jesus is not simply giving the sinner a bit more latitude, but massively multiplying Peter's initial estimate to indicate that that the sinner must always be forgiven. Clearly, forgiveness and love of enemy are central to charity. But does that mean the person with charity simply accepts whatever is done by the neighbor? Absolutely not. Indeed, this passage on forgiveness immediately follows a detailed explanation of how to correct a sinner in a manner that is expressive of, not contrary to, charity. Measures here extend from initial confrontation of the sinner with his sin to expulsion from the community (Matt. 18:15–17). How is it possible to simultaneously love and offer forgiveness to a sinner who acts as enemy, and confront and even punish that person?

Some people wrongly assume that Christian love, due to its insistence on love of all (including enemy) and constant forgiveness, is incompatible with standing up to someone who is harming themselves and others, and certainly incompatible with any punishment that is perceived by the recipient as harmful. But this is not at all true. The gospels are full of stories of Christ confronting people about their actions. Consider the fraternal correction here in Matthew 18, or the numerous occasions where Christ confronts the scribes and Pharisees for their false religiosity (see esp. Matt. 23:13–39), or the famous passage where he tells the woman caught in adultery to "go and sin no more" (John 8:11). In fact, there are also haunting parables told by Jesus of eternal punishment inflicted on those who ignore the needs of those around them (Matt. 25:31–46; Luke 16:19–31). A discussed in chapter 13, humanity's supernatural destiny of union with God does not preclude the possibility of punishment and separation from God.

Of course, in all these cases it is God who judges and punishes people. But Christ makes it clear that humanity shares in the ability to make judgments about sin. In the very chapter we are considering from Matthew, Jesus tells his followers, "whatever you bind on earth shall be bound in heaven, and whatever you loose on earth shall be loosed in heaven" (Matt. 18:18). Though questions need to be addressed as to who can judge (parents? friends? judges? church leaders?), and what punishments are never compatible with charity, making judgments about sin and executing punishment are not incompatible with charity.[16]

---

16. Though we were not yet explicitly discussing charity in chapter 7, this is the context into which to examine the compatibility of Christianity and waging just war. Christian pacifists claim intentional killing of the guilty in warfare is never compatible with charity.

Assuming that all Christians agree that in some cases it is indeed charitable to confront friends, punish children, and even put people in jail, the real question is, how does any of this look different for the person with charity? The answer is that it must always be done for the sake of the happiness of the person judged and punished, even if that person does not recognize it at the time. Correcting wrongdoers is not a matter of harming that individual for the greater good of the community. Given the description in chapter 7 of the common good, the wrongdoer's flourishing and that of the community are intimately intertwined, such that acting for the sake of society can only be truly done when it serves the best interests of the individual, and vice versa. Indeed, in some situations it would be a failure in charity to not confront, punish, or incarcerate someone who was harming themselves and others by their actions. As always, prudence is needed here to determine when such cases arise. And again, we are treading on the next chapter's discussion of the infused cardinal virtues. The point here is that charity, as constituted by constant love of enemy and forgiveness, is indeed compatible with judgment and punishment; but the latter must always serve the former. When wrongdoers are confronted and punished out of hate or selfish motives, or even without concern for the sinner, judgment and punishment are without a doubt incompatible with charity. Christian love must extend to all persons, even the enemy who may be threatening. Of course, the most loving thing to do, both for the enemy and all those involved, may be a prudent maintenance of distance, or perhaps some sort of punishment. But the key is that it must be done for the sake of the genuine happiness of the person loved.

Thus charity as love of God above all else and love of all else in God does make very tangible differences in how we live. The three activities described in this part—worship, love of all persons, and love of enemy and constant forgiveness—are concrete examples of how charity makes a difference in how one lives in this life. Other acts could be added. For instance, along with fraternal correction described above, Aquinas lists almsgiving (from Matt. 6) as an exemplary act of charity. This points us to the following chapter on grace, and particularly how grace transforms the innerworldly activities of cardinal virtues.

Concluding Thoughts

Charity is the form of the virtues and the shape of the Christian life. Self-giving love is the sum of the Christian story and so, unsurprisingly, the virtue that inclines us to live lives of self-giving love is primary in the Christian life. Though it may be difficult to imagine how to love God when our experiential models of love are those toward the people around us, Aquinas uses the example of just such a natural love—friendship—to explain how love of God looks. It is an appreciation of, a seeking to further spread, and enjoyment of, the goodness of God. Charity is indeed primarily love of God, but it is inextricably intertwined with love of others.

Perhaps most important for a book on moral theology, charity makes a concrete difference in how we love people around us. It does not eliminate from our lives what might be called *natural loves*, the host of relationships (parental love, sibling love, friendship, romantic love, etc.) found in people of all times and places and rightly called "loves." Yet it surely does impact our natural loves, transforming them to be lived within the broader context afforded by a truthful vision of the way thing are at the big-picture level. It enables us to seek a more complete happiness for those we love. At times this leads to distinctive acts, as when we are constantly willing to forgive, and when we love all other persons as fellow sons and daughters of God. It leads us to obey the commandments, which may surely (thankfully!) be obeyed by other people but which look different from within the context of the Christian story. So at times it may lead us to acts that do not look distinctively charitable from the outside (taking care of our children, tending to a sick spouse, helping a friend move), but which are actually directed toward an ultimate goal of union with God and others in God. And as we know from chapter 2, our ultimate goal shapes all we do in life.

Thus we say that charity transforms our natural loves. It perfects them, elevating them toward a goal of union with God. The Christian may live a "supernatural" life, but it is also a life where natural loves and activities are done well—indeed, more perfectly. This is why we say grace perfects nature, a claim explained more completely in the following chapter.

Study Questions

1. What is the term "charity" commonly taken to mean? What is its definition in this chapter?
2. What is friendship in general? What three types of friendship does Aristotle distinguish?
3. What about Aristotle's discussion of friendship leads Aquinas to describe charity as friendship with God?
4. Describe two ways that love and God and neighbor can be understood as connected. Which do you find persuasive and why?
5. Why is it important that charity is an act of the will? What role is there for the emotions in Christian love?
6. What does it mean to say that charity is the form of the virtues? How does it shape all our loves in life?
7. Give three examples of distinctive ways charity is lived.

8. Give an example of some way charity transforms a love that is present in those without charity.

Terms to Know

charity, friendships of utility/pleasure/goodness, form of the virtues, natural loves

Questions for Further Reflection

1. In what ways is one's relationship with God like and unlike our friendships with other people?
2. Aristotle distinguishes friendships of goodness from those of utility and pleasure. Given that, from a Christian perspective, charity as friendship of goodness is ideally pleasant and also constituted by a common cause of love of God and others in God, does charity include and transcend Aristotle's two other forms of friendship or simply leave them behind? In other words, is there utility and pleasure in charity?
3. If charity's scope extends to all persons, how useful is friendship for describing charity, since friendship seems to be something we share with certain people and not others?
4. What do the different ways of understanding the relationship between love of God and neighbor have to do with morality of obligation vs. morality of happiness?
5. If charity is a gift from God, can it really be an exercise of one's own will? What does this have to do with freedom of indifference vs. freedom for excellence?
6. Can people who are not Christian have charity? If not, why not? If so, what does it look like?
7. If charity is love of all people, are particular relationships where we are closer to some people (family, friends, spouse, etc.) than others, compatible with charity? Can Christians virtuously have such relationships?
8. How might discussion of charity's scope extending to all persons inform discussions of social justice and human rights? What unique resources can Christians bring to the table in such discussions?
9. If charity demands love of enemy and constant forgiveness, what sorts of punishment are necessarily opposed to charity and can never be done, even if they are claimed to be in the best interests of the person they are inflicted upon?
10. Is it possible for Christians to love the enemy in warfare, and still intentionally kill the enemy? What ramifications does your answer to this question have on the just war/pacifism debate from chapter 7?

11. Should victims (of abuse, oppression, crime, etc.) have charity for their victimizers? Why or why not? If so, what should such charity look like?

Further Reading

The most formative influences on the chapter (beyond the scriptures) are by far Thomas Aquinas's *Summa Theologiae* II–II 23–26 and Augustine's *On Christian Teaching* and *On the Way of Life of the Catholic Church*. C. S. Lewis's *Mere Christianity* and *The Four Loves* also offer excellent descriptions of love in general, and charity in particular. His *The Great Divorce* is an outstanding narrative depiction of what difference it makes to love all things in God (or not). Finally, Pope Benedict XVI's *Deus Caritas Est* is excellent reading on charity, and particularly its relationship to justice and other human loves.

16

GRACE

The Gift of the Holy Spirit for the Virtuous Life

Chapter 14, on the incarnation, described Jesus Christ as the central event in human history. Of course, people can understand the importance of Christ in better or worse ways. In perhaps the most powerful quote in an extraordinary book, C. S. Lewis tries to stave off a false view of Jesus as simply a great moral teacher when he writes:

> I am trying to prevent anyone saying the really foolish thing that people often say about Him [Jesus]: 'I'm ready to accept Jesus as a great moral teacher, but I don't accept His claim to be God.' This is the one thing we must not say. A man who was merely a man and said the sort of things Jesus said [namely, that He was the Messiah, the Son of God] would not be a great moral teacher. He would either be a lunatic—on a level with the man who says he is a poached egg—or else he would be the Devil of Hell. You must make your choice. Either this man was, and is, the Son of God: or else a madman or something worse. You can shut Him up for a fool, you can spit at Him and kill Him as a demon; or you can fall at His feet and call Him Lord and God. But let us not come away with any patronizing nonsense about His being a great moral teacher. He has not left that option open to us. He did not intend to.[1]

1. C. S. Lewis, *Mere Christianity* (San Francisco: HarperSanFrancisco, 2001), 52. For an example of Jesus "saying the sorts of things he said," see John 5:17–30.

311

Why Jesus is more than simply an ethical role model—although he is of course that, too—was explained in detail in that chapter's discussion of the incarnation and how it definitively changed the relationship between God and humanity.

Yet this is not the only reason why Jesus Christ was more than a great moral teacher. The incarnation did not simply have backward-looking impact. In other words, it did not simply wipe the slate clean so humanity could be back on track, in right relationship with God. The incarnation is also a forward-looking event that can be lived out in the ways described at the end of chapter 14 and in chapter 15. And not only does such life in Christ proceed with the incarnation as a model of how to follow Jesus, the incarnate Christ also provides the fuel, if you will, for that journey. Through Jesus Christ, God gives humanity, communally and individually, real help in living lives in Christ. This help is called grace, and explaining its importance in the virtuous life is the point of this chapter.

The chapter proceeds in two sections. The first section defines grace, explains how it works, and offers the famous and powerful autobiographical account of St. Augustine's conversion as an example of grace in action. The second section reexamines the different categories of virtue with the Christian teaching on grace in mind. It clarifies the difference between acquired and infused virtue, and explains the importance of an oft-neglected category of virtue, the infused cardinal virtues. An accurate understanding of these virtues reveals how God's grace not only provides humanity with the three theological virtues of faith, hope, and love, but also transforms how people do innerworldly activities to reflect how they live in Christ.

What Is Grace, and How Does It Work?

Christian teaching on grace is one of the most distinctive, challenging, and often underappreciated and unrecognized parts of the Christian story about the way things are. Really an extension of Christian teaching on the incarnation, it is not only clearly opposed to secular views of the way things are, it also distinguishes Christianity from other faith traditions. The first part of this section will present exactly what the Christian tradition teaches about grace. The second part recounts the famous conversion story of St. Augustine as an example of grace in action.

Defining and Describing Grace

Christians commonly claim that they live "in Christ," or that Christ lives in them (Gal. 2:20, Rom. 8:2). What does this mean? The past two chapters examined some of the central activities of one who lives in Christ: the works of mercy, genuine holiness over wholesomeness, forgiveness, love of enemy, and love of God and all things in God. Much has been said of what a person living in Christ does. Less has been said on how it is done. Explicit and important discussion of grace has been missing.

As Lewis says aptly, Christians do not "act on their own steam."[2] The Christian is "nourishing and protecting a life that he could never have acquired through his own efforts."[3] The source and sustenance of that life is Christ. It is tempting to think that living out Christian discipleship is acting in accordance with Christian beliefs, and in a manner that mimics how Jesus Christ lived on earth. This is certainly true. But Christians think something more happens as well.

> Put right out of your head the idea that these [claims about living in Christ] are only fancy ways of saying that Christians are to read what Christ said and try to carry it out—as a man may read what Plato or Marx said and try to carry it out. They mean something much more than that. They mean that a real Person, Christ, here and now, in the very room where you are saying your prayers, is *doing things to you*. It is not a question of a good man who died two thousand years ago. It is a living Man, still as much a man as you, and still as much God as He was when He created the world, *really coming and interfering with your very self*, killing the old natural self in you and replacing it with the kind of self He has. At first only for moments. Then for longer periods. Finally, if all goes well, turning you permanently into a different sort of thing; into a new little Christ, a being which, in its own small way, has the same kind of life as God; which shares in His power, joy, knowledge, and eternity.[4]

The difference between a great moral teacher (such as, say, Plato) and Christ should now be more completely understood. A great moral teacher does not actively help one in the present to live out what is taught, whereas Christians believe Christ does exactly this. Jesus Christ is the definitive event in human history, not only in a backward-looking way because he cleaned the slate, but also in a forward-looking way in that he lives on, assisting real people to live in Christ.

Grace is the term for this help that God gives people to know and live a more truthful, holy, and virtuous life, directed ultimately toward union with God. The grace of God has always been associated with the Holy Spirit, as when Jesus encountered his disciples after the Resurrection, "breathed on them, and said to them, 'Receive the Holy Spirit'" (John 20:22). The association of grace and the Holy Spirit can be seen in the traditional prayer. "Come Holy Spirit, fill the hearts of your faithful and kindle in them the fire of your love. Lord, send forth your Spirit, and renew the face of the earth." It is also seen in the seven

2. C. S. Lewis, *Mere Christianity*, 63.
3. Ibid.
4. Ibid., 190 (emphasis added).

traditional "gifts of the Holy Spirit," which are God's grace in helping a person to be docile to the promptings of the Holy Spirit. These seven gifts, derived from Isaiah 1:1–2, are: wisdom, understanding, counsel, fortitude, knowledge, piety, and fear of the Lord. Grace can be difficult to specify, for many reasons. One such reason is that if the Christian claim is true—that God is the ultimate source of all that is—what is *not* grace? First of all, anything that is not a help to live more holy and truthful lives is not help from God. So any expressions of our sinfulness, for example, are not in themselves works of God's grace. Second, grace should not be equated simply with goodness. There are indeed many good things that are from God, such as our capacities of reason and will. These things may be crucial on our journey toward our supernatural destiny, or union with God. But the more precise meaning of grace used here is not only what is good or done by God in some sense, but rather what is done by God that directs us to supernatural happiness in union with God. Grace is God's help to do things that are not possible with natural human capacities alone, since they direct us toward our supernatural destiny. Therefore, living a life in Christ, a life of grace, is not simply a matter of being our better selves rather than our sinful selves, and following a rightly formed conscience. It is receiving help from beyond us to direct us toward the ultimate purpose of union with God. "God is the one who, for his good purpose, works in you both to desire and to work" (Phil. 2:13).

One of the primary Christian claims about grace is that God is truly an agent when people live in Christ. This help from God is received in countless ways. One of the more obvious is through other people. Think of all the ways we receive this assistance through others. None of us could have the faith we do without having heard about God from others. Our friends often sustain us in living holy lives. Reading the scriptures, inspired as it is by the Holy Spirit and yet enfleshed in human language written by human authors, is another source of grace. The sacraments are excellent examples of God's real assistance in transforming our lives to be more Christlike. In times of prayer, as Lewis says, God works on us. It is perhaps easier to see how God's assistance comes concretely through prayer, the scriptures, and sacraments, since these are churchy activities. But we should not neglect the importance of how God works on us through other avenues, be they more exalted moments of inspiration from natural beauty, or in the everyday ways that those around us support and encourage us in living holy lives. This is a main reason why friendship is such an essential part of the virtuous life in Christ.

It is easy for the skeptic to see things differently, of course. Why label all of these influences as God's real agency on us? Why not just call them "good influences"? In one sense this is of course correct. All of these occasions are good influences on our lives. But their origin is God and not simply those persons who act as instruments of God's grace in our lives. To use another analogy from Lewis:

> At first it is natural for a baby to take its mother's milk without knowing its mother. It is equally natural for us to see the man who helps us without seeing Christ behind him. But we must not remain babies. We must go on to recognize the real Giver. [5]

Why must there be a real giver behind these influences? If the central claims of the Christian story as presented so far in this book are true, then the life and destiny to which we are called is beyond our human capacities. We could not understand it without help from beyond us, and we could not live in accordance with it without God's help. This life could not be known and lived on our own, understanding "our" not just in individual but also in corporate terms.

In sum, God's grace is at work when we receive help from God to know and do particular things we could not know and do on our own, things that reveal to us and lead us toward our destiny of complete happiness in union with God. It must be acknowledged by Christians that though grace can be described in an intellectually sound manner, the best proof of its existence is not theological discourse, but the real lived experiences of people caught up in the life of God. It is for that reason that we will examine precisely such an autobiographical account below, through the story of St. Augustine. But before proceeding to that story, three further observations about grace will help illuminate that account.

First, what is the relationship between grace and human freedom? In other words, if God is working on us, does that mean that God impedes or usurps our freedom? This is an extraordinarily difficult question, one that Christians have always struggled to articulate in a nuanced manner. A brief answer will have to suffice here. Grace does not usurp or even lessen human freedom. Grace should not be understood to operate in the manner of a possession, such as that depicted in the classic movie *The Exorcist*, where a young girl suffers, against her will, the internal presence of a supernatural being moving her to do involuntary things. Though it is true that we cannot live lives of holiness without God's help, and that even turning to accept that help is a gift from God, it is also true, on the one hand, that we can refuse that help, and on the other hand that when we accept that help it is truly we who are acting. Even though we are being acted on from the outside, we are also cooperating with that influence, and thus our actions under this influence are not only God's but our own.

Consider an imperfect analogy.[6] What skills and good qualities do you possess? Perhaps you play piano or basketball, or write well. These skills are

---

5. Ibid., 190–91.

6. The analogy is helpful in showing how help from the outside can enable rather than impede our freedom. The analogy is imperfect, because skills such as piano playing, basketball, and writing are accessible to humanity as a race on our own, even if individuals require the help

truly your own. They are qualities that mark who you are. But none of them would be possible without the help of others. When a piano teacher holds a child's hands to play keys correctly, or a father teaches a child to shoot foul shots, or a mother assists a child to learn to write, there is real help, or outside agency, at work. The child could not have done it on his own. In fact, the child can resist and never take on the skill. But nonetheless, if the child eventually takes on the skill, it is truly his own even if he is not the origin of the skill. The same is true of grace. God assists us to become the persons who we truly are, but could not be without God's help.

This recalls the second chapter's discussion of freedom, and the difference between freedom for excellence and freedom of indifference. If freedom is understood as simply your ability to choose no matter what is chosen (freedom of indifference), then any outside influence on your choice lessens your own contribution to the choice. Acts of freedom are zero-sum gains, in that the more God helps you in some act, the less free agency is left over for you. From a freedom-of-indifference perspective, therefore, grace is actually an intrusion on your freedom.

But if we understand true freedom as the ability to act well where the action truly comes from us (freedom for excellence), then it is possible to receive help from the outside to live well, and yet still be fully free, since the action is truly from us. In fact, since that external help (grace) enables us to act well, such help makes us more, not less, free than we otherwise would be on our own.

Consider again the example of a piano teacher. Does the teacher impede the child's freedom in teaching him to strike the keys well? At first it is basically all the teacher, moving the child's hands to play. The action is not yet the child's own. But once the skill is gained, the action is genuinely the child's own, *and* only possible with help from outside. The teacher and student's agencies are not rivals operating in a zero-sum gain. The more and better help the teacher gives, the more the child becomes free to play well. Just as it would be foolish to insist that the young pianist's skill is only his own if he developed it without any help, so too is it erroneous to think that God's grace in helping us live holy lives makes our action less our own. Grace heals and enables, rather than usurps, true human freedom.

The second observation concerns the difficulty of life in Christ, and is once again beautifully described by Lewis. Is such life hard or easy, he asks?[7] On the one hand, Christ continually says the disciple must take up his cross and follow Christ. Followers must lay down their lives, and be willing to lose them. This sounds hard. On the other hand, Christ also says "my yoke is easy, and my burden is light" (Matt. 11:30). But yet he still calls it a yoke and a burden!

---

of others to obtain them. Actions that lead us to the supernatural destiny of union with God, however, are only attainable with God's help. The second section further addresses this point.

7. See Lewis, *Mere Christianity*, 195–200, for an excellent discussion of this topic.

Which is it, a yoke and a burden, or easy and light? Lewis says both. It is extraordinarily difficult to lay down our lives, to die to our prideful selves. It is a cross. This can be seen by the many times in our lives when we try to quit a bad habit, or do something difficult we know to be good. Even when we ourselves know it is best to change, or to do what we know is best, so often we resist! We basically try to stay the old selves we have become accustomed to, to remain in charge, but with a change or two around the edges of who we are. This compromise, of wanting to be better persons while staying our old selves, may result in occasional successes but always leads to frustrating failures or the daunting realization that more remains to be done. So we give up or live miserably. By refusing to do the very difficult thing of surrendering ourselves fully to God's direction in grace, we block God's assistance to help us live more holy lives.

But if we take the difficult step of surrendering ourselves to God's grace, life in Christ is easy. God wants our whole selves to be transformed so as to live most fully. If we get out of the way, and let Christ transform us, the grace is there to do so. Too often, like petulant children, we want to do it on our own, and in our way. But when we lay down our lives and allow the life of Christ to blossom in us, not only can we do what seems hopeless on our own; we find that we are living more fully, and are more truly ourselves. Indeed, we find we are living more truthfully, more happily. It is in this sense that Christ meant "my yoke is easy and my burden is light."

This talk of total transformation leads us to the last observation, again through a question posed by Lewis. Does Christ really call us to be perfect (Matt. 5:48)?[8] The answer is yes. Again, in our pride we prefer a little help here and there, but would rather remain firmly at the helm, in control of our lives. Lewis says we are like the person who is afraid to go to the dentist to be relieved of a toothache, since she knows that if she goes the dentist will not simply treat the immediate problem at hand, but will also want to do all sorts of other things that may in the long run be best for her but really uncomfortable in the short run.[9] Similarly, we often turn to God to help us with a pressing need. But we only want God's help with that need. We don't want any tinkering around with the rest of our lives! But Lewis says God is ready to help, yet not interested in fine-tuning our old wayward selves. God wants us completely, and has plans for us that will no doubt take us way beyond the miniscule surrenders we are willing to endure to improve a bit without giving up control. God intends to transform us completely: "You thought you were going to be made into a decent little cottage: but He is building a palace. He intends to come live in it Himself." Lewis continues:

8. See ibid., 201–6.
9. See ibid., 201–2.

The command "be ye perfect" is not idealistic gas. Nor is it a command to do the impossible. He is going to make us into creatures that can obey that command. He said (in the Bible) that we were "gods" and He is going to make good His words. If we let Him—for we can prevent Him, if we choose—He will make the feeblest and filthiest of us into a god or goddess, a dazzling, radiant, immortal creature, pulsating all through with such energy and joy and wisdom and love as we cannot now imagine, a bright stainless mirror which reflects back to God perfectly (though, of course, on a smaller scale) His own boundless power and delight and goodness. This process will be long and in parts very painful, but that is what we are in for. Nothing less. He meant what He said.[10]

As Lewis also notes, the process will not be completed in this life, though God intends to complete it as much as possible before we die.

To summarize this part's depiction of grace, grace is the help that God gives people to know and live more truthful, holy, and virtuous lives in a manner directed ultimately toward union with God. It enables us to do things we could not otherwise do, since they are directed ultimately to our union with God. It is really God acting on us—and not just our better selves—even though it does not defy our freedom. We can resist. If we do not, we will actually become more, not less, free. Though it is extraordinarily difficult in that it entails surrendering our old selves, it is also easy in that God will do the hard work if we only get out of the way and let him. Finally, the goal of our transformation is indeed perfection. This need not discourage us when we fail, but rather serve as a reminder of God's mercy and love in sticking with us to get the job done.

Grace in St. Augustine's Conversion

St. Augustine's autobiographical book *Confessions* is one of the classic works of Western literature for many reasons. We examine it here for only one, albeit important, reason. It is a powerful account of how God's grace works in someone's life. The focal point here will be the eighth chapter (called Book Eight) of his story, where he recounts his definitive conversion to the Christian life. We see beautifully depicted in this account the most central features of grace described above.

At the beginning of Book Eight , Augustine has already been convinced of the truth and wisdom of Christianity. Yet though he has intellectually grasped the persuasiveness of Christianity's story of the way things are, he has not yet allowed his life to be transformed accordingly.

Concerning your eternal life I was now quite certain. . . . What I now longed for was not greater certainty about you, but a more steadfast abiding in you. In my

10. Ibid., 205–6.

daily life everything seemed to be teetering, and my heart needed to be cleansed of old leaven. I was attracted to the Way, which is our Savior Himself, but the narrowness of the path daunted me and I still could not walk in it.[11]

How easy it is for people of faith to resonate with these words! Though our personal reasons and backgrounds may be different, how easy it is for us to sympathize with knowing and wanting to follow Christ wholeheartedly, but yet being still divided and holding back.

What was it that held Augustine back? There were several facets of his old self that he had trouble surrendering, but the one he describes most poignantly is his battle with lust. He was restrained from full conversion with the force of an iron chain. Yet it was no external chain that bound him, but rather "the iron of my own will." In a vivid description of the formation and power of habit (unfortunately here a vice), Augustine claims, "The truth is that a disordered lust springs from a perverted will; when lust is pandered to, a habit is formed; when habit is not checked, it hardens into compulsion."[12] Therefore his newfound will to follow Christ was initially unable to dislodge the earlier habit of lust.

> A new will had begun to emerge in me, the will to worship you distinterestedly and enjoy you, O God, our only sure happiness; but it was not yet capable of surmounting that earlier will strengthened by inveterate custom. And so the two wills fought it out.[13]

Augustine powerfully describes this common experience of being inwardly torn. He notes how we often speak of there being two wills in us, but claims in reality that what may appear to be two wills are really both our own.

> I was the one who wanted to follow [Christ]; and I was the one who wanted not to. I was the only one involved. I neither wanted it wholeheartedly, nor turned from it wholeheartedly. I was at odds with myself, and fragmenting myself.[14]

In an analogy we can all understand, Augustine likens himself at this time to a person awaking from sleep, who knows it is time to get up and even wants to get up, and yet sinks back into sleep as if to say, "one more minute! Let me have a little longer!" (Today we might imagine hitting the snooze bar.) We know from chapter 4 that Augustine is here caught in a state of

11. Augustine, *Confessions*, trans. Maria Boulding, OSB (New York: Random House, 1997), 145.
12. Ibid., 153.
13. Ibid., 153–54. Boulding's translation is modified here. Though she uses "felicity" to translate the Latin *felicitas*, "happiness" is substituted here.
14. Ibid., 163.

incontinence. He knew it was time for him to change his lustful ways, but also felt unready and unwilling to do so. At one point he even pleads to God, "Give me chastity and self-control, but not yet!"[15] The problem, Augustine recognized, was "these 'minutes' never diminished, and my 'little longer' lasted inordinately long."[16]

So at this point in his life story, Augustine felt enslaved, although the source of the chains was his own self, and the bad habits he had willingly developed. Despite a real longing to change his life and follow Christ wholeheartedly, these chains bound him. Augustine's account from the inside of what it feels like to change our old ways is haunting.

> Then I would make a fresh attempt, and now I was almost there, almost there . . . I was touching the goal, grasping it . . . and then I was not there, not touching, not grasping it. I shrank from dying to death and living to life, for ingrained evil was more powerful in me than new-grafted good.[17]

It was as if he were being taunted by his old self, with his wayward desires warning,

> Do you mean to get rid of us? Shall we never be your companions again after that moment . . . never . . . never again? From that time onward so-and-so will be forbidden to you, all your life long.[18]

What person who has struggled to change a bad habit cannot relate to this situation, where in one sense we know it is best for us to change, but in another sense are terrified that by changing we will have to definitively let go of the sinful activity, that former life, that has seemingly become a part of who we are? Augustine reports fearing conversion: "the prospect of being free of all these encumbrances frightened me as much as the encumbrances themselves ought to have done."[19]

The point of Book Eight is not primarily to describe the state Augustine was in, which has been our focus so far. Rather it is to see how God's grace was at work in his conversion. This leads us to a first question regarding grace: does God work on Augustine at his conversion? There can be no doubt that this is how Augustine understands what happens to him. He reports feeling left hanging in the state he was in, unable to fully convert on his own. How would he change? Reminiscent of St. Paul (Rom. 7:24–25), Augustine cries:

15. Ibid., 159.
16. Ibid., 155.
17. Ibid., 165.
18. Ibid., 166.
19. Ibid., 154. See Rom. 7:24–25.

> You set me free from a craving for sexual gratification which fettered me like a
> tight-drawn chain, and from my enslavement to worldly affairs: I will confess
> your name, O Lord, my helper and redeemer.[20]

Augustine is quite clear on this point. It was God who was at work in his conversion: "Let me offer a sacrifice of praise, for *you* have snapped my bonds.
How *you* broke them I will relate."[21] To that next question of how grace works
in Augustine's story we now turn.

The ways God's grace works on Augustine in these pages range from the
mundane to the extraordinary. Augustine reports hearing the conversion stories
of some contemporaries, and all the while thinking that God was at work in-
spiring him to do the same.[22] He reports the steady, silent support of his friend
Alypius at his moment of crisis, an influence that no doubt contributed to his
conversion. He recounts the longtime prayers of his mother, who is overjoyed
at Augustine's eventual conversion. And he details the precise occasion of his
actual conversion, which contains more extraordinary moments of grace: moments of intense, heart-pounding, tearful prayer; being led to the scriptures
by overhearing children sing a song; God's seeming to speak to him directly
through the passage he opens to in the Bible; and, even a vision in which he
is assured by "Lady Continence" that he need not change his life on his own
but can rely on the Lord for help:

> Why try to stand yourself, only to lose your footing? Cast yourself on him [Christ]
> and do not be afraid; he will not step back and let you fall. Cast yourself upon
> him trustfully; he will support and heal you.[23]

This brief overview of Augustine's conversion is full of events, some mundane
and some rather extraordinary, where God's grace was at work on him. But
all these events are reported by Augustine to be vehicles of God's grace, since
through them God led Augustine to himself, and helped him do things he
could have done on his own.

Is Augustine free when he converts? His story is a vivid response to the
more general question about the relationship between grace and freedom.
He clearly describes himself as bound and enslaved before his conversion. He
becomes more free, not less, when he finally surrenders and lets God's grace
go to work on him. This is true in two senses. First, with the help of God's
grace he is able to live out that new will to follow Christ that had sprung up
in him. He is freed to do what he wants to do, rather than be enslaved by his
old habits. Second, in another sense he is more free because he becomes able

20. Augustine, *Confessions*, 155. See Rom. 7:15–25.
21. Augustine, *Confessions*, 145 (emphasis added).
22. See, for example, ibid., 158.
23. Ibid., 167.

to do what is truly best for him. After all, since not only his new will but also his old habits were born in his own will, there really is never a time in his story when he is not doing what he wants. The change is from his wanting two different things (namely, to follow Christ and to remain in lust), but neither wholeheartedly, to wanting what will make him truly happy even when it entails in some sense a loss of his old self. Thus, it is wrong to assume that Augustine's conversion makes him more free if we hold a freedom-of-indifference perspective, since his pre-conversion fragmented will was indeed his own will. Yet from a freedom-for-excellence perspective, it is clear that Augustine grew in freedom by being able to choose to live more fully with God's help.

It should also be clear from Augustine's story that life in Christ is both hard and easy, in the senses described by Lewis. In one sense Augustine's full conversion is tortuous. This entire chapter depicts how difficult it is for him to let go of his old self, to surrender and let's God's life live more fully in him. Then the entreaty of Lady Continence sets him straight. He need not—in fact, cannot—do it on his own. But if he simply trusts in Christ, it will be done for him. One thing that often strikes the reader about the climax of Augustine's conversion is that, in a certain sense, he does not do anything. He simply reports that "the light of certainty flooded my heart and all dark shades of doubt fled away."[24] He tells his friend what happened, and describes himself as suddenly peaceful—that's it. But knowing what Lewis says about life in Christ also being easy, this does not surprise us. Once Augustine surrenders and gets out of the way, the grace of God accomplishes the work. Also reminiscent of Lewis, the work being accomplished is the transformation of Augustine into someone living in Christ, into greater perfection. The process will not come to completion in this life, but God will take it as far Augustine allows.

Grace and the Virtuous Life

The impact that the preceding section's discussion of grace has on moral theology is obvious. Through Christ God actually helps people to live more holy lives. Yet more specifically, what difference does grace have on how we understand the virtues? Answering this question is the purpose of this second section. One of the best ways to understand some entity is to categorize its different manifestations. So when this book first described the meaning of virtue in chapter 3, distinctions such as "cardinal vs. theological" virtue were offered to help us better understand what virtue is. However, at that point the big-picture claims of the second half of this book had not yet been

24. Ibid., 168.

considered. Therefore, some categories of virtue were not addressed. In fact, these omissions led to some misleading assumptions about virtue that can now be corrected. The first part of this section will revisit the different categories of virtue. The second part will explain why one type of virtue that has been neglected thus far in this book, "infused cardinal virtue," is actually a crucial part of moral theology and of living a virtuous life.

Revisiting, and Supplementing, the Categories of Virtue

A habit is a stable disposition in a person that disposes that person to act in a certain manner, with corresponding intentions. Virtues dispose us to act well, whereas vices dispose us to act poorly. One way of categorizing habits is by the sort of activity they concern. For instance, we did this in chapter 12 with the seven deadly sins. When these sins are habits, or vices, they dispose us to consistently act poorly with regard to a certain type of activity (eating and drinking for gluttony, or rectifying injustice with anger, etc.). The same may be said about virtue. In fact, this book is structured by the four cardinal virtues and the three theological virtues. Each of these seven virtues disposes a person to do a certain sort of activity well (believing things about God for faith, or right relations with others for justice, etc.). As we learned in chapter 3, all of these types of activity can be placed into two groups: innerworldly activities, or those that concern God directly. Innerworldly activities are encapsulated in those four main areas—practical decision-making, right relations with others, facing difficulties, or sensual pleasures—that are the basis of the cardinal virtues: prudence, justice, fortitude, and temperance, respectively. The theological virtues faith, hope, and love concern God directly.

We now need to revisit more completely how both of these types of virtues are obtained. The most obvious way the cardinal virtues are obtained is through repetitive, intentional action, as described in chapter 3. If you want to become a generous person, you must repeatedly, and for the right reasons, help those in need with what resources are available to you. By continually performing such actions, a habit develops such that you will be disposed to do more such actions (automatically, with proper intentions) in the future. When virtues are obtained in this manner, that is, by repeated actions we are able to do on our own, they are called acquired virtues.

When one obtains an *acquired cardinal virtue*, one performs innerworldly acts well with an eye toward how they contribute to human happiness. In other words, I drink moderately because I want to maintain bodily health and consistently enjoy this sensual good in its proper place in my life. I am generous because I want to contribute not only to my own well-being, but that of others in my community, since I understand the two as intertwined. People are able to understand, through the use of their reason, natural human happiness as it includes things like bodily health and the common good. These activities concern created human nature, and thus we can figure them out by using our human reasoning (observations, understanding how these activities work, etc.). When we obtain virtues that concern our natural human happiness in this way, we call them *acquired* virtues. Of course, we can use our reasoning poorly—and in fact Christians who understand the pervasiveness of sin know that this happens quite often—but nonetheless people can in principle on their own, as individuals and communities, arrive at truly virtuous ways of doing these activities that serve natural human happiness. It is natural to us, not in the sense everyone does it and does it easily, or even in everyone fully understanding what constitutes natural happiness, but rather in the sense that it concerns human flourishing on matters accessible to our unaided human reasoning.

Yet, as already reiterated throughout the second half of this book, Christians believe that humans are invited by God to share in a greater destiny. This destiny is called, literally, a supernatural happiness, and is constituted by union with the triune God of Jesus Christ, who became man for us to reconcile us with God and make us sharers in the divine nature (2 Pet. 1:4). This is a destiny that far transcends our unaided created nature and unaided powers of reasoning. We could not get there on our own. In fact, we cannot even begin to comprehend this invitation, let alone live it out, without the assistance of God called grace.

So how can this supernatural happiness be understood or achieved? It requires us to become the sorts of people who act in certain ways (i.e., have certain virtues), but we are unable to obtain these virtues on our own. Therefore, God gives us the grace to truthfully understand who God is, and his plan for humanity (faith). He fills us with a longing for union with God, tasted in this life and completed in the next, even when it is not fully available to us now (hope). He bestows on us a love of God and others in God, such that we seek to be unified with God in communion with others (charity). Therefore, people can possess virtues that enable them to pursue their supernatural destiny of union with God thanks to God's help, or grace. Virtues that are given to us by God, and indeed are only possible by the grace of God—since they concern our supernatural happiness—are called *infused virtues*. The three theological virtues faith, hope, and love are all infused virtues.

But what does grace have to do with the cardinal virtues? Christians, like all human persons, live in this created world and continue to engage in innerworldly activities. To do these well they, like all others, need the cardinal virtues of prudence, justice, temperance, and fortitude. At this point it would seem that the only thing distinguishing Christians from non-Christians is the presence of faith, hope, and love. Christians have the infused theological virtues in order to guide them to union with God, a supernatural destiny. But all persons—Christian or not—can have the cardinal virtues that are acquired by the process of habituation and that direct us to do innerworldly activities well for the sake of natural human flourishing. On this reading, in fact, there really is no difference between how Christians act well in the world, and how virtuous non-Christians act well. There is simply a human ethic for innerworldly activities, and so the cardinal virtues incline all people toward the same sorts of action.

There are kernels of truth in saying that Christians and non-Christians both have these acquired cardinal virtues. First of all, for many innerworldly activities, it simply does not matter whether or not one is Christian. If you want to go to a good exercise trainer, it is probably not necessary to ask if he or she is Christian! Physical training is an innerworldly activity, accessible to unaided human reason, that basically looks the same for Christians and non-Christians alike. The same is true of many questions of justice. A non-Christian judge can be just as knowledgeable in American law and render judgments as just as a Christian judge. Second, it is true that Christians can work hard to obtain cardinal virtues concerning innerworldly activities. So Christians can work hard to diet so as to be physically fit, or try to be more patient with people that may annoy them.

However, sometimes innerworldly activities look different for Christians because of their Christian faith. Thomas Aquinas uses the example of fasting.[25] During Lent a Christian may fast and eat less than three square meals a day on, say, Good Friday. To make a sacrifice joining us to the ultimate sacrifice of Christ, and to subordinate our more basic desires for the sake of our deeper desire for the Lord, we forgo eating as much as we normally do. This action concerns an innerworldly activity (eating), and thus is a matter of the cardinal virtue temperance. So the fasting Christian is said to be temperate. But on that same day a virtuous nonbeliever may eat her standard three square meals. She, too, is eating temperately. How to explain this difference?

Some different virtuous actions are explainable due to different circumstances. One person's temperance may entail more food than another's, simply due to a larger body size. But that is not the case here. Both actions are temperate, but they differ, not due to circumstances, but in their very meaning. The nonbeliever is temperate for the sake of natural human flourishing. The Christian is temperate for the sake of union with God. The goal of the former person's temperance is natural human happiness. The goal of the latter person's temperance is the supernatural destiny of humanity's union with God. So the actions differ in meaning, or ultimate goal.

They also differ in source. Though the Christian may work hard to fast, ultimately that temperate act requires the assistance of God's grace. Since we are incapable of acting for the sake of union with God on our own, this temperance is rightly called infused, since eating in this way would not be

25. See Aquinas *Summa Theologiae* I–II 63,4.

possible without God's grace. Hence in this example we have two different types of virtue: the infused cardinal virtue of temperance (in the one fasting during Lent), and the acquired cardinal virtue of temperance (in the nonbeliever eating three squares a day).

Eating is certainly not the only innerworldly activity that is transformed by Christians' call to union with God, and assisted by God's infused grace. Many of the worldly activities of Christians are transformed by our relationship with God, and so are done differently. Consider the cardinal virtue fortitude. Firefighters and other first responders can develop this acquired virtue, risking their lives to help citizens in danger. Christians can do this as well, but see the ultimate act of fortitude to be laying down one's life for one's faith in God, which is called martyrdom. The early church martyrs are fine examples of infused fortitude, as are contemporary examples such as St. Maximilian Kolbe or Martin Luther King Jr. Kolbe was willing to lay down his life in place of a fellow prisoner in a Nazi concentration camp, not simply to save a person with a family, but also in imitation of Christ's willingness to die for us and in hope of future union with God beyond this life.

As for the cardinal virtue justice, surely a virtuous non-Christian can be willing to lay down his life for social justice (e.g., racial or economic equality). But a Christian might do this differently. Anyone who has read Martin Luther King Jr.'s, work knows that he was committed to racial equality not only for the sake of humanity's natural happiness (social justice), but also for the sake of his and humanity's ultimate union with God. He pursued justice in a manner shaped by Christ's injunction to love the enemy, and turn the other cheek. Archbishop Oscar Romero spoke out for economic justice on behalf of the poor not simply because the conditions of his society impeded natural human happiness—which they did—but also because they violated the dignity of people created in God's image, and particularly the poor, for whom God has a special love.

These examples reveal that cardinal virtues, while always concerning innerworldly activities, actually come in two different stripes. And therefore there are ultimately three types of virtues. First, there are infused theological virtues. These concern God directly, and thus are only obtained with God's grace. Second, there are acquired cardinal virtues. They concern innerworldly activities. They are accessible to unaided human reason and acquired by our own efforts. They direct us toward happiness considered simply at the level of our created human nature. Finally, there are also *infused cardinal virtues*. These concern innerworldly activities as well, but they incline us to do innerworldly activities well in the larger perspective of our supernatural destiny. They give a different meaning to those activities (commonly leading to different particular actions), and are possible only with God's grace.

The Importance of the Infused Cardinal Virtues

Why is it important to recognize these three—not two—categories of virtue? Is it simply an abstract theological claim that there are not only infused theological and acquired cardinal virtues, but also infused cardinal virtues? Categorizations are often helpful ways to better understand more about what is being categorized. This is certainly the case with the infused cardinal virtues. People who neglect the existence of this type of virtue fail to see accurately a crucial facet of the Christian life. They may rightly note that people can acquire on their own certain cardinal virtues concerning innerworldly activities. And they might even recognize that God helps people to be in right relationship with him by infusing the theological virtues of faith, hope, and love. But if these two categories of virtue were all that existed, something important would be missing. This is true for three reasons.

First, Christian faith transforms not just a person's relationship with God, but also a person's innerworldly activities. The problem with a two-fold categorization of virtue, which attends only to infused theological virtue and acquired cardinal virtue, is its failure to account for how our worldly activities are transformed by grace. Simply put, Christian faith matters for how we live, including those activities that nonbelievers can do virtuously. We have already considered the case of fasting, which provides an obvious example of Christian faith transforming how one goes about an innerworldly activity. There are many other such examples. Consider the political example of St. Thomas More, who refused to acquiesce to King Henry VIII's demand that he recognize an illegitimate marriage. More's infused justice precluded him from doing so, and his infused fortitude gave him the grace to endure martyrdom because of it. Or consider the contemporary example of the United States bishops, whose stances on political issues differ from our prevailing Republican and Democratic views on justice, in their respect for life at all stages and their preferential option for the poor. This infused justice is not simply another secular form of justice; rather, it is transformed by Christian beliefs. Infused justice leads to, in this case, political actions that are distinctive as compared to acquired justice.

As noted above, sometimes the action performed by someone with an acquired cardinal virtue does look the same as one performed by someone with an infused cardinal virtue. If you want a good fitness trainer, his or her faith commitment is probably of less importance than competence in physical training. And surely people with either infused cardinal virtues or acquired cardinal virtues can pursue racial equality in the manner espoused by Martin Luther King Jr. That said, even in these cases where the external act may be the same, the meaning of the action is still importantly different (for reasons explained in chapters 2 and 15 on the importance of our ultimate goal for how we do all activities that are lower on our triangles). The Christian trainer may understand her work as a way of honoring the bodies God gave us—really as a form of worship. The nonbeliever would not consciously share this perspective. Similarly with King, he understood his work for social justice to be directly related to his own faith and the larger Christian project of helping to further instatiate the kingdom of God. A socially just atheist could surely join King in performing particular actions, and these actions would truly be called just. But the overall meaning of the act, and thus the type of justice, would be different.

Therefore, the first reason why we must attend to infused cardinal virtue is that this category of virtue enables us to explain how Christian faith transforms a person's innerworldly activities. At times, this leads the believer to different sorts of actions. Different sorts of happiness—natural or supernatural—can lead to different understandings of what constitutes truly just, temperate, brave, and prudent action. This is exactly why this book has had to attend to big-picture beliefs about the way things are, in order to fully understand how to live morally in this world. Even when the one with infused cardinal virtue performs acts that appear the same to the external observer as the ones performed by someone with acquired cardinal virtues, those acts nonetheless possess a different overall meaning due to their relation to the supernatural destiny of the person.

The second reason why we must attend to the infused cardinal virtues is that Christians believe people can receive God's grace to help them become virtuous, not just directly in their relationships with God (faith, hope, and love) but also in their innerworldly activities. This is readily seen in our liturgical and prayer lives. We commonly pray for God's help in being more just, temperate, brave, and prudent people. We trust that God's grace also works in these areas. Consider the example of St. Paul from Acts 9. He ceased his unjust persecution of Christians due to God's direct intervention. Or consider St. Augustine's story from earlier in this chapter. He begged for God's assistance to rid himself of lustful desires, and was granted that help, in the famous story of his conversion in the garden.

These are obvious—and dramatic—examples of God's grace helping people with innerworldly activities. Unfortunately, due to the term "infused," and due to the existence of such extraordinary stories of God's grace, people too often assume that infused cardinal virtue is only present when someone has been obviously "zapped" by God's grace in the manner of Paul or Augustine. But God's grace can be just as present and efficacious for people who have less dramatic stories of God's transforming impact on their lives. That grace can be present in the upbringing provided by holy parents, the challenging advice of a close friend, or the helpful example provided by a mentor. We say grace is present anytime someone receives God's help to live in a manner that is ultimately pointed toward his supernatural destiny. Such meaning and ultimate direction for our virtuous action could not be present without God's help, even when that help comes in less dramatic forms.

Differing from Paul and Augustine, Saints Peter and Thomas Aquinas are examples of people who clearly exhibited infused cardinal virtues without extraordinary stories of being zapped by God's grace. That does not mean

God's grace did not transform their lives—it most certainly did. What makes their cardinal virtues infused was that they came from God, and led to actions the ultimate purpose of which was to unite them to God and to neighbors in and through God, which is of course their supernatural happiness, a destiny unknowable, let alone achievable, without God's help. Acquired cardinal virtues may entail actions that look the same, but the ultimate source and ultimate goal of those activities (and hence their meaning) is nonetheless different.

The third and final reason we must attend to the infused cardinal virtues is encapsulated in the famous theological dictum, "grace perfects nature," rather than takes away or leaves it untouched. There has been a great deal of talk in this section about natural and supernatural happiness. But there are two mistakes that are easy to make when discussing these two distinct forms of happiness. First, some assume that they both persist as parallel tracks, with no relationship between the two. This chapter has been very explicit thus far in asserting that this is not the case. Even seemingly nonreligious activities like physical training, eating, and racial equality are indeed transformed in the context of one's supernatural destiny. We do not live natural (or innerworldly) lives sealed off from our supernatural lives. Grace perfects nature, rather than leaving it untouched.

There is also a second error in attending to humanity's two distinct types of happiness. Some recognize that attention to our supernatural destiny impacts our innerworldly activities, but go further and claim that believers actually no longer can be said to seek and experience natural happiness. The natural destiny is taken away and replaced by the supernatural end. Yet this opposite extreme also defies the scholastic dictum that grace perfects nature.

Some examples might help make this clear. Aquinas again uses the example of fasting. Here is a case where infused temperance makes what one eats (e.g., during Lent) different for the believer. The natural end of eating is not taken away; rather, it is fulfilled and transcended in the broader context of one's supernatural destiny. How does fasting respect natural happiness while transcending it? Doesn't it actually defy our natural happiness, since three square meals a day is the path to natural human flourishing, as it concerns eating? Generally, we should eat three square meals a day. But just as we might fast a day before surgery, or "carbo-load" the day before a marathon, three square meals a day is not the only way of achieving natural happiness. Larger goals can shape what constitutes eating well. Furthermore, Aquinas insists that if we were to fast so stringently that it actually harmed our natural bodily health, then we are fasting inappropriately.[26] Thus, grace fulfills and transcends, but does not destroy or leave unfulfilled, our nature.

26. See Aquinas *Summa Theologiae* II–II 147, 1–2. Jean Porter discusses this text in her *Nature as Reason: A Thomistic Theory of the Natural Law* (Grand Rapids: Eerdmans, 2005), 390.

In fact, Christians have consistently maintained that though natural human happiness is in principle accessible to unaided human understanding and action, in reality people are not able to live naturally flourishing lives, due to the reality and pervasiveness of sin. Aquinas claims it is possible to act well in pursuit of natural happiness, but only occasionally and with much error, primarily due to our sinful human condition. Therefore, since God's grace perfects human nature even while transcending it, ironically, complete natural happiness is only possible for those who are assisted by God's grace, even though those same persons are not acting toward natural happiness as their ultimate goal, but rather toward their further goal of an even greater (supernatural) happiness of union with God.

A good example of this is the relationship between love and justice. It is in principle possible to be a just person and have a just society without the theological virtue of charity, or love. However, as the Vatican II document *Gaudium et Spes* and the Pope Benedict XVI encyclical *Deus Caritas Est* both make clear, charity enables one to more perfectly see the beauty and dignity of other persons. This perfects (rather than leaves untouched, or destroys) our ability to be just, giving other persons their due. Thus the person with charity has a different sort of justice. It is still justice, since it concerns innerworldly relations with others. Yet it is transformed by God's grace, and thus rightly called infused rather than acquired justice.

One more example may help illuminate this. Consider two believers who are married. As part of their shared life, they go to church and understand their marriage to be a sacramental bond sustained by God's grace. But that same grace also sustains them in natural aspects of their marriage, aspects of marriage shared by believers and nonbelievers alike. So one spouse may be granted infused virtue to be patient in times of strife, and generous in time and attention. The other spouse may be granted infused virtue to be just in the handling of finances, and chaste in interactions with others. All of these virtues are in principle accessible to unaided reason, and indeed may be acquired by repeated actions and without further reference to any supernatural destiny. But these Christian spouses are granted not only the infused theological virtues of faith, hope, and love, but also infused cardinal virtues to assist them in the natural facets of their marriage, and to transform how those aspects are done in light of their supernatural destiny. In this case grace has clearly perfected—rather than taken away or left untouched—nature in a manner that is more complete with God's grace.

Concluding Thoughts

It is fitting that the climax of a book on living virtuously should come in a chapter on grace, since it is grace that elevates our lives to be directed toward supernatural happiness, and grace that enables us to act well, not only concerning that destiny directly (theological virtue), but also in our inner-worldly activities (cardinal virtue) in light of that destiny. In a sense, this chapter could have come first in the book, since grace is the source and sustenance of the Christian life. Modeling the dictum "grace perfects nature," however, this book instead built its way up to grace, to first show how created human persons "work" (first half of book), and then show how that human nature is perfected and transcended by God's action toward us in grace (second half of the book). We are now prepared to examine two more test cases (concerning having sex and caring for the dying) in light of the claims that the infused theological and cardinal virtues transform our lives in light of the Christian story. But before proceeding to those cases, one more word on the book's structure is in order.

Now that the infused cardinal virtues have been presented, earlier claims need to be understood in an importantly different manner. The presentation of the cardinal virtues in the beginning of this book is by no means inaccurate, but by appearing before this subsequent material on grace it may appear to be unrelated to graced life in Christ. Nothing could be further from the truth. In ways mentioned repeatedly in the second section of this chapter through examples of the saints, the cardinal virtues are only fully understood and lived in the context of graced life in Christ. They are indeed possible for non-Christians, and can be acquired. When they are, they are genuine virtues. But they are not complete, or perfect. For that completion and perfection, they must be understood in reference to humanity's completion and perfection, which is life in union with God, a very participation in God's divine being. This chapter on grace has sought to explain how that is possible. "Thanks be to God through Jesus Christ our Lord" (Rom. 7:25).

Study Questions

1. Define grace. How does it complete reflection on the persistent theme in this book that for Christians, Christ is not simply a great moral teacher?

2. Who is at work when we receive grace? Are humans free when we are given grace?

3. In what ways is living life in Christ hard? In what ways it is easy?

4. Does God call us to be perfect? Explain.

5. State three things that are true about the Christian understanding of God's grace. Give an example of each from the story of Augustine's conversion.

6. In what different ways may virtues be obtained? Give an example of each way.

7. Define infused cardinal virtue and give an example of one. Give three reasons why Christians like Thomas Aquinas have found this category of virtue so important.

Terms to Know

grace, infused virtue, acquired virtue, infused cardinal virtue, grace perfects nature

Questions for Further Reflection

1. How might you respond to a skeptic who thinks that all evidence Christians offer for the reality of grace can easily be otherwise explained?
2. What difference does it make whether you hold a freedom for excellence vs. freedom-of-indifference view of freedom when describing whether someone who receives grace is free or not?
3. When Augustine converts, he is assisted by a vision from Lady Continence. We know what this means from chapter 4; Augustine is given help to contain, or not act upon, his wayward sexual desires. We also know from chapter 4 that continence is good, but is not complete virtue (which would be temperance, or chastity). Should it concern us that God gives Augustine only continence and not, say, a vision from Lady Temperance? What does this say about the grace that God gives? Is it deficient?
4. Why is it important that there is not only one way to obtain virtue? What realities are Christians trying to recognize in saying there are different ways?
5. Can Christians who live in Christ ever have and act out of acquired cardinal virtues? Explain.

Further Reading

Once again it should be clear how formative C. S. Lewis's *Mere Christianity* has been on this discussion of grace, though also once again he is simply stating with typical lucidly the crux of the Christian tradition on this topic. See also the *Catechism of the Catholic Church*, 1965–2011, and 1803–45. A far more in-depth and enormously influential presentation of (the new law and) grace may be found in Aquinas's *Summa Theologiae* I–II 106–14. Augustine's *Confessions* is a must-read in general, and it certainly deserves a reading in conjunction with this chapter. The basis of the argument on the infused cardinal virtues is a close reading of Aquinas's thought on virtue and grace, especially *Summa Theologiae* I–II 55, 63.

17

CHASTITY AND NONMARITAL SEX

Test Case Three

In chapter 5 an example was given of a person thinking about becoming sexually active with her boyfriend. She has well-intentioned reasons to become more sexually involved. She cares for him deeply and wants to physically express her love for him. She also has well-intentioned hesitations about doing so. She knows it will have a huge impact on their relationship, and is not sure how exactly their relationship will handle it, or indeed what their long-term plans together are.

This person is reflecting on how to live out her sex life most virtuously. What does sex mean? Is their relationship ready for it, and what features of a relationship make sex an appropriate activity? The focus on this chapter is how to be virtuous—that is, how to live in a truly fulfilling manner—with regard to sexuality. Writing a chapter on virtuous sex is an enormous task. Reminiscent of the other test-case chapters in this book, there are far too many facts and considerations to address in one chapter. In order to limit its scope, this chapter focuses on one specific question and explores the bigger topic of virtuous sexuality as it concerns this one particular question. The central goal of this chapter is to examine the question of when having sexual intercourse is virtuous and, in particular, whether sex can only be virtuous when a couple is married.

The first section addresses three preliminary questions. First, is this a question that only makes sense for Christians? Second, shouldn't we heed the words of Jesus and "judge not" on delicate questions such as this? And third, what is the basic gist of the traditional position that having sexual intercourse is only virtuous for a couple who are married? All of these questions are important in framing the tone and content of the next section.

That section addresses two crucial topics when answering the question of whether sex is only virtuous in marriage. This section is the fruit of listening to students debate this question for years. They consistently focus their discussions on two questions. First, does sex have any inherent point, or meaning? Clearly, people have sex for some reason. But does the sort of action sexual intercourse is communicate something to one's partner, or does sex simply communicate whatever one wants it to communicate? The second half of section two then explores marriage. Even if one grants that sex means exclusive, permanent love that is open to new life, need one be married to have a relationship marked by these characteristics? Why does a couple need a piece of paper (i.e., a marriage license) to prove this about their relationship?

The Relationship between Sex and Marriage: Preliminary Questions

The real goal of this chapter is to enter into, and take a position on, the debate over whether sex can only be virtuous in a married relationship. That is the task for the next section. But in order to do that well, some preliminary questions must be addressed. First, for what audience does this debate make sense? The first part below argues that this discussion is important not only for Christians, but for all people. Second, what is the tone and ultimate purpose of this debate? The second part explains the difference between making judgments and being judgmental, so as to avoid the latter and seek instead to try to lovingly guide ourselves and others to live most happily. Third, in this day and age, is the view that sex is only for marriage for real? The third part presents a succinct summary of the position that sex can only be virtuous within marriage, so this view is seen as (at least potentially) reasonable, rather than some leftover rule from the olden days. Having treated these three preliminary questions, the reader will be prepared to engage the arguments of section two in depth.

Is Reserving Sex for Marriage (and Even Asking That Question) Only for Christians?

Chastity, and in particular the relationship between sex and marriage, is the first issue explored in this book after the cardinal and theological virtues. Therefore, this is an appropriate place to pause and examine whether: a) this question only makes sense in a Christian context, and b) the answer that virtuous sex belongs only in marriage makes sense only for Christians. The short answer to both questions is no. Sex is an innerworldly activity. Thus, being a sexual person in a good manner (which is what chastity means) is a matter of the cardinal virtues (especially temperance, under which chastity falls). Since the innerworldly activities governed by the cardinal virtues can in principle be figured out, and done well by unaided human reasoning (natural law reasoning), one need not be Christian to be chaste. That said, the Christian person can draw on additional resources to better understand chastity, and has the further assistance of grace in living it out. So sex is a perfect example of how an innerworldly activity that is accessible to natural law reasoning is more perfectly understood in the larger context of Christian big-picture beliefs about the way things are.

Despite the old-fashioned, or even repressive, connotation of the term for some people, *chastity* simply means the virtue of using our sexuality well in our thoughts, desires, and deeds.[1] *Lust* is the opposite of chastity; it is the vice of using our sexuality poorly in our thoughts, desires, and deeds. Though these words have heavy religious overtones (in no small part due to an obsession of some religious people with all things sexual), in reality every human person must determine, either explicitly or implicitly, how to live out his or her sexuality well.

Recall our discussion of rules in the first half of this book. Rules, in the most general sense, are principles that guide our actions (whether well or poorly). One person's rule may be, "have sex whenever and with whomever you want!" Besides the fact that such a person likely does have some restrictions to this rule (e.g., sex must be consensual), note that any rule implies that someone not living according to that rule is not living well. Similarly, many think that deciding when to have sex is a strictly personal question, that it simply up to those involved. Wait until marriage, or do not—that is the couple's choice. But note that even this view is a position, that the only thing that dictates when it is good for a couple to have sex is when they both choose to do so. Both of these views are also moralities, and have guidelines for exercising one's sexuality well or poorly.

So everyone has some vision of how to use their sexuality well or poorly, with rules that guide how one lives that vision out. But the question for this part is not whether sex is an innerworldly activity, but whether the rule "no sex outside marriage" is a rule that people who are not Christian could and do come up with. The answer is clearly yes to the former, and even yes to the

1. Some people are thrown off by the phrasing, "use one's sexuality," as if it implies our sexuality is separate from ourselves, like some tool that may be picked up or put down. That is not intended here. The term is meant to remind us of the claim in chapter 15 about how the way we do certain things (in this case have sex) is shaped by our larger goals in life (in this case charity as love of God). It could equally be said that chastity is being a sexual person well and lust is being a sexual person poorly.

latter. Determining which peoples across times and cultures endorsed this view of chastity is a task for the historian and cultural anthropologist. It is certainly not claimed here that people have always lived out this rule. Nor is it even claimed that *all* peoples have endorsed, let alone lived out, this rule.[2] But this rule has not only been endorsed by Christians. It can be found in people of other religious commitments. It can even be found in contemporary American secular parlance, as evidenced by the recent ad campaign enjoining teens to wait to have sex, with the phrase, "I can wait! I'm worth it!" The presence of commonality between Christians and non-Christians on moral rules concerning innerworldly activities should come as no surprise; as accessible to unaided human reasoning, these activities and the principles that guide how they are done well do not depend on Christian revelation. Once again, the claim here is not that all, or even most, people hold this rule regarding sex. It is simply that both Christians and non-Christians alike have and do hold such a rule to be the path to a happy life.

That said, Christian beliefs do augment, support, and extend the rationale behind the claim that sex belongs in marriage. Most of the debate over sex and marriage below proceeds along natural-law grounds. But that is not to say that distinctively Christian claims are irrelevant for how to live out a virtuous sex life. As explained in chapter 10, the Irish bishops helpfully sum up the entire Christian story with one word: love.[3] The drama of God's love can be seen to play out in the three movements of salvation history: creation, sin, and redemption. Chapter 10 explained the ways that these big- picture beliefs concretely influence how people who hold these beliefs live out their sex lives.

Christian morality, or life in Christ, is simply living in a manner reflective of this story of the way things truly are. Therefore, Christian sexual ethics should not be some arbitrary, externally imposed, repressive set of rules about what not to do. Sadly, Christians share some blame for presenting Christian teaching on sexuality in such a manner. But Christian sexual ethics should be presented and understood as a guide on how to live in accordance with this story of God's love, as it concerns our sex lives. As the Irish bishops beautifully put it, "The Church's whole moral teaching about sex is above all the application to sexuality of God's greatest commandment to charity."[4]

As explained in chapter 10, big-picture beliefs do indeed matter for how we do innerworldly activities like sex. Remembering this can help us sort through the different levels of disagreement that may arise among people discussing

2. A fine example of a very principled and thought-out endorsement of what Christians would see as lust can be found in the Epicurean thinker Lucretius, who advises his readers, by all means, to discharge one's sexual needs as needed but never to make the mistake of falling in love, which is a clear impediment to living the good life! See chapter 10.

3. See Irish Catholic Bishop's Conference, *Love is for Life* (Pastoral Letter, 1985), 15–24. See also Pope Benedict XVI's *Deus Caritas Est* (Encyclical Letter, 2005).

4. Irish bishops, *Love is for Life*, 24.

sexual ethics. One way someone can disagree with, say, the Catholic Church's stance on sex is to contest some or all features of the above story. Such a person might say: "I don't think love is why we are here and how we should live;" or, "There is no such thing as sin in the Christian sense, since it's all good, and people are just growing and learning no matter what they do;" or, "Jesus Christ is not the Son of God, and hence does not offer us grace to help live as sons and daughters of God." Such a person would offer rival big-picture belief commitments. Since these commitments shape how people live virtuously with regard to innerworldly activities, different practical rules regarding sex may result. This is exactly what we saw with Lucretius in chapter 10. Disagreement at this level is not addressed in this chapter.

But disagreement can also arise on a more immediate level when discussing an innerworldly activity such as sex. For instance, someone could agree with the Christian story as presented in the previous paragraphs and think that sex under certain conditions before marriage is living in accordance with that story. Thus Catholics, for instance, may disagree with each other on an issue such as nonmarital sex. This does not, of course, mean that both sides are right. But it does mean that differences on this level will concern not primarily big-picture claims, but rather the meaning of innerworldly activities such as sex and marriage. In fact, two people who disagree on the level of big-picture questions could also conceivably disagree on the meaning of an activity such as sex. That disagreement could be importantly shaped by the different big-picture beliefs, but not reduced totally to differences at that level.

Thus, there are different sources of disagreement on particular moral rules regarding sex: differences in big-picture beliefs that shape how the innerworldly activity of sex is understood, and different understandings of what innerworldly activities like sex and marriage mean, even if there is agreement over those big-picture beliefs. It is the latter sort of disagreement—that is, on the meanings of sex and marriage—that is examined in this chapter.

A Word on Judgment, Blame, and Sin

A second topic must be addressed to set the tone for the second section's argument about whether sex can be virtuous outside of marriage. The purpose here is to say a few words about the point of this inquiry or, more accurately, what is not the point of this inquiry. Many authors who write on the relationship between sex and marriage—and certainly many college students who learn about this topic—are rightly concerned about judgmentalism. Often to a fault, young adults today so frequently refuse to label others' behavior wrong, so as not to judge others. The kernel of truth in this tendency is a refusal to participate when certain (often religious) people use moral issues (often sexual ones) as a way to denounce other people and/or exalt themselves. Surely this is what Jesus was targeting when he counseled his followers, "judge not lest you be judged" (Matt. 7:1).

Yet it is just as sure that what Jesus is not condemning is recognizing faults in ourselves and others. The whole point of the Sermon on the Mount, for instance, is to explain how to live in accordance with the kingdom of God, and doing so entails recognizing, especially in ourselves, what actions run counter to that kingdom. In fact, Jesus gives explicit instruction on how to confront a peer whose behavior is damaging herself and the community (Matt. 18:15–17). Thus, judging in the sense of making distinctions about what is good and bad behavior is clearly not what Jesus denounces. Yet being judgmental, in the sense of using such discussion as a way to demean others or exalt one's self, is surely what must be avoided, according to Jesus.[5]

Thus, the tone of what follows is meant to be one of loving *judgment*, but not *judgmentalism*. As the use of the word "loving" in the previous sentence indicates, judgment is compatible with loving the person judged, whether one's self or another. Judgmentalism is not compatible with love. A good stance to adopt in this difficult discussion is this: how would you address this topic with your teenage child or sibling who sought guidance from you on when to have sex? What lines would you offer him as to when to know the time is right? Only by refusing to offer any response would you avoid making judgments, and that would surely not be in the teenager's best interest as he seeks guidance. Presumably you would tell him what you think is in his genuine best interest, and encourage him to act accordingly. That would be making a judgment, because you want what it best for him. You would hopefully avoid being judgmental, that is, lording it over him or condemning him if he fails. That is the tone of this discussion. We are seeking rules that are not externally imposed obligations, but true guides to a genuinely happy life. Thus, the most loving thing we can do for others and ourselves on challenging questions such as these is to humbly strive to speak the truth rather than tell people what they want to hear, since the truth is what is genuinely best for people.

It should also be noted that the point of the following discussion is not to blame people who do not live in accordance with the best rules. The point is to determine what rules best guide decisions on when to have sex. Of course, that discussion is related to assignment of blame, since if someone deliberately turns away from those rules they are choosing against "right reason, truth, and conscience," which is sin. But assignment of blame to particular persons is a separate, although related, issue. Assignment of blame requires ascertaining what an individual person knew and could have known about

5. Perhaps the finest example of this judgment vs. judgmentalism distinction is the famous story of Christ and the woman caught in adultery (John 8:1). Christ does not refuse to label her behavior sinful. Indeed, the story ends by his saying, "Go and sin no more." Yet Jesus's primary concern in that story is to stop the woman's peers from self-righteously (in that they failed to recall their own sin) denouncing her, rather than lovingly correcting her, as Jesus himself does.

the best way to live. What societal influences have shaped the person? (Recall the importance of formation of conscience.) If someone genuinely believes she is acting well, even though she is not (erroneous conscience), could she have known otherwise (vincible ignorance) or not (invincible ignorance)? As the Irish bishops note, people can feel as if they are acting in a holy and loving manner but actually be wrong and harming themselves and others.[6] If that is the case, it does not necessarily mean the person is without blame. As we know from an earlier discussion, meaning well is not enough; prudence is required to live well. Nonetheless, the assignment of blame is a discussion distinct from what follows.

As a final observation on the tone of this chapter, it should be noted that taking what one believes to be the right stand on this issue does not mean one has always lived up to it. People who hold certain beliefs are often called hypocrites if they fail to live up to them. But that does not necessarily mean they are. Hypocrites are people who claim to believe it is best to live in a certain way, and yet reveal they do not truly believe in that way, since they do not even try to live that way themselves. This is different from truly believing it is best to live a certain way and indeed trying to live it out, but failing at times.

To recall the teenager analogy, hopefully you would teach your child it is best not to talk behind people's backs. Sadly, this does not mean you have always heeded this rule. But you believe it is the best way to live, and you have been disappointed in yourself when you have not lived it out. In this case you are not a hypocrite for teaching this rule. The same is true of sex. If you teach your sibling or child about how to best live sexuality—be chaste— you may not have always lived out what you teach. In fact, sexuality is such a challenging facet of our lives that I would suggest no one is without sin in this area—in thought, desire, or deed. But you are not a hypocrite to teach that, unless you do not really think it the best way to live. Otherwise, we would just have to tell our siblings or children to do whatever they want, because no one is perfect. The point here is that truly loving ourselves and others means wanting our or their true happiness. To help ourselves and others achieve that in the area of sexuality, we must speak the truth lovingly and humbly, always seeking the best way to live, while compassionately recognizing that we and others do fail.

The Relationship between Sex and Marriage

The first two parts of this section have helped set the audience (not just Christian) and tone (humble and loving judgment but not judgmentalism) for the next section's argument on sex and marriage. Before entering into that

6. Irish bishops, *Love is for Life*, 15. See also 74–76, for more on judging vs. judgmentalism.

argument, it is important to succinctly state the rationale of the position that sex is fully virtuous only within marriage. Why? Given the prevalence of sexual intercourse outside marriage in our society, the reasons for following that path are readily available to us. But too often the view that sex is only virtuous within marriage is presented without any adequate explanation of why it is more than some taboo, or residue of the olden days. Is there any reasoning behind this norm? There most certainly is. The task now is to explain that reasoning in preparation for the second section of this chapter, which will explore in more depth the challenges to this reasoning.

What constitutes living out one's sex life chastely, or virtuously? Besides a question of temperance, this is also a question of prudence, since we are seeking to see clearly an innerworldly activity (sex) so as to act virtuously. What norms guide virtuous sex? There are plenty of norms, and many of them are up to individual couples. For instance, different couples may have sex with different frequencies, and go about it in different ways. There are some norms that are absolute in that they apply to all, and their violation always constitutes bad use of sexuality. These are assumed rather than argued here. For instance, lack of consent is incompatible with chastity. Having sex with someone who is married to someone else is incompatible with chastity. There are many rules, or norms, that govern virtuous sex, some absolute and some not. Our more specific question is whether or not having sex with someone without being married to that person is ever virtuous.

Answering this question requires some explanation of what sex means, and what marriage means. These are the two issues that are addressed in more detail in section two. It should be noted now that the traditional norm against sex outside of marriage is not arbitrary as if marriage were some license that enables one to have sex guilt-free. First of all, being married is not the only requirement for virtuous sex. In other words, in the traditional view it is a necessary, but not sufficient condition, for virtuous sex. There are plenty of ways to be lustful while married, even regarding sex with one's spouse. Second, the reason why marriage has long been regarded as a necessary (even if not sufficient) condition for virtuous sex is because both activities—being married and having sex—have been understood to have the same meaning or purpose. In the Christian tradition, marriage is understood by its three goods: fidelity (i.e., exclusivity), permanence, and openness to new life. Even civil marriage is a pledge to remain with one person indefinitely, in a relationship that has long been associated with bearing children.

What does this have to do with sex? Sex is the sort of activity that binds people together (exclusively and over time) and leads to children. This is why Christians and many non-Christians alike have traditionally and today claimed that marriage is the best home, or place, for sex. The *Catechism of the Catholic Church* speaks of a twofold rule to guide sexual intercourse: it must be *procreative* and *unitive*.[7] Since this is what sex as an activity means, people do it virtuously when they do it for these reasons. Sex is procreative when the couple is open to new life, understood not only as being willing to have a child that comes from their sexual union, but also being committed to caring for and raising the child well.[8] Sex is unitive (= unifying) when the couple has committed themselves permanently and exclusively to each other. When these things are true of a relationship, sex is not simply allowed or permitted; it is an appropriate, beautiful, and effective way to live out that relationship. This is why sex and marriage belong together.

Sex before a couple is married is by definition not fully unitive. The man and woman have not committed themselves publicly to stay with each other (and no one else) permanently. In fact, sex before marriage is not even properly procreative. How can this be if a couple is open to having a child that may be conceived from their sexual union? Since the procreative aspect of sex is only fully respected when a couple is open to having and raising the child well, and since marriage is the best environment in which to raise a child, then having sex before marriage also defies the procreative facet of sex.

Some nuances to this basic position must be addressed. First, note that though the claim here is that sex can only be virtuous in marriage, the claim is not that all extramarital sex is equally vicious. Obviously there is an enormous difference between an engaged couple having sex before their wedding, and a casual one-night stand. There is a huge difference between violent sex, and sex between young adults who do love each other but are not ready to commit themselves to each other permanently. But that is not the question here. The question for this chapter is: what is the line a relationship must cross for sex to be virtuous? In other words, what set of conditions should hold true of a relationship in order for the couple to have virtuous sex; and, more specifically, is being married always one of those conditions? Non-married couples may be close to, or far from, that set of conditions. And even people who are married may fail to meet the set of conditions that makes sex virtuous. But the answer offered here is that certain conditions are inherently absent from a non-married relationship that make it best for the couple not to have sex.

Second, saying that marriage is the best relationship to have children is not the same as saying children cannot be raised well by divorced, single, or widowed parents. Thankfully, thriving children have come from all these

7. *Catechism of the Catholic Church*. 2nd ed. (Vatican City: Libreria Editrice Vaticana, 1997), 2363.

8. Note that there are biological reasons, some temporary and some permanent, that may prevent the actual conception of a child. That is why the criterion is "open to new life" rather than having given birth to new life. It is possible to be open to new life but (often sadly) never have a child. What is prohibited by this norm is having sex and at the same time making it infertile. This raises the contested issue of contraception, a related topic but beyond the scope of this chapter.

environments, as they have from broken or abusive households where the parents are married. But recognizing this does not mean that these factors make no difference in how children are raised. All have negative influence on how children are raised, and therefore should not be sought. All of course happen, and when they do we hope (and thankfully have seen) that good can come out of them. But again this is different than purposely acting in a manner that leads to these situations.

This brief overview suffices to present the crux of the argument why sex and marriage belong together. It should go without saying that people often do not live this out. But that is not the focus of this chapter. The focus of this chapter is determining how people who strive to live most fully, most happily, therefore should want to live out their sex lives. According to the position presented thus far, we should want to have sex in, and only in, marriage since the meaning of sexuality corresponds with the meaning of marriage, and thus sex is a beautiful and fitting expression of a marriage relationship. We now turn to address not those who see this as the best way to live and sometimes fail, but rather those who claim this is not the ideal way to live out one's sexuality.

Debating the Possibility of Virtuous Sex Outside of Marriage

The crux of the position on why sexual intercourse is only virtuous in a married relationship relies upon the claim that having sex and being married are human things to do that have corresponding meanings. Thus it makes sense that they belong together. Unsurprisingly then, when people contest this position, the two most common counterarguments are that: a) sex does not have this meaning; and/or, b) marriage does not have this meaning (or at least marriage is not the only relationship that has this meaning). Therefore these counterarguments will be used to structure this second section of the chapter on the debate over the possibility of virtuous sex outside of marriage. The first part addresses the question of what sex means. If sexual intercourse does not, or at least need not always, signify love that is exclusive, permanent, and open to new life, then it could be at home in non-married relationships too. The second part addresses the claim that even if sex does have this meaning, marriage is not the only relationship that truly is exclusive, permanent, and open to new life. To these issues we now turn.

The Purpose, or Meaning, of Sex

What is the point of having sex? In other words, does sex have any meaning or purpose? If so, what is it? What determines the meaning of sex, something about the action itself, or simply whatever the couple wants it to express? And need sex always have the same meaning, or purpose? These are the questions for this first part of this section.

What Does It Mean to Say Sex "Means" Something?

Before examining the important question of what sex means, we must first pause to explain the meaning of the phrase, "what sex means." To say that an activity "means" something is to say that there is a point, or purpose, to the activity. How to determine the point of sex? Rather than start with some abstract discussion of the nature of sexual intercourse, we begin here with the simple observation that our practices—the way we do activities—reveal what we think those activities mean. By examining when people do and do not have sex, we can better specify what that particular action means. Of course, there is not one consistent way people do and do not have sex. But there is significant commonality. By starting there, we can identify the general purpose of sex from common practices, and then use what we find to evaluate differences to see if the different ways all serve that purpose, or if some practices actually defy the general purpose of sex.

Consider an uncontroversial example first. What does a simple sign like a handshake mean? People shake hands when they are entering into, or sustaining, some sort of relationship. It is an embodied sign of peace and goodwill. It may accompany an introduction to a friend's friend, or the closing of a business deal. It may signify affection and friendship for an old friend or acquaintance. Looking at when and how we shake hands with people reveals what that action means. There are certain situations where a handshake would be inappropriate. If you shook your mother's hand after a long absence, she would likely think something amiss! If you offered your hand to someone while still arguing with them about some offense they committed, they would likely think it odd. The gesture would not fit these occasions because of its meaning. Of course, cultural and social factors are very important in specifying the meanings of such bodily acts. But even granting significant cultural variation, there are some boundaries to those variations. In no culture is a punch in the face a sign of friendship and goodwill! Nowhere is sexual intercourse a commonly practiced way of introducing yourself to a new person.

The meaning, or point, of an action is an important way to determine if some gesture is fitting for an occasion. This is a way of looking at the object of the action, to use terminology from chapter 2. But looking at the object of the action alone is not adequate. We must also examine the agent's intention in performing the action. For instance, a handshake may be an appropriate way to close a business deal. But if we learn that one of the partners was actually cheating the other, we would call not just the deal, but also the handshake deceptive. Though there is nothing wrong with the object or meaning of a handshake, that meaning was not intended by the agent. Thus, there was a disconnect between the purpose of the act and the agent's intention. We would call such a person deceptive, and say their act (the handshake) was a lie in some sense, since the person's intention did not match the meaning of the gesture. In all this we would have to attend to the relevant circumstances.

Therefore, when asking what sex means, we are seeking to determine the point or purpose of sex, in order to help us determine in which situations it is appropriate so that we can perform this symbolic act when we mean what it stands for. Note that it is granted here that sex means something, or has some point. If there were no meaning whatsoever to sex, then we would be unconcerned when we had it and with whom, since sex would be pointless, or literally mean nothing. That is obviously not the case, even if there is significant disagreement about what sex means. For instance, if sex literally meant nothing, we could not say it was inappropriate between certain persons (family members, a married person and their lover, doctors and patients, etc.). Thankfully, there are certain situations that are basically unanimously understood as inappropriate venues for sex. To use a more accessible example, if your longtime boyfriend or girlfriend told you they had sex with someone else, it would be nonsensical to be upset about it if sex had no point or meaning. You would have to respond as if they simply held the door for someone, or did some other simple gesture, since it would not mean anything. (In fact, even these gestures have some point.) Clearly, that is not the case, nor would it be the case even if you were told that they did not intend it to mean anything. You would likely reply that even if they intended it to mean nothing, it still did mean something! What is contested is not whether sex has meaning, but which meaning it has.

It is also granted here that sexual intercourse is an expression of love in romantic relationships. There is an important place for cultural studies here, since it has not always and everywhere been the case that the appropriate venue for sex is a romantic relationship of the sort we understand in our own society.[9] Nonetheless, given the scope of this chapter, that investigation will not be done here. Furthermore, the fact that romantic love need not be present in order for there to be virtuous sex (in, say, arranged marriages) does not defeat the following argument about the meaning of sex. The more common question today is at what stage in a romantic relationship is sexual intercourse appropriate. To that question we now turn.

What Does Sex Mean?

So, granting that sex has a meaning and that it has to do with love, what exactly does sex mean? After all, saying sex means "I love you" is not enough. There are plenty of people in our lives whom we love, but with whom we do not have sex (family, friends, mentors, etc.). If sex simply meant I love you, we would have sex with these people. So we have sex not just to say I love you, but to say, "I love you in a certain way," a way that is not true of other people

9. See Lawrence Stone, "Passionate Attachments in the West in Historical Perspective," in *Wing to Wing, Oar to Oar* ed. Amy Kass and Leon Kass (Notre Dame, IN: University of Notre Dame Press, 2000), 38–44. Dame Press, 2000).

whom we also truly love. What types of love does sex express? Even saying that sex means I love you in a romantic way is not enough. What should characterize a romantic relationship where people are having sex? Need there be feelings of romantic love? If feelings of love are needed, do they alone suffice to make sex appropriate? If so, can I have sex with several different people with whom I have such feelings, or have sex with someone I just met that I have a crush on? Our answers to these questions help reveal what we think the meaning of sex is.

In a beautiful description of the meaning of sex, the Irish bishops claim:

> Sexual union says, "I love you", in a very profound way. By sexual union, a man and woman say to each other: "I love you. There is nobody else in all the world I love in the way I love you. I love you just for being you. I want you to become even more wonderful than you are. I want to share my life and my world with you. I want you to share your life and your world with me. I want us to build a new life together, a future together, which will be our future. I need you. I can't live without you. I need you to love me, and to love me not just now but always. I will be faithful to you not just now but always. I will never let you down or walk out on you. I will never put anyone else in place of you. I will stay with you through thick and through thin. I will be responsible for you and I want you to be responsible for me, for us, no matter what happens.[10]

Much of what they claim sex means in this powerful passage is not distinctive to sex. For instance, there are, hopefully, many people in our lives to whom we could say, "I want to share my life and my world with you. I want you to share your life and your world with me." Or, "I love you for just being you." Presumably we could say these things to a friend or family member. But much of what is said here concerns a very particular type of relationship, namely marriage. Several phrases describe faithful exclusivity, such as, "there is nobody else in all the world I love in the way I love you." Even more describe permanence: "I need you to love me, and to love me not just now but always," and, "I will stay with you through thick and thin," and, "I will be faithful to you not just now but always."

In summary, the Irish bishops claim that sex is an embodied form of communication that has an inherent meaning, and that meaning is exclusive and permanent love.[11] It speaks exclusive and permanent love, regardless of whether or not those having sex are intending to say that when they have sex. Due to this meaning, therefore, sex is only appropriate in a relationship where a couple can and has stated just that. They need not be saying it or even thinking of it while having sex, of course! But it must be true of their relationship in order for sex to be an honest act. If it is, then sex is a beautiful, pleasurable, and

---

10. Irish bishops, *Love is For Life*, 9.
11. Another crucial facet of the meaning of sex is described below.

powerful expression of, and further nourishment of, such love. If it is not, the Irish bishops claim that sex is a lie. Two people are saying something with their bodies that they do not intend.

Obviously, the heart of this argument lies in the claim that the point of sex is permanent, faithful love. In order to contextualize the Irish bishops' claim, consider some alternatives. Imagine a graph charting the ascending levels of a relationship, if you will. It starts at two people just meeting and having feelings, or falling for each other. Next, perhaps, comes an expectation that they will see each other again in coming days, weeks, or months. Then comes an expectation of exclusivity. In other words, at some point in the relationship, each expects the other is not seeing someone else, and would rightly feel betrayed if that were the case. Then perhaps things get more serious, such that there is not only exclusivity, but even openness to and discussion of future plans together. At this stage the relationship is at least a factor in decisions of whether to move, what job to take, and so on. This is seen especially in couples where at least one person is going off to or graduating from college, considering a career change, or relocating. At some point there may come an explicit hope, and even expectation, that the two will stay together permanently, often in marriage. If marriage is indeed the goal, then a period of engagement generally precedes the marriage itself.

In this tidy little graph of ascending levels of commitment, three things should be noted. First, the relationship can stop at any one of these and end, or go no further. Second, you could add in, combine, or eliminate any particular stage. The point here is not a precise delineation of how exactly relationships develop. It is simply to specify and imagine where sex enters into the picture. Third, living together is not given as a stage since it can become part of the relationship at nearly any of the above stages.

Our question is, at what stage is sex an appropriate way to express such a relationship? Answering this question reveals what one thinks sex means. If you think sex is appropriate once there is exclusivity, you are simultaneously saying that sex conveys an "I love you" that is exclusive romantic love, and that one should not have sex before that is the case. If you think only those couples who are married should have sex, you are saying that sex means an I love you that is not only exclusive but vowed to be permanent, and open to new life. You are also saying couples who are not in such a married relationship should not have sex.

Clearly there are different people who live out the view that sex is appropriate at each of the spots on this spectrum. So it is tempting to say that sex can mean whatever we want it to mean. For some it's a simply recreational pleasure. For others it's an expression of exclusive self-giving love. For others it's an expression of exclusive self-giving love that is permanent and open to new life. No one can doubt that different people live in these different ways. The question is, does sex have any inherent meaning, such that we might tell someone the relationship they are in is not an appropriate venue for sex because they do not intend to say what sex means?

This is the place people of religious traditions like Christianity commonly cite some authority specific to their tradition and say things like, "the Bible says not to fornicate!" Or, "Genesis 2:24 makes it clear in its claim that the 'two become one flesh' that this is meant to happen in marriage." This is all well and good, and Christian revelation does indeed offer additional resources to enable Christians to better understand innerworldly activities like sex.[12] But since it is an innerworldly activity, we can trust that the reasoning behind these revealed norms can indeed be understood by us using our reason, even if it may be difficult and we do not all see it the same way. So why do the Irish bishops claim sex has the meaning it does, which makes it appropriate and honest only in marriage? What do we know about sex that makes this claim credible? Two answers are offered here.

First, sex is a powerful bodily act that bonds people together physically and emotionally. Sex is pleasurable, but it is more than that. Two people are literally joined in their bodies. Naked and vulnerable, clumsy and awkward, longing and longed for, two people unite bodily in a manner that is more powerful and intimate than other important forms of bodily communication we employ (smiles, handshakes, kisses, etc.) It is not just a sign of love that is already there, although it is that too. It also helps further ingrain that love through its intimacy. Sex works in bonding people together.

There is much evidence for the meaning of sex as powerfully bonding. Scientists describe hormonal changes that sex brings about in partners. But perhaps the most common evidence is the difference sex makes in how partners view each other, and how others view the couple. We assume that a couple who has had sex shares some intimacy that is different than other friendships and intimacies. Friends of each person in the couple generally view that friend's partner as unavailable romantically, somehow connected to their friend in a way that means they are now off-limits. Sex also leads the partners to view one another differently. A bond is established, and even two people who have "hooked up" and had casual sex generally feel awkward if they see each again soon afterward. A bodily connection was made that was disproportionate to their relationship, or lack thereof, on other levels (emotional, mental, spiritual, etc.) It is also why we can tell a partner that we do not intend to get serious despite having sex, and perhaps he or she will agree; yet someone still gets

12. Many Catholic people have found an approach to sexuality called "theology of the body" to be a compelling account of sexuality in the context of faith and discipleship. The theology of the body was explicitly articulated primarily by Pope John Paul II. See his rather dense *Man and Woman He Created Them: A Theology of the Body*, trans. Michale Waldstein (Boston: Pauline Books and Media, 2006). There are also numerous popular portrayals of John Paul's thought, done with varying degrees of accuracy. One particularly popular example is Christopher West's *The Good News about Sex and Marriage* (Ann Arbor, MI: Servant Publications, 2004). Though nearly all contain much that is helpful, no one popular presentation is endorsed here in its totality.

hurt in that scenario, since despite what we say with our words, what we are saying with our bodies is importantly different.

One can immediately object here that this is clearly not the case for some people who have sex casually without a care in the world, who do not seem to be bonded to their partners, or who do not feel awkward after sexual encounters without a proportionate relationship. Granted, there are people like this. But concluding that sex therefore has no inherent bonding meaning is much like saying that we cannot specify what amount of alcohol is virtuous due to the example of alcoholics, who drink too much. Amazingly, even with things like food and drink that are more clearly limited by health concerns, human persons manage to warp themselves, to form bad habits, so as to become persons who are used to all sorts of activities that are actually bad for them. Surely the same can be true of sex.

All of this anecdotal evidence suggests that sex works in bonding people together, even in situations where that does not seem to be the intent. Granted, this is not a knock-down argument proving definitively that sex means exclusive permanent love. Here is a good example of how the meaning of even innerworldly activities may not be uncontested among us even though they are innerworldly (i.e., matters of natural law). But though not demonstrable, the case for the meaning of sex as permanent and exclusive is most persuasive. Loving couples can indeed have sex and bond together even if they do not intend to say they are permanent and exclusive. But in doing so, they use a powerfully intimate form of communication to speak a love that may be strong and genuine, but not fully committed in its exclusivity and permanence. In doing so, they rob sex of its capacity to signify and further nourish a relationship that is truly fully committed. Though sex works, and powerfully bonds people to signify and nourish their faithful permanence, it is only fully effective in its meaning when that is the intention of those who have sex. When it is not, people who have sex outside such a relationship not only lie by speaking with their bodies that which they do not intend; they also dissipate the power of their sexuality and settle for sexual expression that may be genuine and loving, but is simply not all it is capable of being.

Thus far the claim has been that sex has what the Christian tradition has called a *unitive*, or unifying, meaning. It signifies and sustains faithful, permanent relationships. But the second thing that sex means has been neglected so far. Yes, sex seems to bond people together. But if there is one thing that sex does for sure, it is to engender children. Sex is a way to have kids, and is the reason why each of us is here.[13] This is called the *procreative* meaning of sex. The Irish bishops describe it this way:

13. Note that the first children conceived not as a result of intercourse, but through in vitro fertilization, are now young adults. Though this claim is not true of them, it is nonetheless still the case that sex leads to children.

Sexual union speaks of a man's willingness or readiness to "give" a child to a woman as hers, and of a woman's readiness to bear or "have" a child "with him." It speaks of a man and a woman's readiness to openness to share their being in a child which will be "their child," the expression of their love, the bond of their shared life. It speaks of a man's and a woman's desire to "begin a new life together," both in the form of their child and in the form of their shared life around that child.[14]

Again, a couple need not verbally or even consciously have this intention while having sex. But in having sex they are engaging in an act that has this meaning, whether they intend that meaning or not (hence the expression, unintended pregnancy). The Irish bishops eloquently state the Christian tradition's consistent affirmation that sex has a procreative meaning, an affirmation that one clearly need not be Christian to recognize.[15]

Two observations are fitting here concerning the procreative and unitive meanings of sex. First, the Irish bishops go on to describe the interconnectedness of these two meanings of sexual intercourse.

The two meanings of sexual union blend into each other. An act of sexual union which truly and honestly expresses total and life-long and exclusive union between a man and woman is also an act which is open to new life in a child. If the act is deliberately prevented from being open to new life, this can only be by the introduction of some barrier or separation into the life-giving act. But deliberately to introduce separation into an act which intends and says total union is a failure in truth.[16]

Though the Irish bishops emphasize that sexual intercourse which is not open to new life is therefore also not fully unifying, it could also be said that sexual intercourse that is not an expression of faithful permanence is also not fully procreative. This leads to the second observation. The procreative meaning of sex is not simply openness to having a child that is conceived from sex. It is a willingness to care for and raise that child. Justice to the child, and justice to a wider society that is clearly impacted by unintended pregnancy, dictates that having a child occur in relationship where people are committed to care for that child together. As noted earlier in this chapter, sometimes this does not

14. Irish bishops, *Love is For Life*, 11.

15. Of course, given the prevalence and effectiveness today of contraception, a couple can try to prevent sex from being a procreative act, often successfully. But even this separation of procreativity from acts of sexual intercourse seems to acknowledge that inherent meaning of sex. Though this is an obvious occasion to explore the contested issue of the morality of contraception, the scope of this chapter precludes that discussion here. As for the claim that the procreative nature of sex is a consistent claim in the Christian tradition, note that even Christians who affirm the permissibility of birth control do so in ways that purport to respect the procreative nature of sex. Whether that is in fact the case is a topic for another discussion.

16. Irish bishops, *Love is For Life*, 12.

happen. And, thankfully, children can grow up well in environments where that is not the case. But assuming that a child is best raised by parents who love the child and each other, having sex in a manner that is not fully unitive simultaneously offends the procreative nature of sex.

One final argument needs to be addressed before moving on in this chapter. Some claim it is possible to grant the view expressed here that the meaning of sex is only fully respected, and therefore done well, in a relationship that is faithfully permanent and open to nurturing new life. Yet, they continue, while that is their ultimate goal in living out their sexuality, it is possible to engage in sex for a different meaning at certain times in one's life (for pleasure alone, or even for genuine love, but which is not faithfully permanent and open to new life), and then at some later point engage in sex in a manner that fulfills its meaning. Can't we have sex now more casually, or at least not in a fully committed relationship, even while realizing that eventually we want to live out our sex lives in a manner that expresses the full meaning of sex? In fact, perhaps it is important that we do so, in order to try out a relationship on all levels (including sex) before committing exclusively and permanently to the other person!

This is by far the most common objection encountered to the position that sex is only fully virtuous in marriage. In effect these people grant this claim, but think sex can be permissible before such a relationship is present, and simply mean less at the present time. But there is an important problem with this position, and it has everything to do with this book's reliance on developing virtues. A virtue is a habit of using some human capacity (like sex) well. The relevant virtue here is chastity, and the relevant vice is lust. Virtues incline us to acts of a certain sort. They not only incline us to perform certain types of actions, but also to perform those acts with a certain intentionality, and thus meaning. Intentions shape the meaning of our actions, and virtues are inclinations to consistent acts with a certain meaning. People who hold the position just described are in effect developing a habit of exercising their sexuality with a certain meaning, namely, as an expression of pleasure—or perhaps, as an expression of love that is genuine but not fully committed. They are shaping themselves to be the sorts of persons for whom sex means something that is not faithful permanence and open to new life. Such people in effect recognize that sex means something more beautiful and powerful, but develop themselves into people for whom sex means something different. The inconsistency should be clear. But the problem is not simply intellectual inconsistency. If we become what we do through the development of habits, and the full meaning of sexuality is what these people grant it is, then such people in effect prevent themselves from developing sexual habits that will enable them to live most truthfully, most happily. Even should such a couple who truly loves one another eventually get married, their sexual intercourse does not mean faithful permanence open to new life. They have developed it differently. Can they change? Thankfully, yes. But so can people who are greedy, envious, or gluttonous. The fact that people can rectify a bad habit is surely no argument justifying the development of the bad habit in the first place! And, of course, having the habit of exercising their sexuality differently inclines them to do so more in the future.

In summary, this first part of this section has sought to determine what the point, or meaning of sex is. The main claim here is not that sex has some point, or meaning—granted. The first main claim is that due to the sort of action it is, sex has a meaning of exclusive, permanent love that is open to new life. Therefore, sex is done virtuously when this is what the couple intends to express while having sex. If they do not, there is a disconnect between what they say and what they mean. The second main claim is that, due to the way we develop our capacities into virtues or vices, sex has a stable point or meaning even if the couple wishes it to mean different things according to their states of relationship. Both of these claims lead to the conclusion that sex is fully virtuous only in a permanent, exclusive, relationship that is open to new life. That sort of relationship is marriage. To the question of whether that sort of relationship can only be in marriage we now turn.

What's the Big Deal about Marriage?

One of the more surprising things about teaching this topic over the past few years has been that students generally recognize that sexual intercourse has the meaning described in the previous section. The affirmation of sexual exclusivity, and even the recognition that sex is inextricably linked to having children, is less surprising. What is striking is the common recognition that sex means permanent love, and thus is at home in a fully committed relationship. I had always assumed that recognizing this was the end of the discussion. Conclusion: sex is only fully virtuous in marriage. But there is one more step—for many students a rather large one—required to draw this conclusion. Why is being married the only descriptor of a fully committed relationship? This is actually the question that many students spend a clear majority of time debating in their discussions of when sex is fully virtuous.

Even granting the previous view of what sex means, three common objections are offered against the need to be married in order to have such a relationship. First, people understandably gripe that weddings too often say more about wealth and status than they do about a couple's relationship, and so are not morally relevant when discussing when to have sex virtuously. Second, people often claim they can be fully committed without having made marriage vows to each other. And third, people often claim that everything marriage is supposed to signify can be had without a piece of paper that says one is married. These three objections will structure the next part.

What Is Marriage Anyway?

When discussing the moral importance of marriage, one set of arguments that always comes up includes claims such as: "I do not need a dress or big party to know that our love is real;" or "diamond rings, limousines, or tuxedos have more to do with showing how much money you have than with how committed a relationship is." In other words, some of the reasons people dismiss the moral relevance of marriage are based on a rejection of how many people celebrate weddings. What is the difference between marriage and a wedding?

A wedding ceremony is an event. In our society, no matter what one's religious tradition, this often entails a beautiful setting (which may or may not be in a house of worship), fancy dress, expensive meals at lavish event halls, ornate cakes, and open bars. While there may be nothing inherently wrong with any of these features of contemporary weddings, taken together they often suggest that the purpose of the wedding is not simply the celebration of marriage vows, but rather an occasion to display the social status and wealth of those hosting the event. This is not the place to judge what exactly constitutes the virtuous planning of a wedding day; there are other authors who have done a fine job with that issue.[17] The point here is that arguments against wedding-day extravagance (which are often right on target) are not arguments against marriage. Why not?

Marriage is a state of life. It begins with an event, namely, the profession of vows. These vows may or may not be professed with a big wedding. But marriage is the state of living out the vows to love and honor one's spouse "for richer or for poorer, in good times and in bad, in sickness and in health, 'til death do us part." The sense of these vows may be summed up in the word "permanence." The couple promises that nothing—not poverty, not sickness, not bad times—will end their relationship before death. What makes a couple married is not the party. It is the public profession of these vows. It can be done in a quiet religious context. It could be done before a justice of the peace and two witnesses. Or it could be done in an ornate setting. But what makes a couple married is their public vow, or promise, to stay with one another "'til death do us part." The claim that sex is only truly at home in marriage means that it is only fully virtuous in a relationship where the couple has made this public profession.

The permanence of marriage is not simply a religious claim. In fact, the vows cited above ('til death do us part," or sometimes "all the days of our lives") are used in civil marriage services with no religious affiliation. Of course,

---

17. One, in particular, is Julie Hanlon Rubio. See the second chapter of her excellent book, *A Christian Theology of Marriage and Family* (New York: Paulist, 2003). Note that the problem of wedding-day extravagance is not simply a contemporary American issue. See St. John Chrysostom's homilies (discussed in Rubio) to his fifth-century Greek audiences about how Christians should not lose sight of their faith and what is really important when celebrating marriages.

different religious traditions offer further resources for understanding the marriage state. In the Catholic tradition, marriage is one of the seven sacraments, there in the beginning (Gen. 1–2) and then blessed by Christ (John 2, Matt. 19). When marriage is performed not only in a civil but in a sacramental context, a sacramental bond is engendered, echoing the words of Christ himself, "what God has joined together, no human being must separate" (Matt. 19:6). The faithfulness and permanence of marriage is such that St. Paul (following the tradition of several Old Testament prophets) uses this state of life as a metaphor for God's relationship with his people, and in particular Christ's relationship to the church (Eph. 5). Obviously, not all people who are married civilly share all of this understanding of marriage, including Christian traditions where marriage is not a sacrament. And these differences in what marriage means do result in important differences on the question of whether and how a marriage vow can be terminated. Nonetheless, what unites different visions of marriage is vowed permanence.

But how permanent is marriage really? Already the previous paragraph mentioned the termination of a marriage vow. What good is vowed permanence if it is not definitely permanent? Everyone is familiar with the prevalence of divorce in our society. The commonly cited figure is that half of all marriages end in divorce. Given this state of affairs, does it really matter whether or not a couple has taken public vows to stay together for life? This is not the place to sort through the enormously difficult (and for many, painful) question of the morality of divorce, religiously and/or civilly. The simple claim made here is that there is an important different between the loving couple that publicly vows permanence and the one that does not, regardless of the fact that either relationship—or both—may fail. In fact, the very wording of this previous sentence indicates why. Only one relationship is rightly said to have failed: the marriage. For only in that relationship was there a public promise to stay together for life. In the absence of any such promise, we cannot even say the other relationship failed—it just ended. The value of vowed permanence is explored next. It suffices here to note that regardless of the actual longevity of the relationship, assuming marital vows are given with full consent and full intent to be lived out, there is a difference between living in such a state (marriage) and living a committed relationship where that promise is absent. Further reasons for this are given later.

Permanence: Why Bother?

Many will immediately say, why? What is the point of promising to stay with another person in good times and in bad? In fact, this may seem like the last thing a person should want to do. If two people no longer love one another, what is the point of staying together? In one sense this is a valid point. There are many relationships in life, even intimate and important ones such as friendships, that run their course. When they do, we let them go. This is also true of romantic relationships. Many times they run their course and we leave them behind, perhaps with fond memories, but often with pain. So the real question here is what point is there in ever promising in the first place to be with someone in good times and in bad, "all the days of our lives"? If it ends up that way, great. But why commit to it ahead of time, in marriage?

Every person should ask him or herself this question, particularly in considering marriage. It is not simply a rubber-stamp approval of a good relationship. Nor is it the logical next step after dating, falling in love, and becoming exclusive. Nor is it a shared hope that two people will always love each other. It could, of course, be any of these things for a particular couple. But none of these are good enough reasons to publicly vow marriage. Marriage is a commitment to stay together. It is a promise, an act of the will. In our day and age, this promise is generally made in the context of feelings of romantic love, which are fine and beautiful. But those feelings are neither the reason for, nor a solid future foundation of, a marriage commitment. If what one means by love is feeling desire to be with another person, then it actually makes no sense to promise life-long love. One should avoid such commitments, and remain free to leave one's partner if, or when, these desires pass.

Married love is a commitment to share certain goods together in life: an intimate friendship where the good of the other becomes one's own good, an openness to new life in possible children and the raising of those children together, and a participation in the life of a community as a unit (couple or family). It is not a rubber-stamp approval of a relationship, or of sexual intimacy. It is not a statement of the intensity of love a couple shares, and/or a pledge to keep that intensity alive. It is a commitment to go through life together. Its permanence is crucial for two reasons. First, that permanence is the best setting to have and raise children. Second, that permanence makes possible certain facets of a shared life together that are not otherwise possible. The permanence of a relationship means a shared life together, and shared stories. It means being vulnerable to each other in ways that may be avoided outside the commitment of such shared life. It entails a commitment to reconciliation and growth as a couple in the inevitable times of discord. It is not security in the sad sense sought by those who are uncertain and crave certainty; it is commitment in the strong sense of having and building further a common vision of what it means to live a good life.

As such, marriage is actually a radical thing. People change over their lives. Who you are when you marry is not the same exact person you are ten, twenty, or however many years later. The same is true of your spouse. And the world around us changes at least as rapidly. Marriage is the pledge to stay together, to love one another through all of this. It is based on the assumption that there is something life-giving and true about doing so. As a commitment, it may often feel like an obligation, due to difficult situations or our own weaknesses. But from a morality-of-happiness perspective, like the life of virtue itself, marriage properly understood is a source of true happiness.

This discussion of the goods available in vowed permanence has been purposely general so as to apply to all marriages—religious and civil—where such a vow is made. In the Catholic tradition, there are further resources to understand and live out that commitment. One of—if not the—most frequent metaphors in the scriptures used to describe God's relationship with his people is that of marriage. God is the faithful one who always loves and forgives the spouse, his people, even in their times of infidelity. If the scriptures tell us anything about God's love for us, it is that God is faithful forever. Thus Catholics, guided by Ephesians 5, have always seen sacramental marriage as a sign of God's relationship with his people. Combined with Christ's own teaching on the permanence of marriage, this has led Catholics to understand marriage as importantly permanent, a very modeling of God's faithful, enduring love. Of course, given earlier chapters' discussion of self-giving love as the very point of the Christian story (as in who God is, the point of creation, and what we as persons are called to do), it is more clear as to why a couple vows permanence; it is an occasion to embark on a state of life whose very point is the self-giving love of, and service to, another person. In living that life, Christians believe they truly live out, with the help of God's grace, their creation as *imago Dei*.

This is why couples decide—or should be why they decide—to pledge to stay with each other for life. It may be the case that some couples marry who should not, perhaps pressured into marriage as the next step, or seeking societal approval to live together or have sex. Or perhaps they really love each other and seek marriage as a way to proclaim or keep alive that love. Even when couples do understand marriage as a commitment, it is certainly the case that nearly all couples do not fully understand the magnitude and meaning of the marriage commitment when they marry. The claim here is not that a couple should understand fully what lies in store for them in marriage; any long-time married couple will tell you that is impossible. But a couple should understand that they are making a promise, a commitment, that they will make every effort to live into as they grow together.

Can't I Have All That without the Piece of Paper?

Perhaps someone can agree with these claims based on the beauty and importance of committing to stay with someone in the manner described above. Indeed, many couples describe themselves as fully committed, and live out practices reflective of that commitment (living together, having children, shared bank accounts, participation in each other's family lives, etc.). Yet still these couples may question why getting married is necessary to be fully committed. Two responses to this challenge are offered here.

First, if that is indeed their intention, it matters that a couple be able to state clearly that they are promising to stay with each other permanently. Doing so ensures that both persons are on the same page about their relationship, and make clear exactly what that page is! Without any decisive event signifying how the couple understands their relationship, that clarity is lacking. The couple likely shares a similar understanding of what it means to be together which, after all, sustains them in their relationship. But even in the presence of beautiful self-giving love, absent a promise of permanence it is not clear that each person has this understanding of the relationship, namely, as something both are committed to sustaining in good times and in bad, in sickness and in health, and so on. Furthermore, even with a shared understanding of full and mutual commitment, there may be only a vague sense of what full commitment means. After all, "commitment" is a word that requires an object: committed to what? Commitment to feel love for the other person? Even given this book's (chapter 4) claims about the possibility of habituating our emotions, it is an odd thing to commit to have certain feelings. Commit to try real hard to make things work? This is closer to a marriage promise, but note it is not the same as committing to love one another until death. Stating marriage vows not only helps ensure each person in the couple is on the same page, it also helps clarify what it is that they commit to together.

At this point a common objection raised is that a couple may indeed be fully committed but unable to make marriage vows due to being in college or graduate school, student loans or other sources of financial insecurity, military service, and the like. What unites all of these seeming impediments to marriage is that there is some societally imposed constraint that is an obstacle to making a permanent commitment to be together.[18] It is indeed true that all of these things can impede a couple from getting married. But two things should be kept in mind for those in such a position.

First, be careful to distinguish the wedding from being married. Getting married actually costs very little (usually some fees for a state license and blood tests, and perhaps a contribution to a church, if the ceremony is held there). Of course what does not cost little is the big wedding that so many of us envision on the occasion of our marriage vows. The big wedding and its costs may be fine and good, but are not necessary to be married. Of course, societal pressure (especially from parents) on a couple to get married in such a setting may be real, and that may indeed impose hardship on the couple. This is certainly an occasion for fortitude. The couple must endure the difficulty of going ahead with what they, in good conscience, deem most important (if it is their marriage) even without the big wedding, or with the celebration of

18. For an example of this type of argument, saying that sex outside marriage is permissible if such externally imposed obstacles are present, see Phillip Keane, "The Dilemma of Committed Premarital Intercourse," in his *Sexual Morality: A Catholic Perspective* (New York: Paulist, 1997), 105–10.

the marriage delayed to some point after the vows. Or they can decide that it is indeed important to do the big family wedding, and therefore wait to have sex a little longer.

The second observation in situations like this is that often such impediments to marriage are not truly societally imposed, but rather reflections of the fact that due to the age and/or stage in life of the couple, the two people are simply not readily to promise permanent love, even if that state of life is indeed their hope and desire. Young couples may say things like, "we are fully committed to each other but cannot get married" because they are in college or graduate school, because they need to get financially secure, or need to get our careers on track. These may indeed be good reasons to postpone marriage. But then even in the presence of truly self-giving and committed love, there is not full commitment. Full commitment would mean finishing school while together, or establishing financial or job security together. The claim here is not that all couples should do this. It is rather that if they are not ready to, fine and good, but then they are not fully committed. When such challenges come up during marriage rather than before it, the married couple promises to work out the situation and stay together (richer or poorer, sickness and in health, etc.). If a couple before marriage is not willing to promise permanence until the resolution of the challenge, it in effect means their commitment, while strong, is not full. It is conditional upon the resolution of that challenge. That may indeed be a prudent judgment on the part of the couple (or may be an imprudent fear of commitment), but, regardless, it is not the full commitment of promised permanence.

Now to the second response. What if a couple is willing to promise permanence to each other? They are willing to verbally state to one another, and even to others who might ask (like their family members), that they are committed to staying with each other in good times and bad, in sickness and health, and so on. So in this case, they are indeed clear to each about where the relationship stands, and it is not simply really committed, but permanently committed, and indeed promised, to each other. The objection continues, "why do we need a piece of paper (a marriage license from the state or church) to make our marriage legitimate? We know and have even promised our love to each other, and that's enough for us!" What distinguishes this case from the prior one is that there is indeed promised permanence. Yet what distinguishes this case from marriage is the fact that the vow is private rather than public (before others and officially recognized by state and perhaps church). If there is nothing importantly different between marriage and the relationship described in this case, it would seem that sex is fully virtuous in this relationship, which is not marriage. So the question is, what, if anything, makes this relationship importantly different from marriage?

Note that the non-marital relationship, as described here, may be a beautiful and self-giving loving relationship. The claim here is not that this relationship only seems good, but is actually malicious or deceptive. The claim is simply that it lacks something important that marriage has, and that sex is fully virtuous only where all elements that marriage has are present. Furthermore, such a relationship may indeed work out. In fact, most of us likely know people in such relationships who are generous, loving couples, who do indeed stay together, perhaps even longer than (and in a more loving way) than certain married couples we know. No denying that! Yet it is claimed that such couples work out not because of, but in spite of, their lack of public profession of marriage vows.

What distinguishes the couple described here from the married couple is that their promises, or vows, to one another are private. This seems to make sense. After all, what is more personal, and thus seemingly more private, than one's romantic relationship and sex life? If two people know they love one another, and promise that love forever, what could be gained by publicly professing that promise? In fact, to many such a public profession seems to be a crutch, an aid employed by couples who perhaps secretly fear they may not make it, and thus place themselves together publicly so that the public pressures and expectations on married people may help them through tough times. If their love were stronger or pure (i.e., without this public interference), it would be better. In fact, many people assume that it is precisely the public dimension of married relationships that so often leads to their demise!

There are actually several different views here. Some think public profession of vows means nothing. Others think it actually signifies a weaker relationship. Still others think it actually leads to problems since it invites outside interference. What all these have in common is that one can have just as good, if not a better, relationship where permanence is explicitly understood by the couple as the goal of the relationship, and yet never publicly professed. It is not contested here that communal influence on a couple can be an interference, or that some couples may get married as a crutch to help them stay together when they are actually not sure they can or really want to do so. Yet it is claimed here that public profession of vows adds something to the relationship, something that can be a powerful support for married people and indeed a further sign of their commitment to each other.

In the same way that verbal promises between the couple clarify the intent of their relationship to each other, the same is true of a public profession with the broader community. In this case the couple makes it clear to others—family, friends, the state, others who may interact with them in formal or informal ways—that they are a unit, two people bound together for the long haul. Why bother doing this, when the key players, so to speak, in the relationship are the man and woman themselves? Though it is indeed the two people that constitute the couple, as explained in the context of justice in chapter 7 we human persons are social creatures. It is not simply that we are always around other people. Our very identities are shaped by our relations with others.

Therefore, if a person is in a relationship as important as marriage, which will be the primary relationship for that person for the rest of his or her life due to its promised permanence (something that even strong friendships do not formally have), it is only fitting for others who are in relationship with us to be aware of such a central relationship. Public profession of marriage vows does that.

Someone may object, don't the people you care about in your life know that you are in such a relationship? Actually, no. First of all, there are relationships that are not so personal (with the state, insurance companies, a child's school, etc.), where this may not be known, and it is important that it is. Second, even when those close to a couple know they are in a real serious relationship, perhaps one where the couple loves each other deeply and lives together, the couple's loved ones do not know whether or not the couple intends to make that relationship permanent. And thus they do not know how to treat the couple on certain occasions. For instance, should my unmarried friend's partner be included in things I might only invite friends to, or friends with their spouses? If my unmarried friend comes to me while having problems in his relationship, how am I to know if I should support him to try and make the relationship work out, when he and his partner have not publicly promised that they vow to make it work? In the absence of public vows, others have not, in effect, been invited to treat the two people as a couple. Assuming both the primacy of the marital relationship in one's life and the importance of our interactions with others around us, this is a real deficiency.

In addition to these considerations, there is another reason why being married is importantly different than living together, even when living together involves a promise of permanence. Marriage helps people stay together. Rather than simply offering the clear statistics about the increased longevity of couples who are married versus those who live together,[19] let us consider why these statistics are true. One contemporary author describes the weightiness that marriage carries.[20] Though a couple may understand their relationship as their own, once they publicly vow to be married they enter into a state of life that has existed long before them, and will exist long afterwards. There are social responsibilities and expectations that come along with being married, and the couple takes on the power of those centuries-old expectations to help shape their relationship and keep it permanent. This does not, of course, mean that they have no ability to shape their own relationship, or that they must be married in a manner dictated solely by others. But it does mean that they are in effect saying that their relationship is about more than themselves; they are entering into a state of life that is not simply of their own construction.

19. For a helpful overview of sociological data on this question, see Adrian Thatcher's *Living Together and Christian Ethics* (Cambridge: Cambridge University Press, 2002).

20. See Jo McGowen, "Marriage Versus Living Together," in *Perspectives on Marriage*, ed. Kieran Scott and Michael Warren (New York: Oxford University Press, 2001), 125–29.

In doing so they are inviting the support and involvement of others in their community.

Of course, here lies the problem too. The reason why many couples who choose not to marry make that choice is because the weightiness of marriage is experienced as a burden rather than a support. Perhaps their own parents were married and had a horrible relationship which inflicted pain on the children. Perhaps the couple has experienced painful divorce in their families, and the refusal to be married appears an obvious way to avoid such trauma, should hard times arise for them in the future. Given these experiences, it is understandable why people wish to avoid marriage. Yet the question that needs to be asked here is whether the problems against which they react are inherent to marriage (and thus can be avoided by living together without marriage), or whether they are particular to a specific couple. To do so, what must be compared are good marriages and good non-married relationships, to see what differences between the two forms are not simply attributable to characteristics of a particular couple.

One of the assumptions of a public profession of marriage vows is that it is indeed difficult to stay married. In fact, in more difficult times couples report they may stay together simply because they are married. Now this is not a good long-term reason to stay together. The reasons why a permanent relationship is a good thing were discussed previously. Granting that, marriage vows can get people through tough times when they do not feel like being married, but experience their commitment as a burden. In such times marriage vows are a support of the couple's freedom, since they have decided (as evidenced by their vows) that staying together permanently is indeed what is best for them. Marriage promises not only can sustain the couple in times of hardship, but also hopefully act as an impetus not just to endure in hardship, but to work together and address the sources of the difficulty so as to live again in fulfilling relationship with each other. Reminiscent of the second chapter's discussion of freedom for excellence, in this situation the rules (staying together when married) may be experienced as a burden. But living in accordance with them indeed constitutes true happiness.

It is for these reasons that marriage helps a couple stay together. The assumption here, of course, is that this is a good thing, for reasons already described. There may be occasions where this is not so (horrible situations of spousal abuse come immediately to mind). And in such cases separating may indeed be what is best for the couple. But the question for this section is how to best effectuate a couple's commitment to stay together permanently. If a couple avoids marriage, it must be asked if permanence is really their goal. Why not avail themselves of available communal support and expectations to reach that goal? And if such support is not desired in favor of having some sort of pure relationship that is kept together solely by the present desires of the couple, it must be asked to what extent permanence is truly the goal.[21] If permanence is indeed the goal, and a couple feels marriage is actually an impediment to that goal, the argument here is this is not true. Marriage may be experienced as an impediment due to painful experiences in the couple's past. But reminiscent of the first chapter's argument that the remedy to harm inflicted by destructive authorities is not to avoid them altogether but rather to seek genuinely life-giving ones, the best response to destructive experiences of marriage is not to avoid a state of life that actually best serves a stated goal of permanence, but rather to seek out and rely on more life-giving models and experiences of that state. In sum, being married is importantly different than living together in privately promised permanence.

Concluding Thoughts

The bulk of this chapter has been spent discussing one specific question as an entry point into the far broader discussion of when it is virtuous to have sex. The particular question addressed has been whether or not being married is a necessary (even if not sufficient) condition of having virtuous sex. The answer supported here is yes, based mainly on the contention (consistent with this book's focus on intentionality) that the goals or meanings of marriage and sex coincide, such that having sex without marriage reveals that the relationship lacks something signified in marriage necessary to have virtuous sex. A host of arguments have been addressed, but all concern one of two points: whether sex really has a meaning akin to marriage, or whether marriage is the only state of relationship where these goals can be fully sought and lived out. Given the previous chapter's arguments about the existence of infused cardinal virtues, the chapter contains occasional discussion of how certain big-picture Christian beliefs shape the meaning of human activities like having sex and being married. The Christian may do the same acts as a chaste non-Christian, but the former person not only relies of God's grace to live virtuously, but also understands the meaning of virtuous sexuality differently. Since sex is an innerworldly activity accessible to unaided human reasoning (i.e., a natural law activity), much of this chapter's discussion remained at that level. It is hoped this discussion, like the one in the next chapter on end-of-life decision-making, reveals how a topic can be both a natural law issue, and yet also be shaped by one's faith.

It is fitting to end where we started, especially by returning to the early part of the chapter on judgment and judgmentalism. The point in this chapter, as in the entire book, is to try and determine how to live most virtuously, understood as living the most fulfilling life by espousing and acting toward what

---

21. For more on the concept of pure relationship, see David McCarthy, *Sex and Love in the Home* (London: SCM Press, 2004).

will make us genuinely happy. This is difficult for most of us. All of us have likely failed to live up to this challenge as it concerns our sexuality, whether it be in deed or desire. But in order to determine how we ourselves can live, and lovingly support other to live, in a most fulfilling manner, articulating what rules best serve this goal is necessary, even if challenging to understand and live. The need for prudence and fortitude, as well as temperance and justice, is particularly evident here. It is hoped that this chapter can be an occasion for the development of those virtues as it concerns our sex lives.

Study Questions

1. Explain why or why not the question of whether sex belongs in marriage only makes sense for Christians.
2. Describe two different levels on which people could disagree about the question of the relationship between sex and marriage.
3. Distinguish judging from being judgmental. Can one discuss how to have sex virtuously and not be judgmental?
4. What about sex and marriage leads some people to say that sex is only fully virtuous in marriage?
5. What does it "mean" to ask what sex means?
6. What does sex mean? Place yourself somewhere on the continuum of a developing relationship, and say why sex is appropriate at that stage.
7. What is the essence of marriage? How is this different from a wedding?
8. Why would a couple promise to stay together permanently?
9. Does being publicly married add anything to a loving relationship where the partners tell each other they want to be together forever? Why or why not?

Terms to Know

chastity, lust, judgment vs. judgmentalism, sex as language metaphor, unitive meaning of sex, procreative meaning of sex, wedding vs. marriage, marriage as public

Questions for Further Reflection

1. How can we determine whether one has crossed the line from loving judgment to judgmentalism?
2. One goal of this chapter has been to make a certain vision of sex understandable to people. What societal, familial, and church forces are at

work that inhibit the reception of this vision? In other words, how are consciences being poorly (as well as properly) formed on this issue?

3. What impact does the high divorce rate have today on people's reflection on this question?

4. How central is the procreative meaning of sex? Can the position articulated here account for the case of sterile couples? What are the ramifications of one's position on the procreative meaning of sex for questions such as homosexuality, marriage, and contraception?

5. Does permanence makes sense as a good of marriage outside of a Christian perspective?

Further Reading

There is an enormous literature on sex and morality in general, and the relationship between sex and marriage in particular. The official Catholic church document I have found most helpful for teaching is the Irish Bishops' Pastoral Letter *Love is for Life*. David Cloutier's *Love, Reason, and God's Story* is an outstanding introduction to sexual ethics. See also David McCarthy's *Sex and Love in the Home*, Julie Hanlon Rubio's *A Christian Theology of Marriage and Family*, and Richard Gaillardetz's *A Daring Promise: A Spiritually of Christian Marriage*. For a more popular presentation of the position taken in this chapter see Lauren Winner's *Real Sex: The Naked Truth about Chastity*.

18

EUTHANASIA

Test Case Four

Perhaps you have been asked or thought about what you would do if your friend and fellow soldier—wounded in battle and left suffering enormously and near death but without any available medical treatment—begged you to end his life to ease his suffering. This is a horrible situation to imagine, one that, thankfully, few if any of us will ever encounter. But situations where we must decide how to best act toward loved ones who are suffering and near death are sadly not at all uncommon. And given the advanced state of medical technology, the difficulty of end-of-life decision making has only been exacerbated. Decisions today are not only whether to simply care for suffering people until they die, but whether or not to purposely end their lives to ease their suffering. We must also on occasion choose whether or not to use treatments that may themselves hasten the death of a patient. Or we are faced with decisions about whether or not to withhold or remove treatments that appear useless or burdensome, but that nonetheless may keep a person alive.

What all of these decisions have in common is that they impact the length of the patient's life. One common response of bewildered people facing such complicated decisions is, "don't play God!" Nothing seems more God-like than influencing the time of someone's death. But if the aim of those who warn us "don't play God," is avoiding any impact on the length of someone's life, then this advice is misguided. Our decisions in many unavoidable situations truly will impact the length of patients' lives. Should any available treatment be undertaken by a patient, no matter her condition, or can patients opt out of certain treatments? And what of treatments that are undertaken to better or prolong one's life but sadly and unintentionally end up causing death, as regularly happens in the medical world? Are we to stop performing surgeries so as to not play God?

If playing God means making medical decisions that impact the length of someone's life, then doing so is unavoidable. The real task (for the person of faith) is to "play with, rather than against, God." Of course, that is likely what people who say "don't play God" mean. But the rub, if you will, is determining which decisions go against God's will and which do not. In other words, how can we make end-of-life decisions well, or virtuously? Given the complexities of this arena, answering this question requires far more than a simplistic slogan about playing God.

In fact, when we begin to sort out exactly what sorts of decisions constitute playing for or against God, we find that the relevant features of such decisions—intention, patient condition, usefulness of available treatment, and the like—are not accessible only to people of faith. They pertain to an innerworldly activity (end-of-life decision-making) and thus are accessible to people of any or no religious conviction. They are the stuff, if you will, of natural law. This does not mean, of course, that theological commitments do not shape our understanding of such situations and actions; as the previous chapter on sexuality illustrates, they certainly do. As will be seen in the first section of this chapter, faith certainly impacts one's understanding of the meaning (if any) of suffering, or of the extent to which we are willing to live in a manner dependent upon others. The Christian tradition also has specific norms relevant to the issue of euthanasia (such as the sixth commandment, "thou shall not kill"), norms which believers have consistently interpreted as bearing on the case of euthanasia. In short, faith matters for how one does natural-law reasoning concerning innerworldly activities such as end-of-life decision making. Nonetheless, the aspects of euthanasia that make such an act contrary to Christian commitments (i.e., which make it playing against God, or a violation of the commandment) are accessible to persons of any or no religious commitment, and may therefore be discussed accordingly. Hence, this chapter will proceed largely without direct reference to faith commitments, largely because even when discussed in reference to such commitments, the issue of euthanasia demands precision and analysis on matters that do not depend on those commitments.

The purpose of this chapter is to examine how virtuous end-of-life decisions are made in general, and whether or not euthanasia can ever be one such decision in particular. Euthanasia is an enormously large topic. Thorough treatment of this issue would require a book, or books. Therefore, many important facets are left unaddressed here. These include statistics on how and when people do actually die, data from places like Oregon and the Netherlands where forms of euthanasia are legal, discussions of how legalized euthanasia would and does impact the practice of the medical profession, and the impact the legalization of euthanasia would have on vulnerable populations, such as the poor and uninsured.

This chapter takes on three more specific goals. The first section addresses the reasons why people might welcome death, in order to determine whether or when such a stance can be virtuous. The argument of this section is that there are indeed times where it is virtuous to embrace death, although not always. The second section, recognizing that there are a plenitude of ways one might welcome death, defines euthanasia more precisely so as to delineate what exactly is, or should be, meant by euthanasia in debates over this issue. *Euthanasia* is most properly defined as the intentional termination of a patient's life in order to end suffering. The third and final section examines in detail, in light of section one's claim that it may indeed be virtuous at times to welcome death, whether euthanasia as defined in the second section is ever a virtuous response to end-of-life suffering. It concludes that though death may be virtuously welcomed at times, and though genuinely prudent decisions may indeed cause the death of a patient, the intentional ending of a patient's life—even out of the well-meaning desire to end suffering—is never a virtuous act.

The Context for End-of-Life Decisions

Later sections examine more closely the immediate task of this chapter: the definition and morality of euthanasia. But before entering that debate, it would help us to understand better why people would ever desire to die, and whether or not—or when—such a desire can be virtuous. The purpose of doing this is twofold. First, a more careful analysis of people's reasons for seeking death may reveal that this is a bad decision, and realizing why will hopefully lead more people in such situations not to seek death. This has obvious ramifications for the perceived need for euthanasia. But the second reason is to point out that at times it is indeed reasonable to be willing to surrender one's life and welcome death. Simplistic slogans such as "do not play God!" can make it seem as if death is to be avoided at all possible costs. Even among people who oppose euthanasia, however, this need not be the case. It is hoped that this section will enable people to decide more prudently when it is and is not virtuous to embrace death.

In a beautiful article entitled, "The Pressures to Die: Re-conceiving the Shape of Christian Life in the Face of Physician-Assisted Suicide," David Cloutier considers why people seek physician-assisted suicide, which, as explained below, is one form of euthanasia.[1] He focuses on two main reasons: the avoidance of suffering and a desire not to be dependent on others. Cloutier does not dismiss these reasons, but rather hopes to present a more accurate understanding of suffering and dependency so they do not unduly lead people to seek euthanasia. His work is used in this section to help people better decide when and when not to embrace death.

As to the avoidance of suffering, it must be clearly stated that pain and suffering are not good. If they were, then we would purposely impose them on ourselves and others. If they were, we would always be against treatments (such as palliative care or pain relief) whose aim is to diminish pain and suffering. In fact, if pain and suffering were simply good, it is difficult to see how medicine as a profession would make sense. In ways described further below, some people (particularly Christians) do see the possibility of meaning in suffering. Nonetheless, it must be made perfectly clear that saying this is not the same as saying that pain and suffering are good.

The reason why this is important to state at the outset is that, at times, opponents of euthanasia will refer to the meaning and value of suffering to counter euthanasia supporters who cite real suffering as a reason to purposely end the lives of some patients. The problem with responding with arguments based on the value of suffering is that such arguments so often fail to include resources for saying why we do seek to alleviate suffering at times, only to espouse the value of suffering suddenly when it comes to euthanasia. Opponents of euthanasia must be careful in discussing suffering not to make claims that would render unintelligible, even immoral, standard and uncontested medical practices aimed at alleviating pain and suffering. In response to arguments praising the value of suffering in debates over euthanasia, one could respond, "so you are against pain relievers such as aspirin?" People almost never are, and so it is necessary to situate claims about the possibility of meaningful suffering more carefully.

People who cite the value of suffering generally mean two things, both of which are indeed true. First, they mean that suffering can have a purpose. This is something that all people grant. Certain surgical recoveries, physical therapies, burn treatments, and the like all involve significant (at times brutal) pain and suffering. But these are endured for the sake of what is gained by the treatment. If "avoid pain and suffering at all costs" were the appropriate norm governing such situations, we would not do certain virtuous things that we currently do. Therefore, while pain and suffering are not simply good, neither are they to be avoided at all costs.

1. David Cloutier, "The Pressures to Die: Reconceiving the Shape of Christian Life in the Face of Physician-Assisted Suicide," in *Growing Old in Christ*, ed. Stanley Hauerwas, Carole Bailey Stoneking, Keith G. Meador, and David Cloutier (Grand Rapids: Eerdmans, 2003), 247–66.

Cloutier refers to this type of suffering as *educative suffering*. It is endured because the suffering is directly related to—usually the path to—some good that is obtained through the suffering. It is encapsulated by the phrase "no pain, no gain." The meaning of such suffering is easier to grasp, and care-givers can comfort people in these predicaments by reminding them of the light at the end of the tunnel of their pain and suffering. But Cloutier rightly acknowledges that not all suffering is so clearly educative, or a direct path to some good, such as health. Sometimes it seems there is no purpose to suffer-ing. Think of how cruel it would be to say to a terminally ill and suffering patient at the end of life, "no pain, no gain." In certain situations of pain and suffering, there is no obvious gain, or light at the end of the tunnel, which is achieved through a path of suffering.

It is in precisely these situations that supporters of euthanasia assume that such suffering is meaningless, and see no reason to continue such suffering. Indeed, even the Catholic church recognizes that it is completely permissible to seek the alleviation of pain and suffering through palliative care. Yet there is a second reason why people may recognize value even in suffering that is not immediately directed to some good purpose. Here is one place where things are seen differently from the perspective of the Christian story. Without glorifying (or certainly mandating) suffering, Cloutier rightly describes how Christians have always found something potentially meaningful and redemptive in suf-fering. This is a particularly common theme in the letters of St. Paul, who says things like: "when I am weak, then I am strong" (2 Cor. 12:10), and "I rejoice in my sufferings for your sake" (Col. 1:24). What does this mean? Do Christians seek suffering or claim it is simply good?[2]

Absolutely not. Yet a foundational theme of the Christian story is that suf-fering and death are not the last word. Ultimately, God's power, mercy, and love overcome death and suffering. In fact, sometimes in times of suffering we are able to experience more fully the faithfulness and power of God's saving presence, as it can penetrate even the darkest of hours and bring light in the most unexpected moments. This is of course what happened on Easter Sunday after the horror of Good Friday. As it concerns end-of-life decisions, this is not some wishful thought that perhaps the suffering patient will be cured by a miracle—though of course all things are possible with God. Rather, it is a radical laying down of one's life in trust that God is provident, good, and faithful. Christians have consistently reported throughout history that such occasions can be powerful experiences of God's presence and grace. Perhaps there is a renewal of the patient's faith. Perhaps there is overdue reconciliation between members of the family. Perhaps the patient's fortitude in facing death has a transformative effect on the patient's loved ones. What is common to

2. For an extraordinarily powerful reflection on the meaning of suffering, see John Paul II's apostolic letter, *Salvifici Dolores* (Encyclical Letter, 1984).

all such experiences is that the patient's suffering itself is not inherently tied to some gain, and yet some meaning is found in this time of suffering. Hence Cloutier calls it *redemptive suffering*.[3]

Christianity, centered as it is on the story of Good Friday to Easter Sunday, has unique resources to recognize the potential meaningfulness of suffering— again, without idealizing it. So it is less surprising when Christians refuse to avoid suffering at all costs in end-of-life decision making. Yet it should be noted that the refusal to avoid suffering at all costs is not a position particular to Christianity. Even those who support euthanasia in situations of seemingly pointless suffering generally do not advocate involuntary euthanasia for suffering, conscious patients. In other words, their respect for the decision of a patient who does not choose to seek euthanasia in such a situation reveals that they prioritize patient autonomy before the avoidance of such suffering. So even they see the possibility of meaning in such suffering—even if it is simply the meaning of respecting patient autonomy. The simple point here is that though pain and suffering are not good in themselves, and though palliative care to treat them should be readily available, it is not therefore the case that suffering should be avoided at all costs. The avoidance of suffering rightly looms large in end-of-life decision making, but it should not be solely determinative.

The second main reason offered by Cloutier as to why people seek euthanasia is to avoid being dependent on others. How often do we hear aging parents tell their children, "I do not want to be a burden on you"? Anyone who has known or cared for someone at the end of life knows that it can indeed be an enormous burden in terms of time, energy, money, and the displacement of other worthy endeavors. Both for the patient and the caregiver, there is an understandable sense that this is a bad situation to be avoided. But again the question is, at what cost? Without idealizing or glorifying dependency, is it really something to be avoided at all costs, even the cost of ending the dependent terminally ill patient's life?

Cloutier observes that in such an autonomy-minded culture as America today, it is easy to regard dependence as simply a bad thing to be avoided. But he suggests that end-of-life dependence can recall to us just how dependent the good life is for every one of us. We obviously begin life completely dependent, as we often end it. But even as mature adults we depend on those around us: such as family, friends, spouses, and children. We depend on colleagues at work, and fellow citizens who serve the common good of our town or nation. We depend economically on others. Of course others depend on us in so many of these ways. The point here is not to equate these types of dependence with that experienced at the end of life, when even basic bodily functions may require assistance. The point is that being burdened by others, and in turn burdening them, may be a more accurate assessment of our everyday

---

3. Cloutier, "The Pressures to Die."

life than our perceived autonomy, such that end-of-life caregiving, while surely distinctive in its often high demands, is only quantitatively, not qualitatively, different from the dependence at work throughout our entire lives.

There is something true and understandable about the common sentiment to want to avoid being a burden to others. It is indeed a good thing that adults are generally able to provide for and take care of themselves, and pursue activities other than the constant and demanding care of a loved one at the end of life. There are occasions when the mental, physical, emotional, and economic cost of caring for a loved one should influence end-of-life decision making. But just as there can be meaning in suffering, so too can there be meaning and value in dependence. Our understandable fear of placing enormous strain on others should not lead us too quickly to avoid placing any burden, even significant burden, on those around us. Our *mutual dependence*, as Cloutier calls it, is not simply something to be endured, but indeed is constitutive of living a good life. In other words, we are all better off to the extent that we allow ourselves to be burdens to and burdened by others.

One of the best illustrations of mutual dependence advocated by Cloutier can be seen in New York City immediately after September 11th. As a native New Yorker with many friends and family still there, I was regaled in the days after the attacks, not only with stories of the suffering endured, but also with stories of how New Yorkers were changed for a time in how they tended to those around them. The dramatic stories of heroism are well known. But even in ordinary situations people seemed more attentive to others, even strangers. People checked on elderly neighbors. They actually spoke and listened to people at work who previously were simply inhabitants of the same floor in a building. On subways, where every New Yorker knows the standard practice is to shut up and avoid eye contact, people not only spoke to, but actually checked in on, those around them who seemed to be suffering. People were more aware—sadly for too short a time—of their interconnectedness to those around them, and saw clearly that they depended on, and were dependent on, others. Such stories are common in areas ravaged by disaster, including natural disasters. Why does it take such horrible and dramatic events to remind us of our dependency? When these disruptions of our normal way of living occur, are they really reminders of what is true about our mutual dependency, even when we ignore it in more everyday life?

As noted above, this brief discussion of two common things that prompt people to seek euthanasia has been undertaken for two reasons. First, though each reason makes a visceral appeal to our sympathies toward people who wish to end their own lives, neither suffering nor dependency is something that should be avoided at all costs. This is not to glorify or idealize either. But if we fearfully run from each unreflectively, we will be making bad decisions at the end of life whether we seek euthanasia or not. A more accurate understanding of these facets of life enables us to make better end-of-life decisions.

But the second reason these topics are addressed here is to acknowledge that quality-of-life judgments can and must be made during end-of-life decision making. And at times, given the enormous suffering experienced, the burden of ongoing treatment on all involved, and an advanced incurable condition, it may indeed be appropriate to decide to stop fighting the disease and devote one's self to preparing to die. Opponents of euthanasia who deny this do so at their peril, and alienate people whose openness to euthanasia may really be driven by the simple recognition that at times it is appropriate to welcome death. This is a judgment about quality of life, and may indeed mean one dies sooner than if one had continued to fight. But given the advanced state of medical technology today, such judgments at times are necessary.

People of faith cannot avoid making such judgments. Of course, how they are made can vary. They can be made well or poorly. Cloutier's argument about suffering and being a burden means that people can too quickly seek death by wanting to avoid suffering at all costs, or by failing to recognize the proper role of dependency in a good life. But that such judgments are made is unavoidable. What might be good reasons to change one's stance from preserving life to welcoming death? The Catholic church's Declaration on Euthanasia mentions several considerations for such a decision: "the reasonable wishes of the patient and the patient's family"; "the advice of doctors who are specially competent in the matter"; "a wish to avoid the application of a medical procedure disproportionate to the results that can be expected"; "inevitable death is imminent in spite of the means used"; and, "a desire not to impose excessive expense on the family or the community."[4] Of course, reasons are given that may prompt a patient to continue to fight on, such as the desire to unite oneself "with the sufferings of Christ crucified" or to "show generosity at the service of humanity" by assisting in experimental treatments.[5]

Unfortunately, there is no precise measure available to precisely determine in all cases when it is best to decide to stop fighting for life and welcome death. There are clear ways the decision can be made well or poorly, but an accurate appraisal of a particular situation is necessary to best determine what to do on that occasion. There are even occasions when it could be virtuous to either fight on or cease to fight for life; both decisions could be virtuous, depending on the desires of the patient. What is needed here, obviously, is the virtue prudence. What is the best guard to ensure we are being truly prudent in our decision making? It is no guarantee, but a readily available guard is the possession of other virtues. Who are the brave, just, and temperate people in the family who can be relied upon to see clearly how to act well in the challenging situation at hand? Are factors in the decision being weighed

4. *Declaration on Euthanasia* (Sacred Congregation for the Doctrine of the Faith, 1980), iv.

5. Ibid., iii–iv.

properly, or are cowardice, greed, anger, or other vices warping how people are making decisions? Saying this is a matter of prudence is not of course to say that any conceivable decision made is a good one. But it is to say that one can, given circumstances that are sadly not uncommon, make a virtuous decision to welcome death.

We have gone a long way toward recognizing some of the concerns that prompt people to seek euthanasia. It is recognized here both that we do indeed make quality-of-life judgments at the end of life, and that it may be virtuous—even, or perhaps especially, on Christian terms—to no longer fight to live. We are now ready to address the core question of this chapter. Granting a genuinely virtuous decision has been made to no longer fight to live but rather to welcome death, can euthanasia be a virtuous way to act at such a time? The next section attempts to define euthanasia, and the final section offers an extensive treatment of the morality of euthanasia.

Defining Euthanasia

One of the biggest obstacles hindering fruitful discussion of the morality of euthanasia is the difficulty of defining acts of euthanasia. The term "euthanasia" is derived from the Greek, and literally means "good death." But that is far too vague a definition, since there are plenty of good deaths that no one would label euthanasia. More commonly people think of euthanasia in the context of actions deliberately taken that lead to the death of a patient who is suffering and near the end of life. The death is good because it means an end to the patient's suffering. But again, this is far from a definition since "actions deliberately taken" is so vague. Thus, the task of this section is to arrive at a definition of euthanasia.

There are many different ways to distinguish different actions taken at the end of a patient's life. Of course, the main purpose of such distinctions is to say what acts are good and which are bad. So the task of describing different end of life actions is intricately intertwined with discussion of the morality of such acts. This section begins by surveying different ways people have distinguished end-of-life actions. The purpose is to show how they are all inadequate ways of defining euthanasia, save one.

One common way to describe end-of-life decisions is by the *active/passive* distinction. Some people may say, "I am against active euthanasia but am OK with passive euthanasia." I can actually tell what they probably mean when they say this, but the "active/passive" distinction they offer to differentiate good from bad acts is problematic, for two reasons. First, it evacuates any meaning of the term euthanasia itself. If euthanasia can be bad if active, but good if passive, what does the word itself mean? It seems merely to signify a neutral occasion when a suffering patient dies, or some sort of decision that impacts the end of life. The real work of determining what is right and wrong is done by the terms "active" and "passive." Yet this is inaccurate. We do not use the term euthanasia simply to refer to times a suffering patient dies.

Second, these two terms active and passive cannot rise to the occasion of distinguishing good and bad acts. Active euthanasia means something like a suffering patient dying sooner because of some action taken by a caregiver. And passive euthanasia means a patient dying sooner because of a decision by a caregiver (e.g., doctors, nurses, family, or friends) not to take action. But this simply does not work in distinguishing good and bad acts. Sometimes we choose to take actions that in fact lead to the quicker death of a suffering patient, and no one would call this euthanasia. Think, for instance, of surgery for a patient suffering a heart condition. Every surgeon knows there is a risk of a patient dying on the table. Yet knowing this, surgeons still take action, and on occasion actively hasten the death of their patients. But, of course, no one would call this euthanasia. Conversely, there are occasions when we would blame someone for being passive and not helping a suffering patient to live. The point is, euthanasia does not simply signify a neutral situation made good or bad depending on whether or not someone acts or not. First of all, that is not the way we use the term euthanasia; it means more than the death of a suffering patient. Second, the terms active and passive do not adequately distinguish good from bad end-of-life decisions. This is a confusing way of describing decisions at the end of life, and really should be dropped altogether.

Sometimes people distinguish good from bad acts at the end of life by observing the cause of death of the patient. They may say something like, "It is OK to let people die naturally, but we should not cause their death unnaturally." Here what is offered to distinguish good from bad acts is not whether or not the caregiver acts (active/passive) but, rather, what is the cause of death—is it the disease or the caregiver or, as some say, is it *natural* or *unnatural*? We may of course be able to guess what sorts of situations such people are trying to distinguish, but again, the "cause of death" distinction is not an adequate way to consistently differentiate good acts from bad at the end of life. For instance, as the heart surgery example above illustrates, every medical practitioner knows that, on occasion, medical treatment itself may cause the death of a patient. These are not natural deaths. And, conversely, someone may die naturally, but from a completely preventable condition that should have been treated. Therefore, the cause of death is another ultimately ineffective way to distinguish good from bad acts surrounding end-of-life decisions.

Other distinctions are also used to help sort out good and bad acts at the end of life. Some emphasize the importance of consent, and say that if a patient consents to something it is OK, but it is not OK if there is no consent. Surely consent is crucial, but is it really true that whatever the patient wants and consents to is virtuous? We may not blame suffering people for their requests in such states, because there may be duress. But should we honor the request of anyone who gives their consent to have their life ended? Surely not. One last distinction people occasionally offer is based upon who causes death. The claim is usually that a patient causing his own death is OK, but it should not be caused by others. But again this does not work. We surely do not praise any occasion when someone causes their own death. Conversely, if there are occasions where it would in fact be better to end the patient's life, why shouldn't the patient be given assistance in doing so, if needed? To not do so (assuming it was truly the best thing for the patient) seems an injustice to the patient.

Each of the above distinctions tells us something. But the problem with each is that it is unable to serve the role of a consistent rule with which to judge good acts from bad. Often we hear the above terminology used, and we know enough from the context to fill in the rest of the story. So the distinctions may suffice on those occasions. But the problem comes in trying to use them in contested situations where their inadequacy quickly becomes clear. Thus the claim here is certainly not that one is morally blameworthy for using these distinctions. Rather, it is that each is ultimately inadequate in defining euthanasia and determining what actions surrounding end-of-life decisions are good and bad.

Where does that leave us? There is one remaining way both to define euthanasia and sort out good from bad actions during end-of-life decision making, and unsurprisingly, given the concept's importance in this book, it is intention. What defines the act of euthanasia is the intent to end the life of a patient, out of a merciful desire to end the patient's suffering. As the Declaration on Euthanasia states, euthanasia is "an action or omission which of itself or by intention causes death, in order that all suffering may in this way be eliminated."[6] Note the prominence of intention in this definition. Something is euthanasia if there is an intention that the person die in order that suffering be eliminated. Given this way of speaking, euthanasia can be labeled morally wrong and/or illegal without the need for additional qualifiers (like active or passive). Of course, some people do not think euthanasia, even understood as the intentional ending of a patient's life to ease suffering, is morally wrong or should be illegal, but that is a question for the third section of this chapter. The point here is that the definition of euthanasia as an intentional ending of a life (vs. simply action or inaction that does lead to the end of a patient's life) more accurately and consistently distinguishes the type of action to which people refer when they use terms like active vs. passive or natural vs. unnatural.

Observe how this way of defining euthanasia makes sense of all the cases cited above. It works better than the active/passive distinction because euthanasia has a meaning that is not dependent on additional signifiers (active

6. Ibid., ii.

or passive) for moral evaluation. It also explains why the heart surgeon who actively ends her patient's life does not commit euthanasia: she did not intend to end the patient's life (but rather intended to heal the patient). Finally, it explains how certain passive occasions can be morally wrong, namely, if one purposely chooses not to act in order that someone die. In other words, intention can drive inaction as well as action.

See also how this way of defining euthanasia helps explain what people likely mean when they say, "it is OK to let someone die naturally but not to cause their death." They generally do not precisely mean it is bad to cause the patient's death, but rather that it is wrong to intend the patient's death. Again, that is why treatments that do cause death unintentionally are not euthanasia. Conversely, by saying "it is OK to let someone die naturally," they are not praising every occasion where a disease ends a patient's life. Rather, they mean that an intentional decision not to keep treating someone, knowing this means they likely will die of their disease, is not the same as intending to kill someone. That is why the words "let die" are used.

Thus, for the purposes of this chapter euthanasia should be understood as an intentional act. This is how the term euthanasia is understood in Catholic church documents. Yet, note that this is also how euthanasia is best understood, given the current state of law in the United States. Currently, in the United States it is illegal to intentionally end a patient's life, even if that is done to ease their suffering (one exception is treated below). It is not, of course, illegal to cause a patient's death, as evidenced by surgical deaths or other decisions to treat or not treat that may lead unintentionally to a patient's death. Whether or how intending death is different from causing death is a question addressed in detail in the next section. The point is raised here simply to give further credence and support to a definition of euthanasia based on intention, and to point out that this view of euthanasia is not particular to the Catholic church, or based solely on religious reasoning.

Of course, even if all were to agree that this is the best way to define euthanasia, the issue of whether or not it can be virtuous or should be legal is very much alive. In fact, the one exception to the above claim about euthanasia being illegal in the United States is found in the state of Oregon, where physician-assisted suicide is currently legal. *Physician-assisted suicide* (PAS) is when a patient requests a dosage of lethal pills from his physician to be taken with the intention of ending his own life. This is clearly one form of euthanasia, since the intent of both patient and doctor is that the patient ends his own life, with the doctor's "assistance," in order to end his suffering. There are certain conditions that must be met (incurable condition, suffering, imminent death), and more than one physician must attest to this condition. So the law permits only one form of euthanasia (namely, PAS), and only in certain conditions. It is noteworthy here, both as an exception to the general legal prohibition of euthanasia in the nation, and as another example of how euthanasia—even if legalized—is most properly understood on the basis of intention.

How to, and How Not to, Act on This Judgment

The first section's discussion of end-of-life decisions is perhaps the most important practically: guiding people's prudential judgments about when to continue the fight to preserve life, and when to end the fight and await death. But though we have touched upon the reasons driving people to seek euthanasia, we have not yet addressed the core issue in the debate over euthanasia: how to carry out that judgment. In this section of the chapter, let us grant that a genuinely prudent decision has been made by a person with his family that it is indeed time to end the fight. Echoing the words of St. Paul, this person may say, "I have competed well; I have finished the race; I have kept the faith. From now on the crown of righteousness awaits me" (2 Tim. 4:7–8). Due to an incurable condition, great suffering, and an imminent demise, the task at hand is no longer to prolong life but rather to vigilantly await the end of life, and even welcome death.

In what ways can one virtuously await death? The word "await" connotes a passivity. But we know from above that concrete decisions must be made to stop certain treatments, such as to forego certain new types of treatment, or to give painkillers that may impact the length of one's life. It is not enough to say, "just await death." Given the current state of medical technology, a patient's length of life will indeed be influenced by our choices. The real question is how to choose well. And more specifically for this section of the chapter, are there some choices that are never virtuous? Euthanasia has been defined in the previous section as an action or an omission which of itself or by intention causes death, in order that all suffering may in this way be eliminated. Can such an act ever be virtuous?

This section treats this question in three parts. First, it addresses the question of whether or not there really is any difference between intending the death of a patient vs. acting in a manner that hastens or causes that death, even though it is not intended. The second section grants that there is such a difference, and then explores whether there may yet be rare occasions when intending the death of the patient is virtuous. The third section examines the particularly challenging question of how to categorize different types of treatment to determine whether or not their removal necessarily constitutes an intent to end a patient's life. This section concludes that intending the death of a patient is a further step than unintentionally causing a patient's death, or withholding or removing life-sustaining treatments. Not only is intending the patient's death (i.e., euthanasia) a further step, but it is also never virtuous, even when done out of mercy and even when a prudential decision has been made that the time has passed to continue to fight to prolong life.

Intention vs. Foreseen Consequences: Any Real Difference?

One of the main rationales given for the legalization of, or moral permissibility of, euthanasia is that we are in fact already acting in ways that bring about the end of life for people who are at the end of life and suffering greatly. So far this chapter has tried to demonstrate that this is indeed the case. The virtuous person cannot simply not act or decide not to play God; rather, she must act prudently in such situations, since her decisions will indeed impact the length of the patient's life (her own or a loved one's). Yet this section demonstrates that there is still a crucial difference between intending something and simply bringing it about. It is the former that characterizes euthanasia, and enables both the Catholic church and current U.S. law (PAS in Oregon excepted) to disallow it, even while allowing other acts that bring about the end of patients' lives.

Consider a case that prompts euthanasia supporters to make the claim that we are already purposely ending people's lives. It requires a word about *palliative care*, which is treatment for pain given to patients, and especially important at the end of life for those whose conditions entail great suffering. One of the common medical protocols for palliative care is the use of morphine or other opiate drugs to relieve pain. One characteristic of such drugs is that they build tolerance. That is, once one begins taking them, going forward more of the same drug is needed to achieve the same pain-relieving effect. Therefore, incremental increases in dosage are given to patients who are prescribed opiates like morphine for palliative care. However, though the body can endure a high dosage of such drugs if increased incrementally, the body's tolerance for such drugs is not unlimited. In other words, eventually the dose needed to relieve pain can be high enough that it is the drug itself, and not the existing medical condition, that causes the death of the patient, often through respiratory failure.

The question is, if a patient is prescribed such drugs for pain relief, and the drug itself actually ends the patient's life, has the patient's life been intentionally ended? It is tempting to think yes. After all, the caregivers voluntarily gave the morphine. Furthermore, although it is generally not possible to know exactly when one has crossed the line and given a specific dose that will cause death, it is indeed the case that the caregivers know that causing the patient's death is a possibility. Therefore, in this case there is a voluntary action (giving high doses of morphine) that has foreseen consequences. In other words, the caregiver knows that death may result from her treatment. Has the caregiver intentionally ended the patient's life? Though some argue this is the case, careful attention to intentionality using the doctrine of double effect reveals otherwise.

Recall the doctrine of double effect from chapter 8. It helps us determine whether a particular course of action is virtuous or not, when good and bad effects both seem to follow no matter what one does. In this case, a caregiver gives pain relief, which is a good effect. But the pain reliever may hasten the end of the patient's life, which is a bad effect. Alternatively, the caregiver can refrain from giving the pain relief, which has the bad effect of greater suffering for the patient even while it has the good effect of not hastening the patient's death. This is a classic case of double effect. Is it permissible to give the pain relief?

There are three conditions of the doctrine of double effect.[7] The first condition asks whether there is a good intent. In this case the intent is to relieve pain, and so the answer is yes. But couldn't the caregiver's intent really be to end the patient's life? This question requires two answers. First, if the caregiver's ultimate goal is the death of the patient rather than the pain relief of the patient (which is hopefully achieved without ending life, even though it may indeed end the patient's life), then that malicious goal does indeed make the act bad. Second, recall that an intention is a principle that guides action. It is what gives a specific act its meaning, gives shape to the particular act done. If the intent really is to relieve pain, we should expect the patient to be given only the increase in dosage that is needed to secure pain relief. If a very large dose is given initially, someone can say the intent is to relieve pain, but the shape of the act reveals otherwise. The intent was really to end the patient's life, since that is the only meaning that can explain the act of giving a suddenly high dose of morphine.

The second condition of double effect asks whether the evil effect is willed in itself, or is the means to the good effect. Again, if the goal of the act is to end the patient's life, the act is bad. But that need not be the goal here. Indeed, most caregivers see their patients living on with relieved pain and consider their act to have achieved its purpose. And clearly the good effect (pain relief) is not achieved by means of the bad effect (death). Condition two is met.

Condition three concerns proportionality and asks whether the goodness of the good effect outweighs the badness of the bad effect. To determine this, we need to go back to the considerations of the sort addressed in the first section of this chapter: status of illness, prognosis, degree of suffering, toll on family, and so on. We granted, for this section, that such a situation indeed exists. What would be an example of a situation that did not meet this requirement? Imagine you were in a horrible automobile accident, and severely burned, requiring months of burn treatment that should ultimately be successful but

---

7. Recall from chapter 8 that most classic formulations of the doctrine of double effect contain four conditions. The first of the four is omitted here, since it seems superfluous.

will be excruciatingly painful. You are a young married person with small children. You are in horrible pain. Surely pain relief is in order. But in this case, should we risk giving pain relief that may ultimately cause your death (even if that is not the intent), when you will most likely recover, have many years to live, and have a family that awaits you? In this case the good of pain relief does not outweigh the possible bad effect of causing your death.

To euthanasia supporters it seems that we are already willing to voluntarily perform pain-relieving acts with the foreseen consequence of causing death. Therefore, there is no difference between incremental palliative care and, say, injecting a patient with potassium chloride which ends the patient's life and thus his suffering. But the doctrine of double effect reveals the different intentionality of this latter act. Let us grant that condition three, on proportionality, is indeed met in the case at hand, and the ending of suffering by an injection of potassium chloride would indeed outweigh the bad effect of the patient's death, given all the circumstances. What of the first two conditions? As to the first, what is the intent of the act? Recall, an intention is not a vague longterm goal but rather a principle that shapes a particular action. If the particular act (or object) under consideration is an injection of potassium chloride, the only goal that can be driving that immediate act is the death of the patient. That is what potassium chloride does in a person's bloodstream. Thus, the intent is to end the patient's life. Unlike the caregiver providing morphine, who would consider her purpose achieved if the patient lived on with his pain relieved, the one administering potassium chloride would consider her purpose achieved only if the patient died. Of course, that patient would no longer be suffering, since he would be dead. But that leads us to condition two.

Even if we were to grant that the goal (not the intent, which is more immediate) of the injection of potassium chloride were to ease suffering, the evil effect (death) is desired in itself, and indeed is the means to the good effect of cessation of suffering. It is by a cessation of living that suffering is ended. Condition two of the doctrine of double effect is thus not met. Therefore, injecting a patient with a deadly agent such as potassium chloride, in order to relieve suffering, is revealed by the doctrine of double effect to be an importantly different act than the giving of pain relief which may indeed cause the patient's death. What distinguishes them is the presence or absence of an intent to end the patient's life.

At this point, some proponents of euthanasia throw up their arms in exasperation. This type of double-effect analysis seems far too complicated, more like academic hairsplitting than an accurate description of how people do and should make practical decisions. It is indeed true that the palliative care case is complicated, and a perfect example of a hard case that seems to strain the capacities of our practical reasoning. Yet it is suggested here that this is more a result of the particularities of the morphine case than it is the doctrine of double effect. We use double-effect reasoning, and manifest an awareness of the difference between intention and foreseen consequences, all the time.

Consider the heart surgeon who performs risky surgeries. The goal is to heal her patients, which is clearly a good goal. Yet due to the nature of the risky surgery, she knows that (even with no blameworthy negligence) her surgeries will in fact cause the deaths of some (hopefully small) percentage of her patients. She intentionally performs hundreds of surgeries, even while knowing full well ahead of time that she will sadly cause the deaths of some of her patients, patients whose lives would have been longer had they not ended on her surgical table. She has clearly caused the death of some of her patients, and thus we can say that she "killed" people. But is this the same as intentionally ending lives? Of course not. We do indeed grasp the difference between intended acts and voluntary acts with foreseen consequences, even before someone teaches us the doctrine of double effect. Therefore, though analysis of intentionality and the use of the doctrine of double effect may indeed get complicated with hard cases, the source of that complication is life itself, and not the way we go about practical reasoning. It would be a mistake to let a hard case like palliative care prompt us to reject important tools for practical reasoning, such as the careful delineation of intent (rather than reliance solely upon foreseen consequences) and the doctrine of double effect.

What's Wrong with Intending to End a Life You've Already Given Up On?

Of course, demonstrating that intentionally ending the life of a patient who is suffering and near death is different from actions that may cause death does not therefore mean that acts of euthanasia are wrong. It is the purpose of this part to demonstrate why the intentional ending of a patient's life—which is euthanasia—is not only different from other acceptable acts, but also wrong. After all, there are some who recognize the difference intention makes and still claim that in certain rare cases it may be most loving to purposely end the life of a suffering patient.[8] It is important to see the allure of this position. Again, assume we are talking about one of those cases where it is indeed prudent to stop prolonging life. For many, the cessation of treatment will result in a relatively quick death. But what if it does not? What if the suffering goes on, and though death will certainly come, awaiting it is unbearable to the patient? Why not go the extra step and intentionally end this patient's life?

Note how rare this case is. First, clearly the person must be conscious to have unbearable suffering, so we are not talking about any patients that are comatose or in persistent vegetative states. Second, given the advanced state of palliative care today, thankfully it is also the case that few conditions elude

8. See Margaret Farley, "Issues in Contemporary Christian Ethics: The Choice of Death in a Medical Context," *Santa Clara Lectures*, 1 no. 3 (1995): 1–19.

quality pain treatment. Of course, access to quality medical care is definitely lacking not only in the developing world, but even in our own nation, due to injustices in delivery of medical care. Surely everyone who participates in this conversation can be united in pursuing the greater availability of quality palliative care to all who need it.

So though these cases are rare, they do exist. Should we carefully delineate them morally—even legally—and permit the intentional ending of a patient's life only under these rare conditions? This is what the citizens of Oregon have in fact done. But the answer offered here is no, for two reasons. The first is a prudential judgment, meaning it refers not to an absolute norm but rather to a judgment about what is best overall, in this case for the common good of society. Consider the effect of legalizing euthanasia in such rare cases. Would it really remain limited to those rare cases, or would such legalization lead to further practice of and legalization of euthanasia? This type of argument is called a *slippery-slope argument*. It basically says that permitting certain acts may have the unforeseen, or at least undesirable, consequence of leading to acts one did not really intend to permit. For instance, what would happen to vulnerable populations in our society, such as the poor, the uninsured, the lonely elderly, racial minorities—all groups proven to receive less adequate health care than other populations in our society? It is reasonable to suppose that the same pressures alive and well today to limit costly medical care to such populations would lead to explicit, or at least implicit, pressures on such persons to avail themselves of what society has deemed to be an acceptable act at the end of life: euthanasia. This must at least give us pause, especially if we are concerned about the vulnerable among us. And given the rarity of cases that would justify euthanasia to its proponents—and the fact that the very existence of those cases generally betrays the very same injustices in health care that euthanasia opponents fear—the pervasiveness of injustice in health-care delivery to vulnerable populations makes legalization of euthanasia imprudent.

Of course, some slippery-slope arguments sound alarmist fears among people to convince them not to pursue a course of action. These types of slippery-slope claims are the worst of moral arguments.[9] The way to determine whether a slippery -slope claim is a legitimate argument or a case of alarmist fear-mongering is to see how logically connected the immediate course of action is to what is feared down the road. It is true that legislative curbs could be erected to try and ensure that pressure favoring euthanasia not be exerted on vulnerable populations such as the poor and elderly. It is also true that data is mixed from places where euthanasia in some form is legal. In the Netherlands, laws have indeed gotten progressively permissive

9. See James F. Keenan, SJ, "What's Your Worst Moral Argument?" *America* 164 (1993): 17–18, 28–30.

(such that involuntary euthanasia for the nonconscious without advanced directives is now permissible), and numbers are on the rise. In Oregon, where only physician-assisted suicide is legal, there has been no broadening of the laws, and numbers have remained relatively small. So the data is mixed. But given the stakes, and the small number of cases this legitimately concerns, can it really be deemed prudent to legalize euthanasia in our nation today? The answer given here is no.

The second reason why intentionally ending suffering patients' lives is not only different but wrong concerns an absolute norm rather than a prudential judgment. As noted in chapter 8, part of the moral bedrock of the Christian tradition is "that direct and voluntary [i.e., intentional] killing of an innocent human being is always gravely immoral."[10] This is true even where it seems that good may come of the evil act (see Rom. 3:8). Note two key terms in this absolute moral norm. The first is "intentional," which already has been fully explained. The second is "innocent," a word that explains why this norm does not necessarily apply in cases of warfare. Not all killing is the same, and thus recognitions of the permissibility of self defense or warfare do not at all directly translate into the permissibility of euthanasia.

Of course, what the issue of euthanasia offers most distinctly is a case where it seems that intentionally ending the patient's life is in the patient's best interest, since it ends her suffering. Indeed, the patient is presumably asking for it, and others have recognized that it is prudent to stop fighting to prolong life. Surely the prohibition against killing the innocent is meant to protect people. But it seems here that euthanasia in certain rare cases is actually a way to serve the patient's best interests!

We are now at the very crux of the issue. Why is an intent to end a suffering patient's life always and everywhere wrong? It is not enough to say it is playing God, or (more secularly), that it violates human rights, since those answers beg the question. That is, they assume the correct answer in providing their response. We are precisely trying to determine if it is ever a way to honor human dignity, or play with God, to euthanize a patient, much as we trust we are honoring dignity and cooperating with God when we send patients to a surgery even if it turns out to be deadly, or when we give pain killers that actually end up hastening death. Granted, these are non-intentional acts; but why is intentionally ending life always wrong?

One could claim the prohibition of intentional ending of life is an effective stopgap. It helps ensure that the slippery-slope concerns described above do not happen. Or, from a religious perspective, such a prohibition could be seen as a way to leave a gap for God to act, if the decisions we make are somehow wrong; in other words, if we can decide not to prolong life but not to end it,

10. *Evangelium Vitae* (Encyclical Letter, 1995), 57.

then God can intervene and keep the patient alive, if that is God's desire. But this is inadequate. From a secular perspective, it is wrong to instrumentalize those who make up the rare cases, where intending death is appropriate (if that is true), only to guard against possible future harm to people in vulnerable positions. From a religious perspective, presumably God does not need our protection in the form of a purposeful gap to be able to act! Better to do our best to cooperate with God's intentions than see God's agency and our own in tension, and set things up to allow for God to win out in case we are wrong (as if God needs our help!).

This last comment on cooperating with God's intentions addresses our question most directly. Christians believe that God is a God of life, and that death, sin, and suffering are not intended by God; rather, they are deviations from God's plan. It is true, as stated in chapter 13, that God in God's mercy brings enormous good out of even great evils such as death, by bringing people who have died into union with him. But though God allows death to happen, God does not intend death, nor should we.

This answer is one of many answers to our question that are part of the Christian tradition. For instance, euthanasia is interpreted by Christians to defy the divine command, "thou shall not kill." Further, Christians believe that their lives are not their own, but rather gifts from God; and acts directly intended to terminate that gift are sinful. But, the fact, that Christians have additional resources to support the absolute norm against killing the innocent should not mislead one into thinking that this norm is only intelligible, or applicable, to Christians. To the contrary, this is a natural-law norm accessible and applicable to all.

How is it intelligible to those who are not Christian? That it is can be seen in the fact that it is current U.S. law (with the Oregon exception). How it is can be seen by recalling our work on intention in chapter 2. Recall that intentions are not merely transitive (impacting the world around us), but also intransitive (shaping our very selves). Though different acts may lead to the same (transitive) results, it is the intentionality that makes an act intransitive and shapes who we are. Intending to end the life of a patient, even out of mercy, shapes us into people who reject and attack life, rather than people who unequivocally support life, as when we patiently care for the dying. The willingness to intend to end an innocent life, even for the patient's "own good," is not only ripe for abuse, but changes the person so willing to act. Even in the presence of a well-meaning goal of ending suffering, performing acts whose immediate goal is to end life habituates a person into someone who acts against life. As a point of contrast, the person who intentionally administers painkillers, knowing that they may cause death, is still habituating himself into someone who cares for the dying, since that is the intention of the immediate act. This is why intention is what defines euthanasia, and why it is so crucial not to intend to end a patient's life.

The preceding paragraph may make it seem as if the prohibition against intending to end a suffering patient's life is more for the sake of the caregiver than the patient. After all, it is the patient who is suffering, so shouldn't care for that patient take precedence over concern for how the caregiver habituates herself? In fact, this may even appear to be an occasion where the caregiver ought to be willing to give of herself, even at the risk of harm to her character. But this is wrong for two reasons. First, given the discussion of justice in chapter 7, recognition of the common good means that the patient's own good is tied up in the flourishing of those around him, such that it is not actually in the best interest of the patient to be part of a community where intentionally ending life is part of people's character. Second, and related to the first, even in the immediate moment, a caregiver's intention to end life, even if well-meaning, pollutes the caregiving relationship. Rather than being supported by people who care for and suffer with him, the patient is cared for (or is he?) by people who are open to purposely ending his life. One could retort that such an act (euthanasia) would only be done with the patient's consent (indeed, request). Even so, the active consideration of this option in such a situation, particularly at a time of great vulnerability for the patient, diminishes the caregiving encounter in a manner akin to the way intentionally ending a life warps the character in the caregiver. It makes the acceptance of life conditional, and turns a relationship defined by care into a relationship open to elimination of the patient. This is why many authors who write on this issue worry about the involvement of the medical (caregiving) community in the execution of euthanasia.[11] There is a fundamental disconnect between intentional care and intentional elimination.

Withholding or Withdrawing Life-Sustaining Treatment

The preceding parts of the sections have attempted to delineate the difference between intending the death of a patient and offering treatments that may actually cause a patient's death, with a further claim that while the latter may be virtuous, the former never is. But there is another category of actions to consider. Treatments like the administration of painkillers (and even more obvious ones like heart surgery) are clearly intended for the good of the patient, and therefore fall under the doctrine of double effect, even when they in fact lead to a patient's death. The patient's death is a foreseen consequence, though not the intent of these acts, which is why they are distinguished from acts of euthanasia.

One of the reasons that virtuous caregivers are willing to treat patients in ways that may actually hasten their death is that human life, while an extraordinarily

---

11. This is a common topic in the literature on euthanasia. For a brief summary of the issue, see Richard Gula, "Moral Principles Shaping Public Policy on Euthanasia," *Second Opinion*, 14 no. 1 (1990): 73–83.

important good, is not absolute. If life were regarded as an absolute good, then nothing which could threaten it could be undertaken virtuously. This would apply not only to medical procedures such as surgeries and palliative care, but other human activities such as waging war, fighting fires, or even driving cars. Each of the latter is always undertaken by people with the foreseen (but unintended) consequence that it may lead to their death. If preserving and prolonging human life were an absolute value, none of these activities could be virtuous. This position has been called *vitalism*; life should be preserved and prolonged at all possible costs.[12] Thankfully, principled vitalists are few and far between. Few if any would rule out the willingness to sacrifice one's own life for another in a situation such as a with a rescuing mother. And in the medical arena, given the advanced state of technology today, vitalism would mean trying to resuscitate every single person who dies, and using every treatment and piece of technology available at the end of life, no matter what the patient's condition.

A main reason vitalism fails is that it assesses the good of life solely by the length of life. Length of life is not unimportant, for sure, and in general people naturally strive to prolong life. But if length of life alone is considered, prolonging life becomes an absolute norm. This fails to leave any room to make judgments about the quality of life. As chapter 13 on hope and the afterlife endeavors to show, the goal of the truly good life is fullness of life, which is not only measured by duration but by quality. (Virtues are the characteristics that give life such quality.) Firefighters and soldiers make judgments about the quality of life—both for themselves and their communities—and are willing to sacrifice length for quality. The same is true in the medical arena. We should not deny that quality-of-life judgments are indeed made during end-of-life decision making, the point made in section one of this chapter.

The question at issue here is the following: when a quality-of-life judgment is made, such that some particular medical treatment is refused or ceased, with the foreseen consequence that the patient may (indeed, in some cases virtually certainly will) die, what is the intent of such an act? Unlike cases where a treatment intended for the good of a patient unintentionally ends his life (such as heart surgery), here we have a death that results from a purposeful refusal or removal of treatment. Does such a refusal or removal constitute "an action or omission which of itself or by intention causes death?"[13] If so, it is euthanasia, and thus wrong, making it seem the vitalists are right. But if not, what then is the intent of such acts?

Consider two cases. First, a person in a persistent vegetative state (PVS) and unable to breathe is on a respirator to enable him to breathe. Though, of course, such things cannot be declared with total certainly, doctors are virtually certain after months of this condition that the patient will never recover,

12. See ibid.
13. *Declaration on Euthanasia*, ii.

regain consciousness, or breathe on his own. If the family decides to take him off the respirator and he dies, what is their intent? Second, a ninety- year-old woman in the last stages of cancer is in and out of consciousness and in great suffering. At her prior request, and with the support of her family, she has a DNR ("do not resuscitate") order on her medical chart, so that if she were to go into cardiac arrest she would not be revived by her doctors, even if such resuscitation may indeed prolong her life. Does her DNR order constitute an intent to end her life, and thus qualify as euthanasia?

It must be granted that in either case, the act performed (i.e., the object) can be driven by intent to end the patient's life, and thus be an act of euthanasia. (The same, of course, can be said of palliative care.) If this were the case, it would be why the DNR order was given, or why the respirator was turned off, and this aim would be frustrated if the person somehow lived on (particularly in the latter case). But second, these objects may be driven by another intent, namely, the intent to stop prolonging the life of the patient with useless or burdensome treatments. The claim here, which is also the claim of the Catholic church and current U.S. law, is that a caregiver may withhold or withdraw life-prolonging treatment, resulting in the death of the patient, with the intent not to kill the patient but rather to avoid burdensome or useless treatments.

One of the main reasons debates about euthanasia can be so confusing is that people often label such acts euthanasia, most often passive euthanasia. But if the distinguishing feature of euthanasia is an intent to end a patient's life, this is not necessarily the intent behind the act (though again, it may be, and if it is, the act is euthanasia). As in the case of the painkillers, here we have a voluntary act with the foreseen consequence of the patient's death. How can we say death is not intended? This is especially true of this case vs. that of painkillers, since with the administration of painkillers there is at least an obvious alternate intention (relief of pain). What alternate intention exists here, and is this now mere hairsplitting, or worse, self-delusion?

The alternate intent may be to stop prolonging life with treatment that is useless or burdensome (terms examined below). This is obviously the case when some sort of treatment (like CPR) is withheld, as in the ninety- year-old cancer patient. But it is also the case in the removal of the respirator in the PVS patient. Though it may seem the patient is living without treatment, and is then interfered with (by the removal of the respirator, or "pulling the plug"), in reality the situation is better understood as one of ongoing treatment (i.e., the respirator) which is then stopped. The interference was happening all along, and then removed when deemed useless and burdensome. The intent of the act is the withholding or removal of futile treatment. Is this a self-deluding way to say we are not really killing the patient? Not at all. The evidence is the fact that on occasion people do continue to live when taken off a respirator. And certainly people continue to live before their DNR order is respected.

When lives go on, the caregivers support and sustain the patient. They do not consider their aim (intent) frustrated if the person continues to live; their aim was to avoid needlessly prolonging life with treatment. If a person lives on without such treatment, their aim is still achieved! If it were not, presumably they would try to "finish the job" by performing some act (a different object) intended to end the patient's life.

Note two observations about intention when withholding or withdrawing life-sustaining treatment. First, it is certainly true that people may actually harbor a malicious intent (to kill), and legally get away with it by performing an act that cannot be prosecuted, since it may be driven by a legal intent (not to prolong life). When this happens, the act is not virtuous, even if it is not prosecutable. Second, sometimes the intent to not prolong life is accompanied by a hope or desire that the loved one die sooner rather than later. We often hope and pray our suffering loved ones at the end of life may rest in a peaceful death to end their suffering, even while we refuse to end their lives ourselves. In fact, the patient himself may desire a speedy death to be delivered from suffering, and yet refuse to end his own life. The refusal to finish the job and end a life is not an act of cowardice, but the recognition that intending to end a life is a different act than hoping for deliverance from suffering (the point of the last part of this section). Thus family members may actually hope for a speedy death while withholding or withdrawing treatment. Sadly, this often engenders guilt in people in such situations when the patient dies. They may label this a case of having mixed intentions. But again, recall an intention guides actions.. In this case, the hope or wish for a speedy death is not an intention, since it does not drive the action. In such a case we do not, properly speaking, have mixed intentions; we have intentional action accompanied by wishes (that are not intentions). In such a case there should be no guilt, so long as the caregivers are acting to avoid useless or burdensome treatment rather than to end a life, two importantly different intentions even when the foreseen consequences are the same.

The repeated description of treatments as useless or burdensome requires some discussion. Though medical treatments generally prolong life, the point of medicine is not simply to prolong life but rather to enable people to live more fully (a goal that generally coincides with prolonging life). Sometimes medical treatment does not serve this purpose, even though it may prolong life. Two examples are the PVS patient and the ninety-year-old cancer patient already mentioned. In these cases, resuscitation or a respirator would indeed work, in that they prolong life. And in most cases those treatments should indeed be employed. Yet not always. When burdensome to patients and their loved ones, or useless by not serving a medical purpose, then these treatments can be refused.[14] It is essential to note that these two terms refer to the treatment,

---

14. For further discussion of these terms, see Gilbert Meilander, *Bioethics: a Primer for Christians* (Grand Rapids: Eerdmans, 2005), 71.

not to the patient. It is not virtuous to cease treatment because one views a patient's life as useless or burdensome. Even when we judge someone's quality of life such that it is best to no longer fight on, labeling a person useless or burdensome is something else altogether—and incompatible both with respect for persons and with the virtue charity. But a medical treatment may indeed be labeled useless or burdensome.

Another way used to describe useless and burdensome treatments is by calling them extraordinary. *Extraordinary treatments* are those which are burdensome and/or useless, and thus can be refused without intending to end a patient's life. The two cases above are good examples. Another would be the cancer patient whose standard treatment has proven ineffective, but is offered an experimental treatment which would entail moving across the country away from family, significant expense, and far from certain results. Such a treatment would be called extraordinary and could be refused without intending the patient's death. In other words, saying no to such a treatment does not necessarily constitute an intent to die. Note that extraordinary treatments may indeed be virtuously undertaken; they just need not be. Different persons can come to different decisions on such matters and each be virtuous. To add further confusion, the same treatment may be extraordinary in some cases, but not in others. The respirator may be extraordinary for the PVS patient, but not burdensome or useless for a person who is in major surgery and expected to recover. A respirator is used in these latter cases all the time, and if someone were to remove it we could only describe such an act as intended to end the patient's life.

This leads us to the companion term of extraordinary treatment, namely, ordinary treatment. An *ordinary treatment* is one that is not burdensome or useless. Therefore, its refusal or removal can only be driven by an intent to end a patient's life. Sometimes a particular sort of act (object) can be driven by alternative intentions. For instance, one can remove someone from a respirator in order to end his life, or in order to cease burdensome or useless treatment. The act looks the same from the outside, but is importantly different due to intent. Some acts (objects), however, are so clear in their meaning that they can only be driven by one intention. This is what the Declaration on Euthanasia refers to when defining euthanasia as "an action or omission which by itself or by intention causes death."[15] Even if a person tells herself she is doing it for another reason, we say this is self-delusion. For instance, if the ninety-year-old cancer patient acquires an infection that is easily treatable with an antibiotic, that treatment is ordinary. It is not burdensome or useless. If it is refused, there is no explanation for the act other than intending to end the patient's life.

15. *Declaration on Euthanasia*, ii.

Of course, the rub is often deciding whether a treatment is rightly labeled ordinary or extraordinary. Though there is a rationale behind these labels, there is no precise formula available to determine the status of any and all treatments. Some cases are not contested, such as the ones offered so far in this part. Yet others are much more difficult, especially given the fact that usefulness and burden are terms that may be dependent on a patient's particular status, and at different times or with different patients the same treatment may be ordinary or extraordinary. A currently contested example is the administration of AHN, or *artificial hydration and nutrition*. What could be more ordinary than giving a patient food and drink? This is indeed an ordinary treatment in the vast majority of cases. But there are cases of PVS patients who cannot be spoon-fed and who develop horrible infections from tube feeding. In such cases AHN is indeed providing a burden, and nearly all agree in such extreme cases that it can be removed. But what of conscious patients at the very end of life who can receive AHN, even though doing so will prolong their suffering? These are the cases that are debated today.

Debates such as these are dependent not only on clear thinking and precise principles from moral theology (intent, double effect, ordinary/ extraordinary, etc.), but also upon the medical facts of the case which are required in order to make judgments about burden, usefulness, and so on. This should not surprise us; after all we are dealing with an innerworldly activity accessible to unaided human reasoning and thus able to be governed by natural-law reasoning. That analysis cannot be done here. The point of this chapter has been to equip the reader with essential concepts for adjudicating which end-of-life decisions are virtuous, and which are not. With the conclusion of this discussion of ordinary and extraordinary treatments, that task is now complete.

Concluding Thoughts

The painstaking analysis of human action in the preceding parts may lead us to wonder why this chapter is found in the second half of this book. Recall the main claim of the second half of this book is that big-picture beliefs (like the belief commitments of the Christian faith) shape how we engage in innerworldly activities, and thus impact what acts are virtuous or not. That claim is again affirmed here. In terms of this chapter, it is most obviously seen in the first section's discussion of when it is ever virtuous to welcome death. But it is also seen in the goal of medical treatment assumed throughout this chapter: to support and restore life most fully.

Of course, it is also evident in this chapter that Christian beliefs do not uniquely support that goal of medicine. Furthermore, no matter what one's belief commitments, careful action analysis (as seen in the third section) is necessary which is attentive to intentionality, consequences, and so on. Hence, the issue of euthanasia is a particularly appropriate way to end the main body of this textbook. We see here the necessity of prudence, the interconnectedness of prudence and the other cardinal virtues (particularly justice), the importance of object/intention/circumstances, the usefulness of the doctrine of double effect, the place of absolute norms, and the importance of the formation of conscience and the habituation of our desires (particularly our fears concerning death and the end of life). All of these topics—addressed in the first half of this book—are seen here with euthanasia. They all constitute natural-law reasoning, since they concern activities accessible to unaided human reasoning.

All of these topics are also shaped by one's big-picture belief commitments, including those of the Christian story articulated in this second half. So from a Christian perspective, starting from the three theological virtues enables us to see how faith in a God of life leads us to "play with God" by not ever intending the death of innocent persons. Our hope in life eternal allows us not to absolutize earthly life, and yet to see our actions here as continuous with our eternal destiny, such that life here can never be discarded casually or purposely acted against. Our love leads us to care patiently for those who suffer at the end of life, to be with them in their brokenness with trust that loving service to others in times of suffering is indeed the path to new life illuminated by Christ. We trust in God's grace to support us not only in faith, hope and love, but also in the prudence, justice, fortitude, and temperance needed to live virtuously at the end of life. The argument against euthanasia in this chapter is not dependent on resources particular to Christianity. Yet that argument is indeed further illuminated and buttressed by the Christian tradition.

Study Questions

1. Why does this chapter dismiss the helpfulness of the slogan, "don't play God!"?
2. Is suffering simply good? Can there be meaning in suffering? Be sure to explain the difference between educative and redemptive suffering.
3. True or False: "Suffering should be avoided at all costs." Explain your answer.
4. Is dependency ever good? At what point does dependency inhibit a good life?
5. What is it that defines an act of euthanasia according to this chapter? Explain why or why not this way of determining whether an act counts as euthanasia is more helpful than distinctions such as "active/passive" or "natural/unnatural."

6. Give the conditions of the doctrine of double effect. Using it, explain whether or not the administration of painkillers knowing it may hasten death can be a virtuous act.
7. What reasons are given here for why it is wrong to go the extra step and intentionally end a patient's life to relieve suffering?
8. According to this chapter, what constitutes a virtuous intent while withholding or removing treatment? When is such an act virtuous?
9. Explain the difference between ordinary and extraordinary forms of treatment, giving examples of each. Why is it always immoral to withhold or withdraw ordinary treatments?

Terms to Know

educative vs. redemptive suffering, mutual dependency, active/passive, natural vs. unnatural, euthanasia, physician-assisted suicide, palliative care, doctrine of double effect, slippery-slope argument, vitalism, ordinary vs. extraordinary treatment, artificial hydration and nutrition

Questions for Further Reflection

1. If people say in debates over euthanasia, "don't play God!" what do they really mean? What could they say instead, or why is this sufficient?
2. In what ways can we live now, before facing end-of-life decisions, to develop good habits so as to be able to find meaning in suffering, or live out an appropriate sense of mutual dependence?
3. How would you respond to someone who said to you, "I agree with passive euthanasia, but not active euthanasia"?
4. Try to think of examples from everyday life where we can clearly see the difference between voluntarily acting in a way that brings about foreseen consequences, and intending those consequences. Do you agree with the difference between these two?
5. What is your own position on whether or not it can ever be permissible to intentionally end a patient's life in order to relieve suffering?
6. Is artificial hydration and nutrition an ordinary or extraordinary medical treatment? Or can it be either? Explain.

Further Reading

The literature on euthanasia, let alone broader issues in bioethics, is simply enormous. The Vatican's *Declaration on Euthanasia* is a succinct statement on the issue from a moral-theological perspective. See also John Paul II's encyclical

Evangelium Vitae, which offers a powerful exposition of the centrality of affirming life and refusing to intend the death of innocents. The sections focused
on euthanasia are 64–67. John Keown's (ed.) *Euthanasia Examined: Ethical,
Clinical and Legal Perspectives* is a helpful overview of various dimensions
of the issue, including representatives from differing viewpoints. For a helpful examination, from a Catholic perspective, of recent debates over artificial
hydration and nutrition, see Christopher Tollefson (ed.), *Artificial Hydration
and Nutrition: The New Catholic Debate* and Ronald P. Hamel and James
Walters (ed.) *Artificial Hydration and Nutrition in the Permanently Unconscious Patient: the Catholic Debate.*

EPILOGUE

Praying for Virtues

This has been a book on morality, or how we live our lives. It is a book on Christian morality, explaining how the Christian faith infuses and transforms innerworldly life. Yet thus far, the core of Christian life—worship, prayer, and the sacraments—has been barely mentioned! Though the climactic chapter 16 on grace noted how crucial the sacraments and prayer are in receiving God's grace, there has been no sustained attention to the moral importance of liturgical life. This is primarily because the book explores how people do practical reasoning by explaining the hydraulics of human practical reasoning, the relation of such reasoning to our belief commitments, and the manifestation of those commitments in practices. In doing so, the hope has been that we can think and act more intentionally, and more in accordance with the way things really are, as people of faith.

Nonetheless, there is an accurate criticism in noting the lack of attention to prayer and sacraments. Christians are increasingly aware of how liturgical practices are crucially formative for our practical reasoning, and so saying this book is focused on practical reasoning does not adequately justify this omission, which is acknowledged here: the practices we need to consider that manifest and in turn shape what we believe are obviously not only those where we find contested ethical issues, such as drinking alcohol, warfare, sexuality and end-of-life decision making. It stands to reason that for Christians, some of the most important practices are those that explicitly engage God. But rather than quickly summarize why prayer, liturgy, and the sacraments are so morally important, this last chapter has a far more modest goal.

The purpose of this chapter is to look closely at one of the foundations of Christian prayer life—the Our Father, or Lord's Prayer—and explore how its words reveal and further illuminate the life of virtue described in this book. If prayer is part of the good life, and the virtues are a most helpful tool in living and understanding the good life, it should not surprise us that there are clear connections between the virtues and Christian prayer. One of the main organizing principles of this text has been the seven—four cardinal and three theological—virtues of the Christian life. Upon close examination, each of these virtues is readily apparent in the Our Father. The task of this chapter is to look closely at that prayer, with the work of this book in mind, and see what connections can be made between the life of virtue described thus far and the Lord's words in the Our Father. This will serve both as a helpful summary of this book's treatment of the seven main virtues, and a fitting demonstration of the intimate connection between prayer and the life of virtue.

The *Our Father*: A Cornerstone of the Christian Tradition

The Our Father is perhaps the most familiar prayer in the Christian tradition. It is one of the first things learned by children who are taught the Christian faith, said in the celebration of the eucharist, and relied on at other liturgical events (funerals, weddings, etc.). As a prayer, you can count on all Christians knowing it no matter how well formed they have been in their faith or what their current practices are. It is also an ecumenical prayer, cherished by all Christians of any tradition.

Why is this prayer such a foundational part of the Christian tradition? What makes this prayer so special is its origin in the gospels, its context in the gospels, and who offers its words. The prayer appears in both Matthew and Luke.[1] In Matthew it appears in that charter text of the Christian life, the Sermon on the Mount. In the Gospel according to Luke, it appears in a passage where the disciples ask Jesus to show them how to pray. There is something comforting in the Luke passage for those of us who have struggled with how to pray, and wondered if we were doing it right. Here we have Jesus's closest friends, those who have been called by him, who have left everything to follow him, and who have spent countless hours with Jesus during his earthly life. And even they wondered how to pray! Jesus offers no secrets, but rather a straightforward and simple prayer that is nonetheless extraordinarily rich in its content. So

---

1. The Lord's Prayer is found at Matt. 6:9–13 and Luke 11:2–4. The forms are quite similar, though there are differences. Since the Catholic liturgy (and the form commonly recited by Christians) follows Matthew's text, that version is given here.

here we have, in the words of the Savior himself, direct instruction on how to pray to the Father:

> Our Father in heaven, hallowed be your name,
> your kingdom come, your will be done, on earth as in heaven.
> Give us today our daily bread; and forgive us our debts, as we forgive
>   our debtors;
> and do not subject us to the final test, but deliver us from the evil one.[2]

Given the special context in the gospels, the Lord's Prayer has been a central part of Christian tradition from the very beginning. In the Didache, an important early Christian text written around the year 100 AD, the prayer is written out in its entirety, followed by the instruction to pray this three times a day.[3] It has been part of Christian liturgical life from the beginnings of the church. It also quickly became a favorite topic for Christian theologians to write about. Commentaries on the Lord's Prayer number in the hundreds or more. Well-known Christian thinkers like Thomas Aquinas have written entire works on the prayer, and others like Augustine have written extensively on the prayer, even if not devoting an entire book to it.[4] This practice continues today, as evidenced in Fr. Servais Pinckaers, OP's *Sources of Christian Ethics*, where he, following Augustine and Aquinas, aligns different petitions of the Our Father to the Beatitudes (from Matt. 5) and gifts of the Holy Spirit (from Isa. 11).[5] Indeed, one of the four pillars structuring the *Catechism of the Catholic Church*, "Christian prayer," contains an introduction to prayer in general, followed by an extensive commentary on the Our Father.[6] The *Catechism* calls the Our Father the "quintessential prayer of the Church," and notes it has been called "the summary of the whole gospel" (by Tertullian) and the "most perfect of prayers" (by Aquinas).[7] Indeed, this epilogue

---

2. Matt. 6:9–13. This is the translation of the New American Bible, used for scripture readings in Catholic liturgies in the United States. When the prayer is further analyzed below, the more common form used by English-speaking Christians (the same form found in Catholic mass) will be used.

3. Didache, in *Early Christian Writings*, ed. Andrew Louth (New York: Penguin, 1968), 194.

4. See Aquinas's sermons on the Our Father in J. B. Collin's *Catechetical Instructions of St. Thomas Aquinas* (New York: J. F. Wagner, 1939). See also Aquinas's *Summa Theologiae*, English Dominican trans. (New York: Benziger, 1948), II–II 83,9. See Augustine, *Commentary on the Lord's Sermon on the Mount* (New York: Fathers of the Church Series, 1951). See also his *Enchiridion on Faith, Hope, and Love* (Washington, DC: Regnery Gateway, 1961), cxv.

5. Servais Pincakers, OP, *Sources of Christian Ethics* (Washington, DC: Catholic University of America Press, 1995), 155–58.

6. *Catechism of the Catholic Church*, 2nd ed. (Vatican City: Libreria Editrice Vaticana, 1997), 2759–2865.

7. Ibid., 2774–76.

chapter is an attempt to continue in this church tradition of commentating on the words of the Our Father.

The claim here is clearly not to offer the explanation of what the prayer means. For millennia people have plumbed it for limitless wisdom and grace. The more modest goal here is to closely examine the words of the prayer for what insight they might offer into the topic of this book. After all, if this book uses the concept of virtue to explain what is meant by a good life in the context of the Christian story, and if this prayer is the summary of the whole gospel, we should be unsurprised to find close parallels between the virtues and the Lord's Prayer. And that is exactly what we find.

The Structure of the Our Father

The Our Father is such a familiar prayer that it is easy to forget about its words when reciting it. But if we slowly say the prayer, and break from the routine cadence we use in speaking it words, those words reward prayerful analysis and reflection. The first observation to make about the prayer as a whole is that in the Christian tradition since Augustine, thinkers have always recognized that there are seven different *petitions*, or requests, in the prayer. This should not surprise us; after all, if we are praying, it makes sense to ask for something! Indeed, it is comforting to know, should we ever feel odd about continually asking God for things in prayer, that this is exactly what Jesus instructed us to do in the prayer he gave us.[8] But though the familiarity of the prayer may prevent us from noticing it, attending to its sentence structure reveals that there are seven distinct petitions in the prayer, along with several phrases and dependent clauses modifying them. It may help to write the prayer according to these petitions, as follows:

> Our Father, who art in heaven, hallowed be thy name.
> Thy kingdom come,
> Thy will be done, on earth as it is in heaven.
> Give us this day our daily bread,
> And forgive us our trespasses, as we forgive those who trespass against us.
> Lead us not into temptation,
> But deliver us from evil.

The fact that the last four lines are petitions is more obvious: "give us," "forgive us," "lead us," and "deliver us" are all clear requests. Yet the first three

8. See, for instance, Matt. 7:7–11, where Jesus instructs his disciples to "ask and it will be given to you," and "how much more will your heavenly Father give good things to those who ask him." See also Matt 6:6, where Jesus says the Father knows what we need even before we ask.

are less clear: "hallowed be," "thy kingdom come," and "thy will be done." Understanding these petitions requires a discussion of grammar, which is rarely someone's favorite subject. Those who have studied foreign languages, such as Latin or the Romance languages, are familiar with the subjunctive mood for verbs. Though the first three petitions appear to be indicative (i.e., simply indicating something is the case), they are actually in the subjunctive mood, which is rarely used in contemporary English, and when it is we often do not notice it. This particular use of the subjective in Latin is called jussive. It is used not to say something is the case, but as an exhortation that it may be the case. English-speaking students of Latin are commonly instructed to translate the jussive subjective using the word "let," and that may be of help here: "*let* they name be hallowed," "*let* thy kingdom come," and "*let* they will be done." Thus the first three petitions could be rendered in English:

> Our Father who are in heaven, let your name be hallowed
> Let your kingdom come,
> Let your will be done, on earth as it is in heaven.

The addition of "let" underscores the fact that these first three lines are indeed petitions.

In case you are wondering why we do not say it this way, I would suggest two reasons. First, we do! The verbs are indeed in the subjunctive here, and have this meaning, whether we recognize it or not. In fact, that is why we say "be" in the first and third petitions rather than "is." Most people probably think the use of "be" is a reflection of an older use of language (much as we often say "thy name" rather than "your name"), but in English "be" is the subjective form of "to be," rather than "is." Thus, if you have been praying this prayer you have already been asking our Father that his name may be hallowed, that his kingdom may come, and that his will may be done, whether you know it or not! Second, though we could insert "let" with no violence to the meaning of the prayer, old habits do die hard, especially in such important things as a prayer said for so long, and in just such a way in English. Furthermore, given the first point, people are still saying the prayer accurately and can easily be brought to understand that.

Therefore, the first observation on the prayer as a whole is that we have seven distinct petitions. The second observation is related to the first. The seven are divided into two groups: the first three (which use the jussive subjunctive), and the last four (which use the imperative mood). All seven petitions are made to God. But the first three ask in the subjunctive mood things that concern God directly: that God's name be hallowed, his kingdom come, and his will be done. The next four are again addressed to God, but in the imperative mood, concerning things and events that are innerworldly: our bread, our sins, our temptations, and evils that may befall us. Thus the first three petitions beseech

God concerning things that concern God directly, while the last four request of God help with things that are innerworldly.

At this point in the book, the significance of this distinction should be clear. If you did not guess where this chapter was going when it was pointed out there are seven petitions in the Our Father, perhaps you can guess now when it is observed that of the seven, three concern God directly and four concern innerworldly activities in relation to God! The main claim of this chapter is that the Lord's own words in the Our Father both neatly correspond to, and further illuminate, the seven virtues that have been consistently described in the Christian tradition as encapsulating a holy life. The rest of this chapter will examine each of the seven petitions separately, to see how each one corresponds with a virtue, and what it further reveals about that virtue. But before turning to that task an important disclaimer is in order.

Is the claim here that the real meaning of the Lord's Prayer is uncovered by attention to the seven virtues, and that the prayer can now finally be rightly understood after this reflection on it in that context? Absolutely not. A perusal of the scores of commentaries on the Lord's Prayer throughout the Christian tradition reveals an inexhaustible supply of wisdom in these words, much of which does not directly address the seven virtues. In fact, it was surprising to learn that no commentary on this prayer that I could find ever grouped the petitions in this way. Even Aquinas, who organized the whole moral part of his famous moral treatise around the seven virtues, did not organize his commentary on the Our Father in this manner.[9]

Does this mean that an understanding of living the Christian life as encapsulated in the seven traditional virtues is really not there in the Our Father? No; as argued in this chapter it seems clear that the content of the Lords' Prayer does indeed reflect and further illuminate the seven virtues. But the wisdom of God is profound beyond our imagination. So it only makes sense that God's wisdom, which ultimately is one and thus unified, be grasped by different people at different times in different ways. Christians have always espoused what has been called a theological reading of scripture, where the words of scripture can refer to realities beyond the plain senses of the words themselves. The basis of any theological read of scripture must always be the literal words themselves, which act as an anchor to tether our interpretations in truth. Yet as long as that literal sense is respected, application of the words of scripture to our lives or other parts of the Christian tradition can proceed creatively and reverently, confident not only that God's revelation is one, but also that it is rich beyond our grasp and thus always inviting and nourishing further interpretations. Thus the claim here is not that Jesus was really intending to teach his followers about the seven virtues, and now we

9. See Aquinas, sermon on the Our Father in *Catechetical Instructions of St. Thomas Aquinas*. See also his discussion of the Our Father in the *Summa Theologiae* II–II 89,3.

finally got it. Nonetheless, we should not be surprised if Jesus, the word of God incarnate, spoke words that resonate and reverberate with new wisdom for generations to come.

The Seven Petitions of the Our Father

The goal of this section is to examine each of the petitions individually, and reflect on how the particular petition reflects and further illuminates one of the seven main virtues of the Christian tradition. Again, the claim here is neither that each petition offers an exhaustive understanding of one of the virtues, nor that each petition only makes sense in reference to its corresponding virtue. The more modest claim here is that in most cases there is a strikingly clear correspondence between each petition and a virtue, and that we can better understand both the prayer and the virtues by looking at them in relation to each other.

> Our Father, who art in heaven, hallowed be thy name. (FAITH)
> Thy kingdom come, (HOPE)
> Thy will be done, on earth as it is in heaven. (LOVE)
>
> Give us this day our daily bread, (PRUDENCE)
> And forgive us our trespasses, as we forgive those who trespass against us. (JUSTICE)
> Lead us not into temptation, (TEMPERANCE)
> But deliver us from evil. (FORTITUDE)

Faith

The Lord's Prayer begins, "Our Father, who art in heaven, hallowed be thy name." The opening, "Our Father, who art in heaven," applies to the whole prayer, as it is God our Father whom we address in asking what follows. Biblical scholars often comment that the word Jesus used for father, *abba*, is an affectionate term. The prayer begins with an emphasis on God as a close and loving father. Of course, lest anyone doubt this is the same transcendent God who made heaven and earth, the opening address continues, "who art in heaven."

The first petition reads, "hallowed by thy name." What is being asked for here? First consider the word "name." What is in a name? Names have meanings. A name represents who someone is. Think of the importance of your own family name. Or perhaps there is a story behind your first name, or some nickname that loved ones call you. Other cultures ascribe even more obvious importance to names, as particularly witnessed in Native American cultures. The point is that a name is a representation of who someone is. The Jews so reverenced the name of God that they would not speak it aloud, out of respect. Christians give similar reverence to Jesus's name, as seen in the Holy Name devotion, and especially in St. Paul's claim that "at the name of Jesus every knee should bend, of those in heaven and on earth and under the earth" (Phil. 2:10). Thus, the first petition is not primarily about the three-letter word "God," but rather about the reality of who God is.

This first petition is asking that who God is, as represented by God's name, be "hallowed," or reverenced. In other words, it is asking that who God is be known and appreciated for who he is. This is, of course, what the virtue of faith enables people to do. It is the abiding inclination to know the truth about God and God's relationship to humanity. It is also the root of the other theological virtues hope and love, since only when you truly know who God is can you long for complete union with him, and seek him in friendship. In making this petition, we are not simply acknowledging the truth that is known in faith: that God's name is holy. We are also praying that God's holiness be recognized by all people in faith. As the first word of the prayer reminds us, this is not simply an individual prayer but a communal one.

Hope

The second petition reads, "thy kingdom come." The kingdom, or reign, of God is a metaphor to describe that state of affairs where all is happening according to God's will. This is not, of course, to say that anything ever occurs outside of God's providence. Though God's providence penetrates, and ultimately conquers, even the greatest of evils, there is plenty in our world that God does not intend, even if he lets it happen, such as sin, suffering, and death. The kingdom of God is God returning all creation to rightful union with him, and thus the cessation of sin, death, and suffering. Other biblical metaphors for this state of affairs include the New Jerusalem, the last day, and the time when the lion will lay down with the lamb. This is the kingdom for which we pray in the second petition.

What does this have to do with hope? It is the full arrival of God's kingdom for which hope yearns. Upon knowing God and God's plan for humanity in faith, in hope people long for that true fulfillment in union with God. That fulfillment is available only in the next life. But it is in this life that we are given the hope to keep our eyes fixed toward that destiny, rather than be foolishly sidetracked by other things which may be genuinely good, but never ultimately fulfilling. Of course, hope does not only fix us toward the next life. Equipped with this proper perspective, the person of hope can appreciate those non-ultimate goods most properly, and help further inaugurate God's kingdom in this life by living in Christ, in whom "the kingdom of God is at hand." But in the end hope longs for that kingdom referred to by the good thief next to

Jesus on the cross: "Jesus, remember me when you come into your kingdom" (Luke 23:42).

Love

The next and final petition of the group of three that represents the theological virtues is "thy will be done, on earth as it is in heaven." What is asked for here is rather straightforward: that God's will be done on earth just as it is in heaven. What is God's will? We know in faith that God is love (1 John 4:8; 16), and in this petition we pray that God's love reign, not simply in heaven but here on earth as well.

Having studied the theological virtue of love, or charity, we know that it is an act of the will, and something that is done rather than simply felt. And so "thy will be done" recalls for us love. God's love is complete and incessant, and so this petition is in fact asking that we people, created in the image of God and thus able to love, do in fact love one another as God has loved us. Jesus makes it quite clear that his commandment, his will, is that we love one another (John 15:10–17). In this petition we are asking God to infuse us with charity so that we may live this commandment and love God and our neighbor.

It is most fitting that this is the final petition of those representing the theological virtues. First of all, love is the crux of the Christian life. It is who God is, why he created all, and how we are called to participate in God's very nature. Though love is in one sense preceded by faith and hope, in another sense it is love that brings these (and all else) to perfection (see 1 Cor. 13, esp. vs. 7: love "believes all things, hopes all things"). Indeed, all good things in life are nothing without love. Second, though "on earth as it is in heaven" may seem to be a fittingly dramatic conclusion to the previous lines, it is actually most properly a reference to love, and therefore appropriately placed in the third petition. For as important as faith and hope are in this life, they pass away in the next, when we see God face to face and experience full union with him. No need for faith or hope then. But love remains. Love is the very meaning of existence, "on earth as it is in heaven." That is why despite the importance of the three theological virtues faith, hope, and love, "the greatest of these is love" (1 Cor. 13:13).

Prudence

One of the dangers of aligning two groups together and grafting them on to each other as related and mutually illuminating is that the effort is always in danger of being forced, driven more by the desire to align two groups (in this case of seven) neatly than see if their content is really related. It must be admitted that this danger is greatest with the first two petitions of this final group of four: "give us this day our daily bread," and "forgive us our trespasses, as we forgive those who trespass against us." Both of these petitions evoke justice, and neither is obviously about prudence. For instance, "give us this day our daily bread" seems to imply the regulated exchange ("give us" and "daily") that is so importantly a part of justice. It also suggests a crucial emphasis on social justice, begging God that all people have what they need to survive and thrive. Since the point of this chapter is not to claim the only meaning of each petition is fully encapsulated by its corresponding virtue, these insights, and many others, should indeed be kept in mind regarding the fourth petition.

But the petition, "give us this day our daily bread" is aligned here with prudence, for two reasons. First, it is fitting that the first of the four petitions representing cardinal virtues be about prudence, since prudence is the charioteer of, or preeminent among, the virtues. But is the virtue prudence simply imposed on these words, or do the words of the petition themselves have anything to do with prudence? The second reason is that once one has this virtue in mind, the words of the fourth petition do indeed evoke prudence. The priority of prudence makes bread, the basic sustenance for our everyday life, a fitting metaphor for prudence. Thus in this petition we are asking for prudence, the daily bread by which we live out our lives virtuously. After all, it is Christ himself who reminds us that "one does not live by bread alone, but by every word that comes forth from the mouth of God" (Matt. 4:4). And of course the word begotten by the Father is the Son, Jesus Christ, who tells us explicitly that "I am the bread of life; whoever comes to me will never hunger" (John 6:35). He is "the way, the truth, and the life" (John 14:6). In this petition we ask to see things more truthfully—in daily, or innerworldly things—so that we can walk the way of living life to the fullest in our earthly lives. Again, this does not mean we are not also praying for bread in the literal sense, and seeking a more just world where that bread is available. This sense of the petition, and the importance of literal bread for sustaining daily life, is what makes bread an apt metaphor for prudence. For we do not live by bread alone.

Justice

The fifth petition of the Lord's Prayer is enormously rich: "forgive us our trespasses, as we forgive those who trespass against us." As noted in the previous part, just as one could ascribe justice to the fourth petition, prudence also comes to mind with this petition. After all, reminiscent of Barron's windshield analogy for sin in chapter 12, it is only through seeing clearly that we are aware of our sinfulness and our need for forgiveness. The prudent person also sees how interconnected our relationships with God and others are, such that the forgiveness of our sins by God is intertwined with how we forgive others. Nevertheless, this petition seems most obviously about justice, and that is the virtue it is aligned with here.

Justice is the virtue that inclines one to right relations with others. And forgiveness is the reestablishment of right relations after some disruption. Therefore, in this petition we are praying that the order of justice (*ius*) be restored, that right relationship be reestablished between us and God, and between us and other people. It is easy to say this prayer without adequately reflecting on the extent to which these two are bound; we are asking to be forgiven as, or to the extent to which, we forgive others. It should give us pause that we are tying our own forgiveness by God to how well we forgive other people, since so often we are stingy in forgiving.

This petition is a direct repudiation of the attitude of the unforgiving servant in the gospel parable (Matt. 18:21–35). In response to Peter's question about how often we must forgive, Jesus replies not only with the famous "not seven times, but seventy times seven" (meaning always!), but also with the story of the unforgiving servant, who is graciously forgiven a debt by his king he cannot repay, but then proceeds to refuse to forgive a fellow servant a much smaller debt when it cannot be paid. Upon hearing this, the angry king hands over this unforgiving, and ungrateful, servant to the torturers, and Jesus ends the parable with the stern warning, "So will my heavenly Father do to you, unless each of you forgives his brother from his heart" (Matt. 18:35). The point here is not the simplistic "what goes around comes around." It is rather that our forgiveness of our neighbors, or lack thereof, suggests a standard or rule that we think represents the order of justice (again, *ius*), by which they should be judged. And as Christ himself reminds us, "the measure with which you measure will in return be measured out to you" (Luke 6:38).

Temperance

There is an aesthetically pleasing, or beautiful, element to the parallel between the seven virtues and the seven petitions of the Lord's Prayer. For example, the neat separation of the first three petitions from the last four (as seen in the grammatical shift) nicely reflects the difference between theological and cardinal virtue. Similarly, the petitions generally proceed in proper order. For instance, as noted in earlier chapters there is an order to faith, hope, and love, and it is fitting that they appear in the Lord's Prayer in that order. An order is also present in standard treatments of the cardinal virtues. Prudence has a priority, and it is reflected in this interpretation of the Lord's Prayer. Justice is always treated next in order of importance, again, reflected in the prayer. However, the next two virtues treated are generally fortitude and then temperance, since fortitude has historically been seen as closer to one's rational capacities. This chapter's interpretation deviates from that traditional order, and it must, since the last two petitions so obviously represent temperance first and then fortitude. The sixth petition, "lead us not into temptation," is a prayer for temperance.

Temperance is the virtue by which our sensual desires are well-ordered. Temptation is obviously not simply a matter of sensual desires. Indeed, one can be tempted by money, status, or honor. Nonetheless, sensual desire is a particularly obvious and common arena in our lives where we face temptation. Note that in this petition we do not simply ask that there be no temptations in the world. We ask that we be not lead into temptation. One way to understand this is that we may never encounter anything pleasurable or desirable that may tempt us. But another, and I would say more fruitful, way to understand this is that we be not lead into temptation because our desires are moderated by temperance, such that even in the presence of potentially tempting things we see them for what they truly are. We appreciate their beauty and pleasure, but not in a manner that displaces more important goods of this life. A life with no potential temptation is a life without many beautiful delights: delicious food, delectable drink, and pleasurable sexual activity. Yet a temperate life is one where these are indeed partaken with moderation in accordance with one's station in life, and thus truly enjoyed.

Fortitude

Much of what should be said about the seventh and final petition, "deliver is from evil," replicates what was said previously about temperance. First, the traditional order of the cardinal virtues is changed, but the content of the petition so obviously refers to fortitude that this is necessary. Fortitude is the virtue that inclines us to face difficulties well in this life. Evil is certainly one way to describe such difficulties. In the face of sickness and death, social injustice and senseless crime—indeed any such suffering—the virtue of fortitude is required so we may overcome the difficulty at hand (attack), or at least not be overcome by it (endurance).

Furthermore, as was the case with temperance, this petition can be interpreted as asking for two different things concerning evil. We may have always assumed that it means, "let no evil befall us." That is indeed an appropriate prayer. But the words say "*deliver us* from evil." We can be delivered from evil either by not experiencing it, or by not being overcome by it. The first would be nice, but is not fully possible in this life. And so in this petition we pray for fortitude, which allows us to face difficulties well, to be delivered from them by overcoming them, or at least by not being overcome by them.

Closing Reflections on the Petitions of the Our Father and the Virtues

In closing, it may help to make a few more observations about how the seven petitions of the Our Father as a whole are both better understood in reference to, and in turn further illuminate, the seven virtues of the Christian life. First, the prayer for the most part reconfirms the order of the virtues reiterated consistently in the Christian tradition. The three theological virtues are primary; they are the font of the Christian life and so the prayer naturally begins with them. Within this set of three petitions we see the proper order of faith, hope, and love reflected, while the privileged status of love as central to the entire Christian life is also reaffirmed in the third petition, with the triumphant, "on earth as it is in heaven."

Yet while accentuating the primacy of the theological virtues in the Christian life, the Our Father does not neglect the importance of innerworldly activities, and thus it also includes petitions that reflect the four cardinal virtues.[10] Again, something about the proper order of the cardinal virtues is revealed in the prayer, as prudence is aligned with the fourth petition, followed by justice with the fifth. There is deviation from the traditional ordering of fortitude and then temperance, but since both of these virtues help us keep our own ships in order, to recall Lewis's ships analogy, they are closely related to each other.

Furthermore, we should note that there is indeed some overlap among the petitions, which should be unsurprising given the doctrine of the unity of the virtues presented earlier in this book. It is seen most evidently in petitions four and five, each of which seems to suggest both prudence and justice. But it can also be said of other petitions. For instance, the sixth petition's plea to not be led into temptation is granted not only by being given the virtue of temperance, but also by receiving the virtues of fortitude (to stand fast), justice (so our right relations prevent us from pursing certain temptations), and prudence (so we can see clearly what constitutes temptation). Indeed, receiving the theological virtues of faith, hope, and love also transforms the temperance we receive, since we are bolstered in our resistance to temptation by knowing who God is in faith, remaining fixed on God as the source of our complete happiness in hope, and being in true friendship with God and others in charity. This is not to say all the virtues are interchangeable, or that there is really only one virtue. It is rather to say that in the virtuous person, the living out of any one virtue always relies on the presence and support of the other virtues. Thus, it is unsurprising that each of the seven petitions does not echo only one of the seven virtues, even though it is the case that each petition does reflect one of the seven virtues most clearly.

This last point on the unity of the virtues also recalls the discussion in chapter 16 on the importance of the infused cardinal virtues, a category of virtue too often neglected in moral theology today. Nowhere could the reality and importance of this type of virtue be more clearly expressed than in the last four petitions of the Our Father. Recall that these virtues are cardinal in that they concern innerworldly activities in principle accessible to all persons, no matter what religious faith, or none at all. Yet they are obtained not by being acquired by repeated action, but rather by being infused through the grace of

10. Augustine makes this point in his *Enchiridion on Faith, Hope, and Love,* cxv.

God. As such, they enable us not only to do innerworldly activities well, but also to do them with the help of God's grace, and in reference to humanity's supernatural destiny of union with God.

The last four petitions do indeed concern innerworldly activities that may be governed by acquired cardinal virtues. But we know these four are prayers for infused, rather than acquired, cardinal virtues for two reasons. First, we are praying for them! The very fact that we are asking God for the daily bread of prudence, the forgiveness that restores justice, the lack of temptation granted by temperance, and the deliverance from evil that is fortitude indicates that we believe God can indeed give us (or infuse in us) these virtues! That Christians for millennia have been praying in the Lord's Prayer for what can be understood as the four cardinal virtues offers the clearest of evidence that the cardinal virtues can be and are infused in us by God.

Second, since the Lord's Prayer is a unified whole, petitioning God for three theological as well as four cardinal virtues, it makes sense that all these virtues sought concern our supernatural destiny of union with God, whether they directly concern either God or innerworldly activities. One of the defining features of infused virtue is not only that it is obtained by God's grace, but also that it concerns our supernatural destiny of union with God, a destiny that cannot be acquired on our own. As should be clear by the opening "Our Father," and the very fact that we are beseeching God for each of the petitions, all the things sought in the prayer are sought in the context of our relationship with God. Therefore the cardinal virtues that are sought are infused, rather than acquired, virtues.

One final observation is offered here on how the Our Father reflects and further illuminates the seven virtues of the Christian life. It is a challenging point, and so a bit odd to raise at the very end of a chapter, let alone a book. But it brings us back full circle to the opening chapter's discussion of virtue in the context of a morality of happiness. What exactly is being asked for in these petitions? Is it that something change in the world around us, or that something change in us? In other words, is the restless human longing for happiness—of which this prayer is an expression—satisfied by some state of affairs in the world around us, or by we ourselves possessing certain qualities regardless of what the world is like around us?

These questions reflect an ancient debate over the role of what are called *bodily* and *external* goods in the life of happiness. Such goods include health, friends, good fortune, reputation, and the like. They are not fully under one's control. External factors influence whether these goods are present or not. Some thinkers (most notably the Stoics) have thought that happiness, or the good life, can be achieved regardless of whether or not such goods are present. Virtue alone grants happiness, and since they say virtue is totally under one's control, one can be fully happy even when these goods are lacking. Some have quipped that this must mean the Stoic wise person could be "happy on the rack," that is, while being tortured, which seems ludicrous.

On the one hand, there is an allure to this position. We often counsel friends to do what's right, no matter what becomes of them (loss of reputation, job, etc.), by this revealing that we do think being virtuous is far more important than losing such external goods. This is certainly true when a person is willing to bravely sacrifice her health, or even life, for a virtuous cause. But on the other hand, we also pray for the health and safety of others. We are thankful to God for external goods that come our way, such as a good job, friends, or some honor. It is for reasons such as these that Aristotle recognized that even the fully virtuous person is somewhat lacking in full happiness when external and bodily goods such as friendship and health are not present.[11]

What does the Our Father have to do with any of this? Assuming this prayer is one expression of the human longing for happiness, and a divinely inspired manner of doing so, a look at what exactly we are asking for should illuminate this question of where full human happiness lies—and indeed it does. Nearly all the petitions seek some change in what happens outside of us, in the world around us, thus revealing that human happiness is not fully achieved simply by a change in our interior states.

The first way this is obviously true is that we pray *our* Father. This is a communal prayer. And complete human happiness in the Christian tradition is not an individual matter. It is the communion of saints in union with God. Therefore, there is an obvious way that events beyond our control are required for the longing expressed in the prayer to be answered.

Second, nearly all of the petitions ask God that something happen in the world around us. We do not just ask for hope in the kingdom, but that it actually come. We ask that God's will indeed be done, that our daily bread be given, that sins be forgiven, temptations be avoided, and evil not overcome us. All of these things are not fully under our control. Nor is it fully under our control that God's name is hallowed, since this is given by the infused theological virtue faith. But with this petition we are indeed primarily asking for a human (communal) response, since God's name is holy, whether we hallow it or not! Thus, except for the first, each petition does indeed ask God that something be changed in the world around us.

However, every one of the petitions is also answered by the possession of a virtue, revealing the importance of internal qualities for living a happy life. In other words, happiness is not simply something that happens to us; it is something we must actively participate in. So we pray not that God's name is holy (which is certainly is), but that we hallow it. We pray that God's kingdom come, but also for the hope by which we remain fixed on that arrival as our

---

11. See Aristotle, *Nicomachean Ethics,* in *The Basic Works of Aristotle,* ed. Richard McKeon, (New York: Random House, 1941), i.8–11.

proper destiny, and with which we begin to help represent that kingdom in this life. We pray for God's will to be done, which is the reign of God's love. But we are also praying that we participate in that love, which is the theological virtue of charity. We pray to receive our daily sustenance in the literal sense of bread, but also that we live not just by bread alone, but by the Word of God, which among other things means possessing the virtue of infused prudence. We seek right relations between God and us, and us and others, but clearly that requires we possess the virtue justice to participate in those relations. We seek the avoidance of temptations and evil, but this is achieved in this life as much by possessing temperance and fortitude as it is by not facing occasions of temptation and evil. Therefore, in praying the Our Father we are expressing our longing for happiness. We pray that God make changes in the world that are not dependent upon qualities in us. But we also pray, as rational creatures who can understand and participate freely in such a changed world, that we be given God's help in obtaining the virtues needed to become God's friends in inhabiting such a world, in this life or the next.

This last comment suggests an answer to the challenging question of the role of external and bodily goods in human happiness, an answer only available to those who grasp the Christian story of the way things are. For sure, we must actively participate in our complete happiness. Even when faith and hope are no longer needed—when we see face to face, and when the occasion for doing innerworldly activities well has passed—love remains. In the beatific (or happy) vision of heaven, when we partake in the divine nature and see the truth to the fullest extent to which we are capable, and in knowing the truth are fully free, we are accordingly filled with love and joy. But Christians trust that this is not simply a state of mind, an internal disposition, but a reality that the provident God of all ages has brought about. We can participate in supernatural happiness in this life, though it will never be complete given the ongoing presence of sin, suffering, ignorance, and death that remains present in our world. But the future holds a promise not only that we will be made perfect, but also that the completion for which all creation groans in this life will come to pass, and at that point happiness—externally as well as internally—will be complete, and God will be all in all.

Reading Questions

1. What evidence is offered for the importance of the Our Father in the Christian tradition? Why has it been consistently afforded that importance?

2. How is the Lord's Prayer divided into seven distinct petitions? How are these seven further divided into a group of three and a group of four? Explain the basis for this division into two groups.

3. Which virtue is each of the seven petitions aligned with in the chapter? Be able to state one reason why each petition is aligned with its corresponding virtues

4. Explain how each of the following important topics for this book are addressed in some way by the Our Father: the proper order of certain virtues; the unity of the virtues; the reality of infused cardinal virtues; the role of external goods in complete happiness.

Terms to Know

petition, external and bodily goods

Question for Further Reflection

Look at another common Christian prayer (Hail Mary, Prayer of St. Francis, etc.) with the material of this book in mind. What connections can you find between that material and the prayer?

Further Reading

Since this chapter is largely a summary of the book's material with reference to the Our Father, there is little to suggest by way of further reading. For those interested in reading other more extensive commentaries on the Our Father, the works cited in the notes below by Augustine, Thomas Aquinas, and Fr. Servais Pinckaers, OP, are all recommended, along with the *Catechism of the Catholic Church*.

Bibliography

Alighieri, Dante. *The Portable Dante*. Edited by Mark Musa, New York: Penguin Books, 1995.

Annas, Julia. *The Morality of Happiness*. New York: Oxford University Press, 1993.

Aquinas, St. Thomas. *Catechetical Instructions of St. Thomas Aquinas*. Edited by J. B. Collins. New York: J. F. Wagner, 1939.

———. *Disputed Questions on Virtue*. South Bend, IN: St. Augustine's Press, 1999.

———. *Summa Theologiae*. Translated by the Fathers of the English Dominican Province. New York: Benziger, 1948.

Aristotle. *The Basic Works of Aristotle*. Edited by Richard McKeon. New York: Random House, 1941.

Augustine. *City of God*. New York: Penguin Books, 1984.

———. *Commentary on the Lord's Sermon on the Mount*. New York: Fathers of the Church Series, 1951.

———. *Confessions*. Translated by Maria Boulding, OSB. New York: Random House, 1997.

———. *Enchiridion on Faith, Hope, and Love*. Washington, DC: Regnery Gateway, 1961.

———. *On Catechizing the Unlearned*. 187–243 in *Seventeen Short Treatises of St Augustine*. Oxford: J. H. Parker, 1847.

———. *On the Way of Life of the Catholic Church*. Washington, DC: Catholic University of America Press, 1966.

———. *Teaching Christianity*. New York: New City Press, 1996.

Barron, Robert E. *The Strangest Way: Walking the Christian Path*. Maryknoll, NY: Orbis, 2002.

Basil the Great. *On the Holy Spirit*. New York: St. Vladimir's Seminary Press, 1997.

Benedict XVI. *Deus Caritas Est*. Encyclical Letter, 2005. Available online at www.vatican.va.

————. *Spe Salvi*: Encyclical Letter, 2007. Available online at www.vatican.va.

Cahill, Lisa Sowle. *Love Your Enemies: Discipleship, Pacifism, and Just War Theory*. Minneapolis: Fortress, 1994.

Cates, Diana Fritz. *Choosing to Feel: Virtue, Friendship, and Compassion for Friends*. Notre Dame, IN: University of Notre Dame Press, 1997.

Catechism of the Catholic Church. 2nd ed., Vatican City: Libreria Editrice Vaticana, 1997.

Cessario, Romanus. "The Virtue of Hope." In *The Ethics of Aquinas*, edited by Stephen J. Pope, 232–43. Washington, DC: Georgetown University Press, 2002.

Chidress, James, "Niebuhr's Realistic-Pragmatic Approach to War and the Nuclear Dilemma," in Richard Harris, ed. *Reinhold Niebuhr and the Issues of Our Time* (Grand Rapids: Eerdmans 1986), 122–56.

Cloutier, David. "The Pressures to Die: Reconceiving the Shape of Christian Life in the Face of Physician-Assisted Suicide." In *Growing Old in Christ*, edited by Stanley M. Hauerwas, Carole Bailey Stoneking, Keith G. Meador, and David Cloutier, 247–66. Grand Rapids: Eerdmans, 2003.

————. *Love, Reason, and God's Story*. Winona: MN: St. Mary's Press, 2008.

Cook, Christopher C. H. *Alcohol, Addiction, and Christian Ethics*. Cambridge: Cambridge University Press, 2006.

Farley, Margaret. "Issues in Contemporary Christian Ethics: The Choice of Death in a Medical Context." *Santa Clara Lectures* 1, no. 3 (1995): 1–19.

Finnis, John. *Fundamentals of Ethics*. Washington, DC: Georgetown University Press, 1983.

Ford, John. "The Morality of Obliteration Bombing." *Theological Studies 5* (1944): 259–309.

Fussell, Paul. "Thank God for the Atomic Bomb." In *Thank God for the Atomic Bomb and Other Essays*, edited by Paul Fussell, 13–37. New York: Ballantine Books, 1990.

Gaillardetz, Richard. *A Daring Promise: A Spirituality of Marriage*. New York: Crossroads, 2002.

Guardini, Romano. *Eternal Life: What You Need to Know about Death, Judgment, and Life Everlasting.* Manchester, NH: Sophia Institute Press, 1989.

———. *The Last Things: Concerning Death, Purification After Death, Resurrection, Judgment and Eternity.* London: Burns & Oates, 1954.

Guignon, Charles B. *The Good Life.* Hackett Readings in Philosophy. Indianapolis: Hackett, 1999.

Gula, Richard. "Moral Principles Shaping Public Policy on Euthanasia." *Second Opinion* 14, no. 1 (1990): 73–83.

Hall, Paula. *Narrative and Natural Law: An Interpretation of Thomistic Ethics.* Notre Dame, IN: University of Notre Dame Press, 1994.

Hamel, Ronald P. and James Walters, eds. *Artificial Hydration and Nutrition in the Permanently Unconscious Patient: the Catholic Debate.* Washington, DC: Georgetown University Press, 2007.

Harak, G. Simon. *Virtuous Passions: The Formation of Christian Character.* New York: Paulist, 1993.

Hauerwas, Stanley M. and L. Gregory Jones, eds. *Why Narrative? Readings in Narrative Theology.* Grand Rapids: Eerdmans, 1989.

Hibbs, Thomas S. *Virtue's Splendor: Wisdom, Prudence and the Human Good.* New York: Fordham University Press, 2001.

Himes, Michael J. *Doing the Truth in Love: Conversations About God, Relationships, and Service.* New York: Paulist, 1995.

Hollenbach, David. *The Common Good and Christian Ethics.* New York: Cambridge University Press, 2002.

Houser, R. E. "The Virtue of Courage." In *The Ethics of Aquinas,* edited by Stephen J. Pope, 304–20. Washington, DC: Georgetown University Press, 2002.

Irish Catholic Bishop's Conference. *Love is for Life.* Pastoral Letter, 1985. Available at www.ewtn.com/library/bishops/lovelife.htm.

———. *Alcohol: The Challenge of Moderation.* Pastoral Letter, 2007. Available at www.catholiccommunications.ie.

John Paul II. *Evangelium Vitae.* Encyclical Letter, 1995. Available online at www.vatican.va.

———. *Fides et Ratio.* Encyclical Letter, 1998. Available online at www.vatican .va.

———. *Man and Woman He Created Them: A Theology of the Body.* Trans. Michael Waldstein. Boston, MA: Pauline Books and Media, 2006.

———. *Salvifici Doloris.* Encyclical Letter, 1984. Available online at www .vatican.va.

————. *Veritatis Splendor.* Encyclical Letter, 1993. Available online at www
.vatican.va.

Kant, Immanuel *Grounding for the Metaphysics of Morals*, in Ethical Principles, 2nd. ed. Translated by James W. Ellington. (Indianapolis: Hackett
Publishing, 1999).

Kaveny, M. Cathleen. "Wholesomeness, Holiness, and Hairspray," *America.*
March 3, 2003, 15–18.

Keane, Phillip. "The Dilemma of Committed Premarital Intercourse." *Sexual
Morality: A Catholic Perspective.* New York: Paulist Press, 1997.

Keenan, James F. "What's Your Worst Moral Argument?" *America*, Oct. 2,
1993, 164: 17–18, 28–30.

Kelber, Werner H. *Mark's Story of Jesus.* Philadelphia: Fortress, 1979.

Keown, John, ed. *Euthanasia Examined: Ethical, Clinical and Legal Perspectives.* Cambridge: Cambridge University Press, 1995.

King, Jr., Martin Luther. *Strength to Love.* Minneapolis: Augsburg, 1981.

————. "The Quest for Peace and Justice." Nobel Prize acceptance speech.
Dec. 10, 1964.

Knapp, Caroline. *Drinking: A Love Story.* New York: Dial Press, 1996.

Kuo, Meichun, Edward M. Adlaf, Hang Lee, Louis Gliksman, Andrée Dem-
ers, and Henry Wechsler. "More Canadian Students Drink But American
Students Drink More: Comparing College Alcohol Use in Two Countries."
Addiction 97, no. 12 (2002): 1583–92.

Lackey, Douglas. "Why Hiroshima Was Immoral: A Response to Landesman."
Philosophical Forum 34, no. 1 (2003): 39–42.

Landesman, Charles. "Rawls on Hiroshima: An Inquiry Into the Morality
of the Use of Atomic Weapons in August 1945." *Philosophical Forum* 34,
no. 1 (2003): 21–38.

Lewis, C. S. *The Four Loves.* San Diego: Harcourt, 1991.

————. *The Great Divorce.* San Francisco: HarperSanFrancisco, 2001.

————. *Mere Christianity.* San Francisco: HarperSanFrancisco, 2001.

Louth, Andrew, ed., *Early Christian Writings.* New York: Penguin, 1968.

MacIntyre, Alasdair. *Dependent Rational Animals.* Chicago: Open Court,
1999.

Mattison III, William C. "Christian Anger? A Contemporary Account of
Virtuous Anger in the Thomistic Tradition." PhD diss., University of Notre
Dame, 2003.

————. "Christian Anger? Beyond Questions of Vengeance," *Journal for the
Society of Christian Ethics* 24, no. 1 (2004): 159–79.

McCabe, Herbert. *God Still Matters.* London: Continuum, 2003.

McCarthy, David. *Sex and Love in the Home.* London: SCM, 2004.

McGowen, Jo. "Marriage Versus Living Together." In *Perspectives on Marriage: A Reader*, edited by Kieran Scott and Michael Warren. New York: Oxford University Press, 2001.

Meilaender, Gilbert. *Bioethics: A Primer for Christians.* Grand Rapids: Eerdmans, 2005.

————. *Friendship: A Study in Theological Ethics.* Notre Dame, IN: University of Notre Dame Press, 1981.

Miller, Richard B. *Interpretations of Conflict: Ethics, Pacifism, and the Just War Tradition.* Chicago: University of Chicago, 1991.

Murray, Lorraine. "Loving the Lady in the Mirror," *America*, Feb. 17, 2003, 14–16.

National Conference of Catholic Bishops. *The Challenge of Peace: God's Promise and Our Response.* Pastoral Letter, 1983. Available online at www.usccb.org.

————. *The Harvest of Justice is Sown in Peace: A Reflection of the National Conference of Catholic Bishops on the Tenth Anniversary of the Challenge of Peace (November 17, 1993).* Washington, DC: United States Catholic Conference, 1994.

Neuhaus, Richard John. *Death on a Friday Afternoon: Meditations on the Last Words of Jesus From the Cross.* New York: Basic Books, 2001.

O'Donovan, Oliver. *The Just War Revisited.* Cambridge: Cambridge University Press, 2003.

Pieper, Josef. *The Concept of Sin.* South Bend, IN: St. Augustine's Press, 2001.

————. *Faith, Hope, Love.* San Francisco: Ignatius Press, 1997.

————. *The Four Cardinal Virtues: Prudence, Justice, Fortitude, Temperance.* Notre Dame, IN: University of Notre Dame Press, 2003.

————. *Happiness and Contemplation.* South Bend, IN: St. Augustine's Press, 1998.

Pinches, Charles R. *Theology and Action: After Theory in Christian Ethics.* Grand Rapids: Eerdmans, 2002.

Pinckaers, Servais. *Morality: The Catholic View.* South Bend, IN: St. Augustine's Press, 2001.

————. *The Sources of Christian Ethics.* Washington, DC: Catholic University of America Press, 1995.

Plato. *Great Dialogues of Plato.* Edited by Eric Warmington and Philip Rouse. New York: Signet, 1984.

————. *Republic.* Translated by G. M. A. Grube. Indianapolis: Hackett Publishing, 1974.

Pope, Stephen J., ed. *The Ethics of Aquinas*. Washington, DC: Georgetown University Press, 2002.

Porter, Jean. *Nature as Reason: A Thomistic Theory of the Natural Law*. Grand Rapids: Eerdmans, 2005.

———. "The Virtue of Justice." In *The Ethics of Aquinas*, edited by Stephen J. Pope, 272–86. Washington, DC: Georgetown University Press, 2002.

Ratzinger, Joseph. *Eshatology: Death and Eternal Life*. Washington, DC: Catholic University of America Press, 1988.

Rawls, John. "Fifty Years After Hiroshima." In *Collected Papers*, edited by Samuel Freeman, 565–72. Cambridge, MA: Harvard University Press, 1999.

Rhonheimer, Martin. "Sins Against Justice." Translated by Frederick G. Lawrence, in *The Ethics of Aquinas*, edited by Stephen J. Pope, 287–303. Washington, DC: Georgetown University Press, 2002.

Rolheiser, Ronald. *The Holy Longing: The Search for a Christian Spirituality*. New York: Doubleday, 1999.

Rubio, Julie Hanlon. *A Christian Theology of Marriage and Family*. New York: Paulist, 2003.

Sacred Congregation for the Doctrine of the Faith. *Declaration on Euthanasia*. 1980.

Stone, Lawrence. "Passionate Attachments in the West in Historical Perspective." In *Wing to Wing, Oar to Oar: Readings on Courting and Marrying*, edited by Amy A. Kass and Leon Kass. Notre Dame, IN: University of Notre Dame Press, 2000.

Taylor, Charles. *Sources of the Self: The Making of the Modern Identity*. Cambridge: Cambridge University Press, 1994.

Thatcher, Adrian. *Living Together and Christian Ethics*. Cambridge: Cambridge University Press, 2002.

Titus, Craig Steven. *Resilience and the Virtue of Fortitude: Aquinas in Dialogue With the Psychosocial Sciences*. Washington, DC: Catholic University of America Press, 2006.

Tollefsen, Christopher, ed. *Artificial Nutrition and Hydration: The New Catholic Debate*. Dordrecht: Springer, 2008.

Wadell, Paul J. *Becoming Friends: Worship, Justice and the Practice of Christian Friendship*. Grand Rapids: Brazos, 2002.

———. *Friendship and the Moral Life*. Notre Dame, IN: University of Notre Dame Press, 1989.

———. *The Primacy of Love: An Introduction to the Ethics of Thomas Aquinas*. New York: Paulist, 1992.

Walzer, Michael. *Just and Unjust Wars*. New York: Basic Books, 1992.

Walzer, Michael, and Paul Fussell. "An Exchange of Views." In *Thank God for the Atomic Bomb and Other Essays*, edited by Paul Fussell, 23–28. New York: Ballantine Books, 1988.

Weaver, Daniel Fozard. "Conscience: Rightly Formed and Otherwise," *Commonweal* Sept. 23, 2005, 10.

Wechsler, H., B. E. Molnar, A. E. Davenport, and J.S. Baer. "College Alcohol Use: A Full Or Empty Glass?" *Journal of American College Health* 47, no. 6 (1999): 247–52.

West, Christopher. *The Good News About Sex and Marriage*. Ann Arbor, MI: Servant Publications, 2004.

Westberg, Daniel. *Right Practical Reason: Aristotle, Action, and Prudence in Aquinas*. New York: Oxford University Press, 1994.

Winner, Lauren. *Real Sex: The Naked Truth about Chastity*. Grand Rapids: Brazos, 2005.

Yearley, Lee H. *Mencius and Aquinas: Theories of Virtue and Conceptions of Courage*. Albany, NY: State University of New York Press, 1990.

INDEX